It is a privilege and a mark of esteem to be invited to join Taste of Scotland and be included in this book. Many apply for membership but relatively few are chosen. This year there are a number of new entries and some from last year rejected, it is to be hoped temporarily.

Taste of Scotland operates a programme of continual assessment. Every establishment is inspected by at least one inspector, at least once a year to make sure that standards remain high.

The inspectors themselves, under the vigorous supervision of Zandra Macpherson of Glentruim, are all "food professionals", in the sense that their main occupation relates to food preparation, quality control and so on. Inspections are usually incognito - always in the case of new members. The decisions they make regarding membership are not made lightly, and if they are in any doubt, membership will not be offered. In the case of existing members a second opinion may be sought in extenuating circumstances.

Upon being accepted for membership of the scheme, all members pay a small contribution toward the annual marketing of the scheme, as Taste of Scotland is an independent, non-profit making organisation.

This year we have introduced some changes to the Guide. Not only has the layout of each entry been adjusted to give readers a quick idea of the kind of establishment (country house, grand hotel, rural restaurant etc) but there is also comment on the style of cooking to be found and a crucial observation from our inspectors.

It is clear from reading through the inspectors reports this year that there is a clearly emerging style of Scottish modern cooking with its roots firmly in the French and Italian kitchen with some influence from Cuisine Nouvelle and even Eastern traditions.

The reason for this important development is two-fold.

Modern cooking relies upon high quality produce which is absolutely fresh, and therefore capable of being treated very simply, so the natural flavours of the raw materials are allowed to emerge. Scotland is recognised to have the finest raw materials in Europe - indeed we have been described as "the larder of Europe". Think of Aberdeen Angus beef or hill-bred lambs. Think of the game that comes from our mountains and low ground, the shellfish caught off the West Coast, or the white fish landed on the East Coast. Because of our northern latitude there are more hours of sunlight in summer, and the cold winters kill the crop-destroying bugs and fewer pesticides are required for berries, root vegetables, grains and pulses.

The availability of such high quality produce makes modern cooking possible: in the hands of a few outstanding Scottish practitioners, this style of cooking has produced dishes which can rival those produced by chefs anywhere in Europe. Scotland now has more Michelin-starred chefs per capita of population that anywhere else in the UK. It is nothing short of a reformation.

I hope that you find the Guide useful, reliable and accurate. Do write to us if you have any cause for complaint, and if you come upon places that you think should be included let us know.

Laurie Black

Laurie Black
Chairman, of the Taste of Scotland Board

TASTE OF SCOTLAND
*current members are identified
by the 1996 Certificate of
Membership which should
be on display.*

The Taste of Scotland Scheme Ltd is supported by:

- Scottish Tourist Board
- Scottish Enterprise
- Scotch Quality Beef & Lamb Association
- Scottish Salmon Board
- Corporate Members
- Trade Board Members:

  Laurie Black (Chairman, Taste of Scotland Board), Fouters Bistro

  Annie Paul, Taychreggan Hotel

  Eric Brown, Craigendarroch Hotel

Contents

How to use this guide

73 ●————————— Map Reference

Dulnain Bridge

Auchendean Lodge Hotel
Dulnain Bridge, Grantown-on-Spey
Inverness-shire PH26 3LU
Tel: 01479 851347 ●————————— Address & Tel. No. etc
Fax: 01479 851347

On A95, 1 mile south of Dulnain Bridge. ●————— How to Find

| A charming Highland country hotel. |

Type of Building ————— ● ■ Edwardian hunting lodge, with a great view
over the Spey.
Style of Cooking ————— ● ■ Original, talented, eclectic cooking.
Inspector's Comment ————— ● ■ "There is a holistic culinary ethos here, happily
combining French and other influences,
simplicity and sophistication."

Auchendean was built just after the turn of the
century as a sporting lodge and its architectural
detail is influenced by the Arts and Crafts Movement.
The present owners, Eric Hart and Ian Kirk, are
convivial professionals dedicated to giving their ●————— Description
guests a full dining experience. Both Ian and Eric
share the cooking; Eric is a keen mycologist and
finds over 20 varieties of edible wild mushrooms
locally; the hotel's garden also provides vegetables
(including six varieties of potato!), herbs and honey.
Eggs are supplied by the hotel's own hens. Wild
berries, mountain hare, rabbit, pigeon, mallard,
pheasant and home-cured gravadlax are specialities.
The menu changes every night but always balances
a simple main course with something more exotic.

Seasonal Limitations ————— ● Open all year except early Jan to early Feb
Rooms: 7, 5 with private facilities ●————— Accommodation
Bed & Breakfast £15 - £41
Dinner B & B £35 - £64 ●————— Meal Times and Prices
Special Rates for 3+ nights
Dinner 7.30 - 9 pm (d) 4 course menu
Special Diets Catered For ————— ● Vegetarians welcome - prior notice required
No smoking in dining room + one of the
lounges

Menu Specialities ————— ● Home-made gravadlax with mustard and dill
sauce. Roast loin of pork with garlic and rosemary.
Wild mallard duck breast with ceps. Athol brose
cream. Apricot, prune and brandy ice cream.

STB Grading & Classification ————— ● STB Highly Commended 3 Crowns
Credit cards: 1, 2, 3, 5 ●————— Credit Cards
Contact Names ————— ● Proprietors: Eric Hart & Ian Kirk

4

Entries

- Establishments selected by Taste of Scotland are listed in this Guide in alphabetical order under the nearest town or village.

- Island entries are shown alphabetically under Isle.

- A full list of hotels, restaurants etc is given in alphabetical order in the Index at the end of the Guide.

Special diets or requirements

- Where vegetarian menus are available this is highlighted by 'vegetarians welcome' in the entry.

- Other special needs, such as diet or facilities for disabled guests, should be arranged in advance.

Wines and spirits

- Except where otherwise stated, all hotels and restaurants are licensed for the service of wines, spirits, beers etc.

- Most unlicensed establishments which tend to be small guest houses or farmhouses - will welcome your taking your own wine, but again please enquire in advance.

- Where an establishment is shown to have a 'restricted licence' it generally means that residents and diners may be served alcoholic beverages, but members of the public may not call in for a drink.

Lunches

- Nowadays lunchtime eating has become much less formal except in city centre hotels and restaurants. Bar snacks are more usual in some smaller establishments and rural hotels.

- To simplify the choice available, we specify Bar Lunch or Dining Room/Restaurant Lunch in this Guide.

Restrictions on smoking

- Within the information on each establishment, we have noted where there is no smoking permitted in the dining room or restaurant.

- Where an area is set aside for non-smokers, the entry will show 'No smoking area in dining room/restaurant'.

- In addition we have highlighted where no smoking is permitted throughout an establishment or where there are restrictions on smoking in guest bedrooms.

- Entries which do not give any such information are taken to have no restriction on smoking.

Pets

- Pets are accepted in some hotels by arrangement.

  It is wise, however, to confirm this when booking as there may be a small charge and sometimes there is a restriction on the areas within the establishment where pets are permitted.

- Restaurants generally do not accept dogs.

Foreign Languages

- Where establishments have provided us with information on any foreign languages spoken, this has been incorporated within the descriptive paragraph about the establishment.

Meal Prices

- Prices are quoted as a guideline only and Guide readers are advised to check prevailing prices when making their reservation.

- These estimated prices for 1996 were provided by the establishments, based on a three course meal, excluding drinks.

- Where more courses are the norm, this is indicated next to the price band.

Key to Price Bands

(a)	under £10
(b)	£10 - £15
(c)	£15 - £20
(d)	£20 - £25
(e)	£25 - £30
(f)	over £30

- Times of food service are listed to show first and last orders, unless otherwise stated.

Accommodation Rates

- Specimen inclusive terms are listed, once again as a guideline.

- Where a price range is given, the lower price normally indicates the rate per person sharing a double room, and the higher price the rate for single occupancy or per person in a higher quality room.

- The price range may also reflect high and low season fluctuations.

- Where a room rate is offered, this information is shown in the entry.

- Some room rates include breakfast - check with establishment.

Credit/Charge Cards

- Where an establishment accepts credit/charge cards, those taken are listed under the following codes:

Key

1	Access/Mastercard/Eurocard
2	American Express
3	Visa
4	Carte Bleu
5	Diners Club
6	Mastercharge

SWITCH and **DELTA** cards are listed by name where appropriate.

How to Avoid Disappointment

- Make an advance reservation whenever possible.

- Mention you are using the Taste of Scotland Guide.

- **Remember!** Many food items are seasonal and the specialities listed have been selected as an indication of the style of food on offer, but there is no guarantee of availability on any particular day.

- Check if any price changes have taken place since the publication of this Guide.

- Confirm that credit cards are accepted.

Comments

- Taste of Scotland welcomes comments - both good and bad.

- However, if you have an unsatisfactory meal, we would always advise that you speak to the restaurant or hotel manager or proprietor at the time. It gives an immediate opportunity for the situation to be rectified or explained.

- If this fails to solve the problem, do write to the Taste of Scotland Scheme about your experience. While we do not have operational control of any establishment listed, we will pass on your comments for investigation.

- But please let us hear of your good experiences too!

- We like to give our members feedback on comments from the public, so comment slips are provided at the end of this Guide for your use.

Baxters ®

The family of fine foods

Discover
the World of
Baxters

Enjoy the
Baxters Experience

- Free admission
- Free car and coach
parking with facilities for the disabled
- Audio Visual show • Guided factory tour
- The Old Shop Museum -
Where the Baxter Story began
- The George Baxter Cellar - speciality
foods, wines & spirits
- Mrs Baxter's Victorian Kitchen - extensive
international gifts & cookery utensils
- Additional quality retail outlet offering
the "Best of Scotland"merchandise
- Spey Restaurant seating 130
- Herd of pedigreed Highland cattle
- Landscaped grounds and views of the
magnificent River Spey
- Woodland walks and trails
- Family picnic area
- Toilet facilities for the disabled

Coach parties are requested to book in advance.

VISITOR FACILITIES

OPEN 7 DAYS A WEEK - January to December.
9.30 a.m. - 5 p.m. weekdays.
10.a.m. - 5p.m. weekends.

FACTORY TOURS - Weekdays only.
Guided tours of the factory from
9.30 a.m. - 11.30 a.m. and
12.30 p.m. - 4.00 p.m.
(last Factory tour 2.00 p.m. Friday)

Tours subject to availability.

**Parties greater than 10 people,
please book in advance
to avoid disappointment -
an enquiry prior to your visit
should confirm availability.**

FACTORY TOURS ARE NOT AVAILABLE
DURING FACTORY HOLIDAYS.

*All visitor facilities are suitable for the disabled
except for the factory tour.*

**Baxters of Speyside Ltd.,
Fochabers, Scotland, IV32 7LD.
Tel: (01343) 820393**

Baxters ®

*Come and discover the world
of Baxters, part of Scotland's
proud heritage*

The 1995 winners of The Macallan Taste of Scotland Awards are:

Hotel of the Year

The Balmoral Hotel
Edinburgh

Special Merit Award for Newcomers

Braidwoods Restaurant
by Dalry

Restaurant of the Year

The Green Inn
Ballater

Special Merit Award for Achievement

Loch Fyne Oyster Bar
Cairndow

Country House Hotel of the Year

Flodigarry Country House Hotel
Staffin, Isle of Skye

The Macallan Personality of the Year

Christine Morrison
Handa, Lochs, Isle of Lewis

Now in their ninth year the Awards were set up to encourage the pursuit of excellence and by so doing to encourage others to emulate the winners.

The Macallan Single Malt is known for its unique character and unrivalled quality and as such makes the perfect partner for these Awards. This partnership certainly caught the imagination of the public and Taste of Scotland establishments alike with a record number of nominations received in 1995.

The Awards are restricted to establishments which are listed in the Taste of Scotland Guide and thus are already highlighted as leaders in their specific category.

Once again this year we invite Taste of Scotland customers to nominate establishments in which you have received outstanding standards, in addition, Taste of Scotland Inspectors are asked to nominate their favourite places.

Please use the coupons at the rear of this Guide to nominate. Nomination cards are also available at Taste of Scotland member establishments. Letters and postcards are also welcome and taken into consideration.

The categories for the 1996 Awards will remain the same. As in the past the Special Merit Awards will be decided based upon the recommendations received.

Closing date for entries - 31 July 1996

The 1995 Winners have been highlighted in the listings with this symbol

This year for the first time it has been decided to award a further 25 Taste of Scotland establishments with The Macallan 25.

The Macallan 25 is a group of 25 Taste of Scotland members who are recognised for being particularly outstanding in their field.

These 25 establishments have come to our attention through our inspections, nominations from the public for the Awards or letters from users of the Guide.

They are highlighted in the listings and are strongly recommended for the travelling gourmet.

This group of establishments will be reviewed and updated annually.

They are as follows:
Atrium, Edinburgh
Auchterarder House, Auchterarder
Ballathie House Hotel, Perth
Braeval Restaurant, Aberfoyle
Cameron House Hotel, Loch Lomond
The Cellar Restaurant, Anstruther
Chatters, Dunoon
Fins Restaurant, Fairlie
The Gleneagles Hotel, Auchterarder
Isle of Eriska Hotel, Oban
Kilmichael Country House Hotel, Arran
The Kirroughtree Hotel, Newton Stewart
Knockie Lodge, Whitebridge
Knockinaam Lodge, Port Patrick
Le Chambertin at the George Intercontinental, Edinburgh
Lochgreen, Troon
Lynwilg House, Aviemore
Martins Restaurant, Edinburgh
The Peat Inn, Peat Inn nr Cupar
Summer Isles, Achiltibuie
Caledonian Hotel, Edinburgh
The Courtyard on the Lane, Aberdeen
The Cross, Kingussie
Sheraton Grand Hotel, Edinburgh
Turnberry Hotel, Turnberry

Neil's Thoughts on Modern Scottish Cooking

There was a time when the natives of a certain European country which shall remain nameless (suffice to say garlic is heavily involved in their cooking and, dare I mention frogs' legs?) used to say Scotland was a wonderful country to visit, so long as you were not still there for dinner. Well, these days they can eat their words. The standard of cooking and food has improved beyond all measure (except perhaps a measure around the waistline) in the last 20 years.

Part of the reason for this is a global movement towards better cooking. When Scots started travelling in greater numbers abroad, we returned with higher expectations and chefs, themselves, came back with new ideas. The other major factor is Scottish chefs finally cottoned on to what fine natural produce they had at home, set up lines of supply and then worked out how to use it and, if it became necessary, metaphorically, to hi-jack a lorry-load of supplies bound for France they were prepared to do that.

Raymond Blanc the celebrated chef of Le Manoir aux Quat'Saisons, tells a story about

how his uncle, also a chef, at that time working in Scotland, was amazed to see Scots innocently trampling all over fields of wonderful wild mushrooms on their Sunday morning strolls. Not now. These days it is not unusual to surprise a chef in the woods with a basket crammed full of chanterelles hurrying back to prepare them with venison or a joint of lamb.

Things have certainly changed for the better in Scottish kitchens -

just pick any of the restaurants in this Taste of Scotland book - and, more often than not, even foreign visitors can be persuaded to stay for dinner.

Neil MacLean
Food Writer

The Taste of Burns Country 1996

This year sees the Bicentenary of the death of Robert Burns, and in anticipation of the increase in visitors, the restaurateurs and hoteliers of South West Scotland have joined together to promote the produce available in this area.

The areas of Ayrshire and Dumfries and Galloway were Burns' birthplace and his home for most of his life and offer the surroundings for a very special holiday. There are quiet roads, hidden and waiting to be discovered lochs and lochans, green rolling countryside and rugged upland areas such as the Leadhills and Wanlockhead, and marvellous coastal features including sandy bays and rugged cliffs. The two counties, best described as the South West of Scotland, are too often passed by visitors to Scotland heading straight to Glasgow, Edinburgh and further North.

South West Scotland could be the new Lake District, for just one more hour travelling north will take you up into this unspoilt country.

It is with this in mind that the caterers of the area have joined together to form 'The Taste of Burns Country.' There are now around 60 hotels and restaurants featuring fresh local produce, cooked with a light careful hand and offered at prices to please. Participating establishments will display a ceramic plaque outside informing visitors of the welcome waiting. Each offers their own Taste of Burns menu featuring the freshest local produce available that day.

A crucial aspect to the quality of this venture is that all participating chefs will have attended training workshops held by prominent chefs from Scotland's Chefs Association, at which guidance is given in the purchasing and preparation of fresh produce, together with many ideas about cooking and menu composition. The over-riding emphasis is on the presentation of fine Scottish produce, cooked with care to allow the full taste of the food to come through.

Visit the South West of Scotland this year, for a delightful and enchanting holiday with excellent food.

The Tam O' Shanter Experience

Visitors from all over the world will be heading to Scotland in 1996 to celebrate the bi-centenary of the death of Robert Burns, its most famous literary son. Born in Alloway, Ayrshire, in 1759, the man known as the ploughman, the patriot but most notably the poet, left a legacy of words and wisdom which still echoes with resonance in 1996.

Such is his enduring appeal that to commemorate the anniversary, the new Burns National Heritage Park was created in 1995 and received the royal accolade when the Queen opened the Park in July 1995. Comprising the famous Cottage where the poet was born, the Museum, which houses many of his manuscripts, the Auld Kirk at Alloway, the Brig O'Doon and the Monument, set in beautiful gardens, these landmarks are famous in their own right.

However, they have been joined by the Tam O'Shanter Experience, a visitor centre which has a superb gift shop, an introductory audio visual theatre which gives insight into the man and his times, leading into the main event: a state of the art presentation of the tale of Tam O'Shanter, complete with witches, warlocks, thunder, lightening (very frightening) and an astonishing "brig" which descends to allow Tam fortunately to escape, well almost !

After all that excitement, the visitors can enjoy the very best of the best of a taste of Scotland in the restaurant which has a menu to reflect the best of Scottish produce, served in a unique setting overlooking tranquil gardens.

Just as Burns enchanted the lassies in Ayrshire, nearly two hundred years ago, we hope to entice you with flavours and favours as appealing as the words of Robert. Join us for the Burns Experience in 1996 and a taste of Ayrshire hospitality.

See entry page 178

Tam O'Shanter
E X P E R I E N C E

The Burns National Heritage Park brings together Burns Cottage and Museum, the Monument and Gardens, Alloway Kirk and the Brig O' Doon. These world famous Heritage sites have been joined by the new, exciting, Tam O' Shanter Experience.

BURNS
national
HERITAGE
park
Alloway. Ayr

At the Tam O' Shanter Experience enjoy the three-screen audio visual presentation, browse through the Gift Shop, and then take the opportunity to savour the delights of traditional Scottish delicacies - Fish, Cheese, Venison, Patés in the beautifully situated 120 seat Restaurant.

For further details of The Tam O' Shanter Experience and Burns Cottage telephone (01292) 443700

STB Quality Assurance

Since 1985, the Scottish Tourist Board has been inspecting hotels, guest houses, bed and breakfasts, and self catering accommodation, assessing the standards that visitors expect and helping owners and operators meet those standards.

In a two-tier scheme, accommodation all over the country is visited annually and GRADED for quality and CLASSIFIED for facilities.

Grades are based on a wide ranging assessment of quality and service aspects. Each establishment is assessed on its own merits so that any type can achieve the highest grade.

Deluxe
*reflects an **excellent** overall standard*

Highly Commended
*reflects a **very good** overall standard*

Commended
*reflects a **good** overall standard*

Approved
*reflects an **acceptable** overall standard*

These GRADES are awarded by the STB inspectors once they have checked all the important factors that contribute to quality in an establishment. Just as you would, they look for clean, attractive surroundings, well furnished and heated. They sample meals, sleep in the beds, and talk to the staff. Like you, they know that quality should be assessed irrespective of the range of facilities on offer and, of course, they know the value of a warm and welcoming smile.

The CROWN CLASSIFICATION denotes the range of facilities on offer - things such as private bathrooms, lounges, meal provision and so on.

From a basic LISTED classification up to FIVE CROWNS can be added. So more crowns mean more facilities.

The distinctive blue plaques show the awards made by the STB inspectors as a result of their independent annual assessment.

For more information about Grading and Classification of accommodation in Scotland contact :

Scottish Tourist Board, Thistle House, Beechwood Park North, Inverness IV2 3ED

No.1 Princes Street, a wonderful haven in the heart of the city, where sumptuous and elegant surroundings give the atmosphere of a luxury club.

Our Executive Chef, Billy Campbell, presents dishes which feature exciting combinations of fine Scottish produce together with imaginative and creative flair.

For a personal copy of our menu please call 0131 556 2414

THE

BALMORAL

EDINBURGH

A carefully selected range of Scotland's finest quality butchery and game meat products brought to you by one of Scotland's better catering suppliers

SPECIALIST BUTCHERY
& GAME MEAT SUPPLIERS

For more information on our Natural Taste of Scotland products call us on

Our Traditional family business is proud to be a corporate member of Taste of Scotland as this provides us with the opportunity to demonstrate our commitment to supplying Scottish produce of the highest quality.

(John Bain, Partner)

(01651) 851765

Bain of Tarves,
Duthie Road, Tarves, Ellon,
Scotland AB41 0JX
Fax: (01651) 851794

See entry page 107

THE BRAE HOTEL

This former Church Manse overlooking Fort Augustus and with commanding views of the Great Glen and Caledonian Canal makes an ideal base for exploring the Highlands and the many and varied walks in the area. Escape the stress of modern life and relax while enjoying good food and wine.
Open March to end October.

 ★★ Les Routiers Recommended

Scottish TOURIST BOARD HIGHLY COMMENDED LISTED

THE BRAE HOTEL
Fort Augustus, Inverness-shire PH32 4DG
Tel: (01320) 366289 Fax: (01320) 366702

INTERNATIONAL FESTIVAL

BURNS 96

Join us in celebration.

FOR FURTHER INFORMATION CONTACT THE BURNS INTERNATIONAL FESTIVAL HEAD OFFICE
24 SANDGATE AYR KA7 1BY TELEPHONE 01292 288080 FACSIMILE 01292 619622

PRESIDENT: HER ROYAL HIGHNESS THE PRINCESS ROYAL

BURTS HOTEL

Melrose   Roxburghshire

Distinguished family-run town Hotel built in 1722. Tastefully furnished with 21 en suite bedrooms all with modern facilities including Satellite TV, direct-dial telephones, Tea/Coffee facilities, etc.

Elegant restaurant offering both a la carte and table d'hote menus using the best of produce from Scotland's natural larder, prepared and beautifully presented by our chef Gary Moore and his dedicated Brigade. Popular Lounge Bar furnished with over 50 Single Malts on the Gantry and a good selection of Real Ales, serving light, delicious and imaginative Bar Lunches and Suppers daily. Conference facilities, two lounges, private carpark and extensive gardens.

Burts Hotel is the ideal centre for touring the beautiful Border country and enjoying traditional Scottish hospitality. Several golf courses are within easy reach and salmon and trout fishing can be arranged. Game shooting on local estates also available with prior notice.

 AA ★★★⊛   **RAC** ★★★   Scottish HIGHLY COMMENDED   EGON RONAY'S **GUIDES**   Scotland's Commended   THE TASTE OF SCOTLAND *recommended*   SCOTCH BEEF CLUB

For brochure write to Graham and Anne Henderson, Proprietors. Tel 01896 822285 Fax 822870

See entry page 159

See entry page 156

See entry page 79

Sample Menu.

Terrine of Wild Salmon Waverley
served with Drambuie and fresh tarragon.
Haggis Land o'Burns
pan sauté with a dash of local whisky and garnished with oatcakes.
Loch Leven Mussels
lightly braised in garlic, white wine and cream.

❧❧❧

Fillets of Lemon Sole Solway Bay
poached in lemon and presented in a prawn and leek sauce.

❧❧❧

Shellfish Corryvrechan
*scampi, prawns, mussels and queen scallops
poached in a white wine and leek sauce with a dash of coriander.*
Aberdeen Angus Sirloin Steak Auld Alliance
pan sauté and served with an onion and brandy cream sauce.
Breast of Chicken Bannockburn
filled with a vegetable and haggis stuffing and sauté in basil butter.
Roast Haunch of Venison Ben Vorlich
presented in a rich red wine sauce.

❧❧❧

Homemade Peach Cheesecake.
Apple and Ginger Charlotte with Cream.
The 'Other' Macallan
shortbread sandwich filled with soft fruit, ice cream and cream.
Scottish Cheeses
Dunsyre Blue and Ingles Smoked Cheddar with Biscuits.

Clachan Cottage Hotel
**Lochside, Lochearnhead, Perthshire FK19 8PU
Tel (Lochearnhead) 01567-830247**

Clonyard House Hotel

Quietly situated in 7 acres of woodland grounds near the picturesque Colvend Coast; Clonyard is the perfect base to come back to after daily explorations to beautiful Galloway. Fifteen comfortable rooms including twelve on the ground floor, centrally heated rooms, with full facilities and private patios. The hotel is open all year, and has one especially fitted for disabled disabled guests.

Clonyard is noted for its fine food and good value and the restaurant and cocktail bar (where bar meals are served daily) are open to non-residents. There is a special childrens menu and an outdoor play area with an "Enchanted Tree".

Enquiries to J. M. Thompson
Clonyard House Hotel, Colvend, Dalbeattie,
Kirkcudbrightshire
Tel: 01556 630372 Fax: 01556 630422

 Scottish TOURIST BOARD COMMENDED

 AA ★★   **RAC** ★★

see entry page 142

Creebridge House Hotel

Galloway, South West Scotland

Built in 1760 this former shooting lodge to the Earl of Galloway is now an elegant 20 bedroom Country Hotel set in Newton Stewart in 3 acres of private gardens and woodland. 18 hole Golf course 400 yards from the front door. Private Salmon and Trout fishing on the Cree & Bladnoch rivers.

Choose from either the Garden Restaurant or our friendly local Bar where renowned Chef Proprietor Chris Walker and his team cook some of their Taste of Scotland Award winning dishes using fresh local produce. All rooms en suite with colour TV, direct dial phone etc.

Prices from £27.50 bed and breakfast each
Phone or Fax for our brochure
Tel: 01671 402121 Fax: 01671 403258

CRINGLETIE HOUSE HOTEL PEEBLES

Set in 28 acres of gardens and woodland- 2 miles north of Peebles on A703, and only 20 miles from Edinburgh. Magnificent views from all rooms. Consistently recommended for good food, and warm hospitality since 1971.

 ★★★

Johansen Recommended and all main guides

One of the most attractive hotels in Scotland

Telephone (01721) 730 233 Fax (01721) 730 244

See entry page 163

See entry page 185

See entry page 169

See entry page 80

THE Columba Hotel

Tranquil Lochside position with stunning views over Loch Fyne.

Log fired bars with local Malt Whiskies.

Local produce imaginatively prepared.

Extensive, but not expensive, Wine List.

STB
♛♛♛
Commended

Logis of Great Britain

Tarbert, Kintyre, Argyll PA29 6UF Tel 01880-820 808

Coul House Hotel

Our views are breathtaking. The ancient 'Mackenzies of Coul' picked a wonderful situation for their lovely home. Today, Ann and Martyn will give you a warm Highland welcome. You'll enjoy the 'Taste of Scotland' food of chef Bentley, log fires, summer evening piper and 'Skye' and 'Raasay', the hotel's lovable labradors. Why not use our 'Highland Passport' to cruise on Loch Ness, visit Cawdor Castle, sail to the Summer Isles... or follow our 'Highland Heritage' trail to Glenfiddich Distillery, the Wildlife Park, Culloden Battlefield... for golfers, there's a 5-course holiday including championship Royal Dornoch... for anglers, we have our own salmon and trout fishing... there's pony trekking too.

Ring or write for our colour brochure.

Coul House Hotel By Strathpeffer, Ross-shire Tel 01997-421487 Fax 01997-421945

The Wood Makes The Whisky

What makes one malt whisky different from the next?

After all, the ingredients - water, malted barley and a dash of yeast - are simple enough, and the methods of mashing, brewing, distilling and maturing are, broadly speaking, the same. Yet every one is different, I can assure you of this: when I wrote my Pocket Whisky Book I tasted all but a handful of them, and

although it was sometimes difficult to put words to the aromas and flavours, there was never any doubt that they were different.

It is a profound mystery. One well worthy of deep research while you are in Scotland.

The old books all maintain that water is the crucial ingredient: "soft water, rising through peat and flowing over granite". Yet a

fine whisky like Glenmorangie is made from uniquely hard water, and the lighter style of Islay malts (like Bunnahabhain and Bruichladdich) make sure their water doesn't "rise through peat". Modern analysis estimates that water contributes only about 10% to the flavour of the dram.

Is it the barley then and the amount of peat used in malting? Most distillers maintain that the barley variety makes not a blind bit of difference to flavour - although it must be of very high quality. This view has been challenged recently by the well-known whisky writer, Michael Jackson, who tells a fascinating story about Macallan - the only distillery which still uses, exclusively, an old fashioned variety called "Golden Promise" - where the malt buyer was persuaded to use a different variety, and the resulting distillate was noticeably different !

Yeast is discounted as a contributor to flavour, since it is simply the agent which converts the sugars in the malt into alcohol. Distilling methodology - the way the individual still-man runs his stills, and how narrow a "cut" he saves of the spirit run - undoubtedly makes a contribution.

And then we come to maturation.

It used to be said in the Highlands that "The wood makes the whisky", and the evidence of modern research supports this view.

By law, all Scotch whisky must be matured in oak casks: but there are oak casks and oak casks. Long ago the benefits of using a cask which had previously held sherry or bourbon were discovered - or port, rum, brandy or wine, for that matter, though these are rare.

Bourbon hogsheads (as they are called) are far and away the most common today, with a very small proportion of sherry butts (probably only about 10% : they are about ten times as expensive to buy). The Macallan Distillery is the only one to use exclusively sherry-wood for their single malts.

The contribution the cask makes to the flavour of the mature whisky cannot be over-exaggerated. Something of the first incumbent lingers in the wood, and re-emerges, changed, along with the compounds in the wood itself to mellow and colour the sleeping spirit, taming its fire and filling out its flavour.

Bourbon wood tends to impart a light, refined character to the whisky; the effect of sherry-wood depends upon what style of sherry the butt was first filled with - fino and manzanilla yield a light coloured spirit; amontillado and oloroso, rich, dark whisky.

Obviously, with the passage of time and several re-fills, the good things coming out of the wood are reduced in concentration and quantity. So that even an oloroso butt on its fifth or sixth filling with malt whisky will impart only a fraction of the sherry character that it did to its first filling.

Sherried whiskies knock many brandies into a cocked hat as digestifs. The Macallan is the benchmark - rich, smooth and even chocolatey. Then there is a Mortlach, Cragganmore, Balvenie and Strathisla for example. Other distilleries reckon their product benefits from a "sherry finishing" (ie. re-racking into sherry-wood for only the last couple of years of maturation). Glenmorangie pioneered this (they now do an interesting "Port-wood Finish" and are following this with a "Madeira-wood Finish" at the end of 1995). Many others vat together the contents of a number of bourbon hogsheads with a few sherry butts.

It all makes for a fascinating voyage of discovery! Happy tasting.

Charles MacLean
(Author of The Mitchell Beazley Pocket Whisky book, etc.)

HIGHLAND SPRING

❖

ENJOYED IN SCOTLAND'S FINEST WATERING HOLES

You'd expect the finest hotels and restaurants to serve

only the finest natural mineral water. Which is why Highland Spring

Natural Mineral Water, drawn from deep below

the Ochil Hills, Perthshire,   is clearly the Scottish choice.

NATURAL MINERAL WATER

KILFINAN

HOTEL

Discover the true flavour of the West Highlands at this 100 year old coaching Inn on the East Coast of Loch Fyne. Set amidst thousands of acres of unspoilt countryside, it is an ideal base for all outdoor activities and peaceful relaxation. Chef/Manager Rolf Mueller creates exquisite meals using seasonal produce from the adjoining estate and loch.

Luxury and comfort amidst rugged Highland scenery – and all within two hours scenic drive from Glasgow.

A warm welcome awaits you.

AA ❀ ❀ **Food Award**   E G O N RONAY'S GUIDES

STB Highly Commended ♛♛♛

Kilfinan, Nr. Tighnabruaich, Argyll, PA21 2EP
Tel: 01700 821 201 Fax: 01700 821 205

See entry page 144

See entry page 59

The Log Cabin Hotel
& Edelweiss Restaurant

Sample the delights of Scotland's larder in our Restaurant every evening. Cuisine prepared in our kitchens using fresh local produce.

- Uniquely built Hotel & Restaurant
- Bar lunches/suppers served daily
- Scandinavian style Sunday lunch
- Over 100 Malt Whiskies
- Non residents welcome
- Open all Year

Scottish TOURIST BOARD COMMENDED   **AA** ★★ **RAC** ★★   THE TASTE OF SCOTLAND   E G O N RONAY'S GUIDES

Kirkmichael, Perthshire PH10 7NB
Tel 01250 881288 Fax: 01250 881402

See entry page 151

See entry page 189

Loch Melfort Hotel

The finest location on the West Coast of Scotland right beside Arduaine Gardens

For comfort and that mouthwatering "Taste of Scotland" amidst magnificent surroundings

Open End February ~ January 2nd

Spring and Autumn Breaks ~
Christmas and New Year Holidays

AA ★★★ ♛♛♛♛ **STB Commended**

AA *Selected Hotel of the Year Scotland*

Scotland's Commended

and recommended by leading Hotel Guides

Loch Melfort Hotel, Arduaine,
by Oban, Argyll. PA34 4XG

Tel: 01852 200233 Fax: 01852 200214

M A L I N · C O U R T
Turnberry

Experience the Unique

*M*alin Court is thought to be unique in that it offers the facilities of an Hotel and Restaurant along with Residential Care Accommodation. There are seventeen en-suite bedrooms, all tastefully furnished and well appointed.

The Carrick Restaurant provides the best of modern Scottish food prepared by our Award Winning Chef. Only the finest ingredients and quality produce available each day are used.

Malin Court is situated on the beautiful Ayrshire Coast overlooking Turnberry's famous golf course, Ailsa Craig, the Isle of Arran and Maidens Bay. It makes the ideal location for exploring the history and heritage of Burns Country and for visiting the South West of Scotland.

FOR FURTHER INFORMATION :– MALIN COURT HOTEL AND RESTAURANT TURNBERRY, AYRSHIRE. KA26 9PB. TEL : 01655 331457

Taste of Scotland is delighted to welcome the following prestigious companies as Corporate Members of the scheme.

The hamper pictured above is available for purchase by calling Baxters' freephone Tel. No. 0800 186800

NATURAL MINERAL WATER

Highland Spring Limited

Stirling Street, Blackford
Perthshire PH4 1QA

"Highland Spring is Scotland's
finest Natural Mineral Water,
available still, sparkling and
lightly sparkling, and sourced in
the beautiful Ochil Hills
of Perthshire"

Tel: 01764 682444
Fax: 01764 682480

Bain of Tarves

Duthie Road, Tarves
Aberdeenshire
Scotland AB41 OJX

"Catering butchers, game and
venison suppliers"

Tel: 01651 851765
Fax: 01651 851794

Baxters of Speyside Limited

Fochabers, Moray, Scotland
IV32 7LD

"The family of fine foods"

Tel: 01343 820393
Fax: 01343 820286

Matthew Algie & Company Limited

16 Lawmoor Road
Glasgow G5 OUL

"Purveyors of the finest teas and
fresh ground coffee since 1864"

Tel: 0141 429 2817
Fax: 0141 429 3389

The Macallan Distillers Ltd.

The Macallan Distillery
Craigellachie AB38 9RX

"Distillers of The Macallan Single
Highland Malt Scotch Whisky"

Tel: 01340 871471
Fax: 01340 871212

Walkers Shortbread Limited

Aberlour-on-Spey
Scotland AB38 9PD

"The worlds classic pure butter
shortbread"

Tel: 01340 871555
Fax: 01340 871355

Waverley Vintners Limited

PO Box 22, Crieff Road
Perth PH1 2SL

"We offer a full range of wines
from around the world and
exclusive wine agencies"

Tel: 01738 629621
Fax: 01738 630338

Local Tourist Information

For specific information on a particular part of Scotland contact the following:

Aberdeen and Grampian Tourist Board
Tel: 01224 632727
Fax: 01224 848805

Angus and City of Dundee Tourist Board
Tel: 01241 877883
Fax: 01241 878550

Argyll, the Isles, Loch Lomond, Stirling, Trossachs Tourist Board
Tel: 01786 470945
Fax: 01786 471301

Ayrshire and Arran Tourist Board
Tel: 01292 262555
Fax: 01292 269555

Dumfries and Galloway Tourist Board
Tel: 01387 250434
Fax: 01387 250462

Edinburgh and Lothians Tourist Board
Tel: 0131 557 1700
Fax: 0131 557 5118

Glasgow and Clyde Area Tourist Board
Tel: 0141 204 4480
Fax:0141 204 4772

Highlands of Scotland and Skye Tourist Board
Tel:01463 731700
Fax: 01463 731701

Kingdom of Fife Tourist Board
Tel: 01334 474606
Fax: 01334 478422

Orkney Tourist Board
Tel: 01856 872856
Fax: 01856 875056

Perthshire Tourist Board
Tel: 01738 627958
Fax: 01738 630416

Scottish Borders Tourist Board
Tel: 01835 863435/863688
Fax: 01835 864097

Shetland Tourism
Tel: 01595 693434
Fax: 01595 695807

Western Isles Tourist Board
Tel: 01851 703088
Fax: 01851 705244

For general enquiries please contact:

The Scottish Tourist Board
23 Ravelston Terrace, Edinburgh
Tel: 0131 332 2433
Fax: 0131 343 1513

Mansfield House Hotel

WEENSLAND ROAD, HAWICK.
Tel. 01450-373988

Standing in its own wooded grounds overlooking Hawick this charming Victorian House Hotel is now considered one of the best restaurants in the Scottish Borders.

The magnificent Dining Room which has been restored to its original glory makes dining out a real pleasure.

The menus which have a Scottish flavour feature the very best of local and Scottish produce and are complemented by an excellent wine list.

We are sure you will enjoy a memorable meal in the most memorable of surroundings.

See entry page 120

See entry page 58

Mansefield House
HOTEL & RESTAURANT

An impressive former Georgian Manse which has been virtually rebuilt and extended. Mansefield House enjoys an unrivalled reputation for its luxurious decor, excellent food and friendly service. Our restaurant, which specialises in seafood, hosts regular Gourmet evenings accompanied by our pianist.

You will find Mansefield House an ideal base for the many country pursuits which Moray has to offer.

**For further information on weekend breaks, please telephone (Elgin) 01343-540883.
Mansefield House, Mayne Road, Elgin, Moray IV30 1NY**

AA **RAC★★★**

See entry page 103

See entry page 69

Meall mo Chridhe Country House
(c.1790) Ardnamurchan

Dine by Candlelight in our historic dining room overlooking the sea, enjoy the freshest of local fish, game and produce from our walled garden. We make all our own breads, ice creams & sauces and appetising vegetarian dishes.
This country house is the ideal location for touring the West Highlands, handy car ferry to/from Tobermory. Above all peace and tranquillity from todays pressurised lifestyle.
Roy & Janet Smith
Meall mo Chridhe Country House
Kilchoan, West Ardnamurchan, Argyll PH36 4HL
Tel/Fax 01972 510 238

Monachyle Mhor Hotel/Farmhouse

Small family run, 18th Century award winning hotel/farmhouse is set in its own 2000 acres.
All bedrooms, en-suite with the most magnificent views overlooking Lochs Voil & Doine.
The hotel is delightfully furnished with family period furniture & country fabrics.
Robert & Jean Lewis invite you to dine in our restaurant with delicious dishes including game and fresh herbs from our own estate. The farmhouse is fully licensed & non-residents are most welcome to dine with us. We serve unusual bar meals all day. Glasgow/Edinburgh 1 hour. Private fishing & stalking to guests.
Open all year.

♛♛♛
STB Commended
 AA ★★❀❀

Please write or telephone for bookings or further details.
Balquhidder, Lochearnhead, Perthshire FK19 8PQ
Tel 01877-384 622 • Fax 01877-384 305

It's been pouring in Scotland since 1864.
MATTHEW ALGIE
SCOTTISH CHOICE
PREMIUM ROUND TEA BAGS
BLENDING for SCOTTISH WATER
SINCE 1864
250g
88
TEA BAGS
ESTABLISHED
·1864·
MATTHEW ALGIE
Tea & Coffee Merchants
THERE'S ONLY ONE SCOTTISH CHOICE

MAXWELTON HOUSE

*Visit the birthplace of
Annie Laurie made famous by
the well loved ballad.*

House, Gardens, Museum, Chapel, Lunch/Tea Room: Taste of Scotland Award 1993, Gift Shop and Craft Shops

Parking FREE for coaches and Cars

Visitors coming for lunch or tea are welcome to enjoy the extensive gardens and greenhouses, with a varied collection of trees, shrubs and plants.

The Museum, restored from its ruinous state and part of a charming collection of buildings situated about a courtyard, houses early domestic tools and implements of kitchen, dairy, farm and garden, and is well worth a visit.

**Tel: 01848 200 385
or write to: Maxwelton House Trust,
Moniaive, Thornhill, Dumfriesshire, DG3 4DX**

See entry page 161

See entry page 76

THEATRE RESTAURANT

18-22 Greenside Place, Edinburgh EH1 3AA
Reservations 0131-557 8339 Facsimile 0131-557 6520

For the past 18 months Overtures has had a centre stage role on the Edinburgh scene.

Located within the Edinburgh Playhouse but with a separate entrance next to the box office. Overtures has become a popular choice for theatre goers and other diners.

The comprehensive Table D'Hote menu centres on a Scottish/French style of food with every dish using fresh, local produce. For vegetarians there is always a starter and main course

The restaurant is open from Monday to Saturday 6.00pm until late. It is also open at lunchtime on matinee days but private parties can be held by arrangements.

Table D' Hote: 3 Course £16.50

See entry page 101

See entry page 139

THE ROMAN CAMP
COUNTRY HOUSE HOTEL

Nestling in the heart of the beautiful Trossachs, the Roman Camp Hotel offers a magical mixture of gracious living and historic atmosphere.

Surrounded by 20 acres of superb gardens on the banks of the River Teith, the hotel's picturesque interior reflects the original charm of this 17th century building.

All bedrooms have private bathrooms, and facilities which make for a welcoming, comfortable stay. Guests can enjoy peace and tranquillity in a truly unique style.

Fresh produce and fine wines will tempt the most discerning diner and friendly personal service creates an atmosphere of leisured living.

The Roman Camp invites you to relax and enjoy the warmest of welcomes and the greatest of pleasure.

For brochure, tariff and reservations write, telephone or fax.

**The Roman Camp Hotel
Callander FK17 8BG
Telephone 01877-330003 Fax 01877-331533**

ROSEDALE HOTEL

**Portree, Isle of Skye
Tel: 01478 613131 Fax: 01478 612531**

Long established hotel in unrivalled waterfront situation. All bedrooms are en suite and individual in style and character with tv, radio and tea/coffee making facilities. Most rooms face the water. Public rooms include two lounges, one bar and a restaurant with an A.A.Rosette.

Egon Ronay, Ashley Courtenay, Signpost, Les Routiers, Taste of Scotland

AA ★★ ❀   **RAC**★★

Scotland's Cheeses

The climate and geography of Scotland are well suited to cheese-making. The traditional means of using plentiful summer milk, or for conversion into a form suitable for transportation to market from remote areas where there was insufficient market for liquid milk. The short summer-making season in Scotland meant that traditional cheeses usually required to be capable of being stored (matured) through the winter - hence the predominance of hard (pressed) cheese in Scotland and Britain.

At one time most farmhouses or crofts in Scotland had one or more dairy cows and made their own cheese, but the sheer physical effort involved for little financial return and improved transportation of milk changed the scene dramatically. Today there are more than two dozen cheesemakers across Scotland, ranging from the two large industrial Cheddar creameries at Lockerbie and Stranraer operating all year round, to the long established island creameries and to the handful of artisan cheese makers some of whose cheeses are available only locally when milking conditions permit. Several of these can be found on The Isles of Orkney.

Scottish Cheddar accounts for 80% of total output and the main creameries are located at Lockerbie, Stranraer and Campbeltown and on the islands of Bute, Arran, Islay, Mull, Gigha and Orkney. Often the creameries are open to visitors.

The advent of modern temperature controlled facilities and refrigerated transport has led to a re-awakening in artisan cheesemaking in a dozen or more small creameries and farms across the country. For the first time there are now available genuine Scottish speciality cheeses and superb, yet distinctive local versions of internationally popular fine cheeses such as Brie, Camembert, St Paulin and Gruyere. The cheeses invariably reflect great commitment by individual cheesemakers and are well worthwhile seeking out.

Some of these are described below :

Bishop Kennedy:
a 'trappist' cheese of a style made for hundreds of years in the monasteries of France but still relatively unknown in Scotland. Full fat soft cheese, rind washed in malt whisky to produce a distinctive orangey red crust and a strong creamy taste. Runny when ripe.

Bonchester:
small coulommier-style cheese made with unpasteurised Jersey milk. Available mainly March to December.

Bonnet:
mild, pressed goatsmilk cheese from small a Ayrshire dairy. Similar to Inverloch (Isle of Gigha) and Sanday (Isles of Orkney).

Brie:
Howgate Scottish Brie, traditionally made, matures to a runny sticky texture. Also Howgate Camembert.

Brodick Blue:
ewes milk blue cheese from Brodick. Arran Blue is the cows milk version.

Caboc:
(see cream cheese)

Caithness:
a new mild, Danish style wax coated cheese. Also available smoked.

Cream Cheese:
several versions, mostly based on revived traditional Highland recipes and rolled in oatmeal, including Caboc (Ross-shire), Howgate (Tayside) and Lochaber-smoked. Available plain or with peppercorns, garlic or herbs.

Crowdie:
a soft fresh cheese, several versions, mainly available only locally. An ancient Highland crofters cheese originally made using milk left after the cream had separated naturally. Plain or flavoured with peppercorns, garlic or herbs. (Hrasma, Crannog, Gruth Dhu etc.).

Dunlop:
closely resembling Scottish cheddar with soft texture. Mostly creamery-made in blocks on Arran and Islay but also traditionally in Ayrshire (Burns), near Dumfries and at Perth (Gowrie).

Dunsyre Blue:
cows milk farmhouse blue cheese made on the same farm as Lanark Blue, with vegetarian rennet and unpasteurised milk.

Howgate:
established artisan cheesemaker, originally from Howgate near Edinburgh, now located near Dundee. Pioneered the making in Scotland of continental cheeses including Howgate Brie, Camembert and Pentland. Other cheeses include St Andrews, Bishop Kennedy, Strathkinness and Howgate Highland Cream Cheese.

Inverloch:
pasteurised pressed goats cheese from Isle of Gigha. Coated in red wax. Also popular fruit shaped waxed cheeses.

Isle of Mull:
traditional unpasteurised farmhouse cheddar from Tobermory. Cloth-bound.

Kelsae:
unpasteurised pressed cheese made near Kelso from Jersey milk. Similar to Wensleydale but creamier in texture and taste.

Lanark Blue:
unpasteurised ewes milk cheese in the style of Roquefort.

Loch Arthur:
traditional farmhouse organic cheddar from Loch Arthur creamery near Dumfries.

Mull of Kintyre:
small truckle of mature Scottish cheddar coated in black wax. A smoked version is also available.

The Orkney Isles:
distinctive cheddar whose history goes back nearly two centuries, made in two creameries on Orkney. Several seasonal crofting cheeses are sometimes available locally

Pentland:
traditional unpasteurised brie made in small quantities and not widely available (see Howgate)

St Andrews:
award winning full fat, washed rind soft cheese, mild creamy, full flavoured with characteristic golden, orangey rind. (See Howgate)

Scottish Cheddar:
creamery produced cheddar now made in Galloway (Stranraer), Lockerbie, Rothesay and Campbeltown.

Stichill:
unpasteurised creamy Jersey milk Cheshire-style cheese from the Scottish Borders.

Strathkinness:
award wining Scottish version of Gruyere, nearly 50 gallons of milk goes into a cheese! Matured 6-12 months (see Howgate) Limited availability.

Swinzie:
pasteurised, pressed, ewes milk cheese from Ayrshire.

Teviotdate:
vignotte-style, white moulded unpasteurised cheese.

Makers of Fine Cheese

❖ ❖ ❖ ❖ ❖ ❖ ❖ ❖ ❖ ❖ ❖ ❖

St. Andrews • Bishop Kennedy • Strathkinness
Pentland • Howgate Brie • Camembert
Highland Cream Cheese

Established 1966

Howgate Cheese, Camperdown Creamery, Dundee DD2 3QQ. Tel: 01382 811622, Fax: 01382 811722

THE SANDFORD

COUNTRY HOUSE HOTEL

The Sandford Hotel, one of the Kingdom of Fife's most picturesque, listed, country house hotels, is renowned for its fine Scottish and European cuisine and comfortable accommodation.

Seasonal dishes in particular, served in the oak beamed restaurant, are the hallmark of Head Chef, Steven Johnstone. An extensive wine list has been carefully chosen in order to complement the variety of dishes on the extensive table d'hôte menu.

The Sandford is located near to both St Andrews and Dundee, and provides an ideal venue for those touring, fishing, golfing or shooting in this region of Scotland.

Bar Lunch 12.00 to 2.00 pm
Bar Supper and Dinner 6.00 to 9.30 pm
Open January to December (inclusive)
Languages: French, German, Italian

The Sandford Country House Hotel
Newton Hill, Wormit, nr Dundee, Fife DD6 8RG
Tel 01382-541802 • Fax 01382-542136

See entry page 90

Soroba House Hotel

Endowed with panoramic views of Oban Bay and the hills of Morvern, the Soroba House Hotel is situated within nine acres of gardens and woodlands. Away from the hustle and bustle of the town, yet it is near enough to enjoy the town centre's facilities. It is close to the newly opened Lorn and Islands General Hospital.

The Hotel offers bright modern one bedroom suites and two bedroom garden suites. Conference facilities are available for up to 60 delegates.

The Restaurant specialises in traditional cuisine with local seafood and Aberdeen Angus beef. All meals are served from breakfast through to dinner and bar supper.

SOROBA HOUSE HOTEL & GARDEN SUITES
OBAN, SCOTLAND PA34 4SB
TELEPHONE: 01631 562 628

See entry page 166

STRATHISLA
ESTD 1786
CHIVAS REGAL

STRATHISLA DISTILLERY

The Home and Heart of Chivas Regal

A visit includes free coffee and shortbread, visitor handbook, self guided tour of distillery, opportunity to nose a range of whiskies, a complimentary dram of Strathisla or Chivas Regal, souvenir brochure, distillery shop.

Admission Charge

For adults includes a £2 voucher redeemable in the distillery shop. Under 18s free. Please note that children under the age of eight are not admitted to production areas.

Opening Times

Open end January to end November.
Monday to Friday 9.30am - 4.00pm
Saturday 9.30am - 4.00pm July and August

Strathisla Distillery, Keith. *Telephone: 01542 783044*

THE GLENLIVET DISTILLERY VISITORS CENTRE

Enjoy the traditional hospitality of the oldest licensed distillery in the Highlands

Distillery Tour, Free Sample, Whisky and Souvenir Shop, Coffee Shop, Audio Visual Facilities for Disabled People

Open mid March to end of October Monday to Saturday 10.00am - 4.00pm. Sunday 12.30 - 4.00pm
July and August 10.00am - 6.00pm
Coach parties by arrangement. Telephone Glenlivet on 01542 783220. The Glenlivet Reception Centre is 10 miles north of Tomintoul on the B9008.

On the Whisky Trail
"Unhurried since 1824"

® The Glenlivet and Glenlivet are Registered Trademarks

Scottish Salmon

Stir your imaginations with the thought of silver scales gliding through pure, highland waters, and it's not too difficult to reason why gourmets everywhere declare Scottish salmon to be the finest salmon in the world.

Once, Scottish rivers held such abundant stocks of wild salmon that rich and poor could feast on them at will. Poached in vast copper kettles, fresh salmon graced the laird's table and fed the hungry apprentice. The sea captain dined heartily on salmon which had been pickled, smoked and salted for the long voyage.

Today, we too can savour Scottish salmon. Although, sadly, depleted numbers of wild salmon have made it an expensive seasonal delicacy, the Scottish salmon farming industry ensures that the finest quality farmed salmon is available for you to enjoy all year long at an affordable price.

With over 25 years of experience, Scottish salmon farmers nurture their fish in the clear, fast-flowing waters of Scottish lochs and coastal inlets. Their expert husbandry skills, ensure a succulent firm textured salmon with superb flavour.

Indeed, you can unleash your wildest gastronomic designs on salmon. It is succulent poached simply, or equally mouth watering complemented with a rich French sauce or a spicy dip from Thailand.

Salmon is also quick to prepare whether you choose to grill, steam, bake, pan-fry or microwave it. Eat indoors or enjoy salmon al fresco, sizzling on the barbecue and add colour and flavour to the traditional repertoire. In either case, a meal can be ready in less than 20 minutes.

The versatility of salmon goes on and on. Why not try the unique taste of Scottish smoked salmon? Nestled in the highlands and islands, smokehouses use closely guarded secret recipes to cure salmon in a way which will inspire.

Why is salmon increasingly popular? Simply because more people are realising that Scottish salmon is not only tasty and versatile but equally, the healthy choice. Salmon is rich in protein, but also contains calcium, iron and essential vitamins A, B6, B12 and D. It's polyunsaturated fish oils are also a good source Omega 3 fatty acids which can help lower blood cholesterol levels as part of a low fat diet. It's also the slimmers choice too with a 4oz portion of salmon typically containing under 200 calories when steamed or poached.

However, as with all recipes, ingredients are crucial. To ensure you are getting the best from your Scottish salmon look for the Tartan Quality Mark, which is found widely available either as a gill tag attached to a whole fish or as a label on prepacked fresh cuts or smoked salmon.

Only Scottish salmon which are reared in accordance with the stringent standards of the Scottish Quality Salmon scheme are eligible to carry the Tartan Quality Mark, so it is your guarantee that the fish, whether fresh or smoked, is both genuinely Scottish and in peak condition.

Indeed the French, well known for their sensuous delight in food have singled out Tartan Quality Mark Scottish salmon to the first foreign food to carry their prestigious Label Rouge Mark for quality produce. Salmon identified with Tartan Quality Mark/ Label Rouge logos can be found in leading French supermarkets and fishmongers.

Make one of Scotland's finest products a regular feature on your menus. *Enjoy Scottish salmon.*

TARTAN QUALITY MARK
SCOTTISH SALMON

Simply Superior

For details of local stockists
or recipes contact
**The Scottish Salmon Bureau
on 0131 229 8411.**

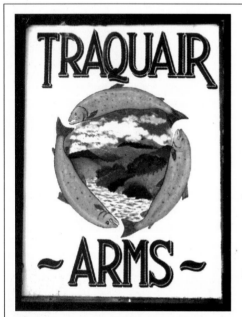

Reputation for Excellence

Like other products with a reputation for excellence it takes time and skill to produce specially selected Scotch Beef.

Taste of Scotland members have a commitment to quality and you will find this reflected in their presentation of Scotch Beef. Alternatively, for your own cooking, look throughout the UK for butchers who are Associate members of the Guild of Scotch Quality Meat Suppliers, and who are identified by the Guild's logo. And whilst in Scotland, look out too for butchers displaying the SFMTA's own 'Shop With Confidence' logo.

For a list of all your local stockists of Scotch Beef and Scotch Lamb phone or fax us:
Scotch Quality Beef and Lamb Association
Tel: 0131 333 5335 Fax: 0131 333 2935

**Winner Gourmet Section and
overall winner of the 1995 Taste of Scotland
Scotch Lamb Challenge:**

Kevin McGillivray,

Ballathie House Hotel, Kinclaven,
Perthshire.

Winner Classic Section:

Suki Barber, Chef/Proprietor,

Old Pines Restaurant with Rooms,
Spean Bridge.

Scotch Lamb

Naturally, one of the Traditional Tastes of Scotland

Scotland, as every gourmet knows, boasts a natural larder which groans with a vast selection of quality foods - amongst them the Scotch Beef and Lamb which have been acclaimed for centuries.

Historically, Scottish cuisine was based on a 'one-pot' system which provided robust, nourishing dishes well suited to the times.

Tradition will always have its honoured place on any nation's tables, but today appetites are more sophisticated, tastes are more international, and chefs more innovative than ever before. Widely appreciative of the natural fine qualities, flavour and versatility of Scotch Lamb, chefs now produce an annually widening selection of Scotch Lamb dishes to please the modern palate and to delight the eye.

The Scotch Quality Beef and Lamb Association which was established more than twenty years ago to let the wider world know more

about these two Scottish specialities has long been associated with the Taste of Scotland scheme. Some years ago this cooperation reached new heights with the establishment of an annual competition for all chefs working in Taste of Scotland restaurants, be they large and small. Competition entries have risen year by year and the event is now divided into two categories. 1995 saw eight finalists - from an initial field of almost eighty chefs - compete for the honour of winning SQBLA's Taste of Scotland Scotch Lamb trophies and titles.

Above

Kevin Mcgillivray, Executive Chef, *Ballathie House Hotel*, Overall Winner (left) - and Stephen Ward.

Left

Suki Barber's prize winning meal, *Old Pines Restaurant with rooms.*

Rolled Saddle of Scotch Lamb with Chestnuts, Truffle and Thyme

Accompanied by a Natural Jus, Wild Mushrooms, Parsnip Mousse and Gratin Potatoes

1995 Taste of Scotland Scotch Lamb Challenge

Winner: Gourmet Section and Overall Winner

Kevin MacGillivray, Head Chef, Ballathie House Hotel,

Kinclaven, Perthshire

Ingredients

2 lb (900g) Scotch lamb saddle

2 oz (50g) chestnuts

1 oz (25g) truffle

2 sprigs thyme

4 oz (100g) wild mushrooms

1 lb (450g) parsnips

2 lb (900g) potatoes

2 pints (1.2L) cream

3 eggs

2 oz (50g) white breadcrumbs

1 oz (25g) garlic puree

seasoning

8 oz (225g) mirepoix vegetables

(carrots, onions, celery, bouquet garni)

6 juniper berries

1 tablespoon thyme jelly

½ pint (300ml) sherry

(Serves 4)

Method

1   Bone a saddle of lamb for rolling. Chop bones and roast for stock.

2   Add the mirepoix of vegetables, juniper berries, thyme jelly and sherry.

3   Cover with water and bring to the boil. Simmer for 45 minutes.

4   Take the lamb fillets and chop finely. Add the diced truffle, wild mushrooms, 1 egg, breadcrumbs and chopped chestnuts.

5   Place the forcemeat into the centre of the lamb saddle, roll and tie for roasting.

6   Roast for 45-50 minutes at GM5\190°C\375°F. Remove and rest prior to carving.

Parsnip Mousse

7   Cook the parsnips until soft, drain and puree.

8   Add the cream and eggs with seasoning and divide the mixture into four dariole moulds.

9   Place in a bain marie to cook for 12 minutes at GM3\170°C\325°F

Gratin Potatoes

10   Peel and slice the potatoes, season dish with garlic, nutmeg, salt and pepper.

11   Line dish with potatoes, cover with cream and cook for 35 minutes at GM5\190°C\375°F.

Sauce

12   Reduce stock until consistency is reached, check for seasoning.

13   Carve lamb onto warm plates with the potatoes and parsnip mousse.

Sauce the plates and garnish with a sprig of thyme.

Filleted Loin of Scotch Lamb on a Bed of Lamb's Liver and Caramelised Onions

with a Rosemary Scented Jus, Glazed New Potatoes and Baby Vegetables.

1995 Taste of Scotland Scotch Lamb Challenge

Winner: Classic Section

Sukie Barber, Proprietor, Old Pines Restaurant with Rooms,

by Spean Bridge

Ingredients

1 loin of Scotch lamb
(approx. 1 3/4 lb) (800g)

8 oz (225g) lamb's liver

1 lb (450g) onions

¼ pint (150ml) sweet white wine

8 oz (225g) any new potatoes

8 oz (225g) each of 3 baby
vegetables in season,

 carrots, turnips, asparagus

4 oz (100g) butter

2 sprigs fresh rosemary

(Serves 4)

Method

1   Fillet the lamb and roast the chopped bones, skin and fat with two cut onions and pepper in a hot oven GM9\240ºC\475ºF until well browned. Reserve the fat and transfer the rest to a saucepan and cover with water.

2   Add two sprigs of fresh rosemary and reduce to make ¼ pint (150ml) of strong stock.

3   Slowly sweat 2 finely chopped onions in butter until soft and golden brown - at least one hour at low heat. As they start to caramelise, add the sweet wine and cook for a further 30 minutes to reduce the wine.

4   Seal the whole fillet in a frying pan using fat reserved from roasting the bones and transfer to an oven and roast for 15 minutes at GM7\220ºC\425ºF allowing sufficient time for it to rest for 10 minutes before carving - the fillet should be pink all through.

5   Cut lamb's liver into fine fingers and fry quickly in butter. While still pink, add and stir into the hot onion mixture.

6   Reheat the jus, adding cold butter to slightly thicken. Taste and check seasoning.

7   Cut the lamb fillet into 4 and slice each piece into 3, leaving the slices all attached at one edge.

8   Fan out these slices on a bed of the onion and lamb's liver. Surround them with lightly boiled baby vegetables and new potatoes glazed with butter. Spoon on the rosemary scented lamb jus *(not over the lamb)* and serve.

A TASTE
of
SCOTLAND
1996

Shetland Islands

121

Lerwick

Orkney Islands

Stromness

120

To Stromness

John o' Groats

Port of Ness

Durness

Balchrick

A836 161 Thurso

A838 205 Tongue

A836

A895 Wick

Altnaharra

A897

8 Kinbrace

157 Lybster

A9

106

118 Stornoway

Isle of Lewis

A859

Culkein

146

155

Lochinver

6

211 Ullapool

Lairg 185 Brora

A837

A839

Harris 116

147 150

22

Kincardine 68 Dornoch

90

A832

198 Tain

North Uist

Gairloch

A835

Invergordon

67

92 55 Cromarty 62 41 80 Elgin Fochabers 85 63

A832

165 166 87 Forres

206 31 112 Nairn 108 Keith 209 Fraserburgh

A890 Inverness A939 28 57 A96 Huntly Banff A98

153 66 102 98 70 A950 Peterhead

179 71 50 173 168

Skye

Benbecula 114

South Uist

81 Kyle of Lochalsh 48 35 A939 129 Inverurie To Lerwick

145 A82 23

95 13 111 Dyce

138 A87 88 214 136 Aviemore 27 5 Aberdeen

Kingussie 137 38 Banchory 1

Canna Rum Ardvasar

Barra 158 Mallaig

17 96 189 Newtonmore Braemar 192

A830 A86 Stonehaven

Eigg 89 Fort William A9

174

15 33 A93

196 25 Glencoe 139 131 144 97 Brechin Johnshaven

Coll 127 178 Pitlochry 9 Montrose

Tobermory 11 A82 3 77 34 86 Forfar A92

123 180 126 30 110

Tiree Ulva Mull 119 172 A85 128 210 59 154 54 100 Arbroath 12

Oban 29 151 60 Dundee 42

Iona 195 Callander 101 75

133 A85 177 Perth Cupar St Andrews

This Map is only intended to give an approximate geographical position for the town or place so numbered in the Guide.

If going to any of the establishments mentioned you need to combine this Map with a proper Road Atlas.

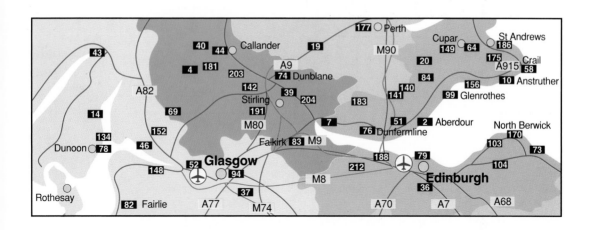

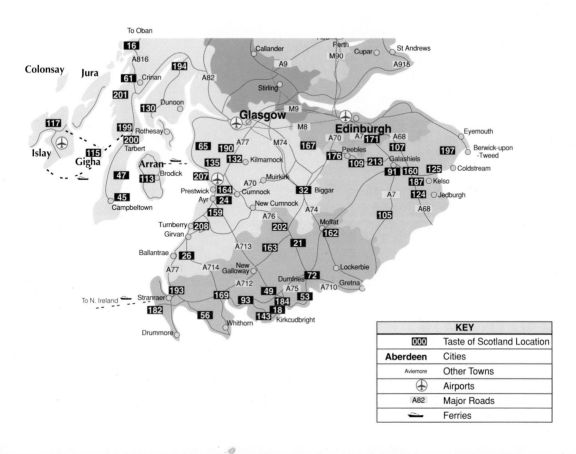

KEY	
000	Taste of Scotland Location
Aberdeen	Cities
Aviemore	Other Towns
✈	Airports
A82	Major Roads
⛴	Ferries

LISTINGS

1996

Credit Card Code	Meal Price Range
1 Access/Mastercard/Eurocard	(a) under £10
2 American Express	(b) £10 - £15
3 Visa	(c) £15 - £20
4 Carte Bleu	(d) £20 - £25
5 Diners Club	(e) £25 - £30
6 Mastercharge	(f) over £30

Aberdeen

Ardoe House Hotel

Blairs, South Deeside Road
Aberdeen AB1 5YP
Tel: 01224 867355
Fax: 01224 861283

B9077, 3 miles west of Aberdeen.

A magnificent hotel in wooded parkland just outside Aberdeen providing excellent accommodation and food.

- Scottish Baronial mansion converted to a comfortable country house hotel.
- Modern and traditional Scottish cuisine.
- "Exquisite dishes with continental influences carefully presented in enchanting surroundings."

Ardoe House is a classic Scots Baronial granite mansion, with towers and corbelled bartizans, crow-stepped gables and crenellations. It was built in 1898 by a wealthy soap manufacturer, 'Soapie' Ogston, for his wife. As day turns to night Ardoe turns into a fairy castle and it is a delight to relax in the original palatial rooms. The bedrooms have private facilities and there are also function rooms available for conferences and weddings. Dining is a la carte, from an extensive menu of unusually treated dishes and imaginative combinations. Chef Paul Bergin draws inspiration from classic French cooking, but gives every dish a spin of his own.

Open all year
Rooms: 71 with private facilities
Room Rate £30 - £150
Special Rates available for 2 nights
Bar Lunch 12 - 2 pm (b)
Dining Room/Restaurant Lunch 12.30 - 2 pm except Sat (b)
Bar Supper 6 - 9.45 pm (b)
Dinner 6.30 - 9.30 pm (d-e) 4 course menu
Dogs accepted at Manager's discretion
Vegetarians welcome

Galantine of Scottish quail filled with a damson and blackcurrant farce. Roast cannon of lamb on a gâteau of tarragon potatoes, baby ratatouille with a rosemary jus. Clootie dumpling with a thistle of ice cream and sweet vinaigrette.

STB Highly Commended 5 Crowns
Credit cards: 1, 2, 3, 5 + SWITCH

Caledonian Thistle Hotel

Union Terrace
Aberdeen AB9 1HE
Tel: 01224 640233
Fax: 01224 641627

City centre.

Traditional city centre hotel.

- Town hotel in the heart of Aberdeen.
- Traditional cooking.
- "The hotel provides old fashioned standards of hospitality in a very convenient location for those visiting Aberdeen."

This large, imposing Victorian hotel overlooks Union Terrace Gardens and is very close to Union Street, the main shopping street of the Granite City. It is well appointed and tastefully decorated in a style which complements the architectural features; bedrooms are traditionally furnished and very comfortable. The Restaurant on the Terrace is of a high standard offering a well balanced table d'hote menu which features local fish and seafood. For less formal eating there is Elrond's Cafe, a spacious bar and restaurant which serves drinks, snacks and a bistro menu. The Caledonian Thistle is a very conveniently located base to explore all that Aberdeen has to offer.

Open all year
Rooms: 80 with private facilities
Bed & Breakfast £45 - £120
Dinner B & B £52 - £135
Room Rate £102 - £140
Special Weekend Rates available
Cafe Bar open all day (b)
Bar Lunch 11 am - 2 pm except Sun Sat (a)
Dining Room/Restaurant Lunch 12 - 2 pm except Sun Sat (b)
Dinner 6.30 - 10 pm Mon to Sat: 6.30 - 9.30 pm Sun (d)
Vegetarians welcome

Layers of Scotch salmon, leeks and filo pastry baked and laced with a watercress, salmon caviar butter sauce. Soft flour tortillas, folded and filled with medallions of lobster tail, guacamole, cheese, peppers, chillies and spices. King scallops baked in shell with chablis cream and chives.

STB Commended 5 Crowns
Credit cards: 1, 2, 3, 5

The Courtyard on the Lane

No 1 Alford Lane
Aberdeen AB1 1YD
Tel: 01224 213795

The Macallan Taste of Scotland Award Winner 1994.

In Aberdeen's west end, between Holburn Street and Albyn Place, just round the corner from Union Street.

A gourmet's paradise in central Aberdeen.

- City centre restaurant and bistro.
- Modern Scottish cooking.
- "First class in all departments."

The Courtyard on the Lane is a small stone building in a cobbled lane in Aberdeen's commercial district. It is a sanctuary of good food and a great discovery. Martha's Bistro (downstairs) serves sophisticated bistro-style dishes, prepared with continental flair, in an informal atmosphere. Upstairs, the Courtyard Restaurant is more formal and encourages you to linger over lunch or dinner. The short, a la carte menus presented here change daily; the choices are imaginative, the treatment creative, the cooking superb. Tony Heath and Shona Drysdale are experienced and accomplished restaurateurs and friendly hosts. They are supported by a loyal clientele, so it is advisable to book.

Open all year except Christmas + Boxing Days, 1 Jan + 2 wks Jul
Bistro Lunch 12 - 2.30 pm except Sun Mon (b)
Dining Room/Restaurant Lunch 12 - 2 pm except Sun Mon (c)
Bistro Supper 6.30 - 10 pm except Sun Mon (b)
Dinner 7 - 9.30 pm except Sun Mon (d)
Closed Sun Mon
Vegetarians welcome

Terrine of west coast scallops and langoustines with a shellfish dressing. Grilled fillets of turbot, brill and halibut with a dill and mustard hollandaise. Loin of local lamb with a gratin of tomatoes and potatoes cooked in stock. Caramelised apple tart with caramel ice cream and toffee sauce. Bistro: char-grilled John Dory on a red pepper sauce. Smoked haddock and tomato omelette. Marinaded pan-fried tuna with an aubergine relish and red pepper puree.

Credit cards: 1, 2, 3, 6 + SWITCH, DELTA
Proprietors: Balgownie Restaurants Ltd

Craighaar Hotel

Waterton Road, Bucksburn
Aberdeen AB2 9HS
Tel: 01224 712275
Fax: 01224 716362

Turn off A96 roundabout at Bankhead Avenue. Follow to end then turn left along Bankhead Road. Straight ahead at crossroads.

A comfortable user-friendly hotel with good restaurant and bar.

- A modern hotel in a residential part of Aberdeen, 5 minutes from the airport.
- Traditional food well-presented.
- "Chef Kenneth Moir and his team produce creative dishes for all tastes, and present traditional food attractively."

This modern hotel is well-placed in relation both to Aberdeen and its airport, and is understandably popular with business people on this account. But its situation is by no means its only attraction. The traditional bar has a lively atmosphere, serves good bar food and has an open log fire. There are a number of attractive 'gallery suites', which have comfortable sitting rooms and bedrooms upstairs. There are also function rooms for conferences, seminars or private dinner parties. In the restaurant you will find friendly service and a wide-ranging choice of modern and traditional dishes, which reflect the excellence of the produce available locally.

Open all year
Note: Christmas Day accommodation by request
Rooms: 55 with private facilities
Bed & Breakfast £25 - £93.90
Dinner B & B from £41.95
Special Rates available
Bar Lunch 12 - 2 pm except Sun Sat (a)
Dining Room/Restaurant Lunch 12 - 2 pm except Sun Sat (a-b)
Carvery Lunch 12 - 2.30 pm Sun only (a)
Bar Supper 6.30 - 10 pm (a-b)
Dinner 7 - 9.30 pm (b-d)
No dogs
Vegetarians welcome

Scottish smoked salmon and watercress terrine with a tomato and basil coulis. Loin of lamb stuffed with a basil mousse, on a wild rowan and mint jelly sauce. Escalope of salmon with fresh chervil and julienne of vegetables baked in filo pastry, served with a cream sauce flavoured with chablis, garlic and chervil.

STB Highly Commended 3 Crowns
Credit cards: 1, 2, 3, 5, 6 + SWITCH, DELTA

Craiglynn Hotel

36 Fonthill Road
Aberdeen AB1 2UJ
Tel: 01224 584050
Fax: 01224 584050

On corner of Fonthill Road and Bon Accord Street, midway between Union Street and King George VI Bridge. Car park access from Bon Accord Street.

A charming small hotel in the centre of Aberdeen offering comfortable accommodation, good food and genuine hospitality.

- An impressive Victorian family townhouse.
- Homely Scottish cooking.
- "A good standard of food, carefully cooked and well-presented."

Craiglynn Hotel was once the home of an Aberdeen fish merchant and has attractive rooms with high moulded ceilings and carved fire surrounds. These features have been carefully preserved by the hotel's owners, Chris and Hazel Mann, as have the parquet flooring and rose-wood panelling in the dining room (which was originally the billiard room). Service is friendly and attentive, and guests are made to feel part of the family. In the handsome dining room menus are short, since everything is prepared from fresh produce (even home-grown) daily, and the cooking homely. The bedrooms are very comfortable and have en suite facilities.

Open all year except Christmas + Boxing Days
Rooms: 9, 7 with private facilities
Bed & Breakfast £31.25 - £57.50
Dinner B & B £46.20 - £72.45
Special Weekend Rates available
Dinner at 7 pm (b)
Reservations required for non-residents
No smoking in dining room + bedrooms
Restricted Licence
No dogs
Vegetarians welcome

Home-made soups. Suprême of chicken with a fresh orange, tarragon and cream sauce. Lamb cobbler. Fillet of trout with almonds. Black cherry crumble. Sticky toffee pudding.

STB Commended 3 Crowns
Credit cards: 1, 2, 3, 5
Proprietors: Chris & Hazel Mann

Faraday's Restaurant

2 Kirk Brae, Cults
Aberdeen AB1 9SQ
Tel: 01224 869666
Fax: 01224 869666

4 miles from city centre on North Deeside Road. On reaching Cults, turn right at traffic lights - Faraday's 100 yards on right.

Faraday's has a deserved reputation for the quality and originality of its cooking.

- Small, atmospheric restaurant in a tastefully converted Victorian electricity station.
- Traditional Scottish cooking, with European, Eastern and African influences.
- "The menus offer interesting combinations of flavours: John Inches' cooking is assured and original."

Michael Faraday, after whom this restaurant is named, was 'The Father of Electricty'. The choice of name is appropriate for a building which was, in Victorian times, an electricity sub-station supplying the district of Cults. The room is long and inviting: its panelled walls decorated with tapestries and memorabilia; its tables of polished wood, with brass candlesticks and linen napery. Vases of cut flowers embellish the window embrasures, and there is a minstrel's gallery at one end. John Inches, Faraday's owner/chef, presents a short menu (five main courses, changing weekly) which he describes as 'Scottish traditional', but which draws inspiration from his extensive travels in France and makes intelligent use of Eastern flavourings and presentation. Faraday's was nominated for the Decanter Wine List of the Year Award.

Open all year except 26 Dec to 10 Jan
Restaurant/Bar Lunch 12 - 2.30 pm except Sun Mon (b)
Dinner 7 - 9.30 pm except Sun (c-d)
Closed Sun
Vegetarians welcome
Facilities for disabled visitors

Crispy filo parcels of smoked rainbow trout with a fresh dill cheese, light lemon and caper sauce. Oatmeal herring fillets with lemon bramley apples and gooseberries. Choux pastry buns filled with coffee ice and served with a coffee bean cream.

Credit cards: 1, 3 + SWITCH
Proprietor: John Inches

Lairhillock Inn & Restaurant

Netherley by Stonehaven
Aberdeenshire AB3 2QS
Tel: 01569 730001
Fax: 01569 731175

From Aberdeen take A90 south for 4 miles to Portlethen/Durris junction. Take Durris road for 2½ miles.

A charming old coaching inn beween Stonehaven and Aberdeen.

■ Small rural restaurant.
■ Modern cooking, with continental influences.
■ "An atmospheric, informal restaurant with an accomplished chef."

Lairhillock is a traditional small coaching inn (originally a farm house) of some antiquity. It stands on the old Stonehaven-Aberdeen road, and was certainly there when Bonnie Prince Charlie took this road north to ultimate defeat at Culloden in 1746. The place has been extensively refurbished by its current owners, Frank and Anne Budd, in a way which enhances the original rustic features (low ceilings, dark beams, carved oak bar front, large open hearth with real log fires). The result is a cosy, informal restaurant and bar with bags of atmosphere. The service is impeccable, and the food excellent. The menu is à la carte or table d'hôte and dishes are named in French - an indication of the style of cooking. Beef comes from local farms; daily fish from Gourdon; fruits from local suppliers. Sauces are interesting and appropriate, and the overall treatment of the food sensitive and unusually good. An interesting wine list features some unusual wines, and some first growths.

Open all year except Christmas + Boxing Days, 1 + 2 Jan
Bar Lunch 12 - 2 pm (b)
Dining Room/Restaurant Lunch 12 - 2 pm Sun (b)
Bar Supper 6 - 9.30 pm Sun to Thu: 6 - 10 pm Fri Sat (b)
Dinner 7 - 9 pm (d)
Vegetarians welcome
Facilities for disabled visitors

Aberdeen Angus fillet topped with haggis and malt whisky sauce. Daily changing fish platters. Wild boar goulash. Seafood crêpes. Stilton and wild mushroom soup. Local lamb with bourguignonne sauce.

Credit cards: 1, 2, 3, 5 + SWITCH, DELTA
Proprietors: Frank & Anne Budd

The Marcliffe at Pitfodels

North Deeside Road, Pitfodels
Aberdeen AB1 9PN
Tel: 01224 861000
Fax: 01224 868860

At the west end of Aberdeen, 2 miles from city centre on A93 Aberdeen-Braemar.

A country house hotel on the outskirts of Aberdeen with full facilities, en suite bedrooms and two restaurants.

■ A large modern building tastefully in keeping with the older house it encompasses.
■ Modern classic cooking with French influences.
■ "A wide-ranging menu to suit all appetites based on Scottish and local produce."

The Marcliffe at Pitfodels is a clever combination of old and new. During 1993 the original old house was restored and substantially added to, in a way which respected the style and feel of the older building. Its atmosphere is luxurious, and enhances modern design with antiques and baronial detailing - the spacious new foyer has a stone flagged floor, comfortable sofas and an open fire. The Marcliffe's proprietors, Sheila and Stewart Spence, are experienced hoteliers and this shows in the attention to detail and the high standard of service in every department. There are two restaurants: the Conservatory, and the Invery Room. Menus in both are well balanced and extensive; and the cooking is accomplished.

Open all year
Rooms: 42 with private facilities
Bed & Breakfast £95 - £145
Dinner B & B £115 - £170
Dining Room/Restaurant Lunch 12 - 2 pm (c)
Dinner 6.30 - 10 pm (d)
No smoking area in restaurant
Vegetarians welcome

Steamed fillet of halibut on a bed of noodles with a butter sauce flavoured with saffron and dill. Pastry casket filled with pasta and a sauce of asparagus, mushrooms and garlic in white wine and cream. Chocolate Marquise with an orange and coriander cream.

STB Highly Commended 5 Crowns
Credit cards: 1, 2, 3, 5
Proprietors: Stewart & Sheila Spence

Maryculter House Hotel

South Deeside Road
Aberdeen AB1 0BB
Tel: 01224 732124
Fax: 01224 733510

B9077 Banchory-Aberdeen (South Deeside Road) c 5 miles from Aberdeen, 1 mile west of B979 and B9077 junction. Signposted.

An historic country hotel outside Aberdeen.

■ Country hotel on the banks of the River Dee.
■ Country house cooking.
■ "Well presented meal in 'ancient' surroundings."

In the early 13th century a powerful Anglo-Norman noble founded a preceptory (college) of the Knights Templar on the south bank of the Dee. The remains of the preceptory is incorporated into Maryculter House - such as the vaulted ceiling in the cocktail bar and the huge open hearth fireplace above the old cellars (which date from 1255). The hotel has five acres of grounds on the banks of the river. The 23 bedrooms are all comfortable and tastefully decorated, as are the public rooms and bars. Food is served both in the bar, 'The Poacher's Pocket' and in the 'The Priory', a more formal dining room where the tables are charmingly dressed with linen and fresh orchids .The former's menu offers an interesting selection of well-priced bistro-style food; the latter's is a solid table d'hôte menu (six main courses) with a broad choice of meat, poultry, fish and vegetarian dishes.

Open all year
Rooms: 23 with private facilities
Bed & Breakfast £25 - £85
Dinner Bed & Breakfast £47 - £65
Bar Lunch 12 - 2.15 pm (b)
Bar Supper 6.30 - 9.15 pm (b)
Dinner 7 - 9.30 pm except Sun (e) 4 course menu
Vegetarians welcome
Facilities for disabled visitors
No smoking in restaurant

Breast of pheasant filled with a mushroom duxelle wrapped in smoked bacon, baked and served with a creamed oyster mushroom sauce. Poached suprême of Scottish salmon with a tomato, mushroom and mustard sauce.

STB Commended 4 Crowns
Credit cards: 1, 2, 3, 5, 6

Thainstone House Hotel

Thainstone Estate, Inverurie
Aberdeenshire AB51 5NT
Tel: 01467 621643
Fax: 01467 625084

On A96 north of Aberdeen (8 miles from airport).

A country house hotel and country club near Aberdeen, winners of Taste of Scotland Scotch Lamb Challenge 1992.

- Converted country mansion.
- Country house cooking.
- "Thainstone ranks among the best country house hotels in Scotland."

This charming house has been modernised to become a comfortable hotel and country club. Behind its imposing facade the house has been radically altered to create a luxurious modern hotel and leisure centre. The executive chef Gordon Dochard (ex Gleneagles) offers both à la carte and table d'hôte menus in 'Simpsons' Restaurant. There is an ambitious and bold feeling about many of the dishes; the presentation is influenced by nouvelle cuisine, but portion sizes and the quality of the raw materials are influenced only by the rich farming country within which Thainstone stands. You can also eat in Cammie's Bar, where the food and atmosphere is more informal. Member of the Scotch Beef Club.

Open all year
Rooms: 48 with private facilities
Bed & Breakfast £39.50 - £99.50
Dinner B & B £55.50 - £129
Room Rate £54 - £125
Special Rates available
Bar Lunch 12 - 2 pm (b)
Dining Room/Restaurant Lunch (Simpsons) 12 - 2 pm (b)
Bar Supper 6.30 - 9.30 pm (c)
Dinner (Simpsons) 7 - 9 pm (e) 4 course menu
Vegetarians welcome
No smoking in restaurant
No dogs

Seared fillet of sea trout with avocado and tomato vinaigrette. Roast fillet of Aberdeen Angus beef with potato rosti and rosemary gravy. Mille feuille of local raspberries with vanilla sabayon. White chocolate candle served upon an almond biscuit.

STB Highly Commended 5 Crowns
Credit cards: 1, 2, 3, 5, 6 + SWITCH

Hawkcraig House

Hawkcraig Point, Aberdour
Fife KY3 0TZ
Tel: 01383 860335

From centre of Aberdour, take Hawkcraig Road (signed 'Silver Sands') through large car park, then to right down very steep access to Hawkcraig Point.

Enchanting waterfront guest house.

- White-washed ferryman's house.
- Accomplished traditional cooking.
- "A really nice, friendly establishment with superb home cooking and hospitality."

This charming old white-washed ferryman's house sits at the water's edge at Hawkcraig Point, next to the old harbour with lovely views of Aberdour Bay and Inchcolm Island's, 12th century abbey. Only half an hour from Edinburgh by road or rail and a pleasant hour's drive from Gleneagles, St Andrews and the East Neuk of Fife. Elma Barrie is a superb hostess whose accomplished cooking encourages guests to return again and again to enjoy the comfort and hospitality of Hawkcraig House.

Open mid Mar to 28 Oct
Rooms: 2 with private facilities
Bed & Breakfast £20 - £26
Dinner B & B £40 - £46
Dinner 7 - 8.30 pm (d) 4 course menu
Open to non-residents booked meals only
Unlicensed - guests welcome to take own wine
Vegetarians welcome
Children over eight years welcome
No smoking throughout
No dogs

Home-made soups. Fresh crab, lobster, halibut and salmon from Pittenweem. Herb-crusted rack of lamb. Prime Roast beef. Hazelnut gateau with Scottish raspberries. Chocolate brandy roulade. Scottish cheeses.

STB Deluxe 3 Crowns
No credit cards
Proprietor: Elma Barrie

Farleyer House Hotel

by Aberfeldy, Perthshire
PH15 2JE
Tel: 01887 820332
Fax: 01887 829430

From A9 follow Aberfeldy at crossroads next to Blackwatch Inn turn right for Kinloch Rannoch and Castle Menzies. Through Weem village and past castle after ½ mile on right hand side of road.

An award-winning country house hotel in beautiful surroundings.

- A small, formal and intimate hotel, rightly renowned.
- Elegant Scottish cuisine with nouvelle cuisine influences in presentation.
- "Gracious living in a unique ambience."

In the heart of the old Castle Menzies estate, Farleyer was built as a croft in the 16th century. Enlarged twice since then Farleyer retains its air of calm opulence. Thirty-four acres of grounds enhance the house's tranquillity. Its Bistro offers imaginative Scottish cooking in a relaxed and informal atmosphere. The set menus in the Menzies Restaurant make the most of the outstanding quality of local game, meat and fish.

Open all year
Rooms: 11 with private facilities + 4 in grounds (Gillies Cottage)
Bed & Breakfast £70 - £80
Dinner B & B £90 - £100
Special Rates available
Bistro Lunch 12 - 2.30 pm (c)
Lunch (Menzies Restaurant) - private parties only
Bistro Dinner 6 - 9.30 pm (c)
Dinner (Menzies Restaurant) 7.30 for 8 pm (f) 4 course menu
Vegetarians welcome
Facilities for disabled visitors
No smoking in Menzies Restaurant
Dogs not allowed in hotel - kennel provided

Salad of pan-fried Skye scallops. Escalope of wild Tay salmon with a fresh herb sauce. Roast Highland 'rib eye' steak with an Aberfeldy malt sauce. Poached pears in red wine with Farleyer's vanilla ice cream. Selection of Scottish cheeses.

STB Deluxe 4 Crowns
Credit cards: 1, 2, 3, 5, 6 + SWITCH, DELTA
Resident Managing Director: Nick White

Guinach House

by The Birks, Aberfeldy
Perthshire PH15 2ET
Tel: 01887 820251
Fax: 01887 829607

On A826, south-west outskirts of Aberfeldy, on road to 'The Birks', Guinach is signposted from Urlar Road.

This small hotel is run by international Master Chef Bert MacKay and his wife, Marian, it has received the STB 'Glenturret Best Hotel in Perthshire' Award.

- This Victorian house is set in three acres of secluded gardens and birch woods with stunning views across Perthshire.
- Sophisticated cuisine combining a range of national and international influences.
- "Inspired Scottish cooking with a hint of French, using a delightful blend of flavours and textures".

Guinach House is a seven-roomed hotel immersed in the rolling countryside around Aberfeldy. It is an ideal location for those who simply wish to relax in tranquil surroundings and indulge in gastronomic inspiration. For those who prefer to build up an appetite more actively, there are nearby facilities for swimming, golf, fly fishing and riding. The MacKays are attentive and friendly hosts who run Guinach more like a home than a hotel. Bert's culinary expertise allows him to create rich and varied menus, while maximising on the availability of fresh local produce.

Open all year except Christmas + Boxing Days
Rooms: 7 with private facilities
Bed & Breakfast from £37.50
Dinner B & B from £58.50
Dinner 7 - 9.30 pm (d) 4 course menu
Vegetarians welcome
No smoking in dining room

West coast mussels cooked in white wine with onions and herbs. Local oak-smoked venison. Grilled halibut steak with a lemon and prawn butter, set on braised sorrel. Fillet of beef topped with diced chicken liver with capsicums masked in a Madeira wine sauce. Layers of shortcake with strawberries. Profiteroles with hot chocolate sauce.

STB Highly Commended 3 Crowns
Credit cards: 1, 3
Proprietor: Albert MacKay

Braeval Restaurant

nr Aberfoyle, Stirling
FK8 3UY
Tel: 01877 382 711
Fax: 01877 382 400

Situated on the A81, 1 mile outside Aberfoyle, next to the golf course.

A small restaurant which ranks among the best in Britain.

- A country restaurant with a formidable reputation.
- Outstanding modern Scottish cooking.
- "Nick Nairn has won many awards, all of them deserved. To eat here is a memorable experience."

Nick Nairn was the youngest Scottish chef ever to win a Michelin Star (in 1991, retained ever since). A former merchant seaman, he is self-taught (like so many leading chefs!) and opened Braeval with his wife, Fiona, in 1986. Since then he has won many awards, including the Macallan/Decanter 'Best Restaurant' of the Year. He presents a set four course menu (choice of desserts) at both lunch and dinner, and is happy to discuss special requirements (e.g. vegetarian) prior to arrival. The menus change daily according to the produce available - important, since Nick cooks in the straightforward modern manner which allows flavours to speak for themselves. He has evolved his own style: simple, but with flair and imagination. Nick also runs a cookery school at Braeval. Member of the Scotch Beef Club.

1wk Jun + 2 wks Oct
Open all year except 1 wk Feb,
Dining Room/Restaurant Lunch 12.30 - 1.30pm
Sun only (c) 4 course set menu
Dinner 7.30 - 9.30 pm Tue to Sat (e)
4 course set menu
Closed Mon
Vegetarians welcome - prior notice required
Facilities for disabled visitors
Note: Guests are asked not to smoke pipes or cigars. Cigarettes permitted at coffee stage only

Artichoke soup with seared scallops. Warm salad of seabass with lemon and herb dressing. Seared beef fillet with roasted red peppers, home-dried tomato and red wine jus. Chocolate soufflé pudding with chocolate sauce and cinnamon ice cream.

Credit cards: 1, 3 + SWITCH, DELTA
Proprietors: Nick & Fiona Nairn

The Scottish Wool Centre

Riverside Car Park, Aberfoyle
Stirlingshire FK8 3UG
Tel: 01877 382850
Fax: 01877 382854

Adjacent to main car park in Aberfoyle, southern gateway to the Trossachs.

Coffee shop, visitors centre and craft shop in the Trossachs.

- Coffee shop and restaurant.
- Home cooking.
- "What better location than in the heart of the Trossachs to stop for a snack."

The visitors centre presents 'The Story of Scottish Wool' - a live theatre display spanning 2,000 years, 'where all the stars are on four legs'. Next door is a craft display area, where you can watch spinners and weavers, a knitwear and woollens shop and a gift shop. Outside there is a kiddie's farm, and, at the weekends, sheepdog trails and pipe bands. The restaurant which is part of all this activity is self-service and provides meals all day. The baking is especially good, and snacks and light meals are its forte. It has a stable feel, with pine furniture and old photographs.

Open all year except Christmas Day + New Year's Day
Food available 9.30 am - 5.30 pm summer:
10 am - 4.30 pm winter (a)
Unlicensed
Vegetarians welcome
Facilities for disabled visitors
No smoking area in restaurant

Home-made soup e.g. leek and potato, cauliflower and black pepper, feather fowlie. Scotch lamb hot pot. Beef casserole with chunky vegetables and dumplings. Garden vegetable crumble. Weekend roasts e.g. pork with a herb and apple crust, honey roast ham with orange and ginger sauce, leg of lamb with rosemary and garlic. Home-made steak pies. Wide selection of home baking.

No credit cards

Hazlehurst Lodge

Ballater Road, Aboyne
Aberdeenshire AB34 5HY
Tel: 013398 86921

On A93 on western side of Aboyne.

Charmingly refurbished lodge-house restaurant.

- Country restaurant with rooms.
- Imaginative home cooking.
- "Chef Anne Strachan uses fresh herbs and vegetables in a very creative way to add flair to traditional menus."

This rose-granite building with its' beautifully laid out gardens was once the coachman's lodge of Aboyne Castle. It has been artistically decorated to create an intimate, welcoming atmosphere in which guests enjoy the best of the cooking. Anne Strachan combines traditional home cooking with an imaginative approach to sauces and accompaniments to create memorable dishes. Her wine list is personally selected from top growers, mainly French, and is very reasonably priced given the quality of the wines on offer. There are three bedrooms, all individually designed, with full private facilities. Throughout the house there is evidence of a discriminating taste at work with unusual, specially commissioned furniture and artworks.

Open Feb to Dec
Rooms: 5, 4 with private facilities
Bed & Breakfast from £25
Dining Room Lunch available for special bookings
Dinner 7.30 - 9.30 pm (d)
No smoking in dining room + bedrooms

Spring vegetable soup with a shank of lamb stuffed with basil pesto. Gamebird terrine with ceps served with a chanterelle sauce. Brill with dill, tarragon and chardonnay butter served with crab soufflé, in a bisque sauce. Layers of vegetables and herb pancakes en brioche, with a red pepper sauce. Floating caramelised meringue on a custard cream accompanied by brandied peach.

STB Deluxe 3 Crowns
Credit cards: 1, 2, 3, 5
Proprietors: Anne & Eddie Strachan

The White Cottage Restaurant

Craigwell, Aboyne
Aberdeenshire AB34 5BP
Tel: 013398 86265

On main A93 Aberdeen-Braemar, 2½ miles east of Aboyne.

Charming cottage in Royal Deeside.

- Small restaurant with one bedroom.
- Creative Scottish cooking.
- "Laurie Mill's enthusiasm is evident in the care he takes to produce well-cooked imaginative food complemented by interesting wines."

In the heart of Royal Deeside the restaurant also has one bedroom available for guests. The conservatory attached to the original stone-built cottage is a light airy room which matches the tasteful decor. Fresh flowers, scrubbed wooden floors and open log fires enhance the country cottage feel. Menus are interesting and well-balanced with unusual combinations of flavours and a predominant use of fresh local produce. The wine list is carefully combined with a mix balance of French and New World wines all reasonably priced. The restaurant also specialises in a range of beautifully prepared, home-cooked hampers which must be ordered in advance.

Open all year except 24 Dec to 4 Jan
Rooms: 1 with private facilities
Bed & Breakfast from £18.50
Dinner B & B £26.50 - £39.50
Special Rates available
Bar Lunch 12 - 3 pm except Mon (a)
Dining Room/Restaurant Lunch 12 - 3 pm except Mon (b)
Bar Supper 6 - 9 pm except Mon (a-b)
Dinner 7 - 9 pm except Mon (d)
Closed Mon
Restaurant Licence
Vegetarians welcome
Facilities for disabled visitors
No smoking in restaurant
No dogs

Welsh rarebit. Moules marinières. Carrot and lovage soup. Fisherman's pie. Smoked salmon and scrambled eggs. Saffron sea-cakes. Baked River Dee wild salmon with lemon and tarragon. Home-made puddings. Gigha cheeses.

Credit cards: 1, 3
Proprietors: Laurie & Josephine Mill

Summer Isles Hotel

Achiltibuie
Ross-shire IV26 2YG
Tel: 01854 622282
Fax: 01854 622251

Prestige Award Winner 1991

10 miles north of Ullapool turn west off A835 and continue for 15 miles along single track road.

Award-winning country hotel in the West Highlands.

- A country hotel in a converted croft house.
- Innovative modern Scottish cooking.
- "Mark and Geraldine Irvine are delightful hosts who do their utmost to make sure guests enjoy their stay."

Achiltibuie is another world. The village itself is a straggle of white cottages at the end of which you find the hotel, facing out over the bay to the Summer Isles and the Hebrides beyond. It is an unlikely setting for an outpost of civilisation and fine cooking. Proprietors Mark and Geraldine Irvine are natural hosts, and after a day exploring, fishing, walking or bird-watching you return to dinner served promptly at 8pm. Menus are simple with limited choice; the produce used is fresh, cooked with imagination and assurance and presented with flair. Everyone who goes there leaves reluctantly, determined to return.

Open 3 Apr to 10 Oct
Rooms: 11 with private facilities
Bed & Breakfast £34 - £65
Dinner B & B £67 - £99
Special Rates available for 6+ nights
Bar Meals available all day (b)
Dining Room/Restaurant Lunch 12.30 - 2 pm (b)
Dinner at 8 pm (f) 5 course set menu - booking essential for non-residents
Vegetarians welcome - prior notice required
No smoking in restaurant

Cream of spinach soup with garlic croûtons. Home-made breads. Stilton soufflé served with mixed salad leaves. Turbot and sole in a cream sauce. Lemon flan and orange and ginger sorbet. Hazelnut gâteau with summer fruit. Superb cheese trolley.

STB Highly Commended 3 Crowns
No credit cards
Proprietors: Mark & Geraldine Irvine

7
Alloa

The Gean House
Gean Park
Tullibody Road, Alloa
Clackmannanshire
FK10 2HS
Tel: 01259 219275
Fax: 01259 213827

Prestige Award Winner 1992

A907 from Kincardine Bridge or Stirling. Park entrance on B9096 Tullibody, less than 5 minutes from Alloa Town Hall roundabout.

A delightful, richly decorated, family-run hotel.

■ Country house hotel.
■ Modern cooking, with many influences.
■ "Truly fantastic Edwardian interiors, gorgeous bedrooms and an experienced chef make a stay here a great pleasure."

The Gean (the word is Scots for a wild cherry tree, and refers to the number of these which surround the house) is an unspoilt Edwardian mansion. Built in 1912, it is meticulously maintained by its owners, Paul and Sandra Frost. Head Chef Shane Jarman (formerly of St James Court, London, and therefore having a wide répertoire of cooking styles and dishes at his command) heads a talented brigade. Friendly and well-run, very reasonably priced, imaginative food, The Gean House is delightful. Twenty four hour service facility.

Open all year
Rooms: 7 with private facilities
Bed & Breakfast £60 - £80
Dinner B & B £75 - £95
Special Weekend Rates + nightly rates
Oct-end Mar
Light Meals served all day until 10 pm
for non-residents (b)
Dining Room/Restaurant Lunch 12 - 2.30 pm (b)
Dinner 7 - 9.30 pm (d)
Vegetarians and special diets welcome
Facilities for disabled visitors
No smoking in dining room
No dogs

West Coast crab and red pepper cakes with a toasted cumin dressing. Saddle of Ayrshire lamb roasted with a leek and kumquat soufflé served with caramel sauce. Warm pear and almond tart with vanilla ice cream. Cappuccino mousse with toasted marshmallows.

STB Deluxe 4 Crowns
Credit cards: 1, 2, 3, 5, 6 + DELTA
Proprietors: Sandra & Paul Frost

8
Altnaharra

Altnaharra Hotel
Altnaharra by Lairg
Sutherland IV27 4UE
Tel: 01549 411222
Fax: 01549 411222

A836, 21 miles north of Lairg.

An old coaching inn, recently refurbished, in a remote situation.

■ Country hotel and restaurant.
■ Imaginative traditional cooking.
■ "A delightful isolated spot with a long history."

Anne Tuscher felt an immediate affinity with this isolated and beautiful part of central Sutherland so she bought the well-known hotel, which had been built as a coaching inn in the early 19th century and has catered for anglers for at least a century. It had been partly rebuilt in 1957, and during 1994/95 was completely overhauled. Fishing themes (prints and ornaments), are complemented by open fires and comfortable country house furniture. Anne is a warm and welcoming host, and the atmosphere is informal and friendly. The place is very popular with sportsmen and with locals. The short table d'hôte menus make good use of local fish and game.

Open 1 Mar to 1 Nov
Rooms: 16 with private facilities
Bed & Breakfast £40 - £50
Dinner B & B £49 - £59
Bar Lunch 12 - 2.30 pm (a)
Bar Supper 5 - 10 pm (a)
Dinner 7 - 10 pm (c)
Vegetarians welcome
No smoking in dining room

Terrine of smoked fish with whisky. Escalope of Pork with Madeira sauce. Grilled fresh herrings in oatmeal. Steaks. Platter of cold meats and seasonal salads. Fruit flan. Selection of fine cheeses.

Credit cards: 1, 3
Proprietor: Anne Tuscher

9
Alyth

Drumnacree House
St Ninians Road, Alyth
Perthshire PH11 8AP
Tel: 01828 632194
Fax: 01828 632194

Turn off A926 Blairgowrie-Kirriemuir to Alyth. Take first turning on left after Clydesdale Bank - 300 yards on right.

A small country hotel winner of the Glenturret 'Best Restaurant Meal of the Year'.
Also recommended by Good Food, and Egon Ronay Guide.

■ Converted mansion.
■ Modern Scottish and international cooking.
■ "Food cooked to perfection and of supreme quality."

Drumnacreee House is situated at the foot of Glenisla in the old market town of Alyth. The southern aspect of the town and the surrounding acres of raspberry fields lend the place the feel of a mediterranean vineyard. Allan and Eleanor Cull run their hotel most efficiently and create a relaxing atmosphere. They both do the cooking and draw from their years of international travel to create unusual menus as well as more traditional ones all of which are accompanied by home-grown organic vegetables and herbs from the kitchen garden; the dishes express a national content while being inspired by foreign impulses and are attractively described and presented. Allan also cures his own fish and game.

Open 1 Apr to 20 Dec
Rooms: 6 with private facilities
Bed & Breakfast £32 - £60.50
Dinner B & B £52 - £80
Special Weekly Rates
Dinner 7 - 10pm Tue to Sat: Sun Mon residents only (c)
Restricted Licence
Vegetarians welcome - prior notice required
Facilities for disabled visitors
No smoking in dining room + bedrooms

Home-cured salmon gravadlax. Duck leg confit with Chinese sauce. Pan-fried fillet of Tay salmon with a beurre blanc and chive sauce. Fillet of venison on rosti with a chanterelle mushroom sauce. Home-made truffles.

STB Highly Commended 3 Crowns
Credit cards: 1, 3
Proprietors: Allan & Eleanor Cull

The Cellar Restaurant
4 East Green, Anstruther
Fife KY10 3AA
Tel: 01333 310378

Prestige Award Winner 1993

From the seafront road on the harbour turn up into the town by The Ship and first right up into East Green.

> A small restaurant in Anstruther with a large reputation.

- Converted cooperage and smoke-house.
- Fish, classic cooking.
- "Peter Jukes buys his fish locally and daily, and prepares it with passion and respect."

For over 20 years The Cellar has had a strong reputation for its cooking, especially its fish. Approached via a small courtyard, inside it has log fires, open beams, polished tables, and an atmosphere of integrity. The latter word might be equally applied to the chef-proprietor, Peter Jukes, whose culinary philosophy is to allow the intrinsic flavours of the highest quality raw materials to emerge naturally. He is helped in this by being able to buy very fresh fish, from boats which return to harbour daily rather than weekly. His cooking has variously been termed 'sympathetic', 'rustic' and 'correct'; meat and fish is minimally cooked, and his restrained and acquiescent sauces complement the central ingredient rather than dominate. The end result is highly sophisticated. He also has one of the best wine lists in Scotland. Member of the Scotch Beef Club.

Open all year except Christmas/New Year
Dining Room/Restaurant Lunch 12.30 - 1.30pm
Tue to Sat (b)
Dinner 7 - 9.30 pm Tue to Sat (e) 4 course menu
Closed Sun Mon
Facilities for disabled visitors
No smoking in restaurant

Crayfish and mussel bisque. Grilled suprême of East Neuk halibut flavoured with citrus juices, served with hollandaise sauce. Turbot and Western Isles scallops braised in chardonnay and enriched with cream. Medallion of beef fillet with oyster mushrooms and Dijon mustard sauce. Strawberries with a warm caraway sauce anglaise.

Credit cards: 1, 2, 3
Proprietor: Peter Jukes

Invercreran Country House Hotel
Glen Creran, Appin
Argyll PA38 4BJ
Tel: 01631 730 414/456
Fax: 01631 730 532

Just off A828 Oban-Fort William at head of Loch Creran, 14 miles north of Connel Bridge.

> An idyllically positioned family hotel in the wilds of Glen Creran.

- Secluded country house with stylish modern appeal.
- Modern Scottish cooking.
- "Well worth travelling out of your way to visit".

The hotel commands stupendous mountain views, built perched on a hillside enjoying uninterrupted views over idyllic Glen Creran. The house itself is strikingly different, cleverly designed to make the most of its situation, yet not in the slightest out of place in this secluded picturesque glen. Splendid public rooms with spacious terraces, and large comfortable bedrooms, contribute to the overall feeling of luxury. The three generations of the Kersley family who own and run the hotel do so with unassuming charm and friendliness. The food lives up to the high standards that mark this place featuring local meats and seafood in traditional recipes presented to delight the eye and please the palate, served within a delightful dining room. Member of the Scotch Beef Club.

Open 1 Mar to 31 Nov
Rooms: 9 with private facilities
Bed & Breakfast £45 - £70
Dinner B & B £75 - £98
Special Rates available
Bar Lunch 12.30 - 1.45 pm (a)
Dining Room/Restaurant Lunch 12 - 1.45 pm (c)
Dinner 7 - 8 pm (e) 4 course menu
Vegetarians welcome
Children over five years welcome
No dogs
No smoking in dining room

Fresh Port Appin prawns with a tomato and lime dip. Pan-fried breast of pigeon on a pool of Cumberland dressing. Blairgowrie raspberry cranachan. Chilled Atholl Brose.

STB Deluxe 4 Crowns
Credit cards: 1, 3
Proprietors: The Kersley Family

The Stewart Hotel
Glen Duror, Appin
Argyll PA38 4BW
Tel: 0163 174 268
Fax: 0163 174 328

A828 - Fort William 17 miles; Glencoe 10 miles; Oban 30 miles.

> A traditional Highland lodge in a historic setting.

- Small country hotel.
- Traditional Scottish cooking with innovative touches.
- "The hotel embodies traditional notions of hospitality and is an ideal base for the traveller exploring a wonderful part of Scotland."

A classic Victorian hunting lodge which has retained many of its original features and thus combines the best of the old and the new. The hotel is set in its own grounds and overlooks Loch Linnhe, ten miles from Glencoe. The whole area is steeped in history, factual and fictional. It was the scene of the famous Appin Murder in 1751, and the setting for Robert Louis Stevenson's masterpiece, Kidnapped. The bedrooms are in a modern annexe and are comfortable and pleasantly furnished. The public rooms are in the older part of the house and are on a grander scale. Food is excellent, with a table d'hôte menu that changes daily, and distinctively Scottish menus, accompanied by an extensive and knowledgeable wine list. The gardens are a delight.

Open 1 Apr to 15 Oct
Rooms: 19 with private facilities
Bed & Breakfast £35 - £45
Dinner B & B £65 - £75
Special Rates available for 3 nights
Bar Lunch 12 - 2 pm (a)
Bar Supper 6 - 7.30 pm (a)
Dinner 7 - 9 pm (d) 4 course menu
Vegetarians welcome
No smoking in dining room

Loch Linnhe prawns served with garlic butter on a bed of samphire. Tail of monkfish encased in filo pastry served on a light spinach sauce. Pan-fried suprême of chicken on an onion confit. Fresh fruit brûlée.

STB Commended 4 Crowns
Credit cards: 1, 2, 3, 5, 6
Proprietors: The Lacy Family

Arbroath

Byre Farm Restaurant
Redford, Carmyllie
Arbroath DD11 2QZ
Tel: 01241 860245

On B961 Dundee-Brechin. From Forfar, take
Carnoustie road to turn off for Redford. From
Arbroath, turn off at Condor and follow Redford
sign.

> Rural restaurant near Arbroath.

- ■ Converted steading.
- ■ Home cooking.
- ■ "Real farm cooking."

The Byre Farm Restaurant is tucked away in the
fertile farmlands of Angus and as its name suggests
it has been converted from a single storey cottage
with a byre at one end. The inside is light and airy,
charmingly decorated with a homely feel. The
cooking is wholesome, no-nonsense traditional.
Anne Law, the owner/cook, obtains fish from
Arbroath and meat and vegetables from local
farms. As well as lunch and dinner, a traditional
high tea is served - complete with home-baked
scones and cakes.

Open all year except New Year/first wk Jan
Restaurant Lunch 12 - 2.30 pm (a)
Supper 6 - 7 pm (a)
Dinner 6.30 - 8 pm (b) except Sun Mon -
reservations only
Facilities for disabled visitors
No smoking in restaurant

Farmhouse soup with home-made brown rolls.
Potted smoked fish pâté with bannocks. Home-
made steak pie with light puff pastry. Angus Glen
venison in rich gravy. Lamb wrapped in pastry
parcel with redcurrant sauce. Arbroath smokie
warmed in lemon butter.

Credit cards: 1, 3
Proprietor: Anne Law

Letham Grange Hotel & Golf Courses
Colliston By Arbroath
Angus DD11 4RL
Tel: 01241 890373
Fax: 01241 890414

From A92, Arbroath, take A933 to Colliston
and turn right at sign to Letham Grange.

> A gracious and beautifully restored baronial
> mansion.

- ■ A grand country house hotel preserving the best
  of the past.
- ■ Modern/traditional Scottish cuisine.
- ■ "The sumptuous luxury of country house
  living."

With its period features - original panelling,
sculptured ceilings, period paintings - faithfully
and carefully restored to their original splendour of
1884, its Victorian builders would recognise a great
deal at Letham Grange. This is enhanced by every
modern comfort and a range of outdoor pursuits
from two 18-hole golf courses to curling in the
hotel's own 300 acre grounds. In its magnificently
panelled Rosehaugh Restaurant the hotel offers
both à la carte and table d'hôte dishes that draw on
fresh local produce, imaginatively cooked. The
menus are well-balanced and reasonably priced.
The wine list is extensive if unremarkable. The
hotel stocks over 90 single malt whiskies, some
from now defunct distilleries.

Open all year except Christmas + Boxing Days
Rooms: 20 with private facilities
Bed & Breakfast £62.50 - £79
Dinner B & B £81.75 - £97.75
Special Rates (min 2 nights stay)
Bar Lunch 11 am - 5 pm (a)
Dining Room/Restaurant Lunch 12.30 -
2.30pm (b)
Bar Supper 5 - 8.30 pm (a)
Dinner 7 - 9.30 pm (c)
Vegetarians welcome
Facilities for disabled visitors

Marinated rack of Highland lamb roasted with
kidneys and garlic. Aberdeen Angus fillet of beef
stuffed with haggis with a mustard sauce. Timbale
of Arbroath smokie served with coriander
mayonnaise. Auchmithie lobster with a delicate
cheese sauce. Honey-roasted half duck with a sweet
and sour sauce. Dover sole soufflé with a saffron
sauce.

STB Commended 4 Crowns
Credit cards: 1, 2, 3, 5, 6 + SWITCH

Ardelve

Loch Duich Hotel
Ardelve
by Kyle of Lochalsh IV40 8DY
Tel: 01599 555213
Fax: 01599 555214

Off A87 from Fort William and Inverness (via
Loch Ness), 7 miles from Kyle of Lochalsh/
Skye ferry.

> An old drovers inn, overlooking Eilean Donan
> Castle.

- ■ Country hotel.
- ■ Traditional Scottish cooking.
- ■ "An enthusiastic young chef who makes good
  use of local produce."

The hotel was established over 300 years ago as a
resting place for drovers, driving their cattle from
Skye to the southern markets, and the present
building was erected by Farquhar MacRae in 1896.
The MacRaes were Captains of Eilean Donan on
behalf of the Mackenzies of Seaforth (they were
known as 'Mackenzie's shirt of mail' on account of
their loyalty). Eilean Donan itself is the archetypal
West Highland castle, and the most photographed,
so the hotel has a classically lovely view. It is owned
by Iain and Karin Fraser, who have modernised and
upgraded the hotel. Their chef, Stephen Crockett is
a local man and presents an extensive à la carte
menu. His enthusiasm for his job is infectious!

Open 21 Mar to 19 Dec + 28 Dec to 2 Jan
Rooms: 18, 5 with private facilities
Bed & Breakfast £22 - £28.50
Special New Year Rates
Bar Lunch 12 - 2 pm (a)
Dining Room/Restaurant Lunch 12.30 - 2 pm
Sun only (a)
Bar Supper 6 - 9 pm (b)
Dinner 7 - 9 pm (c)
No smoking in dining room
Vegetarians welcome

Smoked salmon mousse. Casserole of venison with
red wine. Honey glazed rack of lamb with fresh
mint. Fresh prawns in a creamy Pernod sauce.
Baked rainbow trout with leek and Stilton filling.

STB Commended 2 Crowns
Credit cards: 1, 3, 6
Proprietors: Iain & Karin Fraser

14

Ardentinny

Ardentinny Hotel
Ardentinny, Loch Long, nr Dunoon
Argyll PA23 8TR
Tel: 01369 810 209
Fax: 01369 810 345

12 miles north of Dunoon. From Gourock-
Dunoon ferry, take A815 then A880. Or scenic
drive round Loch Lomond A82 and A83 then
A815 through Strachur, and over hill to
Ardentinny.

> Rural family-run hotel.

- ■ 18th century coaching inn.
- ■ Modern/traditional Scottish cooking.
- ■ "An most attractive old inn, well known for its
  food."

This delightful droving inn built in the 1700s lies
on a small promontory on Loch Long and is
surrounded by the glorious Argyll Forest Park. The
hotel's gardens stretch down to the lochside and
pier for those arriving by yacht (the hotel has its
own moorings). Informal lunches and suppers can
be eaten in the Buttery or patio garden, or guests
may prefer a more formal dinner in the relaxed
atmosphere of the dining room. There is
outstanding cuisine with many traditional Scottish
dishes using local produce. The menus demonstrate
culinary confidence and incorporate some
international influences.

Open 15 Mar to 1 Nov
Rooms: 11 with private facilities
Bed & Breakfast £20 - £45
Dinner B & B £39 - £75
Special Rates available
Bar Lunch (Patio Garden/Buttery) 12 - 2.30 pm
Mon to Sat: 12 - 5.30 pm Sun (b)
Bar Supper (Buttery) 6 - 10 pm (c)
Dinner 7.30 - 9 pm (d)
Vegetarians welcome
No smoking in dining room

Collops of roe deer glazed with Arran mustard and
honey, served with beetroot and redcurrant
quenelles. Ardentinny clam chowder. Saddle of
lamb topped with honey and rosemary croustade
served with a rich port sauce. Variety of shellfish.
Fillet of plaice poached with white wine and chive
butter sauce, and a timbale of buttered mange tout.

STB Commended 4 Crowns
Credit cards: 1, 2, 3, 5, 6 + SWITCH, DELTA
Proprietors: John & Thyrza Horn, Hazel Hall

15

Ardnamurchan

Feorag House
Glenborrodale Acharacle
Argyll PH36 4JP
Tel: 01972 500 248

Corran Ferry to Salen on A861. Then B8007
along Loch Sunart to Glenborrodale.

> A handsome new house on the shores of Loch
> Sunart in Glenborrodale.

- ■ A country house with wonderful views.
- ■ Delightful home cooking.
- ■ "What a treat to stay here: friendly hosts and
  delicious food."

Feorag House was designed and built by its present
owners, Peter and Helen Stockdale, in 1994 on the
wooded northern shore of Loch Sunart. It has a
lovely situation, within yards of a rocky inlet and
facing south. The view can best be appreciated from
the large balcony attached to the sitting room, with
open log fire, or in less clement weather, from the
broad bay windows in the luxurious dining room.
Altogether, the house has been sensitively designed,
furnished and decorated to a high standard. The
food is delicious: both Peter and Helen cook and
bake on their Aga; everything is fresh and local.
Their friendliness and hospitality is overwhelming.
A real find!

Open all year
Rooms: 3 with private facilities
Bed & Breakfast £25 - £45
Dinner B & B £43 - £63
Rates incl afternoon tea with home baking
Special Rates for 3+ nights
Residents only
Unlicensed - guests welcome to take own wine
Dinner 7.30 - 8.30 pm (c) 4 course menu
Vegetarians welcome - by arrangement
Children over 10 years welcome
No smoking in dining room + bedrooms
Dogs by arrangement

Princess scallops in garlic provencal and toasted
crumb top. Seafood selection of scallops, salmon,
monkfish, whiting in dill and brandy sauce. Loin of
Scottish lamb in cranberry and red wine sauce.
Medallions of pork fillet with soured cream and
marinated mango in white wine. Home-made
honey and ginger ice cream with hazelnut biscuit.
Home-made sorbets. Wild bramble and apple
meringue.

STB Deluxe 3 Crowns
Credit cards: 1, 3
Proprietors: Peter & Helen Stockdale

Meall mo Chridhe Country House
Kilchoan, West Ardnamurchan
Argyll PH36 4LH
Tel: 01972 510238
Fax: 01972 510238

From Corran Ferry by A861, then along B8007
by the side of Loch Sunart.

> The most westerly Georgian country house on
> the UK mainland.

- ■ Old Georgian country house built in 1790 in a
  lovely situation.
- ■ Country house cooking.
- ■ "The best of Scottish produce served in a
  comfortable family home."

Meall mo Chridhe (pro. 'me-al-mo-cree') means
'little hill of my heart'. The house was built as a
manse in 1790, and has the classical proportions of
that period (it is now a Grade II Listed building). It
stands within its own 45 acres, with splendid views
over Kilchoan Bay and the Sound of Mull. Its
resident owners are Roy and Janet Smith, whose
goal is to offer 'good food, peace and tranquillity'.
The dining room is candlelit and guests share a
magnificent polished mahogany table. The four
course set menu (three starters; three puddings)
uses only fresh local produce; vegetables and herbs
are grown in the walled garden; the cooking is
imaginative and fresh. Bring your own wines and
spirits (no corkage).
Guests are made most welcome at Daisy Chain
Crafts - run by Janet.

Open New Year + 1 Apr to 31 Oct
Rooms: 3 with private facilities
Bed & Breakfast £33 - £46
Dinner B & B £59 - £72
Special Rates for 3/5/7 day breaks
Dinner at 7 pm (e) 4 course menu
Unlicensed - guests welcome to take
own wine + spirits
Vegetarians welcome
No smoking throughout

Queen scallops. Ardnamurchan fish soup. Fresh
salmon in filo pastry served with sorrel sauce.
Blackcurrant sponge pudding. Home-made breads,
sorbets and ice creams.

STB Highly Commended 3 Crowns
No credit cards
Proprietors: Roy & Janet Smith

Arduaine

Loch Melfort Hotel
Arduaine, by Oban
Argyll PA34 4XG
Tel: 01852 200233
Fax: 01852 200214

On A816, 19 miles south of Oban.

> An award-winning country hotel in a splendid situation.

- Informal and friendly hotel with the emphasis on welcome.
- Fresh, imaginative Scottish cuisine.
- "The finest location on the west coast."

Under its owners Philip and Rosalind Lewis, the Loch Melfort Hotel deserves its growing reputation and such past awards as 'Hotel of the Year Scotland,' 1992. It is dramatically situated with panoramic views across Asknish Bay to the islands. Originally the home of the Campbells of Arduaine, the hotel has been sensibly and tastefully extended to take maximum advantage of the magnificent land and seascape. The renowned Arduaine Gardens are adjacent to the hotel grounds. Both in its dining room and Chartroom Bar, the hotel offers the best of fresh local produce - particularly sea food and shellfish - and an imaginatively balanced wine list.

Open 24 Feb to 4 Jan
Rooms: 26 with private facilities
Bed & Breakfast £30 - £47.50
Dinner B & B £37.50 - £65
Special Spring/Autumn Breaks available
Morning coffee + afternoon teas 10 am - 6 pm
Bar Lunch 12 - 2.30 pm (a-c)
Bar Supper 6 - 9 pm (a-c)
Dinner 7.30 - 9 pm (e)
Facilities for disabled visitors
No smoking in dining room

Omelette roulade with mushroom and tomato filling. Own gravadlax with a dill and sweet mustard dressing. Langoustine from Luing with home-made mayonnaise. Whole plaice marinated in yoghurt and spices and grilled. Roast topside of Aberdeen Angus beef with a horseradish dumpling in a Yorkshire pudding. Guard of lamb with a herb and green peppercorn crust with a sloe sauce. Chocolate and walnut tart. Raspberry and lemon pavlova.

STB Commended 4 Crowns
Credit cards: 1, 3, 6 + SWITCH
Proprietors: Philip & Rosalind Lewis

Arisaig

Arisaig House
Beasdale, by Arisaig
Inverness-shire PH39 4NR
Tel: 01687 450622
Fax: 01687 450626

1991 Prestige Award Winner

Just off A830 Fort William-Mallaig, 3 miles east of Arisaig village on A830.

> One of the most distinguished hotels in the West Highlands. AA 3 Red Stars and 2 Rosettes (for cooking).

- A benchmark country house hotel in a lovely situation on the west coast.
- Classic Scottish cooking, with strong French influences.
- "The fish was just so good and fresh it was out of this world".

Arisaig House was built in 1864. The garden has many fine old specimen trees, and falls, in formal terraces, down to the beach from which Bonnie Prince Charlie escaped to France. The high standard set by Ruth and John Smither and their family is apparent throughout: public and private rooms are tastefully furnished, and the staff are highly trained, courteous and efficient: the service is first class. Their priority is to provide 'peace and quiet and gentle luxury to the weary traveller'. Arisaig House's chef (a son-in-law of the owners) marries fresh local produce (notably seafood from Mallaig) and personal inspiration, both table d'hôte and à la carte. The owner modestly admits to being old fashioned in selecting an (excellent) wine list which is predominantly French.

Open 1 Apr to 31 Oct
Rooms: 12 + 2 suites with private facilities
Bed & Breakfast £75 - £115
Special Rates available
Bar Lunch 12.30 - 2 pm (b)
Dining Room/Restaurant Lunch 12.30 - 2 pm (c-d)
Dinner 7.30 - 8.30 pm (f) 4 course menu - booking essential
Restricted Licence
Children over 10 years welcome
No dogs
Vegetarians welcome - prior notice required

Squat lobsters and watercress mousse. Mallaig turbot fillet with mussels and white wine. Chocolate Marquise.

STB Deluxe 4 Crowns
Credit cards: 1, 2, 3 + SWITCH
Proprietors: Ruth, John & Andrew Smither

The Old Library Lodge & Restaurant
High Street, Arisaig
Inverness-shire PH39 4NH
Tel: 01687 450 651
Fax: 01687 450 219

In centre of village on seafront.

> A village inn on the west coast overlooking the sea.

- Small restaurant with rooms.
- Classic French cooking with distinctively Scottish influences.
- "Alan Broadhurst's cooking is truly creative using traditional French cuisine as a starting point for a fresh, well-balanced modern Scottish menu."

The Old Library Lodge and Restaurant enjoys an attractive situation on the seafront in Arisaig with fine views out over the small Hebridean isles. The building itself is a 200 year old stone built stable converted into a restaurant of character with accommodation attached. A cheerful and welcoming atmosphere prevails not least in the dining room where guests choose from a table d'hôte menu with a choice of five of everything - starters, main courses and puddings. The menu is fresh, simple and well-balanced featuring, naturally enough, a wealth of locally caught fish and seafood attractively cooked and presented. The comfortable accommodation is in a wing of terraced bedrooms with balconies overlooking the terraced garden. Breakfast is something to look forward to.

Open Easter to end Oct
Rooms: 6 with private facilities
Bed & Breakfast from £30
Dinner B & B from £50
Special Rates for 3+ nights
Restaurant Lunch 11.30 am - 2.30 pm (a)
Dinner 6.30 - 9.30 pm (c)
Restricted Licence

Mussel and fennel soup with home-made bread. Rolled local sole filled with salmon served with a cream and chive sauce. Fillet of venison with a rowanberry and red wine sauce. Grilled Mallaig scallops on a vegetable ragoût. Rhubarb fudge crumble. Creme brûlée.

STB Commended 3 Crowns
Credit cards: 1, 2, 3 + SWITCH, DELTA
Proprietors: Alan & Angela Broadhurst

Balcary Bay Hotel

Auchencairn, nr Castle Douglas
Kirkcudbrightshire DG7 1QZ
Tel: 01556 640217/640311
Fax: 01556 640272

A711 Dalbeattie-Kirkcudbright to Auchencairn.
Then take 'no through road' signposted Balcary
(single track) for 2 miles.

An idyllically situated country house hotel in an
area of rare natural beauty. Which? 'Regional
Hotel of the Year' 1993.

- Superb country house dating back from 1625
  set standing close to the beach of Balcary Bay.
- Modern Scottish cooking.
- "My meal was beautifully cooked....a perfect
  example of Scottish cooking at its best and most
  original."

This house stands in a splendidly exposed position
by the Solway Firth, in three acres of grounds.
Under the personal care of resident managers
Graeme and Clare Lamb the service is friendly and
efficient, and the hotel is maintained to
accommodate guests in considerable comfort. Most
have spectacular views. The hotel has been recently
extended and refurbished; the restaurant, cocktail
bar and conservatory are now handsome public
rooms. A short table d'hôte menu is offered in the
restaurant, featuring fresh local specialities as well
as an extensive à la carte menu.

Open Mar to mid Nov
Rooms: 17 with private facilities
Bed & Breakfast £45 - £50
Dinner B & B £50 - £70
Special Rates for 2+ nights Spring/Autumn: for
3 + 7 nights Jun to Sep
Bar Lunch 12 - 2 pm (a)
Dining Room/Restaurant Lunch 12 - 1.45 pm
Sun only (a): à la carte lunch by reservation
only Mon to Sat (c)
Dinner 7 - 8.30 pm (c)
Vegetarians welcome

Grilled trout fillets cooked in an orange butter.
Saddle of venison roasted on a bed of hazelnuts,
with a rich red wine sauce.Noisettes of lamb with a
gin and juniper berry sauce.

STB Highly Commended 4 Crowns
Credit cards: 1, 3 + SWITCH, DELTA
Proprietors: Ronald & Joan Lamb, Graeme
& Clare Lamb

Collin House

Auchencairn, Castle Douglas
Dumfries & Galloway DG7 1QN
Tel: 01556 640292
Fax: 01556 640276

Turn off A711 east of Auchencairn, signposted.

A country house hotel on the Galloway coast.

- Listed 18th century house.
- Modern Scottish cooking.
- "The best crab bisque I have ever tasted."

This is a charming example of a well-restored
country house. It was built in 1750 and careful
conversion and restoration by the owners has
turned it into a discreet and relaxed hotel. Both
public and private rooms have antique furniture
and there is a refined period air about the place.
The hotel has a lovely outlook over Auchencairn
Bay and Hestan Island which adds much to the
general ambience. At dinner there is a small
regularly changing menu, which makes interesting
use of fish and game. The dishes on the whole are
light with sustaining flavours and compassionate
sauces, the chef/owner John Wood concentrates on
using well-hung meat, home-cured produce and
fresh ingredients and allows their natural flavours
to emerge.

Open Mar to Jan
Rooms: 6 with private facilities
Bed & Breakfast £39 - £42
Dinner B & B £67 - £70
Special Rates for 3+ nights
Dinner 7.30 for 8 pm (e) 4/5 course menu
Dinner for non-residents by reservation only
Table Licence
Vegetarians welcome - prior notice required
No smoking in dining room
Children over 11 years welcome in dining
room
Dogs by arrangement

Lobster bisque. Crab soup with rouille. Risotto of
smoked venison with cèpes. Hot kipper pâté with
shallot butter sauce. Noisettes of Scottish lamb on a
bed of spinach with port wine sauce. Escalope of sea
bass filled with its own mousseline and served with
basil scented juices.

STB Deluxe 3 Crowns
Credit cards: 1, 3
Proprietors: Pam Hall & John Wood

Auchterarder House

Auchterarder
Perthshire PH3 1DZ
Tel: 01764 663646/7
Fax: 01764 662939

Off B8062 Auchterarder-Crieff, 1 mile from
village.

A majestic country house hotel; member of the
'Small Luxury Hotels of the World'.

- Baronial-style 19th century mansion.
- Country house cooking, with modernist
  overtones.
- "Unusual combinations and inventive
  creations."

Ian and Audrey Brown, the proprietors of this
sumptuously appointed red sandstone mansion,
make every effort to create the atmosphere of a
country house. The magnificent public rooms
retain a strong period style and have many echoes
of past elegance in the furnishings and decor. The
house itself is surrounded by 17½ acres of
manicured lawns and mature woodland, making it
a peaceful refuge from the outside world. The food
served in the dining room has a refined country
house feel, with elements of surf and turf; plenty of
seafood and game cooked with pleasing and
enhancing sauces and accompaniments. Member
of the Scotch Beef Club.

Open all year except Christmas period
Rooms: 15 with private facilities
Bed & Breakfast £65 - £100
Special Dinner B & B Rates for 2+ nights
Dining Room/Restaurant Lunch - by
reservation only (b-e)
Victorian teas in Winter Garden
Conservatory 3 - 5 pm
Dinner - by reservation only (c-f)
Vegetarians welcome - prior notice required
No children

West coast mussel stew spiked with Pernod,
complemented with herb dumplings. Collop of
Aberdeen Angus beef with fresh langoustine tails,
served with a gingered shellfish and coriander
sauce. Braised turbot fillet edged with a light pesto,
presented on a warm dill and tomato dressing.
Baked chocolate spiced pudding with honey ice
cream and toddie sabayon.

Credit cards: 1, 2, 3, 5 + SWITCH
Proprietors: Ian & Audrey Brown

Duchally House Hotel
Duchally, by Auchterarder
Perthshire PH3 1PN
Tel: 01764 663071
Fax: 01764 662464

Just off A823 Crieff-Dunfermline, 2 miles south of Auchterarder.

> Recently refurbished country hotel.

- ■ Granite Victorian country house.
- ■ Good hotel cooking .
- ■ "Much thought and imagination goes into the planning of the menus."

This hotel is hybrid of original 19th century architecture and modern extensions, standing in 27 acres. Despite its rather severe exterior, inside it retains some of the Victorian features, including a fine staircase, some attractive fireplaces (there are open log fires in all the public rooms) and a panelled billiards room. The restaurant is attractively decorated and furnished, and both table d'hôte and à la carte menus are presented; dishes are traditional and familiar, but are cooked to order and well-presented.

Open all year except Christmas Eve, Christmas + Boxing Days
Rooms: 15 with private facilities
Bed & Breakfast £35 - £50
Dinner B & B £50 - £60
Special Rates for 2+ nights
Bar Lunch 12 - 2.15 pm (a)
Dining Room/Restaurant Lunch 12 - 2 pm (b)
Bar Supper 6 - 9.30 pm (a)
Dinner 7 - 9.30 pm (d)
Vegetarians welcome
Facilities for disabled visitors
No smoking area in restaurant

Fillet of Scottish salmon steamed with lemon butter and garden herbs. Pan-fried fillet of halibut with apples and a light cider sauce. Fillet of Scotch beef in a pepper, brandy and cream sauce.

STB Highly Commended 4 Crowns
Credit cards: 1, 2, 3, 5, 6
Proprietor: Arne Raeder

The Gleneagles Hotel
Auchterarder
Perthshire PH3 1NF
Tel: 01764 662231
Fax: 01764 662134

½ mile west of A9, 10 miles north of Dunblane, 1 mile south of Auchterarder.

> Scotland's most famous hotel.

- ■ Palatial Edwardian resort hotel.
- ■ Several restaurants and styles of cooking.
- ■ "Gleneagles is a total experience, where the past and the future meet!"

When Gleneagles, the first 'resort hotel' opened in 1924, the Morning Post's headline ran 'The Scottish Palace in the Glens; The Playground of the Gods'. This is no exaggeration. The effect is awesome, Gleneagles has six restaurants of one kind or another - from brasseries or 'school meals' (in the Dormyhouse grill) to afternoon tea and light lunch (in the Drawing Room). Gourmets seek out the Strathearn - glittering with silver, crystal chandeliers and fine china. Executive Chef, Alan Hill, presents à la carte and daily changing table d'hôte menus for lunch and dinner. The style of cooking might be described as 'modernised-classical, in the grand hotel tradition'. Member of the Scotch Beef Club.

Open all year
Rooms: 234 with private facilities
Bed & Breakfast from £100
Dinner B & B from £150
Special Rates available on request
Food available all day - Clubhouse Grill + Equestrian Centre (a)
Dining Room/Restaurant Lunch (Strathearn) 12.30-2.30 pm Sun only (d)
Dining Room/Restaurant Lunch (Drawing Room) 12- 2.30 pm (d)
Dinner (Clubhouse) 7.30-10 pm except Sat (e)
Dinner (Strathearn) 7.30-10 pm except Sat (f)
Note: please telephone in advance for non-residential dining in Strathearn Restaurant, Clubhouse Grill and Equestrian Centre
Vegetarians welcome
No smoking area in restaurants

Smoked Scottish salmon. Rosette of beef with wild mushrooms and grated potatoes. Nougatine wafers with home-grown strawberries.

STB Deluxe 5 Crowns
Credit cards: 1, 2, 3, 5, 6 + SWITCH

Ardchoille Farm Guest House
Dunshalt, Auchtermuchty
Fife KY14 7EY
Tel: 01337 828414
Fax: 01337 828414

On B936 just outside Dunshalt village, 1½ miles south of Auchtermuchty. 1 hour's drive from Edinburgh, 20 minutes from St Andrews or Perth.

> A spacious, well-appointed guest house with views over the Lomond Hills. 1 mile from the historic village of Falkland.

- ■ A farmhouse built in 1957 where guests' comfort is a priority.
- ■ Traditional, good home cooking, using only fresh ingredients.
- ■ "Run on the best guest house lines."

From the embroidered linen napkins you can tell that attention to detail is the aim of Ardchoille's proprietors Donald and Isobel Steven. They succeed in making you feel like a guest in their own elegantly furnished home. Wonderful home-made shortbread is available in the en suite bedrooms. Freshly prepared meals of local produce are served at a long mahogany table set with fine china and crystal in the comfortable dining room, husband Donald serves the food that Isobel cooks. Breakfasts are "the best we've ever had". The personal touch is evident throughout this excellent guest house. Ardchoille's location makes it an excellent base for touring, golf or just relaxing.

Open all year except Christmas/New Year
Rooms: 3 with private facilities
Bed & Breakfast £25 - £45
Dinner B & B £45 - £60
Dinner 7 - 8 pm (d) 4 course set menu
Dinner for non-residents by prior arrangement only
Unlicensed - guests welcome to take own wine
Vegetarians welcome - prior notice required
No smoking throughout, No dogs

Venison pâté with port wine jelly topping. Home-made cauliflower and courgette soup. Chicken breast stuffed with apricots in a light savoury lemon sauce. Fresh garden vegetables. Tuille basket with home-made vanilla ice cream and fresh strawberries.

STB Highly Commended 3 Crowns
Credit cards: 1, 3
Proprietors: Donald & Isobel Steven

Auldgirth by Dumfries

Low Kirkbride Farmhouse
Auldgirth
Dumfries DG2 0SP
Tel: 01387 820258
Fax: 01387 820258

From Dumfries take A76 Kilmarnock for 2 miles, then B729 to Dunscore. Beyond Dunscore at crossroads go right. After 1½ miles take first left. Farm first on left.

> Guest house in rolling Dumfriesshire farmland.

- Farmhouse family bed and breakfast.
- Home cooking.
- "A choice of duck, hen or pheasant eggs for breakfast!"

This is a working farm with a prize-winning herd of Friesian cattle and lots of sheep, so there is much to entertain those who love the countryside and farming life. It is located in remote rolling countryside just north of Dumfries. The traditional farmhouse is surrounded by outbuildings and has a lovingly tended garden to the front. The guest rooms are comfortable with a domestic appeal about them. Dinner is provided for residents with substantial helpings of wholesome home-made dishes using home-grown produce wherever possible. You will be joined by Zan Kirk and her family, who cook, serve and entertain you in their friendly and happy home.

Open all year except Christmas Day
Rooms: 2
Bed & Breakfast £15 - £18
Dinner B & B £25 - £28
Special Rates for 3+ nights
Dinner 6 - 9 pm (b)
Residents only
Unlicensed
Vegetarians welcome
No smoking in bedrooms
No dogs

Home-made soup. Carbonnade of beef. Roast leg of Low Kirkbride lamb. Rabbit casserole. Bramble and apple pie. Scotch trifle. Banoffi pie.

STB Commended Listed
No credit cards
Proprietors: Joe & Zan Kirk

Aultbea

Aultbea Hotel & Restaurant
Seafront, Aultbea
Ross-shire IV22 2HX
Tel: 01445 731201
Fax: 01445 731214

Off A832, on the shores of Loch Ewe.

> A family-run hotel on the shores of Loch Ewe.

- A traditional West Highland Hotel.
- Traditional Scottish cooking.
- "A cheerful place, offering good reliable local fare."

The earliest part of the hotel was build by the Earl of Zetland in the early 1800s, and the hotel's principal restaurant is named after him. Aultbea also serves teas, coffees and snacks all day long in its Waterside Bistro housed in a conservatory, with fine views over the Isle of Ewe to the mountains of Torridon. Peter and Avril Nieto have owned the hotel for nearly ten years and have established a firm reputation for their service and cuisine. Daily changing table d'hote and a la carte menus are offered; good generous menus, with locally landed seafood being something of a speciality.

Open all year except Christmas Day
Rooms: 8 with private facilities
Bed & Breakfast £25 - £39
Dinner B & B £46 - £60
Special Rates available
Waterside Bistro 9 am - 9 pm (a)
Bar Meals 11 am - 9 pm (b)
Dinner 7 - 9 pm (d)
Vegetarians welcome

Lobster bisque. Rainbow trout with smoked salmon, topped with a gooseberry sauce. Medallions of venison sautéd with shallots and topped with a red wine and redcurrant jus. Athol Brose.

STB Commended 4 Crowns
Credit cards: 1, 3 + SWITCH
Proprietors: Peter & Avril Nieto

Aviemore

Lynwilg House
Lynwilg, by Aviemore
Inverness-shire PH22 1PZ
Tel: 01479 811685
Fax: 01479 811685

The Macallan Taste of Scotland Award Winner 1992

A9 Perth-Inverness, take Lynwilg road 1 mile south of Aviemore.

> A beautiful country house built in the 1930s.

- Country house hotel overlooking the Cairngorms.
- Traditional imaginative cooking.
- "Dinner at Lynwilg is an occasion to look forward to."

Lynwilg is an impressive country house, built by the Duke of Richmond, standing on high ground looking out over the Cairngorms one mile south of Aviemore. The house is set in four acres of attractively landscaped gardens with a well-planned kitchen garden which provides much of the fruit, vegetables and herbs used in the daily changing menus. Marjory Cleary presents a set menu each evening; her inventiveness and flair in the kitchen mean that every meal is special. Comfortable, well-furnished bedrooms, roaring log fires, croquet on the lawn and fishing on a private loch are all indications of a relaxed country house style. There is a private self-catering cottage in the grounds which sleeps four.

Open 27 Dec to 31 Oct
Rooms: 4 with private facilities
Bed & Breakfast £25 - £30
Dinner B & B £42 - £50
Dinner 7 - 8 pm (c) 4 course menu
Unlicensed - guests welcome to take own wine
Vegetarians welcome
No smoking in restaurant
Dogs by arrangement

Seasonal soups. Wild mushrooms. Terrines. Pâtés. Casserole of assorted seafood in a cream and bay leaf salsa. Fillets of venison in a port and redcurrant jus. Local game. Lime sorbet with lemon tuilles. Drambuie chocolate roulade. Local cheeses. Home-made breads.

STB Highly Commended 3 Crowns
Credit cards: 1, 3
Proprietor: Marjory Cleary

The Old Bridge Inn

Old Dalfaber Road
Aviemore PH22 1PU
Tel: 01479 811137
Fax: 01479 810270

At south end of Aviemore, take B970 ski road (Cairngorms) for 300 yards then take turning on left for another 300 yards.

A cosy Highland pub nestling beside the river Spey.

- A friendly, informal place of great hospitality.
- Pub food at its best.
- "Everything a Highland inn should be."

Only minutes on foot from the centre of Aviemore, The Old Bridge Inn has the air of a country pub. This quaint and unpretentious building offers pub food as it should be - freshly prepared and cooked. Proprietor Nigel Reid and chef Norma Hutton concentrate on fresh local produce for their extensive and imaginative menu. Rightly popular, they even make their own ice cream. There is a special children's menu. In the evenings, the menu is based on food cooked on a large chargrill. In the summer the inn holds regular Highland ceilidhs, with pipers and Scottish dancing.

Open all year
Bar Lunch 12 - 2 pm Mon to Sat (a): 12.30 - 2.30 pm Sun (b)
Bar Supper 6 - 9 pm (a)
Vegetarians welcome
No smoking area in restaurant

Home-made broths. Orcadian buidhe. Seafood bake. Poached brill with lemon sauce. Game pie topped with flaky pastry. Chargrill prime Scottish venison chop with a port and cranberry sauce. Ecclefechan tart. Scottish cheeses.

No credit cards
Proprietor: Nigel Reid

The Rowan Tree Restaurant & Guest House

Loch Alvie, by Aviemore
Inverness-shire PH22 1QB
Tel: 01479 810207
Fax: 01479 810207

1½ miles south of Aviemore on old A9 (B9152) overlooking Loch Alvie.

Restaurant and guest house, with horn carving visitor attraction and all day tearoom.

- A small restaurant and guest house on Speyside.
- Traditional Scottish fare.
- "The Rowan Tree offers good, sound, wholesome family type cooking in an attractive and relaxing setting."

One of the oldest hotels in Strathspey, The Rowan Tree is fast establishing a reputation as a place to find traditional quality Scottish food. A four course table d'hôte dinner menu offers generous portions of dishes with a distinctly Scottish theme and there is a comfortable lounge to enjoy a pre-dinner drink and peruse the wine list. George and Gillian have recently added a tearoom offering delicious home baking, sandwiches and salads to complement the opening of Speyside Horn and Country Crafts - Strathspey's newest visitor attraction where guests can see the traditional craft of horn carving and visit the craft shop.

Open New Year + 19 Jan to 1 Nov
Note: Jan to Mar, closed Sun to Thu except 12 Feb to 23 Feb
Rooms: 10, 6 with private facilities
Bed & Breakfast £17.50 - £25
Special Rates available
Tearoom menu 10 am - 5 pm except Sun (a)
Scottish High Tea 5 - 6.30 pm except Sun (a)
Dinner 7.30 - 9 pm except Sun (c)
Closed Sun
Vegetarians and children welcome
No smoking area in dining room

Parcels of smoked Scottish salmon filled with a salmon and chive mousse. Highland lamb and apple pie flavoured with rosemary. Salmon steak with a tangy herb and lemon butter. Local Badenoch venison cooked in a red wine and cranberry gravy. Rowan Tree Delight - home-made Scotch pancakes topped with soft fruits, hot syrup and fresh cream.

Credit cards: 1, 3
Proprietors: George & Gillian Orr

The Boathouse

4 South Harbour Street
Ayr KA7 1JA
Tel: 01292 280212
Fax: 01292 288718

At end of Fort Street on riverside, overlooking harbour.

Restaurant and bar in Ayr.

- Harbourside eaterie.
- Bistro-style and modern Scottish cooking.
- "Unusual dishes, like saddle of hare and fillet of ling, prepared with style."

This quayside restaurant is aptly named, since 100 years ago it housed the local lifeboat. The theme is justifiably nautical, with a racing scull suspended from the roof and oars around the walls. The oak-panelled restaurant is on two levels with tiny windows and exposed rafters. A bar is at one end of the room, and here a bistro-style menu is served, which also offers baked potatoes and open sandwiches. The main restaurant menu is a la carte and original, promising interesting combinations - a starter of 'braised oxtails with old Madeira and a rich meat essence', for example.

Open all year
Bar Lunch 12 - 2.30 pm (b)
Dining Room/Restaurant Lunch 12 - 2.30 pm (d)
Bar Supper 6.30 - 9.30 pm except Sat (b)
Dinner 6.30 - 9.30 pm (d)
Facilities for disabled visitors
Note: No pipes or cigars in restaurant

Home-cured Scottish salmon with cucumber and shallot relish, roquette leaves and pear vinaigrette. Fresh mussels with orange butter sauce. Noisettes of lamb with a tapenade scented jus. Pan-fried monkfish on a saffron, spring onion and chilli beurre blanc. Scottish venison with a liquorice and red wine sauce. Ayr landed hake with a saffron and Noilly Prat sauce.

Credit cards: 1, 2, 3, 5
Proprietors: Robert Jones & Heather Clark

Dunure Anchorage

Harbour View, Dunure
nr Ayr KA7 4LN
Tel: 01292 500295

In Dunure village, off A719 (coast road) about
6 miles south of Ayr.

> Restaurant in conservation village.

- Harbourside eaterie.
- Modern/Bistro cooking.
- "A wonderful old world atmosphere."

The Smith family bought the Dunure Anchorage
four years ago, it was run down and has required a
great deal of care and attention to refurbish the
building to its present high standard. The
restaurant is part of a row of Grade-A Listed
fishermen's cottages on the harbour of this
enchanting and historic little village. Mr Smith
offers an individual style of cooking which still
satisfies traditional tastes. He concentrates on
providing good quality meat and game offering the
customers whatever sauces they prefer, from the
traditional au poivre to a Japanese teriyaki
marinade or Mexican jalapeno cream, and many of
the dishes are bistro-style. Ready access to fresh fish
is a boon and service is efficient and friendly.

Open all year
Note: only open Fri to Sun in Jan/Feb
Bar Meals 12 - 2.30 pm Mon to Fri;
12 - 9.30 pm Sat Sun (b)
Meals available all day Jul to Sep (incl)
Dinner 6 - 9.30 pm (c)

Tarragon chicken cheesecake. Plaice, watercress
and salmon terrine with home-made lemon
vinaigrette. Noisettes of lamb with a grape and port
sauce. Poached fillet of salmon on a bed of fresh
spinach with a cream, vermouth and parsley sauce.
Haunch of venison braised gently with redcurrants
and wine.

Credit cards: 1, 3 + SWITCH, DELTA
Proprietors: The Smith Family

Fairfield House Hotel

12 Fairfield Road, Ayr
Ayrshire KA7 2AR
Tel: 01292 267461
Fax: 01292 261456

From Burns Statue Square, down Miller Road.
Turn left (A719 Maidens) then immediate right
into Fairfield Road.

> Splendid town house with Hospitality Comfort
> and Restaurant Awards, and 4 AA Stars and 2
> Rosettes.

- Luxury town house hotel.
- Modern French cooking.
- "Old fashioned hospitality and good food make
  Fairfield House a place to return to."

A Victorian mansion which was once the home of a
Glasgow tea merchant. The decor is sumptuous,
with a clever use of appropriate fabrics and
furniture to create an authentic and luxurious
atmosphere. There is a superb Leisure Club with
pool, sauna, steam room, whirlpool and
gymnasium. Guests have a choice of places to eat:
The Fleur de Lys is a sumptuous formal restaurant;
the Brasserie, a large Victorian-style conservatory
serving informal meals and the 'Directors' and
'Churchills' are private dining rooms. Choose from
carte du jour or house recommendations. The food
is excellent: fresh, interesting, creative; cooked and
presented in the modern style.

Open all year
Rooms: 33 with private facilities
Bed & Breakfast £65 - £110
Dinner B & B £80 - £140
Room Rate from £60
Special Rates for 2+ nights
Bar Lunch 12 - 2 pm (b)
Dining Room/Restaurant Lunch 12 - 2 pm (c)
Bar Supper 6 - 10 pm (b)
Dinner 7 - 9.30 pm (d) 4 course menu
Vegetarians welcome
Facilities for disabled visitors
No smoking in restaurant

Salmon mousseline wrapped in leeks, with cherry
tomato salad and dill dressing. Breast of chicken in
a herb pastry crust stuffed with apricots, cream
cheese and hazelnuts. Casserole of monkfish tails,
with smoked bacon, pine kernels and tomatoes,
glazed with cheese. Medallions of beef in a sharp
red wine vinegar and strawberry essence with
snipped tarragon and peppercorns.

STB Highly Commended 4 Crowns
Credit cards: 1, 2, 3, 5, 6 + SWITCH

Fouters Bistro Restaurant

2A Academy Street, Ayr
Ayrshire KA7 1HS
Tel: 01292 261391
Fax: 01292 619323

Town centre, opposite Town Hall.

> Historic basement restaurant in Ayr.

- Converted bank vaults.
- Modern Scottish cooking.
- "I will never forget the fricassee of lobster.
  Simply superb."

Situated in a converted basement of the 18th
century British Linen Bank building, in an old
cobbled lane opposite the Town Hall in Ayr, Fouters
has been a restaurant since 1973, and is one of the
best places to eat in South West Scotland. Laurie
and Fran Black create a bright and cheerful
atmosphere; white walls and stencils give a casual,
continental feel to this underground sanctuary. It
has been one of the most popular restaurants in Ayr
since it opened. The style of cooking is inspired by
the traditional French kitchen, and makes good use
of the fish and shellfish from Ayr Fish Market, game
in season from local estates and top quality Ayrshire
beef and dairy products. Menus are supplemented
by daily 'chef's specials'. Now the proud owners of
second AA Rosette. Member of the Scotch Beef Club.

Open all year except 24 to 27 Dec, 1 to 3 Jan
Restaurant Lunch 12 - 2 pm except
Sun Mon (b)
Dinner 6.30 - 10.30 pm except Mon (d)
Closed Mon
Vegetarians welcome
Special diets catered for
Children welcome

Hot smoked salmon. Fouters pâté. Lobster bisque.
Brioche with Summer Isles smoked chicken.
Salmon in pastry. Medley of local seafood. Lobster
dishes. Medallions of beef with wild chanterelle
mushrooms. Bread and butter pudding. Crème
brûlée. Cloutie dumpling. Scottish cheeses.

Credit cards: 1, 2, 3, 5, 6 + SWITCH
Proprietors: Laurie & Fran Black

The Hunny Pot

37 Beresford Terrace
Ayr KA7 2EU
Tel: 01292 263239

In the town centre of Ayr, close to Burns' Statue Square.

Coffee shop in Ayr.

- ◼ Small informal town tearoom.
- ◼ Home baking/cooking.
- ◼ "One of those places that used to be common but are now hard to find."

Felicity Thomson runs this quaint coffee shop in Ayr which has the theme of Winnie the Pooh - thus accounting for the curious spelling in its name! There are teddy bears everywhere and the motif reigns on the menu with references to the characters of Milne's books. The food is simple plain fare, with masses of home baking and light snacks available all day. In Poohspeak a Hunny Pot is his favourite place for "a little snackerel of something" - what more need one say?

Open all year except Christmas + Boxing Days, 1 + 2 Jan
Meals served all day from 10 am - 10 pm
except Sun: 10.45 am - 5.30 pm Sun (a)
Traditional Afternoon Teas served
2 - 5.30 pm Sun
No smoking area in restaurant

All home-made soups, scones, brown sugar meringues, cakes and dish of the day. Puddings include seasonal fruit crumbles, hazelnut meringue cake. Scottish cheeses with oatcakes.

No credit cards
Proprietor: Felicity Thomson

Northpark House

Alloway Village, Ayr
Ayrshire KA7 4NL
Tel: 01292 442336
Fax: 01292 445572

Alloway Village, near Burns' cottage, 2 miles from Ayr town centre.

A charming, well-restored small country house hotel and restaurant in the heart of Burns country.

- ◼ An award-winning, family-run establishment of excellent reputation.
- ◼ Outstanding and varied traditional cuisine.
- ◼ "Immaculate taste and charm."

Robert Burns was born almost next door to Northpark, an early 18th century farmhouse that has been sympathetically extended and converted. Surrounded by Belleisle's two fine golf courses, it stands in its own grounds. Although the hotel has five well-appointed bedrooms, it is best known for its four unique restaurants, grouped around a central conservatory which serves light meals and snacks. In each of the restaurants, both table d'hôte and à la carte menus offer the best of local produce cooked with flair but without pretention. With 95 bins, the wine list befits the cuisine.

Open all year
Rooms : 5 with private facilities
Bed & Breakfast £40 - £80
Dinner B & B £59 - £99
Bar Lunch 12 - 2.30 pm (a)
Dining Room/Restaurant Lunch 12.30-2.30 pm (c)
Dinner 7 - 9.30 pm (c-d)
Vegetarians welcome
Facilities for disabled visitors
Two dining rooms non-smoking

Pan-fried scallops with a delicate vermouth and tomato cream glazed under a crisp parsley crust. Baked breast of chicken with a haggis stuffing set on a light whisky cream. Pan-fried whole lemon sole with capers. Loin of Scotch lamb served with a Stilton and pear purse. Grilled suprême of wild salmon on an Arran mustard and tarragon cream.

STB Highly Commended 4 Crowns
Credit cards: 1, 2, 3, 5, 6 + SWITCH
Proprietors: Graeme & Rosamond Rennie

The Stables Coffee House

Queen's Court, Sandgate
Ayr KA7 1BD
Tel: 01292 283704

To the rear of the old courtyard at the corner of Sandgate and Newmarket Street.

A small, charming town centre restaurant and tearoom.

- ◼ Unmistakably Scottish fare and atmosphere in a Georgian corner of Ayr.
- ◼ Ethnic Scottish cooking.
- ◼ "A taste of the past in the present."

Proprietor Ed Baines is a man of firm opinions. At the Stables, a converted block built of local stone in the 1760s, he caters for those who wish distinctively Scottish fare, from tea and a scone to a full meal. You will find neither burgers nor chips in his non-smoking restaurant. The cakes, scones and iced cream are excellent and made on the premises, the family smokehouse at Craigrossie always produces something interesting. Enjoy a glass of silver birch wine with farm-made cheeses and fresh oatcakes or one of the traditional dishes listed below. This is an iconoclastic establishment, but what Ed Baines does, he does well.

Open all year except 25, 26 Dec + 1, 2 Jan
Open 10 am - 4.45 pm Mon to Sat: 12.30 -
5 pm Sun - summer only (a)
Vegetarians welcome
No smoking in restaurant

Home-baking. Haggis. Stovies. Ham and haddie pie. Tweed kettle. Clootie dumpling. Farm-made cheeses. Fruit wines from Moniack Castle.

No credit cards
Proprietor: Ed Baines

Ballachulish

Ballantrae

Ballachulish House
Ballachulish
Argyll PA39 4JX
Tel: 0185 581 1266
Fax: 0185 581 1498

From roundabout south of Ballachulish Bridge take A828 Oban. Signed on left, 200 yards beyond Ballachulish Hotel.

> A charming guest house in Argyllshire with a family atmosphere.

- An 18th century country house, immersed in history and beautiful countryside in a remote corner of Scotland's west coast.
- Home cooking; local fish a speciality.
- "We will cook your catch for breakfast!"

Ballachulish House is steeped in history. It has been the seat of the Stewarts of Ballachulish since the 16th century, although it was burned down by Hanoverian troops in 1746. Indeed the final order for the massacre of Glencoe was signed here. Today Ballachulish House offers quiet, peace and comfort to the traveller. The rooms are spacious and elegantly furnished with antiques; log fires throughout the year ensure a warm and relaxed ambience; the en suite bedrooms have spectacular views over Loch Linnhe and the Morven Hills and in keeping with the rest of the house are comfortable and well decorated. The owners, Liz and John Grey, treat visitors to their home as personal guests. The dining room is situated in the oldest part of the house, has a low ceiling and looks out to the garden. Surrounded by period furniture, antiques and glassware, a simple but elegant table d'hote menu is presented. The cooking is simple and unfussy, the produce local.

Open all year except Christmas + New Year
Rooms: 6, 4 with private facilities
Bed & Breakfast £32 - £38
Dinner B & B £55 - £61
Dinner 7.30 - 8 pm (d) 4 course menu
Restricted Hotel Licence
Vegetarians welcome
No smoking in dining room + bedrooms

Pan-fried scallops with fresh garden herbs, cream and wine sauce. Roast venison with rowan jelly. Gooseberry and elderflower tart. Scottish cheeses.

STB Highly Commended 4 Crowns
Credit cards: 1, 3 + DELTA
Proprietors: John & Liz Grey

Balkissock Lodge
Ballantrae
Ayrshire KA26 0LP
Tel: 01465 831537
Fax: 01465 831537

Take first inland road off A77, south of River Stinchar at Ballantrae (signed to Laggan caravans) and follow for 2¼ miles. Turn right at T-junction and continue along single track 'no through road' to its end, c.1½ miles.

> A quiet country guest house, run by Adrian and Janet Beale.

- An early 19th century shooting lodge.
- Innovative Scottish cooking with international influences.
- "I was able to take the delicious dishes that we had eaten away in the shape of Janet's book."

Just south of the picturesque fishing village of Ballantrae, deep in rural Ayrshire you will find Balkissock Lodge - once a sporting retreat, now a relaxed and atmospheric small guest house. The owners are considerate and attentive hosts, and Janet spends most of her long days in the kitchen, preparing her imaginative meals. The menu is table d'hôte and à la carte and guests are asked to make their dinner choices in the afternoon, so that everything can be freshly prepared. Janet is an experienced cook, and hosts occasional gourmet and speciality events for food lovers. The guest house also has an adjacent cottage, which may be rented.

Open all year
Rooms: 3 with private facilities
Bed & Breakfast from £26.50
Dinner B & B £31.50 - £37.50
Special Rates for 4 nights
Dinner 7 - 7.30 pm (b-c)
Non-residents by prior arrangement
Unlicensed - guests welcome to take own wine
Vegetarians welcome
No dogs
No smoking throughout

Deep-fried Bonchester cheese with apricot relish. Cullen skink. Venison flavoured with home-grown rosemary and cooked with prunes and red wine. Pheasant cooked with Madeira, pecan nuts and juniper berries. Asparagus and mushrooms crêpes.

Credit cards: 1, 3
Proprietors: Adrian & Janet Beale

Cosses Country House
Ballantrae
Ayrshire KA26 0LR
Tel: 01465 831 363
Fax: 01465 831 598

From A77 at southern end of Ballantrae, take inland road signed to Laggan. Cosses is c. 2 miles on right.

> A former shooting lodge and home farm in lovely grounds.

- A charming converted farmhouse.
- Gourmet country house cooking.
- "A corner of Paradise; perfect food and lovely situation."

Now a country house, standing in 12 acres of glorious gardens and woodland in a fold in the hills, Cosses was built as a shooting lodge and became the home farm for nearby Glenapp Estate. It is the home of Robin and Susan Crosthwaite, and guests are made to feel they are part of the family. They grow their own vegetables, herbs and some fruit, and Susan - a Cordon Bleu chef - presents delicious, four course, table d'hôte menus which feature local seafood and game, Scottish cheeses and home- made petit fours (the menus are often discussed with guests beforehand). Two cottage suites are provided within the courtyard and there is a double bedroom en suite within the house itself.

Open 20 Jan to 23 Dec
Rooms: 3 with private facilities
Bed & Breakfast £30 - £35
Dinner B & B £48 - £55
Special Rates for 3+ nights
Dinner 7 - 9 pm (c) 4 course menu
Dinner for non-residents by reservation only
Vegetarians welcome

Terrine of salmon, sole and prawns, served warm with a Newburg cream sauce. Herb crêpes filled with Dunsyre Blue cheese served with fresh tomato sauce. Ailsa Craig lobster with herb mayonnaise and salad Elona. Fillet of Ayrshire lamb with a rosemary, Madeira and redcurrant sauce. Brandy snap cones filled with rhubarb fool.

STB Deluxe 3 Crowns
No credit cards
Proprietors: Susan & Robin Crosthwaite

Ballater

Balgonie Country House
Braemar Place
Ballater AB35 5RQ
Tel: 013397 55482
Fax: 013397 55482

Prestige Award Winner 1993.

Off Braemar Road (A93), a few hundred yards west of Church Green.

A country house hotel in the heart of Deeside; winners of the AA Hotel Inspectors 'Selected Hotel of the Year 1994' Award (2 Rosettes for Cuisine); 2 Red Stars.

■ Tranquil Edwardian mansion in four acres of mature gardens with views up Glen Muick.
■ Traditional and innovative recipes using fresh local produce.
■ "French and Scottish cooking; very creative, first-class presentation and unforgettable flavours."

Balgonie is five minutes walk from Ballater on Royal Deeside and its spacious gardens overlook Ballater Golf Course. The resident proprietors, John and Priscilla Finnie, pride themselves on maintaining a friendly but unobtrusive service. The nine en suite bedrooms are very comfortable and tastefully furnished. The dining room is the heart of Balgonie providing an inviting cuisine using locally sourced fish and game. When in season, herbs and soft fruits from the garden are always found on the menu. French and German is spoken.

Open Mid Feb to early Jan
Rooms: 9 with private facilities
Bed & Breakfast £35 - £55
Dinner B & B £62.50 - £82.50
Special Rates available
Dining Room/Restaurant Lunch 12.30 - 2 pm (c) - reservation only
Dinner 7 - 9 pm (e) 4 course menu - reservation only
Facilities for disabled visitors
No smoking in dining room
Vegetarians welcome

Sauté of Chicken livers cooked with smoked bacon, sage, Cognac and cream, with a timbale of pilaff rice. Medallions of Aberdeen Angus fillet with a fricassée of mushrooms and a red Burgundy jus. A light raspberry fool layered with fresh fruits.

STB Deluxe 4 Crowns
Credit cards: 1, 2, 3, 6 + SWITCH, DELTA
Proprietors: John & Priscilla Finnie

Craigendarroch Hotel & Country Club
Braemar Road, Ballater
Royal Deeside AB35 5XA
Tel: 013397 55858
Fax: 013397 55447

On A93 western end of Ballater, near Balmoral.

A resort hotel with full leisure and sports facilities.

■ Victorian country house.
■ Modern grand hotel with fine dining and bistro cooking.
■ "Here you may expect a special occasion and a memorable meal."

This house was built in the 19th century for the Keiller family (the inventors of marmalade) and has been converted into a modern resort hotel with time-ownership lodges and every imaginable facility. The food on offer has all the feel of a large hotel with a brigade of chefs working busily to support the restaurants. The Oaks is a classy formal restaurant, serving interesting and imaginative dishes prepared by the talented young executive chef, Eric Fausserier. Eric trained in France and Switzerland before starting at Craigendarroch as a sous-chef six years ago, and both continental and classic influences are detectable in his beautifully presented dishes. In The Clubhouse Restaurant, which adjoins the pool area in the Leisure Club, the bistro-style food is fast, comprehensive and unsophisticated - good grub for all the family, and some dishes may be taken away.

Open all year except 7 to 12 Jan
Rooms: 44 with private facilities
Bed & Breakfast £47.50 - £97.50
Dinner B & B £67.50 - £117.50
Special Rates available
Lunch (Clubhouse Restaurant) 12 - 3 pm (a-c)
Dinner (Clubhouse Restaurant) 5 - 10 pm (a-c)
Dinner (The Oaks) 7 - 10 pm (c-f)
Vegetarians welcome
No smoking in The Oaks

Terrine of Deeside game: venison, pheasant and pigeon terrine with apricots and pistachio nuts served with quenelles of red onion marmalade and pickled walnut vinaigrette. Pan-fried roulade of salmon on a bed of buttered spinach served with a butter sauce with tomato, sorrel, solferino of vegetables and topped with crispy leeks.

STB Highly Commended 5 Crowns
Credit cards: 1, 2, 3, 5 + SWITCH, DELTA

Darroch Learg Hotel
Braemar Road, Ballater
Aberdeenshire AB35 5UX
Tel: 013397 55443
Fax: 013397 55252

On A93 at western edge of Ballater on road to Braemar.

Country house hotel on Royal Deeside.

■ Victorian period house overlooking Ballater and Royal Deeside.
■ Interesting modern Scottish cooking, with international influences.
■ "Iced Drambuie parfait with warm waffles and a marmalade sauce tasted even nicer than it sounded."

Darroch Learg was built in 1888 as a country residence when Royal Deeside was at its most fashionable. The hotel enjoys a wonderful situation, high up on a rocky hillside, with excellent views. The house has period charm and has retained the comfortable atmosphere of the family home it once was, with two drawing rooms (smoking and non-smoking). The dining room and spacious conservatory allow diners to enjoy the wonderful outlook south to the hills of Glen Muick. The short table d'hôte menu (two main courses) offers top quality local meat from the excellent local dealers confidently and expertly prepared in unusual combinations and sauces.

Open 1 Feb to 31 Dec closed Christmas
Rooms: 20 with private facilities
Bed & Breakfast £35 - £50
Dinner B & B £57 - £72
Special Rates for 3+/7+ nights
Bar Lunch 12.30 - 2 pm (b)
Dining Room/Restaurant Lunch 12.30 - 2 pm Sun only (b)
Dinner 7 - 8.30 pm Sun to Thu: 7 - 9 pm Fri Sat (d)
Vegetarians welcome - prior notice required
No smoking in dining room

Casserole of fresh queen scallops, langoustines and smoked mussels steeped in a Noilly Prat and dill sauce. Suprême of wild Dee salmon on a bed of mixed beans in a watercress, lemon balm and carrot sauce. Roasted stuffed saddle of lamb scented with garlic and parsley, with baked shallots and baby turnips in a thyme flavoured lamb jus.

STB Highly Commended 4 Crowns
Credit cards: 1, 2, 3, 5 + SWITCH
Proprietors: Nigel & Fiona Franks

The Deeside Hotel

Braemar Road, Ballater
Aberdeenshire AB35 5RQ
Tel: 013397 55420
Fax: 013397 55357

On west side of Ballater, set back from A93 Braemar road.

A small, family-owned hotel standing in an acre of garden.

- Pink granite town house.
- Traditional food.
- "An unusually good selection of malt whiskies."

The Deeside is an attractive pink granite building, set back from the main road with an informal well-maintained garden. It is a family-run establishment with eight en suite bedrooms, two of which are situated on the ground floor. The house is welcoming and in the sitting room there is an impressive painted frieze of wild animals; the original Victorian mantelpiece and tiled fireplace has been retained. Through an open archway from the lounge bar is the dining room with its varnished wooden floor and oil paintings of mountain scenery on the walls. In the evening meals are available in both the restaurant and bar where you can also sample a good selection of Scottish real ales and malt whiskies.

Open 10 Feb to Dec closed Christmas Day
Rooms: 8 with private facilities
Bed & Breakfast £20 - £30
Dinner B & B £34 - £44
Special Rates available
Bar Lunch 12 - 2 pm Sun only (b)
Dining Room/Restaurant Lunch 12 - 2 pm
Sun only (b)
Bar Supper 6 - 9 pm (b)
Dinner 6 - 9 pm (b)
Vegetarians welcome
Facilities for disabled visitors
No smoking in restaurant

Fish soups and chowders. Baked mussels with garlic and parsley butter. Home-made game pie. Roast rack of lamb with garlic and rosemary. Fillet of Orkney salmon with leeks and ginger baked in puff pastry. Pigeon casserole. Dark chocolate roulade with strawberries, raspberries and cream.

STB Commended 3 Crowns
Credit cards: 1, 3
Proprietors: Donald & Alison Brooker

The Glen Lui Hotel

Invercauld Road, Ballater
Aberdeenshire AB35 5RP
Tel: 013397 55402
Fax: 013397 55545

Off A93 at western end of Ballater.

A town hotel with a country feel overlooking the golf course and Lochnagar.

- A small country house-style hotel standing in two acres of grounds.
- Modern Scottish cooking, with some French influences.
- "Every course was outstanding."

A house which has been much added to, most recently by the addition of a wrap-around conservatory/restaurant overlooking the golf course. Accommodation is comfortable (some currently being upgraded); service polite, friendly and well trained. The courses of the table d'hôte menu (four starters, four main courses) are titled in French - 'votre plat principal', etc - but you forgive all when you discover that the owner is himself French, and that the cooking is sublime. The plain menu descriptions do not do justice to the confidence and artistry each dish demonstrates. A family-style 'bistro menu' is also offered. There is a very comprehensive wine list with vintage wines.

Open all year
Note: Possible renovation Jan/Feb - please telephone
Rooms: 19 with private facilities
Bed & Breakfast £28 - £38
Dinner Bed & Breakfast £42 - £58
Special Rates available
Bistro Lunch 12 - 2 pm (b)
Dinner (Bistro) 6 - 9 pm (b)
Dinner (Garden Restaurant) 6 - 9 pm (c)
Vegetarians welcome
No smoking in restaurant + conference room

Oyster mushrooms and baby leeks sautéd in garlic butter with a tarragon and whisky cream under puff pastry. Poached suprême of Orkney salmon with a white wine, cucumber and dill velouté. Scottish cheeses.

STB Highly Commended 4 Crowns
Credit cards: 1, 2, 3, 6 + SWITCH
Proprietors: Serge & Lorraine Geraud

The Green Inn

9 Victoria Road
Ballater AB35 5QQ
Tel: 013397 55701
Fax: 013397 55701

In centre of Ballater on village green.

A quality restaurant with rooms; Jeffrey Purves, who has a justified reputation for his cooking, and his wife provide delicious food in intimate and comfortable surroundings.

- A two-storey granite building, once a temperance hotel.
- Modern regional Scottish cooking, with good use of international influences.
- "A very tempting menu with superb presentation and combination of flavours."

Jeff Purves' reputation is well deserved: his cooking is innovative and imaginative, draws inspiration from other traditions (Oriental, for example) and applies this to the excellent local produce available on Deeside. Chef specials change daily, often treat classic Scottish dishes in an unusual way and combine flavours with assured confidence. An outstanding selection of Scottish cheeses is always available. Jeff Purves' cooking adopts a 'healthy' approach - using cream only when necessary, replacing sugar with honey, and so on - and he is also delighted by the challenge of vegetarian cooking, but requests advance warning to do it justice. Service from Carol is friendly and helpful in the intimate dining room.

Open all year except 2 wks early Dec +
Christmas Day
Rooms: 3 with private facilities
Bed & Breakfast £25 - £30
Dinner B & B £44.50 - £50
Special Rates available
Dining Room/Restaurant Lunch 12.30 - 2 pm
Sun only (a)
Dinner 6 - 9 pm (d)
No smoking in dining room
Vegetarians welcome

Peppered duck breast on a shallot cream with a red wine hot and sour sauce served with chicken and spring onion dumpling. Creme brulée with a compote of rhubarb in a warm ginger butter sauce.

STB Commended 3 Crowns
Credit cards: 1, 3, 6
Proprietors: Carol & Jeffrey Purves

Hayloft Restaurant
Bridge Square, Ballater
Aberdeenshire AB35 5QJ
Tel: 013397 55999
Fax: 013397 55999

Central Ballater, close to the bridge.

A highly atmospheric restaurant by the River Dee in the centre of Ballater.

- Converted 19th century stables.
- Home cooking and fresh light meals.
- "Traditional and unpretentious cooking with a wide menu choice at attractive prices."

The old stable building stands beside the river in the centre of town and has been converted into a licensed restaurant. The interior makes a theme of its former function, retaining many of the original features, with hay bales and items of riding tack decorating the room. The restaurant has a high wooden ceiling and has been set out on two levels with a long gallery running along one side. Pine tables and chairs, horse brasses and other paraphenalia add to the peculiar rustic atmosphere here. The varied menus offer both daily specials and traditional dishes (plus pizzas, pastas and children's specials), cooked simply with attention to presentation. The service is cheerful and there is a delicious range of home baking available during the day.

Open all year except 2 wks mid Dec
Note: Nov to Mar closes 1½ days per wk
Light Lunch 11 am - 2.30 pm (a-b)
Restaurant Lunch 11 am - 2.30 pm (a-b)
Dinner 6.30 - 9.30 pm (a-b)
Vegetarians welcome
Facilities for disabled visitors
No smoking area in restaurant

Orkney herring marinated in dill, sherry and juniper berries. Breast of Gressingham duck, cooked pink, served with home-made orange sauce. Grilled local salmon steak with parsley butter. Escalope of venison served with hollandaise sauce. Chargrilled prime Aberdeen Angus steaks. Sticky toffee pudding. Summer pudding.

Credit cards: 1, 2, 3, 5, 6 + SWITCH, DELTA
Proprietors: Brodie & Winifred Hepburn

The Delnashaugh Inn
Ballindalloch
Banffshire AB37 9AS
Tel: 01807 500255
Fax: 01807 500389

From A9 Aviemore, take A95 via Grantown-on-Spey, or A941 from Elgin, to Ballindalloch.

A stylishly refurbished country inn on Speyside.

- Old drovers inn with a lovely situation.
- Home cooking.
- "Use of fresh Scottish produce - good balance."

The Delnashaugh Inn dates back to the 16th century, when it provided rest and food for the drovers as they took their cattle to the markets in the south. Today it is popular with sportsmen, particularly fishermen: it stands within the Ballindalloch Estate and overlooks the valley of the River Avon, which joins the Spey not far from the hotel; fishing, shooting and stalking can be arranged. It was completely refurbished recently, in a way which respects the original atmosphere and character of the old inn. The inn's proprietors, David and Marion Ogden, present a simple table d'hote menu (three starters, three main courses), often featuring salmon and game from the estate. The cooking is traditional and tempting.

Open 4 Mar to end Oct
Rooms: 9, 8 with private facilities
Bed & Breakfast £40 - £55
Dinner B & B £55 - £70
Bar Lunch 12 - 2 pm (b)
Dinner 7 - 8.30 pm (d)
Vegetarians welcome
Facilities for disabled visitors

Smoked local venison served with warm onion marmalade. Roast breast of Ballindalloch wild duck with plum sauce. Baked wild Spey salmon served with hollandaise sauce.

STB Highly Commended 4 Crowns
Credit cards: 1, 3
Proprietors: David & Marion Ogden

Monachyle Mhor Farmhouse/Hotel
Balquhidder, Lochearnhead
Perthshire FK19 8PQ
Tel: 01877 384 622
Fax: 01877 384 305

North of Callander A84 to Balquhidder. 4 miles beyond village at end of lochside.

A small, award-winning farmhouse hotel in the Perthshire hills.

- Family-run establishment of great character .
- Elegant Scottish/traditional cooking.
- "Modern comfort in a beautiful country setting."

In Rob Roy country of mountains and lochs, Monachyle Mhor sits in its own 2,000 acres in the heart of the Braes o' Balquhidder. The hotel's views over Lochs Voil and Dione are breathtaking. Proprietors Rob and Jean Lewis fully deserve their reputation for hospitality. All rooms are comfortable and have bathrooms en suite. Both the restaurant and cosy bar serve imaginative, good food that makes the best of fresh, local produce. House wines are simple but sound. Monachyle has 2 AA Stars and 2 Rosettes. There are also three self-catering cottages, equipped and appointed to the same high standards as the hotel.

Open all year
Rooms: 5 with private facilities
Bed & Breakfast £27.50 - £35
Dinner B & B £45.50 - £57
Bar Lunch 12 - 2 pm (a)
Dining Room/Restaurant Lunch 12 - 2 pm (c)
Bar Supper 5 - 7 pm (b)
Dinner 7 - 9 pm (c-d)
Vegetarians welcome
No dogs

Hot salmon soufflé served with sorrel sauce. Entrecote of venison on a carrot and courgette pancake with prunes, garlic and Burgundy. Monachyle grouse served with a wild raspberry jus and home-made sage stuffing. West coast scallops with ginger and spring onions with squid ink tagliatelli. Figs poached in a claret syrup. Marzipan, date, brandy and chocolate wedge.

STB Commended 3 Crowns
Credit cards: 1, 3
Proprietors: Rob & Jean Lewis

Perthshire Visitor Centre

Bankfoot
Perth PH1 4EB
Tel: 01738 787696
Fax: 01738 787120

6 miles north of Perth on A9. Follow signs for
Bankfoot.

> Just off the A9, this is a good place to break a
> journey.

■ Waitress service restaurant, plus shop and
   'Macbeth Experience'.
■ Country kitchen restaurant with good home
   cooking.
■ "Good food, easy parking, good comfort stop."

'The Macbeth Experience', which is the focus of this
visitor centre, is a multi-media exploration of
Scotland's mis-judged 11th century warrior king.
Next door is a well-stocked shop (knitwear, glass,
books, foods and whisky, gifts and souvenirs) and a
comfortable friendly restaurant, offering home
baking and snacks (baked potatoes, pizzas, burgers,
sandwiches, toasties, omelettes, vegetarian snacks,
etc) as well as a selection of freshly cooked meals
listed on a blackboard. There is a large car park
adjacent, and a children's play area.

Open all year except Christmas + New Year's
Days
Note: Open 9 am - 8 pm Apr to end Sep: 9 am -
6 pm Mon to Thu Oct to Mar:
9 am - 7.30 pm Fri to Sun Oct to Mar
Food served all day: specials from 12 noon
Last orders 8 pm summer
Table Licence
Vegetarians welcome
Facilities for disabled visitors
No dogs

Home-made soups. Roast chicken with oatmeal
stuffing. Steak and kidney pie. Poached trout and
almonds. Home-made desserts: clootie dumpling,
carrot cake, cheesecake topped with seasonal fruits.
Selection of home baking.

Credit cards: 1, 3
Proprietors: Wilson & Catriona Girvan

Chrialdon Hotel

Station Road, Beauly
Inverness-shire IV4 7EH
Tel: 01463 782336

On A862 main road through Beauly, 12 miles
from Inverness.

> A small hotel just off the main street in the
> centre of Beauly; an ideal touring base for the
> Highlands.

■ Red sandstone Victorian detached town house.
■ Scottish home cooking.
■ "Clean flavours of fresh food delicately balanced
   by simple but effective sauces."

Surrounded by a very well tended garden in the
town of Beauly, the Chrialdon is elegant yet
informal with spacious rooms in a homely
environment. The hotel is run by Anthony and
Jennifer Bond, who are welcoming and helpful
hosts and who pay attention to the small details
and needs which make for a memorable stay. The
proprietors offer short but well-balanced menus,
using only such fresh produce as is seasonally
available; the cooking is simple, creative and tasty -
and extremely good value for money. It is no
wonder the Chrialdon has such a good local
reputation.

Open 1 Mar to 31 Oct
Rooms: 8, 6 with private facilities
Bed & Breakfast £22 - £28
Special Rates for 3+ nights
Dinner B & B £42 - £48
Dinner 7.15 - 8 pm (d) 5 course menu
No smoking in dining room
Residents only
Vegetarians welcome

Avocado pear with wild prawns on a bed of summer
leaves. Pan-fried wild venison steak with a sauce of
juniper berries and redcurrant jelly. Chocolate,
raisin and brandy ice.

STB Commended 3 Crowns
Credit cards: 1, 3
Proprietors: Anthony & Jennifer Bond

Mullardoch House Hotel

Glen Cannich, By Beauly
Inverness-shire IV4 7LX
Tel: 01456 415460
Fax: 01456 415460

Take A831 from either Beauly or
Drumnadrochit to Cannich. 8 miles west of
Cannich on single track road toward Loch
Mullardoch.

> A country house hotel in a stunning location.

■ Edwardian hunting lodge whose character has
   been carefully preserved.
■ Traditional Scottish cooking.
■ "The hotel is spacious, elegant and extremely
   comfortable with breathtaking views."

Converted from a hunting lodge originally built for
Chisholm of Chisholm in 1912, Mullardoch House
Hotel has recently undergone major refurbishment
to a very high standard. The hotel looks out over
Loch Sealbanach to the Affric mountains beyond
and is the perfect base for those wishing to enjoy
countryside pursuits such as walking, climbing,
fishing and boating. The area is one of great,
unspoilt beauty and is extremely rich in wildlife -
early risers have even spotted otters playing at the
lochside. Accommodation at the hotel is spacious
and comfortable and great care is taken to make
guests feel at home hence an abundance of books,
magazines and games in the public rooms. The
hotel's chef specialises in traditional Scottish
cooking using fresh produce, no mean achievement
given the remote location.

Open all year
Rooms: 7 with private facilities
Bed & Breakfast £25.50 - £46.50
Dinner B & B £42.50 - £63.50
Meals available all day (c)
Dinner 7.30 - 8.30 pm (c) 4 course menu
Restricted Licence
Vegetarians welcome
No smoking in dining room

Home-made breads. Home-grown herbs. Locally
landed langoustine with lime mayonnaise.
Poached wild Scottish salmon with hollandaise
sauce. Prime Scottish beef steaks. Local
strawberries. Home-grown rhubarb crumble.

STB Highly Commended 3 Crowns
Credit cards: 1, 2, 3
Proprietors: Andy & Helen Johnston

Biggar

Hartree Country House Hotel
Biggar
Lanarkshire ML12 6JJ
Tel: 01899 221027
Fax: 01899 221259

Just off A702 on western outskirts of Biggar.

> Country house hotel in its own grounds in rural countryside.

■ Old sandstone baronial mansion.
■ Good Scottish cooking.
■ "Justifiably famous locally for its fresh food!"

Hartree is an historic country house with parts dating from the 15th century, although it is mainly Victorian and set in seven acres of peaceful wooded countryside. It is not far from Biggar, and offers a good base from which to tour this part of the Borders. The house is charming and has retained many baronial features in its interior - heavy mouldings and panelling, a marble floor in the lobby and carved fireplaces. The grand dining room offers an interesting menu with daily changing 'specials' and many Scottish specialities. Almost equidistant from Edinburgh and Glasgow. Over 100 Malt Whiskies.

Open all year except Christmas Day + Jan
Rooms: 14 with private facilities
Bed & Breakfast £25 - £45
Dinner B & B £37 - £65
Special Rates available
Dinner 6 - 9 pm (b-c)
Vegetarians welcome
Dogs by arrangement

Chicken breast stuffed with haggis. Prime beef with local Broughton ale, served with a puff pastry lid. Salmon fillet with cream, saffron and wine sauce. Prime fillet steak stuffed with prawns, served with a mushroom and cream sauce.

STB Commended 4 Crowns
Credit cards: 1, 2, 3, 5, 6 + SWITCH, DELTA
Proprietors: John & Anne Charlton,
Robert & Susan Reed

Skirling House
Skirling, by Biggar
Lanarkshire
ML12 6HD
Tel: 01899 860274
Fax: 01899 860255

In Skirling village overlooking the village green. 2 miles from Biggar on A72.

> Architecturally unique, this splendid house is also wonderfully hospitable.

■ Small de luxe guest house overlooking the village green in Skirling.
■ Good home cooking.
■ "The cares of my week washed away within minutes of my entering this gorgeous, hospitable home!"

Private houses in the Arts and Crafts style are not common in Scotland, and to find one which retains so many of its original features is a great joy. The house was built in 1908 for Lord Gibson Carmichael and is now the home of Bob and Isobel Hunter, for whom nothing is too much trouble if it makes your stay more enjoyable. Bob presents a four course set menu each evening (guests preferences are sought in advance), based upon the fresh produce available locally that day; he cooks with a light touch and his dishes are very well executed. Everything is home-made, including breads, ice cream and preserves. "This place is a real gem."

Open 1 Mar to 31 Dec
Rooms : 3 with private facilities
Bed & Breakfast £25 - £40
Dinner B & B £40 - £55
Dining Room/Restaurant Lunch - by arrangement only
Dinner at 8 pm (c) 4 course menu
Restricted Hotel Licence
Residents only
Vegetarians welcome
No smoking throughout

Warm salad with smoked venison. Fillet of salmon in a horseradish and parsley crust. Breast of chicken with a mustard sauce and dark onion confit. Red pepper tart. Iced orange soufflé. Banana toffee crumble with a banana sorbet.

STB Highly Commended 3 Crowns
No credit cards
Proprietors: Bob & Isobel Hunter

Blair Atholl

Atholl Arms Hotel
Blair Atholl
Perthshire
PH18 5SG
Tel: 01796 481205
Fax: 01796 481550

1 mile from A9. Opposite Blair Castle.

> Traditional Highland hotel steeped in history.

■ Baronial-style hotel.
■ Modern British cooking.
■ "Martin Hollis has an excellent reputation as an innovative chef."

The Atholl Arms built in 1832 is a traditional hotel which has built up a reputation for good food, comfort and friendly service over many years. Chef Martin Hollis brings with him the reliable cooking from his previous restaurant.

Open all year
Rooms: 31 with private facilities
Bed & Breakfast £26.50 - £36.50
Dinner B & B £45 - £55
Special Rates available
Bar Lunch 12 - 2.30 pm (a)
Dining Room/Restaurant Lunch 12.30 - 3 pm Sun (b)
Bar Supper 6 - 9 pm (b)
Dinner 7 - 9 pm (c)
Vegetarians welcome
Facilities for disabled visitors
No smoking in dining room

Rolled breast of pheasant with an orange, sage and horseradish filling served on a whisky and orange caramel sauce. Oban mussels cooked in white wine, shallots and cream. Seared escalopes of salmon with lemon chutney. Drambuie and cooked oatmeal parfait with raspberries and glazed sabayon sauce.

Credit cards: 1, 3

Woodlands

St Andrews Crescent, Blair Atholl
Perthshire PH18 5SX
Tel: 01796 481 403

A9, 7 miles north of Pitlochry.

A charming guest house in Blair Atholl.

- Attractive town house.
- Home cooking.
- "You are treated like a friend by Dolina MacLennan, who is a very good cook and convivial host."

Sheltered in its own gardens down a small lane off the main Blair Atholl thoroughfare, Woodlands is a warm and welcoming home. And no ordinary home either for owner and hostess Dolina MacLennan is an enchanting character and a well-known Gaelic singer and actress. Her idiosyncratic home has all the charm of an old Scottish family house, with creaking floorboards and over-excited plumbing! Dolina's guests return again and again, revelling in her delightful company and generous hospitality. Sherry is offered in the sitting room in the early evening before dinner is served. Dolina seeks out the finest fresh foods, from Hebridean seafood to Highland venison and game, all cooked simply and carefully in the best tradition of home cooking.

N.B. Opening times variable, depending on filming commitment
Rooms: 4
Bed & Breakfast £18 - £20
Dinner B & B £30 - £35
Dinner from 7.30 pm (c)
Dinner for non-residents by arrangement
Unlicensed - guests welcome to take own wine
Vegetarians welcome

Jugged kippers and kedgeree for breakfast. Home-made bread and preserves. Game soups. Rannoch venison in wine and juniper berries. Seafood from the islands. Local pheasant. Lewis salmon. Nut roasts and vegetarian dishes. Scottish cheeseboard.

No credit cards
Proprietor: Dolina MacLennan

Glenshieling House

Hatton Road, Blairgowrie
Perthshire PH10 7HZ
Tel: 01250 874605

Follow A93 heading north towards Braemar. ½ mile on right hand side, Globe petrol station, turn right and follow signs (250 metres).

Former jute-mill manager's house on the River Ericht.

- Country house hotel.
- Contemporary cooking, with international influences.
- "An experienced, amusing and enthusiastic chef."

A Georgian-style house - well proportioned - built for a Blairgowrie mill manager during the reign of Queen Victoria, Glenshieling is now owned and run by Adrian and Virginia Stirling. Of Scots descent, Adrian was brought up in East Africa and travelled widely in Europe - both factors which have influenced his cooking. He was trained in France and at Gleneagles, and describes his cooking as 'robust'. He is confident and convivial, uses fresh local produce and presents a nightly changing table d'hote menu (six starters, six main courses - one of which is always vegetarian).

Open all year except Christmas Day
Rooms: 7, 4 with private facilities
Bed & Breakfast £19.50 - £28.50
Dinner B & B £37.45 - £46.45
Special Rates for 3+ nights
Restricted Hotel Licence
Dinner 7 - 8.30 pm (c)
Vegetarians welcome
No smoking in dining room
Dogs by prior arrangement

Crisp tartlet lined with Tay smoked salmon topped with creamy scrambled egg. Sea fresh fillets of east coast lemon sole lightly coated in fresh breadcrumbs, grilled with butter and banana flavoured with lemon. Prime Aberdeen Angus steak thinly sliced with savoury pork stuffing and braised in gravy until tender. Thin pancake filled with Blairgowrie strawberries and kirsch.

STB Highly Commended 3 Crowns
Credit cards: 1, 3
Proprietors: Adrian & Virginia Stirling

The Boat Hotel

Boat of Garten
Inverness-shire
PH24 3BH
Tel: 01479 831258
Fax: 01479 831414

Leave A9 north of Aviemore, take A95 then turn off for Boat of Garten. 4½ miles from A9.

A small village hotel with a country house atmosphere.

- Neat country hotel in an attractive village.
- Traditional Scottish cooking.
- "Excellent service and a pleasant, fresh meal in attractive surroundings."

Boat of Garten takes its name from the ferry which crossed the Spey at this point: the hotel is an excellent base from which to explore the many attractions of Upper Speyside. The hotel is privately owned by Bruce and Jean Wilson - attentive and experienced hosts who are supported by a professional and friendly staff. Although it has 32 bedrooms and a large airy restaurant, The Boat manages to retain the atmosphere of a small, personal hotel. Guests have compared it to a country house. The food, chosen from a four course table d'hote menu, is well conceived, with interesting combinations of flavour. The service is excellent. The hotel is extremely popular with golfers, birdwatchers, hill walkers and small groups.

Open 21 Dec to 30 Nov
Rooms: 32 with private facilities
Bed & Breakfast £39 - £49
Dinner B & B £59 - £69
Special Rates available
Bar Lunch 12.15 - 2.15 pm (a)
Bar Supper 6.30 - 9 pm (b)
Dinner 7 - 9 pm (d) 4 course menu
Vegetarians welcome
No smoking in restaurant

Escalope of Spey salmon poached in white wine court bouillion and set onto a sauce of freshwater crayfish. Rosettes of venison pan-fried in a bramble, redcurrant and port wine sauce. Loin cutlets of Highland lamb with a sauce of honey, mint and wild garlic. Pot-roasted breast of duck with root vegetables and game glaze.

STB Commended 4 Crowns
Credit cards: 1, 2, 3, 5, 6 + SWITCH, DELTA
Proprietors: Bruce and Jean Wilson

Heathbank - The Victorian House

Boat of Garten
Inverness-shire PH24 3BD
Tel: 01479 831 234

Situated in village of Boat of Garten.

> Country hotel set in heather and herb gardens run by Graham and Lindsay Burge.

- ■ Victorian house with painstakingly designed interiors.
- ■ Innovative with French influences.
- ■ "Dinner is a leisurely affair and although there are few choices the results were individual and unusual."

Built at the turn of the century, Heathbank retains much of its period charm. Bedrooms, including two with four poster beds, are filled with Victoriana - fans, lace, tapestries and mirrors. Each is individually designed by Lindsay Burge, the joint-owner. Her skills are particularly apparent in the new conservatory dining room, which has a Rennie Mackintosh theme with furniture tailor-made by local craftsmen. Lindsay's husband Graham is a highly qualified and experienced chef (including membership of the Association Culinaire Française) and presents a simple table d'hôte menu which features whatever he has found to be best in the market that day. His cooking influences are eclectic and incorporate several different styles of European preparation and presentation.

Open 26 Dec to 31 Oct
Rooms: 7 with private facilities
Bed & Breakfast £22 - £35
Dinner B & B £38 - £52
Dinner at 7 pm (c) 4 course menu
Restricted Licence
No smoking throughout
Vegetarians welcome

Smoked venison with plum mousse. Cream of lovage soup. Duck breast marinated in honey, spices and garlic served with lime and ginger sauce. Escalope of Spey salmon wrapped in smoked bacon with a sauce of white wine, cream and Scottish grain mustard. Home-made ice creams and sorbets. Home-made jams and marmalades. Home-made bread.

STB Highly Commended 3 Crowns
No credit cards
Proprietors: Lindsay Burge & Graham Burge AHCIMA

36
Bonnyrigg

Dalhousie Castle Hotel and Restaurant

Bonnyrigg nr Edinburgh
Midlothian EH19 3JB
Tel: 01875 820153
Fax: 01875 821936

A7, 7 miles south from Edinburgh or north from Galashiels. Turn right/left at B704 junction - ½ mile journey.

> Castle hotel.

- ■ Historical building with some superb features.
- ■ Traditional Scottish cooking.
- ■ "By candlelight, surrounded by mystique, enjoy the fresh local produce served at Dalhousie Castle."

Splendour and history surrounds this 13th century castle which was built over 700 years ago by the Ramsays of Dalhousie. Situated amongst acres of forest, parkland and pasture yet close to Edinburgh and gateway to the north. Dalhousie is a memorable place to visit. In a unique dungeon setting the cooking is traditional Scottish with French influences serving fresh local produce at its best.

Open from 22 Jan (all year)
Rooms: 25 with private facilities
Bed & Breakfast £42.50 - £62.50
Dinner B & B £64 - £86
Special Rates available
Bar Lunch 12 - 2 pm (a)
Dining Room/Restaurant Lunch 12 - 2 pm (b)
Dinner 7 - 9 pm except Sat (d) 4 course menu
Vegetarians welcome
No smoking in dining room
Dogs in bedrooms only

Timbale of scallop and chicken on an Armagnac and tarragon essence. Tournedos of Scottish beef and veal on a parsnip galette with a sorrel and lime sauce. East coast sea bass baked with ginger, thyme, vermouth, fine herbs, tomato and caviar butter. Warm apple, chocolate and almond tart with a Madeira sabayon. Poached pear stuffed with crowdie cheese and walnuts.

STB Highly Commended 4 Crowns
Credit cards: 1, 2, 3, 5 + SWITCH
Proprietor: Neville Petts

37
Bothwell

The Grape Vine Restaurant & Cafe Bar

27 Main Street, Bothwell
Lanarkshire G71 8RD
Tel: 01698 852014
Fax: 01698 854405

On main street in Bothwell, ½ mile off M74 (East Kilbride exit).

> Informal restaurant/coffee shop/pub.

- ■ Village pub with restaurant.
- ■ Good standard cooking.
- ■ "Everything on offer here."

The Grape Vine is in the centre of of the picturesque conservation village of Bothwell. Whether for informal dining - a light meal or snack in the bar - or a more leisurely experience in the restaurant, both are available all day. Menus, prepared under the aegis of head chef Paul Reilly, cover a very wide selection of familiar choices, including burgers and grills, pizzas and pasta, to smoked salmon, lamb and duck.

Open all year except Christmas + Boxing Days, 1 + 2 Jan
Food Service 10 am - 10.30 pm (a-c)

Peppered smoked salmon. Gâteau of haggis. Lamb with spinach and herb crust. Roast breast of duck with juniper and sloe gin. Baby scallops with saffron and chillis. Fillet steaks. Scottish salmon with pesto.

Credit cards: 1, 2, 3, 5 + SWITCH
Proprietor: Colin Morrison

38

Braemar

Braemar Lodge Hotel
Glenshee Road, Braemar
Aberdeenshire AB35 5YQ
Tel: 013397 41627
Fax: 013397 41627

On main A93 Perth-Aberdeen road, on the edge of Braemar.

A neat Victorian shooting lodge at the head of Glen Cluine.

- Small country house hotel.
- Country house cooking.
- "Friendly and cosy shooting lodge, providing good food."

Wood panelling, log fires, antique furniture, lovely grounds - all the attributes one would expect of a Victorian shooting lodge. Edna and Sarah Coyne bought Braemar Lodge in October 1994, and have upheld the lodge's gastronomic reputation, which included an AA Rosette. Edna presents a straightforward four course table d'hôte menu (two main courses), cooked with imagination and flair and well-presented in a tastefully decorated candlelit dining room. Both she and her daughter, Sarah (who waits and assists in front of house), are friendly and attentive hosts. It is not surprising that Braemar Lodge is so popular.

Open 26 Dec to 31 Oct
Rooms: 5 with private facilities
Bed & Breakfast £35 - £58
Dinner B & B £57 - £80
Special Rates available
Dinner 7 - 8.45 pm except Sat (d) 4 course menu
Vegetarians welcome
No smoking in dining room

Cullen skink. Salad of Orkney scallops in bacon tossed in an orange dressing. Salmon escalope in white wine, fresh herbs and watercress sauce. Sirloin steak in a whisky and tarragon sauce. Venison fillet in a Guinness and port sauce. Cranachan.

STB Highly Commended 3 Crowns
Credit cards: 1, 3
Proprietors: Sarah & Edna Coyne

39

Bridge of Allan

The Royal Hotel
55 Henderson Street, Bridge of Allan
Stirlingshire FK9 4HG
Tel: 01786 832284
Fax: 01786 834377

On main street of Bridge of Allan (junction 11, M9), c. 2 miles north of Stirling.

A traditional town centre hotel of distinction.

- A medium sized, privately owned hotel.
- Good traditional/modern Scottish cuisine.
- "Fine food, peace and pleasure in a busy world."

Built in 1842, this impressive Victorian hotel stands in the middle of Bridge of Allan, home to Stirling University. Carefully restored and refurbished, its atmosphere is of gracious comfort. Under its new chefs, the hotel's restaurant offers seasonal table d'hote menus that make the most of fresh, local produce. The King's Bar serves freshly prepared light meals and snacks at reasonable prices. The wine list of 55 bins is wide-ranging and fairly priced. Service is cheerful and considerate.

Open all year
Rooms: 32 with private facilities
Room Rate £39.50 - £54.50
Special Rates available
Bar Lunch 12 - 2.30 pm (a)
Dining Room/Restaurant Lunch 12 - 2.30 pm Mon to Sat: 12 - 6 pm Sun (a)
Bar Supper 6 - 9.30 pm Mon to Sat: 6 - 8.30 pm Sun (a)
Dinner 7 - 9.30 pm Mon to Sat: 7 - 8.30 pm Sun (c)

Loch Fyne mussels in white wine, cream and parsley. Warm Highland venison with rowanberry jelly and seasonal leaves. Poached Scottish Tay salmon with a Champagne and chive sauce. Medallions of beef in a Madeira sauce. Steak Diane cooked at the table. Grilled whole lemon sole with lemon and herb butter.

STB Commended 4 Crowns
Credit cards: 1, 2, 3, 5, 6 + SWITCH, DELTA

40

Brig O' Turk

The Byre Inn
Brig O' Turk, The Trossachs
Perthshire FK17 8HT
Tel: 01877 376292

North of Callander on A84, turn onto A821 at Kilmahog: Brig O' Turk 5 miles.

A country restaurant in the Trossachs.

- A characterful rural hostelry.
- Modern Scottish cooking.
- "This is Scottish fare with a modern touch served in a place with stacks of character."

The Byre nestles in a tranquil and beautiful little hollow on the western fringe of Brig O' Turk. It is a an understated whitewashed building, converted into a timbered bar full of farm relics and atmosphere. The restaurant is adjacent to the bar. Blackboard menus offer an interesting choice of freshly prepared dishes at very reasonable prices. Presentation is exquisite - almost nouvelle, however the content is more substantial than this might suggest - and attractive colours and intrinsic flavours are emphasised. Appealing fish and game dishes are the strength of the menus and a vegetarian choice is always offered. The Byre is understandably popular with both local people and visitors to the Trossachs.

Open all year except 9 Jan to 6 Feb
Note: closed Wed Nov to Mar
Bar Lunch 12 - 2.30 pm 12 - 3 pm Sun (a)
Dining Room/Restaurant Lunch 12 - 2.30 pm 12 - 3 pm Sun (a)
Dinner 6 - 9 pm (c)
Facilities for disabled visitors
No smoking in restaurant

Smoked salmon with scrambled eggs. Grilled Tay salmon topped with fresh dill butter. Suprême of chicken filled with skirlie in a leek sauce. Lamb cutlets pan-fried with garlic and rosemary. Quail stuffed with herbs, chestnuts and apricot on a rich red wine sauce. Sirloin steak pan-fried with wild mushrooms and Madeira. Guinea fowl served with an orange sauce.

Credit cards: 1, 3
Proprietor: John Park

Brodie

Brodie Countryfare
Brodie, by Forres
Morayshire IV36 0TD
Tel: 01309 641555
Fax: 01309 641499

On A96 between Forres and Nairn.

Popular self-service restaurant.

- Cafeteria within a shopping complex.
- Home baking and traditional meals.
- "Good family fare."

This is a rustic-style theme restaurant within the Brodie Countryfare complex. Ideal for a rainy day when you can browse through all the lovely crafts on sale and then eat a meal (at any time of the day), either outside on the picnic benches or inside in the eating area which has a conservatory. The à la carte menu offers freshly made soups and baking, salads and a long list of snacks and desserts; the 'chef's specials' are more substantial.

Open all year except Christmas + Boxing Days, 1 + 2 Jan
Food service 9.30 am - 5 pm Apr to Oct:
9.30 am - 4.30 pm Nov to Mar (a)
Facilities for disabled visitors
Restaurant is non-smoking with small smoking area

Home-made soups. Dish of day prepared from fresh ingredients daily e.g. steak and kidney pie, peppered pork, beef olives. Salad bar a speciality. Seasonal soft fruit. Selection of home baking and desserts.

No credit cards
Proprietor: Kathleen Duncan

Broughty Ferry

South Kingennie House
Licensed Restaurant
Kellas, by Broughty Ferry
Dundee DD5 1BJ
Tel: 01382 350 562

From A92 Dundee-Arbroath, take B978 to Kellas then road to Drumsturdy to signpost for South Kingennie, 2 miles.

Converted farmhouse.

- A quiet and formal restaurant in a tranquil country setting.
- Modern British cuisine.
- "Impeccably run with guests in mind."

Originally a farmhouse, South Kingennie deserves its excellent local reputation. Owned and run by Peter and Jill Robinson, it serves inexpensive and imaginative table d'hôte meals in a long, elegant dining room. Peter's stylish and imaginative cooking is matched by Jill's supervision of the front of the house. Atmosphere and service are relaxed and friendly. The wine list is comprehensive. Tasting notes are clear and helpful.

Open all year except Boxing Day + 1 Jan, last wk Jan + first wk Feb
Bar Lunch served in Restaurant 12 - 2 pm except Mon (b)
Dinner 7 - 9 pm Tue to Fri (c): Sat (d)
4 course menu
Closed Sun evening + Mon
Vegetarians welcome
Facilities for disabled visitors

Baked fillets of sole finished with smoked salmon and lemon sauce. Sirloin steak seasoned with garlic, served with Madeira sauce and shallots. Medallions of venison haunch finished with burgundy sauce and bacon. Loin of new season lamb glazed with mint hollandaise. Fillets of Scottish salmon with vermouth sauce, tomato and cucumber.

Credit cards: 1, 3, 6 + SWITCH, DELTA
Proprietors: Peter & Jill Robinson

Cairndow

Special Merit Award
for Achievement

Loch Fyne Oyster Bar
Cairndow
Argyll PA26 8BH
Tel: 01499 600217/600264
Fax: 01499 600234

A83 Glasgow-Oban-Campbeltown, at head of Loch Fyne near Cairndow.

Renowned seafood restaurant.

- Converted farm steading.
- Fresh seafood.
- "A haven for anyone travelling in the west. A place with a great reputation."

In 1978 John Noble and Andrew Lane started a business which sets out to make the best possible use of the wonderful fish and shellfish of Loch Fyne, historically the most famous fishing loch on the west coast (during the mid-nineteenth century 670 boats were based here, and and its oyster-beds supplied all Edinburgh). Their plan was to re-establish the oyster beds and, as well as offering them for sale generally, to establish an oyster bar on the loch where people could sample them, and other seafood - cooked, cured, or simply served for the purist on ice. The restaurant eschews 'haute cuisine'; dishes are very simply prepared, so the fresh natural flavour of the seafood can be enjoyed. Meals served throughout the day, and the adjacent shop (and tree nursery) permits 'carry-outs'.

Open all year except Christmas Day + New Year's Day
Menu available throughout the day 9 am - 9 pm (d)
Note: closes 6 pm Mon to Thu Nov to 31 Mar
Vegetarians welcome

Fresh rock oysters from Loch Fyne. Queen scallops roasted with bacon. Bradhan rost (salmon smoked in a hot kiln) served hot with a whisky sauce. Shellfish platter - fresh oysters, langoustines, queen scallops, brown crab and clams. Spicy seafood chowder.

Credit cards: 1, 3, 5 + SWITCH, DELTA
Proprietors: Andrew Lane & John Noble

Highland House Hotel

South Church Street, Callander
Perthshire FK17 8BN
Tel: 01877 330269

Just off A84 (main street through town centre).

Family-run town hotel, winner of 'Best Place to Stay' in area tourism awards.

- Georgian town house.
- Home cooking.
- "A good meal every evening."

The inviting appearance of this neat Georgian house with roses round the door is matched by the warm and welcoming haven within. In the small dining room overlooking the street you will enjoy the home-cooked offerings of the enthusiastic Dee Shirley who creates interesting dishes, presented on table d'hôte menus, using the fresh produce she can obtain. Dee and her husband David have earned a strong local reputation for their high standards and cheerful hospitality.

Open 1 Mar to 5 Nov
Rooms: 9, 8 with private facilities
Bed & Breakfast £19.75 - £28
Dinner B & B £29 - £45
Special Rates available
Bar Supper 7 - 8 pm (a-b)
Dinner 7 - 8 pm (b-c)
Vegetarians welcome and special diets catered for
No smoking in dining room + bedrooms
Dogs accepted at proprietors' discretion

Home-made soups and pâtés. Scottish lamb chops with port and redcurrant sauce. Local salmon steak with seafood sauce. Vegetarian dish of the day. Selection of desserts. Scottish cheeses. Children's menu available.

STB Commended 3 Crowns
Credit cards: 1, 2, 3
Proprietors: David & Dee Shirley

Roman Camp Hotel

Callander, Perthshire
FK17 8BG
Tel: 01877 330003
Fax: 01877 331533

Signposted off main route through Callander (A84).

A renowned country house hotel of dignity and charm.

- Close to the town, yet set on the banks of the River Teith.
- Outstanding Scottish cuisine.
- "The grace of a French château, the intimacy of a country cottage."

Designed and built for the Dukes of Perth in 1625, the Roman Camp has been a hotel since 1939. Under the guidance now of Eric and Marion Brown, it maintains its atmosphere of elegance. With its 20 acres of beautiful gardens, old library and secret chapel, the hotel offers the peace of the past alongside every possible modern convenience. The dining room, hung with tapestries and lit by candles, boasts a particularly fine painted ceiling. The best of fresh local produce is imaginatively used to create the finest Scottish cuisine, complemented by an excellent wine list. Service is unhurried and impeccable.

Open all year
Rooms: 14 with private facilities
Bed & Breakfast £42 - £77.50
Dinner B & B £76 - £111.50
Special Rates for 2+ nights
Dining Room/Restaurant Lunch 12 - 2 pm (c)
Dinner 7 - 9 pm (f) 4 course menu
Vegetarians welcome
Facilities for disabled visitors
No smoking in restaurant

Ravioli of lobster with foie gras, summer truffle and a truffle oil dressing. Terrine of pigeon and smoked bacon with pickled baby vegetables. Fillet of Scottish lamb with sweetbreads and a wood mushroom soufflé. Chilled chocolate fondant cake with a prune and malt whisky sauce.

STB Highly Commended 4 Crowns
Credit cards: 1, 2, 3, 5, 6 + SWITCH
Proprietors: Eric & Marion Brown

Seafield Hotel

Kilkerran Road, Campbeltown
Argyll PA28 6JL
Tel: 01586 554385
Fax: 01586 552741

On the shores of Campbeltown Loch - 4 minutes walk from town centre.

A charming and informal small town hotel.

- A friendly, warm and welcoming home from home.
- Straightforward, good plain cooking.
- "Hospitality away from home."

This Victorian villa overlooks Campbeltown Loch. Built by the founders of Springbank Distillery, locals maintain it was the first house in the town to be fitted with a bath. Proprietors Alastair and Elizabeth Gilchrist have recently carried out considerable refurbishments, enhancing the hotel's homely charm. It is well run throughout. The dining room's menus offer a range of dishes to suit all tastes. RAC Restaurant Award.

Open all year
Rooms: 9 with private facilities
Dinner 7 - 8.30 pm (c)
Bed & Breakfast £30 - £40
Special Rates for 3+ nights
Bar Lunch 12.30 - 2 pm (a)
Dining Room/Restaurant Lunch 12.30 - 2 pm
Mon to Sat (a): Buffet Lunch Sun (b) 4 course menu
Bar Supper 5.30 - 8.30 pm (b)

Home-made soups. Haunch of venison roasted with bacon, served with redcurrant and port wine sauce. Leg of lamb cooked with root ginger, with a brandy and mushroom sauce. Scallops, scampi tails and white fish poached lightly with spring onion, vermouth, cream and cheese. Medallions of fillet steak pan-fried with whole grain mustard, whisky, mushrooms and tomato.

STB Commended 3 Crowns
Credit cards: 1, 3
Proprietors: Alastair & Elizabeth Gilchrist

White Hart Hotel

Main Street, Campbeltown
Argyll PA28 6AN
Tel: 01586 552440/553356
Fax: 01586 554972

On main street in centre of town.

Distinctive small hotel in town centre.

- Busy town hotel.
- Traditional Scottish cooking.
- "A general air of activity and industry indicates the popularity of this well-known establishment."

The attractive, white-painted hotel is quite a landmark in this charming West Coast fishing port and market town and is ideally situated for the new Campbeltown - Ballycastle Irish ferry. Campbeltown and The Mull of Kintyre, although relatively remote, are well established on the visitor trail and the hotel is obviously a popular stopping off point. Machrihanish Golf Course nearby is another reason for the hotel's success. The building dates back to 1728 and has been thoroughly modernised to bring it up to today's standards of comfort. Menus are based on traditional Scottish style with a modern twist and offer generous portions at extremely good value for money. The Conservatory, which opens out to a beautiful well-established courtyard garden, is an ideal place for a simple lunch or floodlit supper.

Open all year except 1 to 4 Jan
Rooms: 17 with private facilities
Bed & Breakfast £34.50 - £36.50
Dinner B & B £48 - £50
Special Weekend Rates available
Bar Lunch 12 - 2 pm except Sun (a)
Dining Room/Restaurant Lunch 12 - 2 pm except Sun (a)
Bar Supper 5.30 - 9 pm except Sun - winter (a)
Dinner 7 - 9 pm except Sun - winter (b)
Vegetarians welcome

Baked ramekin of prawns, mushrooms and cheese. Braised Jura venison casserole in red wine. Noisettes of Mull of Kintyre lamb, surrounded with a mushroom duxelle wrapped in a lattice pastry, served with redcurrant and brandy sauce. Tournedos of fillet beef on a rosti potato pancake served with prawns on an Islay mustard sauce.

STB Approved 2 Crowns
Credit cards: 1, 3
Proprietors: P Stogdale & B Kennedy

Kirkton House

Darleith Road, Cardross
Dunbartonshire G82 5EZ
Tel: 01389 841 951
Fax: 01389 841 868

Cardross is mid way between Helensburgh and Dumbarton on the north bank of the Clyde. At west end of Cardross village turn north off A814 up Darleith Road. Kirkton House drive ½ mile on right.

Pleasant accommodation in a tranquil location by the River Clyde.

- Farm guest house.
- Home cooking.
- "Homely, informal and unpretentious."

Kirkton House is a converted, late 18th century farmhouse built around a courtyard. It sits above Cardross village, looking over the River Clyde towards Greenock - a good base from which to explore Glasgow, if you are looking for rural tranquility. Kirkton's owners, Stewart and Gillian Macdonald, are relaxed and friendly, and set out to make your stay as pleasant as possible. The public rooms have their original stone walls and rustic fireplaces - the fire in the lounge is lit on chilly evenings. Kirkton has all the facilities of a small hotel, serves a homely dinner and a wonderful breakfast.

Open all year except Christmas + New Year
Rooms: 6 with private facilities
Bed & breakfast £27 - £29.50
Dinner B & B £44.50 - £55
Special Rates available
Snacks served throughout day
Dinner 7.30 - 8 pm (c) 4 course menu
Residents only
Restricted Licence
Vegetarians welcome
Facilities for disabled visitors (downstairs rooms only)
No smoking in dining room

Cockles and mussels in brandy cream sauce. Grilled venison steak. Breast of chicken in a mushroom and pepper sauce topped with crisp breadcrumbs. Pork in a light ginger sauce. Banana flambé with ice cream smothered in caramel sauce. Raspberry meringue roulade.

STB Highly Commended 3 Crowns
Credit cards: 1, 2, 3 + DELTA
Proprietors: Stewart & Gillian Macdonald

Carradale Hotel

Carradale
Argyll PA28 6RY
Tel: 01583 431223
Fax: 01583 431223

From Tarbert (Loch Fyne) 26 miles via A83, B8001 and B842. From Campbeltown about 17 miles on B842.

An hotel overlooking the little fishing port.

- Country hotel in its own grounds.
- Innovative/traditional cooking.
- The menu sets out to please all preferences with simple fare well presented and flavoured."

Quite the most prominent feature of the village, the Carradale Hotel occupies a splendid location above the harbour in its own grounds and gardens, and enjoys lovely views across the Kilbrannan Sound to Arran. You will be kindly received by Marcus and Morag Adams who have been steadily improving the hotel's facilities over the past few years. The menus present local fish and meat with unusual and accomplished coulis and sauces. The cooking has a delightful freshness about it and each dish is well balanced. Carradale offers pleasant beach and forest walks. The hotel has squash courts, sauna, solarium, mountain bikes, game fishing and an adjacent 9 hole golf course.

Open all year except 24 to 26 Dec
Rooms: 14 with private facilities,
3 children's rooms (adjacent to parents' rooms) + 1 family suite
Bed & Breakfast £20 - £35
Dinner B & B £35 - £50
Special Rates available
Bar Lunch 12 - 2 pm (a)
Bar Supper 6 - 7.30 pm (a)
Dinner 7.30 - 9 pm (c)
Vegetarians welcome
No smoking in restaurant

A trio of home-made red, roe and Sika venison pâtés with oatcakes and cranberry jelly. Noisettes of Kintyre hill lamb with an Arran goats cheese and rosemary crust. Oven-baked wild Lussa river salmon stuffed with Carradale landed clams and langoustine served with wild rice and an asparagus hollandaise. Home-made orange and Grand Marnier ice cream.

STB Commended 3 Crowns
Credit cards: 1, 3
Proprietors: Marcus & Morag Adams

Carrbridge

Dalrachney Lodge Hotel

Carrbridge
Inverness-shire PH23 3AT
Tel: 01479 841252
Fax: 01479 841382

On A938 to Dulnain Bridge, c. 400 yards from Carrbridge.

> Victorian shooting lodge in peaceful setting.

- Country hotel, formerly a hunting lodge of the Countess of Seafield.
- Traditional Scottish cooking: extensive bar meal menu.
- "Comfortable, spacious accommodation and a wide choice of food."

Dalrachney Lodge is a traditionally built Highland shooting lodge standing in 16 acres of peaceful grounds on the banks of the River Dulnain. Decor throughout the hotel is of a high standard with comfortable, spacious bedrooms and well-maintained public rooms. There are also two self-contained houses within the grounds which are available on a self-catering or serviced basis. The Lodge Restaurant is an typical period dining room with a bright, open outlook. At lunch a wide-ranging bar menu is presented, augmented by a dish of the day - this can be eaten in the restaurant or in the bar. For dinner, both à la carte and table d'hôte menus are offered. Provision is made for anyone with food allergies and special needs and there is always a good vegetarian choice. RAC 3 Star.

Open all year
Rooms: 16 with private facilities
Bed & Breakfast £25 - £40
Dinner B & B £50 - £65
Special Rates available
Bar Lunch 12 - 2 pm (a)
Dining Room/Restaurant Lunch 12 - 2 pm (b)
Bar Supper 5.30 - 9.30 pm (a-b)
Dinner 7 - 9 pm (c): (d) 5 course menu
Vegetarians welcome
No smoking area in restaurant

Grilled rainbow trout with pan-fried mushrooms and prawns. Duck marinated with honey, lemon and rosemary.

STB Highly Commended 4 Crowns
Credit cards: 1, 2, 3, 6 + SWITCH, DELTA
Proprietor: Helen Swanney

Ecclefechan Bistro

Main Street, Carrbridge
Inverness-shire PH23 3AJ
Tel: 01479 841374

Main road Carrbridge, on Carrbridge by-pass off A9 north of Aviemore.

> A small town bistro.

- Informal Restaurant.
- Traditional home cooking.
- "This restaurant has received accolades in France."

This is a pleasant wayside pit-stop on the way through Carrbridge. It is an immaculate family-run establishment which offers food of all sorts from home-baking to rich substantial meals all reflecting the traditions of Scottish cooking, and sometimes with a hint of international influence. Lunch and dinner are available when you can have unpretentious and robust fish soups, steaks, game and seafood dishes and throughout the day there is a wonderful array of home-baked delicacies to enjoy with coffee or tea. There is something to suit everyone's appetite and pocket here.

Open all year except Nov, Christmas Day
Open 10 am - 3 pm except Tue (a)
Dinner 6.30 - 9.30 pm except Tue (b)
Closed Tue
Vegetarians welcome
Facilities for disabled visitors

Hebridean skink - a creamy fish soup with pieces of salmon, smoked fish, prawns etc. Local smoked salmon. Scottish prawns with dill. Yorkshire pudding with roast beef in gravy. Venison in claret. Steak Blairgowrie. Ecclefechan tart.

Credit cards: 1, 3
Proprietors: Duncan & Anne Hilditch

Castle Douglas

Longacre Manor

Ernespie Road, Castle Douglas
Kirkcudbrightshire DG7 1LE
Tel: 01556 503576

Off A75 Dumfries-Stranraer (eastern exit) to Castle Douglas, c. 3/4 mile.

> A small but appealing country house on the outskirts of Castle Douglas.

- Pantiled country house with a fine woodland garden and lawns.
- Good home cooking.
- "Consistent and fresh appeal of home cooked dishes."

This friendly small hotel is run more like a home than a hotel; Elma and Charles Ball are solicitous hosts and set out to make sure your stay is pleasant and relaxing. The hotel has a polished period feel, with an oak-panelled reception hall, a real fire in the elegant drawing room, and plaster mouldings in the dining room where guests dine in company from a splendid refectory. There are superb views from the en suite bedrooms, two of which have four posters. The food served here is absolutely fresh and of local origin. The à la carte menu changes daily and offers a balanced selection of classic dishes and interesting sauces.

Open all year
Rooms: 4 with private facilities
Bed & Breakfast £27.50 - £35
Dinner B & B £42.50 - £50
Special Winter Rates for 3+ nights
Dinner 7 for 7.30 pm (c)
Dinner for non-residents by prior arrangement
Restricted Licence
Vegetarians welcome
Children over 10 years welcome
Dogs welcome
No smoking in dining room

Cream of watercress soup. Solway smoked salmon pâté. Noisettes of Galloway lamb. Roulade of sole filled with scallop and crab. Sticky toffee pudding and butterscotch sauce. Raspberry cranachan. Scottish cheeses.

STB Highly Commended 3 Crowns
Credit cards: 1, 3 + DELTA
Proprietors: Charles & Elma Ball

50	51	52

Chapel of Garioch

Pittodrie House Hotel

Chapel of Garioch, nr Inverurie
Aberdeenshire AB51 5HS
Tel: 01467 681444
Fax: 01467 681648

Off A96 just north of Inverurie 21 miles north of Aberdeen, 17 miles north of airport.

> An imposing country house hotel.

■ Scottish baronial mansion, incorporating many architectural details of its long history.
■ Traditional Scottish cuisine.
■ "A rustic historic house, full of antiques and atmosphere."

Standing in the shadow of Bennachie in 2,000 acres of gardens and parkland, Pittodrie House originally belonged to a branch of the family of the Earls of Mar, the estate being granted to them by Robert the Bruce for their loyalty at the Battle of Bannockburn. The house was built in 1480 and was subsequently burnt down by the Marquis of Montrose. What was left was reconstructed into a Z Plan castle in 1675 and added to in the Baronial style in 1850. The latter influence is reflected in the opulent interiors of the public rooms, and the period atmosphere has been carefully maintained throughout the hotel. In the dining room the robust table d'hôte menus are well balanced and offer just the kind of dishes one would expect in a grand country house, accompanied by herbs and vegetables from the hotel's own garden and a delicious selection of desserts.

Open all year
Rooms: 27 with private facilities
Bed & Breakfast £45 - £95
Dinner B & B £58 - £120
Special Rates for 2+ nights
Bar Lunch 12 - 2 pm except Sun (b)
Dining Room/Restaurant Lunch 12.30 - 2 pm (c)
Dinner 7.30 - 9 pm (e) 4 course menu
Vegetarians welcome

Carrot and orange soup. Pigeon breast with bacon, plum and port sauce. Smoked Loch Fyne seafood with dill dressing. Grilled fillet steak with smoked salmon and mustard sauce. Pan-fried salmon with samphire. Banana and toffee cheesecake served on a chocolate sauce. Orange and vanilla custard tart on a lemon and lime syrup.

STB Commended 4 Crowns
Credit cards: 1, 2, 3, 5, 6 + SWITCH, DELTA

Cleish

Nivingston House

Cleish, nr Kinross
Kinross-shire KY13 7LS
Tel: 01577 850216
Fax: 01577 850238

In country, 2 miles from junction 5 on M90.

> A Victorian mansion standing in 12 acres of gardens.

■ Country house hotel .
■ Good country house cooking.
■ "An uncomplicated menu demonstrating unpretentious creativity."

Nivingston House is a tranquil place, standing as it does in 12 acres of gardens, with fine views over the rolling Stirlingshire countryside, yet it is only a couple of miles from the M90. The building is a pleasing example of an old Scottish country house which has been extended with care, using different styles of architecture. Its location is ideal for reaching Edinburgh and Glasgow, not to mention St Andrews and the north. The atmosphere is comfortable and welcoming, with log fires and broad armchairs. In the pleasant, candlelit dining room, you will enjoy good quality country house cuisine, with interesting sauces.

Open all year
Rooms: 17 with private facilities
Bed & Breakfast £45 - £65
Dinner B & B £50 - £75
Special Rates available
Bar Lunch 12 - 2 pm (a)
Dining Room/Restaurant Lunch 12 - 2 pm (c)
Dinner 7 - 9 pm (e)
Vegetarians welcome

Chicken liver parfait with an orange and port marmalade. Sirloin steak with a Dijon mustard and red wine sauce. Raspberry brulée.

STB Highly Commended 4 Crowns
Credit cards: 1, 2, 3, 6 + SWITCH, DELTA
Proprietor: Allan Deeson

Clydebank

Beardmore Hotel

Beardmore Street, Clydebank
Dunbartonshire G81 4SA
Tel: 0141 951 6000
Fax: 0141 951 6018

Between Glasgow and Loch Lomond. Off A82, 8 miles from M8 junction 19.

> A modern, international hotel in an attractive setting.

■ Newly built within its own grounds, with views over the River Clyde.
■ Award-winning, imaginative, international cuisine.
■ "Light and airy, and with all the facilities you might expect."

Part of the HCI International Medical Centre Complex, the Beardmore Hotel is an ultra-modern red brick building with striking green roofs. A leisure club, purpose-built conference centre and 168 air-conditioned bedrooms complete its range of facilities. Executive chef James Murphy trained with Anton Mossiman at the Dorchester and at Maxim's in Paris. This is reflected in a cuisine that is creative and distinct, extending over a well-stocked buffet in the hotel's spacious Brasserie as well as an à la carte menu. The service is efficient, friendly and relaxed.

Open all year
Rooms: 168 with private facilities
Bed & Breakfast £50 - £100
Dinner B & B £53 - £83
Room Rate £90 - £180
Special Rates available
Brasserie Lunch 12 - 2.15 pm (b)
Dinner 7 - 10 pm (c)
Vegetarians welcome
Facilities for the disabled

Haggis loaf with green olives. Confit of duck with lentils. Roasted peppers and aubergines with ricotta cheese. Haunch of Rannoch Moor venison with Highland thyme and oregano jelly. Combination of Tay salmon: smoked, marinated and pan-fried. Mango and pear clafoutis.

STB De Luxe 5 Crowns
Credit cards: 1, 2, 3, 5

Clonyard House Hotel
Colvend, Dalbeattie
Dumfriesshire DG5 4QW
Tel: 01556 630372
Fax: 01556 630422

4½ miles south of Dalbeattie on A710 Solway coast road. 18 miles west of Dumfries.

> Small country house hotel.

■ Victorian country house.
■ Hotel catering.
■ "Extensive menu with large and varied range."

This is a typical 19th century house in a pleasant location amidst wooded grounds, containing an aviary (there is also a parrot in the hall!). It has 15 bedrooms with private facilities, a large cocktail bar and a dining room overlooking the lawns. The à la carte menu is an extensive list of familiar favourites, cooked to order; the table d'hôte menu offers traditional dishes prepared fresh each day.

Open all year
Rooms: 15 with private facilities
Bed & Breakfast £27.50 - £38
Dinner B & B £42 - £53
Special Rates available
Bar Lunch 12 - 2 pm (a)
Bar Supper 6 - 9.30 pm (a)
Dinner 7 - 9 pm (c)
Facilities for disabled visitors

Mussels baked in a fresh herb butter. Home-made soup with fresh baked rolls. Solway salmon with watercress sauce. Loin of lamb served on a small spinach pancake, with a tarragon sauce. Seafood - scallops, prawns, scampi and mussels - in chardonnay. Baked halibut with a light mousseline sauce.

STB Commended 4 Crowns
Credit cards: 1, 2, 3 + SWITCH
Proprietors: Nick, David & Joan Thompson

The Deil's Cauldron Lounge Bar & Restaurant
27 Dundas Street, Comrie
Perthshire PH6 2LN
Tel: 01764 670352

On A85 west end of Comrie.

> Lounge bar/restaurant in Comrie.

■ 18th Century town building.
■ Auld Alliance cooking.
■ "Simple menu; well cooked food."

The Deil's Cauldron is an attractive bar and restaurant which has been created from a 200 year old Listed building in the village. There is a rugged charm about the interior, with its exposed stone walls lined with prints and old photographs. There is a choice of home-cooked dishes which will accommodate all tastes, appetites and pockets. The standard can be gauged by the regular local custom and the popularity of the restaurant amongst visitors. No surprises or disappointments.

Open all year except Christmas Day,
31 Dec to 2 Jan
Note: Nov to Mar advisable to check opening times
Bar Lunch 12 - 2.30 pm except Tue (a)
Dining Room/Restaurant Lunch 12 - 2.30 pm except Tue (b)
Bar Supper 6 - 9 pm except Tue (b)
Dinner 6 - 9 pm except Tue (c)
Closed Tue
Vegetarians dishes available
Separate dining room for non-smokers

Grilled goats cheese with salad and walnut dressing. Smoked Tay salmon. Noisettes of venison with honey and gin sauce. Fillet of lamb served on spinach with a wine and redcurrant sauce flavoured with rosemary. Poached fillet of salmon with lemon butter sauce. The Angler's Lunch - grilled fillet of trout with almonds, fresh vegetables and a baked jacket potato.

Credit cards: 1, 2, 3
Proprietors: Robert & Judith Shepherd

The Granary
Drummond Street, Comrie
Perthshire PH6 2DW
Tel: 01764 670838

On main street of Comrie (A85 west of Crieff) - opposite garage.

> A small, welcoming coffee shop on the main street of Comrie.

■ A charming little tea-room/coffee shop with the comfortable air of an Edwardian coffee shop.
■ Good home baking.
■ "What better place to eat a light lunch or tea - and the baking is a special boon".

The Granary is an old fashioned building in the centre of the bustling village of Comrie. The large windows with sunny flowered curtains look towards the Perthshire hills and the antique mahogany counter is laden with a mouth-watering display of home baking. Local watercolours decorate the walls, and a rich collection of home-made jams and chutneys crowd the shelves. Proprietors Liz and Mark Grieve have made The Granary a special place with a warm and welcoming atmosphere, tempting customers with a delicious choice of food. There is a good selection of ground coffees and teas (including fruit and herbal infusions). The full menu is available all day and visitors can purchase cakes and scones, breads and preserves to carry out.

Open 2 Mar to 28 Oct
Food available 10 am - 5 pm Tue to Sat:
12 - 5 pm Sun (a)
Closed Mon
Unlicensed
Vegetarians welcome
Facilities for disabled visitors
No smoking throughout

Home-made soups. Baked potatoes with fillings. Ploughman's lunch with home-made soda bread. Toasties. Lemon and blueberry meringue. Banoffee pie. Sticky toffee pudding. Raspberry roulade. Mincemeat crumble cake. Lemon gâteaux. Traybakes and scones. Variety of home-made ice cream.

No credit cards
Proprietors: Mark & Elizabeth Grieve

Tullybannocher Farm Food Bar

Comrie
Perthshire PH6 2JY
Tel: 01764 670827

Just outside Comrie on A85 Lochearnhead road.

A popular, informal bistro/restaurant on the banks of the river Earn.

- A self-service, relaxed and ideal place to break your journey.
- The best of farmhouse cooking.
- "A fine atmosphere in a marvellous setting."

Just outside the picturesque village of Comrie, Tullybannocher is ideally placed for those enjoying a drive along Loch Earn. It stands in beautiful woodland, is easy to pull in to and offers ample car parking. The decor of this large log cabin is simple. It offers a wide range of inexpensive and freshly-prepared meats, fish and quiches and simple but good salads. The smell of home baking is refreshing and real. In fine weather, the rustic tables on the restaurant's rolling lawn are understandably popular.

Open 1 Apr to 14 Oct
Food served all day (a)
Lunch from 12 noon (a)
Supper 6 - 9 pm (b)
Table Licence
Vegetarians welcome
Dogs allowed outside only

Home-baked ham. Local smoked trout. Venison. Steak pie. Home-made quiches. Coronation chicken. Hot dishes of the day. Fresh strawberry flan. A large selection of home baking. Supper menu: steaks, seafood and salmon.

No credit cards
Proprietor: Peter Davenport

Coul House Hotel

Contin, by Strathpeffer
Ross-shire IV14 9EY
Tel: 01997 421487
Fax: 01997 421945

On A835 to Ullapool, 17 miles north-west of Inverness.

A country house near Strathpeffer; 1992 RAC 'Small Hotel of the Year'.

- 19th century mansion converted into an elegant hotel.
- Country house cooking.
- " A starter of fresh prawns was followed by delicately smoked sliced venison; a wonderful combination."

This elegant country house hotel commands fine views over unspoiled Highland scenery, little changed since its original inhabitants, the Mackenzies of Coul lived here. The spacious public rooms have open log fires and the recently refurbished en suite bedrooms are comfortable and tastefully decorated. Resident proprietors, Martyn and Ann Hill, are hospitable and welcoming. The bar lunches are notable - and the 'Kitchen Bar' itself is very popular with locals. 'Mackenzie's Taste of Scotland Restaurant' offers table d'hôte and à la carte lunch and dinner menus which focus on Scottish specialities. The hotel has some salmon and trout fishing; pony trekking and guided rambling is available locally.

Open all year
Rooms: 21 with private facilities
Bed & Breakfast £35 - £58
Dinner B & B £49.50 - £80.50
Special Rates for 3 nights
Bar Lunch 12 - 2 pm Mon to Sat: 12.30 - 2 pm Sun (a)
Dining Room/Restaurant Lunch 12 - 2 pm (b) by arrangement only
Bar Supper 5.30 - 9 pm (a)
Dinner 7 - 9 pm (e) 5 course menu
Vegetarians welcome

Terrine of mixed local game with brandy and herbs served with wholemeal toast. Summer Isle scallops dusted in flour and lightly pan-fried. Scottish cheeses.

STB Highly Commended 4 Crowns
Credit cards: 1, 2, 3, 5 + SWITCH
Proprietors: Martyn & Ann Hill

Corsemalzie House Hotel

Corsemalzie, Port William
Newton Stewart
Wigtownshire DG8 9RL
Tel: 01988 860254
Fax: 01988 860213

Halfway along B7005 Glenluce-Wigtown, off A714 Newton Stewart-Port William or A747 Glenluce-Port William.

Sporting country house hotel.

- Victorian country mansion.
- Traditional hotel cooking.
- "Well-cooked Steaks."

This 19th century house with its own 40 acre estate is a popular venue for those who enjoy the pursuit of country sports. The sprawling gardens and woodlands around the house are most attractive and peacocks strut proudly across the lawns, with the occasional courageous pheasant which has avoided the pot, ducking between them. The menus are familiar in this style of establishment with an emphasis on red meat and game, served with a range of sauces.

Open 1 Mar to 31 Jan except Christmas + Boxing Days
Rooms: 15, 14 with private facilities
Bed & Breakfast £34 - £55
Dinner B & B £46 - £71
Special Rates available
Bar Lunch 12.30 - 2 pm (a)
Dining Room/Restaurant Lunch 12.30 - 2 pm (b)
Bar Supper 7.15 - 9 pm (b) 5 courses
Dinner 7.30 - 9 pm (c)
Vegetarians welcome
Dogs accepted (small charge)

Filo parcels filled with spinach and Scottish cream cheese. Whole local fresh prawns with garlic butter. Smoked Bladnoch salmon. Local lamb cutlets en croûte. Jumbo Luce Bay Scampi with seafood sauce. Torhouse trout stuffed with prawns.

STB Commended 4 Crowns
Credit cards: 1, 2, 3
Proprietor: Peter McDougall

Craigellachie

Craigellachie Hotel
Craigellachie
Banffshire AB38 9SR
Tel: 01340 881204
Fax: 01340 881253

On A941, 12 miles south of Elgin.

> An imposing hotel in its own grounds just off the main square of the viilage, with the River Spey at the foot of the garden.

■ A large 19th century country hotel, refurbished in 1995.
■ Country house cooking.
■ "Splendid views, very comfortable rooms, good cooking."

Located at the heart of whisky country, within the attractive Speyside village of Craigellachie, this imposing hotel is decorated to a high standard and in excellent taste. It is comfortable and well run; the elegant interior is matched by the attentive and unobtrusive service. The bedrooms, some with four poster beds and all with private facilities, have lovely views over the river and the countryside beyond. The kitchen uses fresh produce as far as practicable, and carefully sources delicacies from all around Scotland - from Ayrshire smoked bacon to Sheildaig shellfish. The lunch and dinner menus are à la carte, change daily and feature robust, traditional dishes, given an imaginative twist by a very competent chef, who offers cookery workshops and 'epicurean evenings'. The hotel also has modern leisure facilities.

Open all year
Rooms: 30 with private facilities
Bed & Breakfast £49.50 - £62.50
Dinner B & B £77.50 - £90.50
Special Rates available
Bar Lunch 12.30-2 pm (a)
Dining Room/Restaurant Lunch 12.30-2 pm (b)
Dinner 7-9.30 pm (e) 4 course menu
No smoking in dining room
Vegetarians welcome

North Sea fish and dill cakes with warm tartare sauce. Baked Guinea fowl breast with a lentil and mushroom casserole. Glazed tartlet of woodland mushrooms and goats cheese. White chocolate cheesecake.

STB Highly Commended 4 Crowns
Credit cards: 1, 2, 3, 5

Crail

Hazelton Guest House
29 Marketgate, Crail
Fife KY10 3TH
Tel: 01333 450250

In town centre opposite tourist office and Tolbooth.

> A town guest house in Crail.

■ Victorian terraced house.
■ Creative Scottish cooking using fresh local produce.
■ "Innovative and attractive sounding menus with good range and combinations."

Hazelton is situated in the centre of Crail opposite the famous 16th century Tolbooth in Marketgate. Owners Alan and Rita Brown extend a warm welcome to their guests whom they accommodate in seven warm comfortably furnished bedrooms. The dining room overlooking Marketgate is airy and well-appointed. Breakfast, is chosen from a well-balanced traditional menu. The dinner menu changes daily and is imaginative and interesting, always including fresh fish or seafood and red and white meat dishes, home-smoked specialities appear frequently. The Browns' attention to detail combined with the relaxed and friendly atmosphere and the high standard of Rita's award-winning culinary skills ensure that guests return time and again.

Open Feb to Nov
Rooms: 7
Bed & Breakfast £16 - £18
Dinner B & B £31 - £33
Dinner at 7 pm (b) except Mon Tue - unless by prior arrangement
It is requested that guests select their menu by 4 pm
Residents only
Vegetarians welcome
Dinner menu not suitable for children
No dogs

Local crab and haddock in filo pastry with dill and white wine sauce. Tenderloin of pork in an orange cream sauce with ginger. Breast of chicken in a cream and mushroom sauce flavoured with gin and juniper berries. Tayberry crumble.

STB Commended Listed
No credit cards
Proprietors: Alan & Rita Brown

Crianlarich

Allt-Chaorain Country House
Crianlarich
Perthshire FK20 8RU
Tel: 01838 300283
Fax: 01838 300238

Off A82, 1 mile north-west of Crianlarich.

> Small country hotel.

■ Informal country house.
■ Home cooking.
■ "Lots of Scottish emphasis on the presentation and flavours of the food."

This house is perched on a hill in its own grounds overlooking the scenic countryside of Benmore and Strathfillan. Its owner, Roger McDonald, runs the hotel personally and takes pride in maintaining an unobtrusive, homely atmosphere. Each evening he presents a different dinner menu for guests in the charming wood-panelled dining room where you will share one of three large tables with others staying in the hotel. The dishes are interesting, with a strong traditional Scottish theme; the cooking is much appreciated by guests. A 'trust' bar is available in the attractive drawing room where a log fire burns throughout the year.

Open 18 Mar to 19 Oct
Rooms: 8 with private facilities
Bed & Breakfast £30 - £46
Dinner B & B £45 - £51
Special Rates available
Dinner 7 - 8 pm (c)
Residents only
No smoking in dining room, bedrooms + main lounge
A sun lounge is set aside for those who wish to smoke

Home-made soups - spicy parsnip, carrot and orange. Local salmon and trout. Lamb steaks with a haggis crust. Traditional steak and kidney pie. Home-made desserts - orange meringue pie, bread and butter pudding, cranachan, Ecclefechan tart, cloutie dumpling.

STB Commended 3 Crowns
Credit cards: 1, 3 + SWITCH, DELTA
Proprietor: Roger McDonald

Crieff

Crieff Visitors Centre
Muthill Road, Crieff
Perthshire PH7 4AZ
Tel: 01764 654014
Fax: 01764 652903

On A822 leading out of Crieff to the south.

A visitors centre with a number of attractions.

- Self-service, cafeteria-style restaurant.
- Home baking and light meals.
- "A generous slice of home-made chicken liver pâté with rough oatcakes was enough to set me up for a good day's walk."

This self-service restaurant is part of a visitor complex of showroom, shops, audio-visual display and garden centre beside two rural factories producing thistle pattern Buchan pottery and paper-weights. The restaurant itself is a large, light and airy building, with glass, brick and pine being used most successfully in its design and construction. It is a very busy establishment and is self-service. The range of food on offer goes from familiar starters, to soups, hot main courses, fresh salads and ending with an impressive array of home baking. It is good value and the produce used is all local and fresh, ideal for the family as there are special children's meals on the menu.

Open all year but closed Mon Tue Dec to Feb
Food service 9 am - 6 pm (a)
(Note: hours restricted in winter)
Vegetarians welcome
Facilities for disabled visitors

Credit cards: 1, 2, 3 + SWITCH, DELTA

Murraypark Hotel
Connaught Terrace, Crieff
Perthshire PH7 3DJ
Tel: 01764 653731
Fax: 01764 655311

Turn off A85 at Connaught Terrace, uphill to residential part of town.

Hotel set in its own grounds in Crieff, with pleasant gardens and comfortable accommodation.

- Victorian sandstone villa, at the 'Gateway to the Highlands'.
- Traditional Scottish cooking.
- "Home-made food with strong emphasis on local produce."

This 19th century family home standing in its own gardens in a residential part of Crieff has been converted by Noel and Ann Scott into a sound family hotel ideal for a golfing holiday and popular with local people. Bedrooms all have en suite facilities. The small restaurant has an uncrowded atmosphere and overlooks the pleasant gardens. Menus (lunch and dinner) are table d'hôte and à la carte, and always offer fresh produce. Breakfasts are famous.

Open all year
Rooms: 20 with private facilities
Bed & Breakfast £35 - £48
Dinner B & B £50 - £65
Bar Lunch 12 - 2 pm (b)
Bar Supper 7.30 - 9.30 pm (c)
Dinner 7.30 - 9.30 pm (d) 4 course menu
No smoking in restaurant
Vegetarians welcome

Fresh mussels. Venison and pork pâté. Scampi poached in white wine with leeks, cream and freshly grated ginger. Char-grilled venison with a brandy and green peppercorn sauce. Chicken poached in lemon juice, spices and vegetables garnished with deep-fried scampi tails. Poached salmon and scallops with dill and yoghurt sauce.

STB Commended 4 Crowns
Credit cards: 1, 2, 3, 5, 6 + SWITCH
Proprietors: Ann & Noel Scott

Smugglers Restaurant
Glenturret Distillery
The Hosh, Crieff, Perthshire PH7 4HA
Tel: 01764 656565
Fax: 01764 654366

Signed from A85 in Crieff and from A822 (Sma' Glen) at Gilmerton (off A85 to east of Crieff).

Two restaurants in a converted distillery building, offering a range of good quality food for both formal and informal occasions.

- An 18th century bonded warehouse in the grounds of one of Scotland's oldest distilleries.
- Traditional Scottish fare.
- "The unashamedly Scottish menu offers a selection of popular national dishes."

Glenturret makes a strong claim to being Scotland's oldest distillery. It was established in 1775 although the site was used by illicit distillers and smugglers long before then. It was the first distillery to encourage visitors, and now attracts over 215,000 people per annum with a heritage centre, exhibition museum and shop as well as two restaurants. Smugglers, on the first floor of the warehouse is self-service but has high standards of cooking. The Pagoda Room which extends from Smugglers and is a smaller more formal setting, offers efficient and friendly waitress service. In good weather visitors can sit at tables on the balcony. The menus feature Highland venison, beef and salmon. Coffee, afternoon tea and home baking are also available during the day. Dinners and parties are welcome at Glenturret by prior arrangement.

Open all year except Christmas + Boxing Days, 1 + 2 Jan
Note: closed weekends Jan Feb
Bar Lunch (Smugglers) 12 - 2.30 pm (a)
Dining Room/Restaurant Lunch (Pagoda Room) 12 - 2.30 pm (b)
Dinner - by private arrangement only
Complete facilities are no smoking but a smoking area is provided in Smugglers Restaurant
Disabled access
Vegetarians welcome

Glenturret smoked salmon. Home-made soups. Venison in illicit whisky sauce. Highland beef in red wine sauce. Tay salmon. Haggis neeps and tatties. Steak pie. Smugglers chicken. Glenturret ice cream. Cranachan.

Credit cards 1, 2, 3

Crinan

Crinan Hotel
Crinan, Lochgilphead
Argyll PA31 8SR
Tel: 01546 830261
Fax: 01546 830292

Prestige Award Winner 1991

A82 Glasgow-Inveraray, then A83 to
Lochgilphead. Follow A816 (Oban) for c. 5
miles, then B841 to Crinan.

One of Scotland's most famous hotels; a haven
for yachtsmen.

■ Country hotel with a spectacular location.
■ Modern Scottish cooking.
■ "Lock 16 may well be Britain's best seafood
restaurant."

The tiny village of Crinan lies at the north end of
the Crinan Canal which connects the Firth of Clyde
(via Loch Fyne) to the Atlantic. The plain white,
family-owned hotel rises conspicuously above the
holding basin and has stupendous views over a
pattern of islands to the north and west. The hotel's
small and exclusive Lock 16 Restaurant is in the
top storey of the building and its picture windows
enjoy the view to the full. Seafood is the speciality
here. It is freshly landed daily below the hotel.
Indeed so much does the chef rely on the catch of
the day that he will often not know until 5 pm what
his menu will be. The hotel's main restaurant, the
Westward, offers a brief and delicious table d'hôte
menu (prefaced by the local shipping forcast!)
which features prime beef, wild venison and hill
lamb, as well as fish. A new Gallery Bar has been
built on the rooftop of the hotel with panoramic
views of the sea and mountains. In the bar are
pictures by Frances Macdonald (Mrs Ryan).

Open all year incl Christmas
Rooms: 22 with private facilities
Bed & Breakfast £115 - £140
Dinner B & B £170 - £190
Special Winter Rates available
Bar Lunch 12.30 - 2.30 pm (a)
Dinner (Westward Restaurant) 7 - 9 pm (e)
Dinner (Lock 16 mid Apr to end Sep only) at
8 pm except Sun Mon (e-f) - booking essential
Vegetarians welcome.

Mussels marinière. Locally smoked wild Scottish
salmon. Loch Crinan prawns Corryvreckan. Local
lobster. Scottish beef dishes.

STB Highly Commended 4 Crowns
Credit cards: 1, 2, 3 + SWITCH
Proprietors: Nick & Frances Ryan

Sealgair
c/o Wave Yacht Charters
1 Hazel Drive
Dundee DD2 1QQ
Tel: 01382 668501
Fax: 01382 668501

Classic cruising yacht based at Bellanoch, by
Crinan, Argyll.

■ Charter yacht.
■ Home cooking.
■ "Even without the benefit of a keen appetite,
the food on Sealgair is wonderful."

This magnificent 46 foot wooden ketch is equipped
to the highest standards for comfort, performance
and safety and is maintained in top condition,
Sealgair (which is pronounced 'Shallachar' and is
Gaelic for 'hunter') was the first cruising yacht to
be invited to join Taste of Scotland and the high
standard of food served on board continues to
delight her guests. Crewed by an experienced
husband and wife team, both are dedicated to
ensuring guests have a relaxing holiday enhanced
by tasty and imaginative meals. Normally crusing
the west coast of Scotland under Category 1
classification, Sealgair is available for longer more
adventurous journeys. Six guest berths. Fully
bonded. YCA membership. French spoken.

Open 1 May to mid Sep
Cabins: 4
Daily rate £60 per person, per day, minimum
charge £300 - includes all meals +
accommodation
Special Rates available
Unlicensed - guests welcome to take own wine
Vegetarians welcome
No smoking in dining area + cabins
No dogs

Tasty soups: spicy tomato, carrot and ginger.
Starters: marinaded red peppers, fresh asparagus
with foaming hollandaise. Venison with cranberry
and juniper. Herb crusted salmon. Lamb with a
bramble sauce.

No credit cards
Proprietor: Wave Yacht Management Ltd

Cromarty

The Royal Hotel
Marine Terrace, Cromarty
Ross & Cromarty IV11 8YN
Tel: 01381 600217
Fax: 01381 600217

Across Kessock Bridge from Inverness on A9.
Turn right approx 2-3 miles. Follow signs, 17
miles.

Traditional family-owned Scottish country
house hotel.

■ In historic village with splendid views.
■ Traditional Scottish cooking.
■ "A friendly family-owned hotel."

This traditional hotel has been around for over 150
years and overlooks the beach and harbour of the
ancient and historic village of Cromarty (all
bedrooms share this splendid view - watch out for
the bottle-nosed dolphins which live in the
Cromarty Firth). The public rooms are pleasantly
furnished and the dining room is bright and sunny.
Friendly, well-trained staff offer a table d'hôte menu
which features classic Scottish dishes. The food is
simply presented but of a high standard Children's
selection on menu.

Open all year
Rooms: 10 with private facilities
Bed & Breakfast £25 - £35
Dinner B & B £40 - £50
Special Rates available
Bar Lunch 12 - 2 pm (b)
Dining Room/Restaurant Lunch 12 - 3 pm (c)
Bar Supper 5 - 9 pm (b)
Dinner 5 - 9 pm (c)
Vegetarians welcome

Mushroom and nutmeg soup. Whole prawns.
Cromarty crab salad. Wild trout and salmon.
Lobster. Game pâté. Nairn smoked salmon and
asparagus rolls. Grilled local salmon and lemon
butter. Lamb cutlets with honey and lemon glaze.
Local steaks. Mandarin charlotte.

STB Commended 3 Crowns
Credit cards: 1, 2, 3
Proprietors: John & Brenda Shearer

Cullen

Bayview Hotel & Restaurant
Seafield Street, Cullen
Banffshire AB56 2SU
Tel: 01542 841031

A98 between Banff and Fochabers -
overlooking Cullen Harbour.

> A really charming hotel in a picturesque fishing
> village on the Moray Firth.

- ■ A small town hotel converted from a quayside
  house commanding views over the harbour and
  the bay beyond.
- ■ Seafood a speciality.
- ■ "Good choice of seafood."

A delightful, typical east coast town house, close to
the harbour at Cullen with lovely views over the
Moray Firth. This is a pleasant haven from which
to explore the surrounding countryside and historic
local fishing villages. The proprietor, David Evans,
runs the hotel himself, and provides friendly service
and a comfortable stay. He also makes full use of
the hotel's location by maximising on the excellent
choice of fresh fish available daily, and the à la
carte menus feature an excellent variety of fresh
produce, imaginatively presented.

Open all year except Christmas Day
Rooms: 6 with private facilities
Bed & Breakfast £25 - £35
Bar Lunch 12 - 1.45 pm (a)
Dining Room/Restaurant Lunch 12 - 1.45 pm
Sun only (b)
Bar Supper 6.30 - 9 pm (b)
Dinner 6.30 - 9 pm (c)
Vegetarians welcome
No dogs

Home-made soups. Grilled skate wings with
cucumber batons in a nut-brown butter. Poached
darne of local salmon in a Champagne sauce.
Escalope of pork pan-fried with apples, peppers and
spring onions in a cider and cream sauce.

Credit cards: 1, 3
Proprietor: David Evans

The Seafield Arms Hotel
Seafield Street, Cullen
Moray AB56 2SG
Tel: 01542 840791
Fax: 01542 840736

Situated on A98 (main road through Cullen) up
from town square.

> A charming old town hotel with lovely
> bedrooms, a lively bar and a smart dining room.

- ■ A 17th century coaching inn in the heart of
  Cullen.
- ■ Good hotel catering.
- ■ "Fresh, simple and traditional fare; I
  particularly like the Clan Grant tartan rugs!"

The Seafield Arms is an impressive former coaching
inn, built by the Earl of Seaforth in 1822. The
statistical Account of Scotland in 1845 stated: "The
Seafield Arms... has no superior between Aberdeen
and Inverness." The character and hospitality of
this hostelry are still evident. The staff are smart,
polite and attentive; the accommodation
comfortable and traditional. All the 25 bedrooms
were refurbished in 1995. The place is popular with
local people and the bar offers a range of over 100
whiskies to enjoy before a roaring fire. A wide-
ranging menu caters for all ages and preferences.

Open all year
Rooms: 25, 23 with private facilities
Bed & Breakfast £29 - £35
Special Rates available
Bar Lunch 12 - 2 pm (a)
Dining Room/Restaurant Lunch 12 - 2 pm (b)
Bar Supper 6 - 9 pm (b)
Dinner 6 - 9 pm (c)
No dogs
Facilities for disabled visitors
Vegetarians welcome

Seafield Arms Cullen skink - a local traditional
smoked haddock soup. Hot prawns with crispy
bread. Poached fillet of salmon served with
broccoli and a lemon flavoured hollandaise sauce
with lime slices. Breaded breast of chicken cooked
in butter with pineapples, served with a separate
spicy tomato sauce. Char-grilled steaks.

STB Commended 4 Crowns
Credit cards: 1, 2, 3, 6 + SWITCH, DELTA
Proprietors: Herbert & Alison Cox

Cupar

Eden House Hotel
2 Pitscottie Road, Cupar
St Andrews
Fife KY15 4HF
Tel: 01334 652 510
Fax: 01334 652 277

Overlooking Haugh Park, Cupar. On A91 road
to St Andrews, 8 miles west of St Andrews.

> An attractive hotel, stylishly refurbished.

- ■ Country house hotel.
- ■ Adventurous country cooking.
- ■ "Enthusiastic new owners."

Eden House Hotel has style. The house itself is
Victorian - built for a merchant and reflecting the
pompous grandeur favoured by the period. It has
been very well refurbished, in a way which respects
the original but allows for modern comforts. The
house overlooks the Haugh Park, on the outskirts of
the town, and a large conservatory has been built
on to accommodate the restaurant. It also has an
'annexe' in the road-side gate-house. The Vizan
family, who bought the house in 1995, run it with
enthusiasm and attention to detail. The cooking
makes use of local meat and fish and favours
interesting and richly flavoured sauces.

Open all year
Rooms: 11 with private facilities
Bed & Breakfast £24 - £39
Dinner B & B £40 - £50
Special Rates for 3 nights + weekend
Bar Lunch 12 - 2 pm (b)
Dining Room/Restaurant Lunch 12 - 2 pm (c)
Bar Supper 6.30 - 10 pm (b)
Dinner 6.30 - 10 pm (c)
Vegetarians welcome
Facilities for disabled visitors
Dogs welcome outside only

Button mushroom flambé in whisky with Stilton,
white wine and cream sauce in a puff pastry case.
Saddle of venison with a crème de cassis and
cranberry sauce. Sirloin steak with a brandy and
moutarde de meaux sauce. Butterscotch cheesecake
with butterscotch sauce.

STB Commended 3 Crowns
Credit cards: 1, 2, 3
Proprietors: Laurence & Mary Vizan

Ostlers Close

Bonnygate, Cupar
Fife KY15 4BU
Tel: 01334 655574

Via A91/A92 to centre of Cupar.

An award-winning, cottage-like town centre restaurant of distinction and charm.

- A cosy and comfortable establishment in a narrow Cupar lane.
- Elegant Scottish cuisine.
- "An enviable reputation, well-deserved."

Nestling in a lane or 'close' just off the market town of Cupar's main street, Ostler's is a simply and unpretentiously decorated small restaurant. Chef/proprietor Jimmy Graham deserves the excellent reputation he has earned for his imaginative cooking. His treatment of fish and shellfish is outstanding, but he applies the same flair to Scottish meat and game. Given such quality, a meal here - complemented by a small but good wine list - is excellent value for money. Amanda Graham looks after guests with courtesy and charm.

Open all year except Christmas + Boxing Days, 1 Jan, first 2 wks Jun,
Dining Room/Restaurant Lunch 12.15 - 2 pm except Sun Mon (b)
Dinner 7 - 9.30 pm except Sun Mon (d-e)
Closed Sun Mon
Vegetarians welcome - prior notice required

Local seafood broth. Pan-fried terrine of goats cheese and potato served with mixed salad leaves. Roast saddle of lamb served with a herb scented sauce. Fillet of turbot with langoustines and asparagus on a fresh herb butter sauce. Roast fillet of beef served with a green peppercorn sauce. Selection of seafood with a shellfish stock.

Credit cards: 1, 3, 6 + SWITCH, DELTA
Proprietors: Jimmy & Amanda Graham

Special Merit Award for Newcomers

Braidwoods Restaurant

Drumastle Mill Cottage,
by Dalry
Ayrshire KA24 4LN
Tel: 01294 833544

A737 Kilwinning-Dalry. On southern outskirts of Dalry, take road to Saltcoats for 1 mile and follow signs.

An outstanding restaurant deep in the Ayrshire countryside.

- A converted 18th century miller's cottage surrounded by rolling farmland.
- Innovative modern Scottish cooking.
- "The food was the best I had eaten this year"

This restaurant was converted in 1994 from two long and low cottages by Keith and Nicola Braidwood into a tasteful contemporary restaurant. The owners have been described simply as 'two of Scotland's best younger chefs'. They are both highly qualified, with impressive track records (Shieldhill, Murrayshall, Peat Inn, Inverlochy Castle, etc) and demonstrate their skills daily in wonderfully original combinations of flavour, textures and unusual ingredients. Their table d'hôte menus give an unexpected, and wholly successful, twist to classic dishes. Raw materials are carefully sourced locally. A truly gourmet experience.

Booking essential.
Open 23 Jan to 31 Dec except 1 wk Oct
Dining Room/Restaurant Lunch 12 - 2 pm except Mon Tue (b)
Dinner 7 - 9.30 pm except Sun Mon (d)
4 course menu
Closed Mon
Table Licence
Vegetarians by arrangement
No smoking throughout

Warm mousseline of lemon sole centred with smoked salmon on ribbons of cucumber, glazed with a horseradish and chive hollandaise. Pan-fried loin of woodland roe deer on savoury Du Puy lentils with port and thyme sauce. Honey glazed breast of Gressingham duck with a confit of its own leg and a caramelised cranberry and ginger essence. Trio of caramel puddings. Banana brûlée. Praline mousse.

Credit cards: 1, 2, 3 + SWITCH, DELTA
Proprietors: Keith & Nicola Braidwood

Daviot Mains Farm

Daviot, Inverness IV1 2ER
Tel: 01463 772215
Fax: 01463 772215

On B851 (B9006) to Culloden/Croy, 5 miles south of Inverness.

Working farm, recommended by Elizabeth Gundrey's Staying off the Beaten Track.

- Early 19th century Highland farmhouse.
- Home cooking.
- "Well cooked traditional and modern dishes."

Daviot Mains is a 19th century Highland farmhouse 5 miles south of Inverness and a short drive from Culloden Moor. This warm and friendly home is run by Margaret and Alex Hutcheson where delicious meals are thoughtfully prepared from fresh, locally sourced ingredients, following traditional and modern recipes. Log fires burn in both sitting room and dining room where guests are offered a light supper of tea and home baking around 10 pm.

Open all year except Christmas Eve, Christmas Day, 31 Dec + New Year's Day
Rooms: 3, 2 with private facilities
Bed & Breakfast £16 - £22
Dinner B & B £26 - £34
Special Rates for 3+ nights Oct to Apr (excl Easter + Christmas holiday period)
Dinner at 6.30 pm except Sun Sat 4 May to 21 Sep incl; except Sun rest of year (b)
Unlicensed - guests welcome to take own wine
Vegetarians welcome - prior notice required
Special diets on request
No smoking throughout
Dogs accepted by arrangement

According to season - home-made soups, fresh local salmon and trout, Scottish meats, vegetables and cheeses. Local fruits and home-made puddings.

STB Highly Commended 2 Crowns
Credit cards: 1, 3
Proprietors: Margaret & Alex Hutcheson

Dingwall

Kinkell House

Easter Kinkell, Conon Bridge
Ross-shire IV7 8HY
Tel: 01349 861270
Fax: 01349 861270

One mile from A9 on B9169, 10 miles north of Inverness.

> A well appointed hotel with a reputation for high class cooking.

- Small country house hotel.
- Country house cooking.
- "The setting sun floods the restaurant; a wonderful view and great cooking."

Once a large farmhouse, Kinkell stands in its own grounds on the Black Isle, overlooking the Cromarty Firth, towards Ben Wyvis and the hills of Wester Ross. It is the home of Marsha and Steve Fraser, and retains the atmosphere of a private house, with appropriate period furnishings and log fires. The excellence of Marsha's cooking has won Kinkell an AA Rosette, the hotel has also been awarded AA 5Q Premier Select. She presents interesting and well balanced à la carte menus for lunch and dinner (five main courses; changing daily) featuring fresh local produce with both classic and innovative treatments. The restaurant is popular, and non-residents are asked to book in advance.

Open Mar to Dec
Rooms: 3 with private facilities
Bed & Breakfast £28.50 - £43.50
Dinner B & B £48 - £63
Special Rates available
Dining Room/Restaurant Lunch 12.30 - 2 pm except Sat (b) - reservation essential: Group parties by arrangement Sat
Dinner 7 - 9 pm (c) - reservation essential
Vegetarians welcome
No smoking area in dining room + bedrooms

Warm salad of pigeon breast and wild mushrooms on tossed leaves. Savoury crusted salmon fillet and scallops with a lime and coriander tartare sauce. Peppered sirloin steak with mushroom and onion marmalade. Collops of venison fillet with port and rowanberry sauce. Iced chocolate and Drambuie parfait with red berry coulis.

STB Highly Commended 3 Crowns
Credit cards: 1, 3
Proprietor: Marsha Fraser

Dornoch

Dornoch Castle Hotel

Castle Street
Dornoch IV25 3SD
Tel: 01862 810216
Fax: 01862 810981

In the centre of the cathedral town of Dornoch, 2 miles off A9.

> Unique castle hotel.

- 15th century tower house.
- Country house cooking.
- "The history of this old castle adds something indefinable to the dining experience."

Part of the original tower, with its dungeons and turnpike stairway (and a charming panelled cocktail bar) are still intact, although there have been many additions over the centuries. There is a new wing of bedrooms and the public rooms including The Bishop's Room restaurant in the old palace kitchens, where there is a choice of table d'hôte and à la carte menus (an attractive and well-priced bar menu is also available) The food served here is of a traditional country house style with, rich seafood and game dishes making frequent appearances. After dinner, relax in the sitting room, which looks out on the terrace and walled garden.

Open 28 Mar to 31 Oct
Rooms: 17 with private facilities
Bed & Breakfast £32.50 - £41
Dinner B & B £51 - £60
Special Rates for 2+nights
Bar Lunch 12.15 - 2 pm Mon to Sat: 12.30 - 2 pm Sun (a)
Dining Room/Restaurant Lunch 12.15 - 2 pm Mon to Sat: 12.30 - 2 pm Sun (a)
Bar Supper 6 - 9 pm Mon to Sat: 6.30 - 9 pm Sun (a)
Dinner 7.30 - 9 pm (c) 4 course menu
Vegetarians welcome
No smoking in restaurant

Avocado with soft poached quail egg and béarnaise sauce. Ragôut of wild forest mushrooms. Parsnip soup with cumin. Roast loin of lamb with rhubarb and mint compote. Collops of monkfish on a nest of shredded courgettes with caramelised shallots and tomato and basil butter sauce. Chilled strawberry and Drambuie iced soufflé.

STB Commended 4 Crowns
Credit cards: 1, 2, 3, 6 + SWITCH, DELTA
Proprietor: Michael Ketchin

The Royal Golf Hotel

1st Tee, Dornoch
Sutherland IV25 3LG
Tel: 01862 810283
Fax: 01862 810923

From A9, 2 miles into Dornoch town square.

> The hotel is appropriately named, being adjacent to the first tee.

- Seaside golfing hotel.
- Traditional Scottish cooking.
- "A warm welcome from Donald Macleod, General Manager, combines with exciting cooking by Martyn Woodward."

The Royal Golf is a traditional Scottish hotel, within yards of the first tee of the famous golf course of the same name, and having a broad, picture-windowed modern extension overlooking the course and the sandy beaches of the Dornoch Firth beyond. The restaurant also benefits from this splendid view. Here Chef Martyn Woodward - who came 2nd in the 1995 Scottish Chef of the Year Competition - presents a well-priced table d'hôte menu featuring local fish, poultry, beef and lamb. The cooking is first rate and presentation attractive.

Open Mar to Dec
Rooms: 30 with private facilities
Bed & Breakfast £39 - £69
Dinner B & B £36 - £75
Special Rates for 2+ nights
Bar Lunch 12 - 2 pm (a)
Bar Supper 6 - 9 pm (b)
Dinner 7 - 9 pm (c) 4 course menu
Vegetarians welcome

Fresh vegetables and wild mushrooms stir-fried and simmered in cream and saffron, served with a timbale of rice. Smoked salmon parcel filled with prawns.

STB Commended 4 Crowns
Credit cards: 1, 2, 3, 5

The Mallin House Hotel

Church Street, Dornoch
Sutherland IV25 3LP
Tel: 01862 810335
Fax: 01862 810810

Down to centre of town, turn right.

| Comfortable town hotel popular with golfers. |

- Family-run hotel close to historic golf course.
- Modern Scottish cooking.
- "Under Linda and Malcolm Holden's relaxed style of management this hotel has won a well-deserved reputation for quality."

The hotel is a mere 200 yards from the Royal Dornoch Golf Course, one of the finest and oldest links courses in the world. As you would expect, it is very popular with golfers: its bar, in particular, is a refuge from the rigours of the course, with an exceptionally good range of bar meals including lobster and a special 'malt of the month' promotion. An extensive à la carte menu offers a good choice of local produce with superb, locally caught seafood as something of a speciality. Food is imaginatively prepared with unusual sauces and accompaniments. The restaurant itself has magnificent views of the Dornoch Firth and the Struie Hills. Accommodation is very comfortable with recent new additions and improvements including a residents' lounge.

Open all year
Rooms: 11 with private facilities
Bed & Breakfast £28 - £30
Dinner B & B £43 - £50
Bar Lunch 12.30 - 2.15 pm (a)
Dining Room/Restaurant Lunch 12.30 - 2.15 pm (c)
Bar Supper 6.30 - 9 pm (a)
Dinner 6.30 - 9 pm (c)
Vegetarians welcome
Facilities for disabled visitors: wheelchair ramp
Kennel for dogs

King scallops with diced red onions, fresh herbs and flamed with Pernod. Rack of spring lamb roasted with rosemary, with port wine sauce and a tartlet case filled with rowanberry jelly. Whole local lobster in hot garlic and herb butter. Fresh salmon escalope filled with crab and lemon forcemeat served with a sauce of prawns, mushroom and dry white wine.

STB Commended 3 Crowns
Credit cards: 1, 2, 3 + SWITCH, DELTA
Proprietors: Malcolm & Linda Holden

Buchanan Arms Hotel

Main Street,
Drymen by Loch Lomond
Stirlingshire G63 0BQ
Tel: 01360 660588
Fax: 01360 660943

A811 Balloch (Loch Lomond)/Stirling. The hotel is in a roadside position in the pretty village of Drymen, c. 7 miles east of Balloch.

| A resort hotel offering comfortable accommodation, extensive leisure facilities and a wide choice of food. |

- An old coaching inn near Loch Lomond, with extensive modern facilities.
- Traditional Scottish, with international influences.
- "A large, interesting menu at a very reasonable price."

The Buchanan Arms is an 18th century coaching inn and retains the feeling of such an establishment, although it has been extensively modernised. It has long been popular with visitors to picturesque Loch Lomondside, attracted by, among other features, the hotel's well-equipped leisure complex. The exterior of the building, which is on the principal street in Drymen, itself still has a period charm; inside the public rooms are spacious and comfortable. Light meals and snacks are served in the conservatory; the main restaurant, called 'Tapestries', offers both à la carte and table d'hôte menus which include continental dishes as well as Scottish classics.

Open all year
Rooms: 51 with private facilities
Bed & Breakfast £55 - £75
Dinner B & B £54 - £59 (min 2 nights stay)
Special Rates available
Light Meals/Snacks (Conservatory) 12 - 2.30 pm (a)
Dining Room/Restaurant Lunch (Tapestries) 12.30 - 2.30 pm (a)
Dinner (Tapestries) 7 - 9.30 pm (c)
Facilities for disabled visitors
Vegetarians welcome

Terrine of Highland game scented with herbs. Roast rib of Scottish beef flavoured with thyme and rosemary served with glazed baby onions, asparagus spears and a port wine jus. Brandy snap scrolls set on a dark chocolate sauce with coffee ice cream.

STB Commended 4 Crowns
Credit cards: 1, 2, 3, 5, 6 + SWITCH, DELTA

A Taste of Speyside

10 Balvenie Street, Dufftown
Banffshire AB5 4AB
Tel: 01340 820860
Fax: 01340 820860

| Popular restaurant in whisky country. |

- Informal town restaurant.
- Good home cooking.
- "The Scottish theme prevails - tartan, whisky and well-cooked Scottish fare."

The restaurant is situated in malt whisky heartland and was originally set up as a whisky tasting centre and restaurant. To this day one of its major attractions is the superb selection of malt whiskies on offer. Situated close to the centre of Dufftown the restaurant revels in its Scottishness, evident in its tartan inspired decor and style of cuisine, but in a tasteful, rather than a mawkish way. You will find simple fare that makes the most of local ingredients, cooked and presented with style. This is home cooking at its best, enhanced by a well-chosen wine list with a predominance of reasonably priced New World wines.

Open 15 Mar to 31 Dec
Note: Closed lunches 1 Nov to 31 Dec, + Mon Tue 1 Nov to 31 Dec
Bar Meals 11 am - 5.30 pm (a)
Restaurant Lunch 11 am - 5.30 pm (a)
Dinner 6 - 9 pm (b)
Vegetarians welcome

Cullen skink. A Taste of Speyside Platter. Large local scampi cooked in a birch wine sauce. Prime Scottish beef steak with a grain mustard cream and malt whisky sauce. Medallions of roe deer in a Madeira sauce. Heather honey and malt whisky cheesecake topped with walnuts, with fresh cream and raspberry coulis. Hot fruit dumpling with Drambuie cream.

Credit cards: 1, 2, 3
Proprietors: J Thompson & R McLean

Dulnain Bridge

Dumfries

Dunbar

Auchendean Lodge Hotel
Dulnain Bridge, Grantown-on-Spey
Inverness-shire PH26 3LU
Tel: 01479 851347
Fax: 01479 851347

On A95, 1 mile south of Dulnain Bridge.

A charming Highland country hotel.

■ Edwardian hunting lodge, with a great view over the Spey.
■ Original, talented, eclectic cooking.
■ "There is a holistic culinary ethos here, happily combining French and other influences, simplicity and sophistication."

Auchendean was built just after the turn of the century as a sporting lodge. The present owners, Eric Hart and Ian Kirk, are convivial professionals dedicated to giving their guests a full dining experience. Before dinner you are served drinks in the drawing room and introduced to the other diners - this makes for an interesting evening, with conversations whirling round the dining room between tables. Both Ian and Eric share the cooking; Eric is a keen mycologist and finds over 20 varieties of edible wild mushrooms locally; the hotel's garden also provides vegetables (including six varieties of potato!), herbs and honey. Eggs are supplied by the hotel's own hens. Wild berries, mountain hare, rabbit, pigeon, mallard, pheasant and home-cured gravadlax are specialities. The menu changes every night but always balances a simple main course with something more exotic. As a New Zealander Ian has created an extensive cellar including over 30 special wines from his home country. French spoken.

Open all year except early Jan to early Feb
Rooms: 7, 5 with private facilities
Bed & Breakfast £15 - £41
Dinner B & B £35 - £64
Special Rates for 3+ nights
Dinner 7.30 - 9 pm (d) 4 course menu
Vegetarians welcome - prior notice required
No smoking in dining room + one of the lounges
Home-made gravadlax with mustard and dill sauce. Roast loin of pork with garlic and rosemary. Wild mallard duck breast with ceps. Athol brose cream. Apricot, prune and brandy ice cream.

STB Highly Commended 3 Crowns
Credit cards: 1, 2, 3, 5
Proprietors: Eric Hart & Ian Kirk

Station Hotel
Lovers Walk, Dumfries
Dumfriesshire DG1 1LT
Tel: 01387 54316
Fax: 01387 50388

Just outside town centre opposite railway station.

A traditional railway hotel in Dumfries.

■ Victorian, red sandstone grand hotel.
■ Hotel cooking.
■ "A pleasant, old fashioned hotel."

This hotel is a typical 19th century station hotel, built in 1896 by the London Midland Scottish Railway Company and retains some of the grandeur and elegance built in to such hotels - ornate plasterwork and mouldings, spacious public rooms, and so on. All the hotel's 32 bedroooms have recently been refurbished. The dining room has also been redecorated but still has an attractive grand hotel atmosphere. A la carte and table d'hôte menus are presented here in the evening, featuring Solway salmon and shellfish, and Dumfriesshire beef and lamb, cooked in familiar ways. Next door to the hotel there is a bistro - stone floor tiles, plain wooden tables and beamed ceilings - which offers a set price lunch and a well-priced menu of bistro-style food.

Open all year except Christmas + Boxing Days
Rooms: 32 with private facilities
Bed & Breakfast £35 - £65
Dinner B & B £50 - £80
Special Rates for 2 nights
Bar Lunch 12 - 2 pm (a)
Bar Supper 5 - 10 pm (a)
Dinner 7 - 9.30 pm (b)
Taste of Scotland applies to main restaurant only
Vegetarians welcome
No smoking area in restaurant

Oak-smoked salmon cornets with prawns and Marie Rose sauce. Locally-made haggis served on warm oatcakes. Sirloin steak in a sauce with mushrooms flavoured with Drambuie. Seafood platter with salmon, mussels, prawns and cockles. Selection of Scottish cheeses.

STB Commended 4 Crowns
Credit cards: 1, 2, 3, 5 + SWITCH, DELTA

The Courtyard Hotel & Restaurant
Woodbush Brae, Dunbar
East Lothian EH42 1HB
Tel: 01368 864169

From A1 take A1087 to Dunbar. At south end of High Street, take road towards seashore.

Charming restaurant with rooms overlooking the beach at Dunbar.

■ Converted fishermans' cottages on the seafront.
■ Country cooking with classic French influences.
■ "The owner is such a food enthusiast, he'll travel to Northern Ireland for lunch."

This little hotel is tucked away off Dunbar's main street, facing out to sea, and literally washed by the salt water during high tides. Self-taught chef/owner Peter Bramley has won a strong reputation for the quality of his cooking since opening in 1990. He welcomes you with friendly and affable courtesy whether you are staying in one of the comfortable modern bedrooms or simply eating in his restaurant. He describes his cuisine as 'unpretentious country cooking', but it is more than this. The menus are imaginative, with interesting and exciting combinations and classic French influences. Everything is fresh, and, as one would imagine in a fishing port, fish and shellfish is something of a speciality (ordered at sea, via a ship-to-shore telephone!) A friendly, relaxed place, full of character.

Open all year except Christmas Day night
Rooms: 7, 2 with private facilities
Bed & Breakfast £22 - £42
Dinner B & B £35 - £55
Dining Room/Restaurant Lunch 12 - 2 pm (a)
Dinner 7 - 9.30 pm (b)
Vegetarians welcome

Rolled lemon sole stuffed with pesto and served with salad. Fennel and aubergine quiche. Noisettes of lamb with a Madeira and tomato sauce. Roast breast of Barbary duck with a cassis sauce. Parsnip and nut cake with Chantilly cream. Bread and butter pudding.

STB Commended 2 Crowns
Credit cards: 1, 2, 3
Proprietor: Peter W Bramley

Dunblane

Cromlix House

Kinbuck, by Dunblane
Perthshire FK15 9JT
Tel: 01786 822125
Fax: 01786 825450

Off A9, B8033 to Kinbuck, through village,
cross narrow bridge, drive is second on left.
From Crieff A822 to Braco, then B8033
Kinbuck.

> A baronial mansion recalling the splendours of
> a bygone age.

■ A highly praised hotel with the atmosphere of a
much loved home.
■ Outstanding modern/traditional Scottish
cuisine.
■ "A taste of Cromlix is a taste of serenity."

Proprietors David and Alisa Assenti succeed in
exemplifying the true traditions of country house
hospitality, treating each of their guests as a
cherished friend. Under head chef Stephen
Robertson, Cromlix takes only the best of fresh
produce, either from the estate or procured locally,
and produces imaginative meals for the
discriminating palate. Menus change daily. The
wine list is discerning and extensive. Awarded
among other prizes the STB's coveted Deluxe 4
Crowns, Cromlix is indeed a 'totally relaxing,
seemingly effortless, well run ship'. Member of the
Scotch Beef Club.

Open all year except mid Jan to mid Feb
Rooms: 14 with private facilities
Bed & Breakfast £60 - £100 Oct to Mar: £70 -
£120 Apr to Sep
Dinner B & B £95 - £135 Oct to Mar: £105 -
£155 Apr to Oct
Special Rates for 2+ nights Oct to Mar
Light Lunch & Snacks 12.30 - 1.30 pm (a-b)
Dining Room Lunch 12.30 - 1.15 pm:
Sun Sat only Oct to Mar (d)
Dinner 7 - 8.30 pm (f) 5 course menu
Vegetarians welcome
No smoking in dining rooms

Poached Tay salmon crowned with mushroom
duxelle and hollandaise over a herb cream sauce.
Cutlets of Perthshire lamb with a garlic and savoy
cabbage crust flavoured with a shallot and
rosemary reduction. Extensive vegetarian menu.

STB Deluxe 4 Crowns
Credit cards: 1, 2, 3, 5, 6
Proprietors: David & Ailsa Assenti

Dundee

The Old Mansion House Hotel

Auchterhouse by Dundee
DD3 0QN
Tel: 01382 320366
Fax: 01382 320400

Take A923 out of Dundee to Muirhead, then
B954 for 2 miles - hotel entrance on left.

> A small, luxury country house hotel beautifully
> situated in the Sidlaw hills.

■ A formal and elegant establishment of old
fashioned virtues.
■ Fine Scottish/modern cuisine.
■ "A hotel which is hard to fault."

This 16th century baronial mansion has been
carefully and lovingly converted by its present
owners, Nigel and Eva Bell. Magnificent
plasterwork and fine vaulted ceilings are matched
by fine furnishings to retain all the graciousness of
the past. All rooms are well-appointed. Outside, the
hotel's 10 acres of grounds offer squash and tennis
courts, a croquet lawn and a heated swimming
pool. In the splendid dining room, with its fine
Jacobean fireplace, chef Campbell Bruce offers
outstanding and reasonably-priced cuisine that
combines imagination and style with the best of
local produce. Service is attentive, formal and
impeccable.

Open 6 Jan to 25 Dec
Rooms: 6 with private facilities
Bed & Breakfast £75 - £95
Bar Lunch 12 - 1.50 pm (a)
Dining Room/Restaurant Lunch 12.30 -
1.50 pm (b)
Bar Supper 7 - 9.20 pm (b)
Dinner 7 - 9.20 pm (d)
Vegetarians welcome
No smoking in restaurant

Peppered Tay salmon with watercress and potato
salad. Whole Pittenweem prawn tails with
cucumber, apples and curry sauce. Parcel of pork
with hazelnuts and spinach served with lemon
thyme sauce. Banana and ginger crème brûlée.

STB Highly Commended 4 Crowns
Credit cards: 1, 2, 3, 5, 6 + SWITCH
Proprietors: Nigel & Eva Bell

The Sandford Country House Hotel

Newton Hill
Wormit, nr Dundee
Fife DD6 8RG
Tel: 01382 541802
Fax: 01382 542136

Near to B946 junction with A914 route which
links Forth Road Bridge, Edinburgh, with Tay
Bridge, Dundee.

> An historic 20th century building on the Tay.

■ Country house hotel.
■ Modern Scottish cooking.
■ "Attractive hotel, with friendly service and well-
cooked, generous meals."

A Listed building, designed in the Arts and Crafts
style and built at the turn of the century for the
Valentine (card manufacturers) family of Dundee.
It stands in seven acres of gardens and policies, part
of which is given over to Newton Hill Country
Sports, where you can powder a few clays, try your
hand at off-road driving or or improve your casting
over Newton Farm Loch. Unusually good bar meals
are offered (à la carte) and also a daily table d'hôte
menu of dishes freshly made from whatever is
available in the market. German, Italian and some
Japanese spoken.

Open all year except 4 to 6 Jan
Rooms: 16 with private facilities
Bed & Breakfast £50 - £60
Dinner B & B from £57.50
Bar Lunch 12 - 2.30 pm (a)
Dining Room/Restaurant Lunch 12 -
2.30 pm (a)
Bar Supper 6 - 9.30 pm (a)
Dinner 7 - 9.30 pm (c)
Vegetarians welcome
Facilities for disabled visitors
No smoking in restaurant

Crail crab soup with prawn dumplings fresh herbs
and a little cream. Fillet of salmon roasted in a nut
brown balsamic butter with fresh pasta, spring
onion, coriander and chilli. Medallion of beef fillet
with shredded horseradish in a claret sauce. Fillet of
rock turbot in a potato crust with basil and wholegrain Arran mustard.

STB Highly Commended 4 Crowns
Credit cards: 1, 2, 3 + SWITCH

Dunfermline

The Shaftesbury Hotel & Rachel's Restaurant

1 Hyndford Street, Dundee
Angus DD1 1HQ
Tel: 01382 669216
Fax: 01382 641598

West end of Dundee, off A90 (formerly A85) Perth-Dundee. Follow signs Sinderins and University.

A fine, small town house hotel and restaurant in a residential district.

■ A friendly establishment in the City of Discovery.
■ A wide range of traditional British/Scottish cooking.
■ "Always something tasty."

Built in 1870, this red sandstone former 'Jute Baron's' mansion has been carefully and sympathetically converted by its owner, Dennis Smith. The bedrooms are comfortable and well-furnished. The restaurant, which takes its name from the maker of a Victorian sampler found during the hotel's renovations, has a good local reputation. An attractive blend of the old and the new, it offers a freshly cooked and well-presented, varied à la carte menu.

Open all year
Rooms: 12 with private facilities
Bed & Breakfast £30 - £49.50
Dinner B & B £40 - £50.50
Special Rates available
Dinner 7 - 8.45 pm except Sun (b)
Residents only Sun
Vegetarians welcome
No smoking in restaurant

Arbroath smokie soup. Smoked salmon pâté. Home-made haddock and sole fish cakes served with a spicy tomato sauce. Baked escalope of chicken filled with haggis, served with home-made crab apple jelly and a butter and cream sauce with strips of vegetables. Collops of beef fillet with sauté of onions, a little chicken liver pâté, wrapped in puff pastry, served with a mushroom sauce.

STB Highly Commended 3 Crowns
Credit cards: 1, 2, 3, 5
Proprietor: Dennis H Smith

Strathdon Hotel

277 Perth Road, Dundee
Tayside DD2 1JS
Tel: 01382 65648

On main Perth road, in Dundee's west end - close to Ninewells Hospital, Dundee Airport and the University.

A small, intimate, family-run town centre hotel.

■ Fine views over the River Tay.
■ Good modern British cooking.
■ "For people who care about food."

Proprietor/chef Ian Hornsby and his wife, Carole, take great pride in ensuring their guests feel at home in this Edwardian terraced hotel. The atmosphere is cosy and comfortable. Ian's passionate commitment to good food is reflected in cuisine that is distinguished for its quality and freshness, using only the pick of local produce. The menus represent excellent value for money.

Open all year except Christmas Day + 1 Jan
Rooms: 10 with private facilities
Bed & Breakfast £24 - £35
Dinner B & B £41 - £52
Dinner 7 - 8.30 pm except Sun (c)
Restricted Hotel Licence
Vegetarians welcome
No smoking in restaurant
No dogs

Game parfait presented in a casket of puff pastry on a warm sherry and sesame seed vinaigrette. Gigot chop of new season lamb pan-fried in rosemary butter, presented on a minted tarragon sauce and topped with croûtons, grapes and mushrooms. Terrine of smoked salmon, lemon sole and spinach with dill flavoured mayonnaise.

STB Commended 3 Crowns
Credit cards: 1, 3
Proprietors: Ian & Carole Hornsby

Davaar House Hotel & Restaurant

126 Grieve Street, Dunfermline
Fife KY12 8DW
Tel: 01383 721886/735365
Fax: 01383 623633

From M90 Junction 3 to Dunfermline, follow A907 Kincardine into Carnegie Drive. Right into Chalmers Street, then second left to Grieve Street.

Small, family-run town hotel and restaurant.

■ Victorian town house.
■ Home cooking.
■ "Proudly billed as home cooking the food does succeed at its goal."

Davaar House was built at the turn of the century and retains such features as a splendid oak staircase, marble fireplaces and elaborate cornices. It is centrally situated in a residential area of Dunfermline. There is an appealing, chintzy, appearance to the hotel. The food is cooked by Doreen Jarvis who creates traditional dishes with intuitive flair and, using the best fresh vegetables, supplied by her husband Jim, who has his own fruit and vegetable business. Davaar also has the honour of its own label 12 year old whisky.

Open all year except Christmas Day, 26, 31 Dec + 1 Jan
Rooms: 8 with private facilities
Bed & Breakfast £27.50 - £42
Dinner B & B £40 - £58
Room Rate £38 - £58
Special Weekend Rates available
Dining Room/Restaurant Lunch (b) - by appointment
Supper 6 - 8.30 pm except Sun (b)
High Tea 4 - 6.30 pm Sun (a)
Dinner 7 - 8.30 pm except Sun (c)
Restricted Licence
Vegetarians welcome
Facilities for disabled visitors
No smoking in restaurant, No dogs

Home-made vegetable soups. Steaks with mushroom and crushed peppercorn sauce. River Tay salmon baked in a paper parcel served with Arran grain mustard sauce. Home-made apple and red plum crumble. Shortbread fingers with whisky and toffee ice cream.

STB Commended 3 Crowns
Credit cards: 1, 3
Proprietors: Jim & Doreen Jarvis

Dunkeld

Keavil House Hotel

Main Street, Crossford
by Dunfermline
Fife KY12 8QW
Tel: 01383 736258
Fax: 01383 621600

Junction 3, M90, 7 miles from Forth Road
Bridge. Take A985 then right after bridge. From
Dunfermline take A994.

An attractive country house near Dunfermline.

■ Country house hotel.
■ Traditional Scottish cooking.
■ "The high standards achieved here in every
department are an example to similar
establishments."

Crossford village is just outside Dunfermline, and
Keavil House is on the Main Street, standing in 12
acres of gardens and woods. As well as having two
restaurants to choose from, the hotel also has a
swimming pool, gym and sauna/solarium, etc.
Staff are smart and well-trained; rooms are very
comfortable. There is a choice of à la carte or table
d'hôte menus which offer both traditional and
more adventurous dishes, all of them well-cooked
and presented. Keavil is part of the Best Western
group of hotels, but is much, much better than the
average.

Open all year
Rooms: 33 with private facilities
Bed & Breakfast £42.50 - £49
Dinner B & B £59.50 - £67.50 (min 2 nights
stay)
Special Rates for Dec + Jan
Bar Lunch 12 - 2 pm (a)
Dining Room/Restaurant Lunch 12 - 2 pm (b)
Bar Supper 6 - 10 pm except Mon Tue (b)
Dinner 7 - 9 pm (c): (d) 4 course menu
Vegetarians welcome
Facilities for disabled visitors
No smoking in restaurants
Dogs not allowed in public rooms

Warm quenelles of salmon and sweet cicely/saviar
sauce. Salad of warm forest mushrooms, lardons
and croûtons. Rosette of charantais melon/summer
fruit compote. Medallions of venison on a casserole
of mousseron and shallots. Grilled halibut on a
juniper berry, tomato and gin sauce. Roast wild
boar with haggis stuffing on a peppered jus.

STB Commended 4 Crowns
Credit cards: 1, 2, 3, 5 + SWITCH
Hosts: Mark Simpkins & Stephen Owen

Royal Dunkeld Hotel

Atholl Street, Dunkeld
Perthshire PH8 0AR
Tel: 01350 727322
Fax: 01350 728989

From A9 follow signs for Dunkeld. Over
Telford's Bridge, hotel in prominent position on
Atholl Street.

Popular county town hotel on the tourist trail.

■ Privately owned hotel in scenic market town.
■ Traditional Scottish cooking.
■ "The hotel provides a diversity of eating styles
from a traditional carvery to an innovative, a la
carte menu full of the unexpected."

The hotel was completed in 1809, the same year as
the famous Telford Bridge which spans the River
Tay in Dunkeld. It was once a coaching inn and
has been carefully modernised to provide attractive
and comfortable accommodation. Food in the
hotel's restaurant is very good indeed with a choice
between a reasonably priced carvery and an à la
carte menu that contains many surprises. The chefs
have clearly taken the time to construct a well
balanced menu with excellent choice and very
appealing vegetarian options. Along with the
restaurant there is the informal Gargoyles bistro
where bar meals are served.

Open all year
Rooms: 35 with private facilities
Bed & Breakfast £20 - £45
Special Rates for 2/3 nights
Bar Lunch 12 - 2.30 pm (a)
Dining Room/Restaurant Lunch 12 - 2 pm (b)
Bar Supper 5 - 9.30 pm (a)
Dinner 7 - 9.30 pm (c)
Vegetarians welcome
Facilities for disabled visitors
No pipes or cigars in restaurant

Saddle of venison marinated in red wine and fresh
herbs, cooked in a rich game sauce with
mushrooms and spiced pear, topped with a pear-
shaped pastry crouton. Home-made blackcurrant
mousse set on a light sponge and topped with a
blackcurrant glaze.

STB Commended 3 Crowns
Credit cards: 1, 2, 3, 5, 6 + SWITCH, DELTA
Proprietors: Graham & Ann Rees

Stakis Dunkeld House Resort Hotel

Dunkeld
Perthshire PH8 0HX
Tel: 01350 727771
Fax: 01350 728924

A9 to Dunkeld, hotel lies c. 1 mile east of
village.

A luxury country house hotel set in idyllic
surroundings.

■ Highly regarded as offering the best of the old
and the new.
■ Outstanding Scottish cuisine with flair.
■ "Elegant, original and individual."

Built originally for the Seventh Duke of Atholl, this
Edwardian house has been sympathetically
extended and restored to form a rare combination
of country house and luxury hotel. The hotel sits
within its own 280 acre estate on the banks of the
River Tay and has a private 2-mile salmon beat. An
excellent leisure centre includes an indoor pool.
Outdoors, the hotel offers all-weather tennis courts,
a croquet lawn and clay-pigeon shooting. Menus in
the dining room are intended to satisfy the most
discerning of palates. The table d'hôte menu offers
four choices for each course. It should be noted that
during the quiet season the dining room is not
always available at lunchtime. Dishes are well
balanced and use fresh, local ingredients.
Presentation and service round off a pleasurable
experience.

Open all year
Rooms: 86 with private facilities
Bed & Breakfast £56 - £126
Dinner B & B £73 - £151.75
Room Rate £92 - £162
Special Rates available
Bar Lunch 12 - 2 pm Mon to Sat: 12 - 2.30 pm
Sun (a)
Dining Room/Restaurant
Lunch 12 - 2 pm Mon to Sat: 12 - 2.30 pm
Sun (b)
Dinner 7 - 9.30 pm Mon to Sat: 7 - 9 pm Sun (e)
Vegetarians welcome

Timbale of smoked trout mousse with strips of
smoked salmon with a lemon and dill dressing.
Pork fillet with woodland mushrooms and brandy
sauce. Casserole of Highland game with a
Burgundy and shallot sauce.

STB Highly Commended 5 Crowns
Credit cards: 1, 2, 3, 5 + SWITCH

Dunoon

Ardfillayne Hotel
Beverley's Restaurant
Bullwood Road, Dunoon
Argyll PA23 7QJ
Tel: 01369 702267
Fax: 01369 702501

At west end of Dunoon (A815).

Country house on the outskirts of Dunoon.

- Country house.
- Scottish/French cooking.
- "An unusual marinaded cut of wild boar was a high point of dinner."

A traditional country house situated in a 16 acre wooded estate on an elevated position overlooking the Firth of Clyde on the outskirts of Dunoon, the hotel retains the atmosphere of a bygone era. The interior of the house is crammed with antique furniture, Victoriana, bric-a-brac and an interesting collection of clocks. Beverley's Restaurant is decorated with lace, crystal and silverware with an extensive à la carte menu. Service is formal and the cooking applies classical French techniques to traditional Scottish recipes. Bill McCaffrey, the owner, also has an extensive cellar of wines he has bought at auction.

Open all year
Rooms: 8 with private facilities
Bed & Breakfast £35 - £45
Dinner B & B £58 - £68
Dinner 7 - 9 pm (d) - advance booking required
Restaurant closed Sun evening in winter
Vegetarians welcome - prior notice required
No smoking in restaurant

Fresh oysters. Smoked salmon. Broccoli and almond soup. Roast marinated wild boar. Sliced fillet of Aberdeen Angus beef. Grilled wild salmon and parsley butter.

STB Deluxe 4 Crowns
Credit cards: 1, 2, 3, 5
Proprietor: Bill McCaffrey

Chatters
58 John Street, Dunoon
Argyll PA23 8BJ
Tel: 01369 6402

The Macallan Taste
of Scotland Award Winner 1994

On John Street, Dunoon,
opposite the cinema.

Charming, award winning small restaurant in popular seaside resort.

- Town restaurant in converted traditional cottage.
- Traditional, French influenced Scottish cooking.
- "One of the best meals I have eaten this year."

Now in its fifth year of operation in the capable hands of Rosemary MacInnes this restaurant has picked up several awards including the Macallan Special Merit Award 1994. The young chefs are very enthusiastic, original and extremely competent. Credible and well balanced à la carte menus are presented for lunch and dinner (six starters, six main courses); every dish is an unusual and successful combination of flavours and textures, and each demonstrates considerable talent. There is also a sophisticated bar lunch menu which can be enjoyed in the newly built lounge extension opening out onto a small garden. In spite of its excellence and distinction, Chatters has a friendly, informal atmosphere and is very popular with locals for coffee and afternoon tea, with home baking.

Open 17 Feb to 31 Dec except Christmas Day
Bar Lunch 12 - 2.30 pm except Sun (b)
Dining Room/Restaurant Lunch 12 - 2.30 pm except Sun (c)
Bar Supper 6 - 10 pm except Sun (b)
Dinner 6 - 9.30 pm except Sun (c)
Closed Sun
Table Licence
Smoking discouraged

Warm tartlet of wild mushrooms on a Stilton and asparagus sauce. Baked breast of Guinea fowl and mango on a bed of honey and ginger glazed carrot ribbons on a natural jus. Fillet of Loch Fyne salmon, topped with a mousseline of scallops, wrapped in puff pastry. Collops of Scottish beef with pickled walnuts and wild mushroom dumpling with a juniper and port wine reduction.

Credit cards: 1, 3
Proprietor: Rosemary Anne MacInnes

Enmore Hotel
Marine Parade, Kirn
Dunoon, Argyll PA23 8HH
Tel: 01369 702230
Fax: 01369 702148

On seafront near Hunters Quay ferry, on road to Dunoon.

Seafront hotel near Dunoon.

- 19th century villa.
- Modern Scottish cooking.
- "Blessed with great local shellfish, and a talented chef to make the most of it."

Originally built in 1875 as a country retreat for a wealthy Glasgow businessman, the house has been enlarged over the years into a luxurious small hotel. It has ten en suite bedrooms, and the public rooms are attractively furnished with reproduction period pieces. There is a colourful garden, a squash court, a private beach and golf and fishing are within easy reach. The limited choice menu guarantees the freshness of the produce - 'creel caught crayfish' and Loch Fyne scallops - and the hotel's own garden provides herbs and vegetables. Chef/proprietor, David Wilson, has an AA Rosette, and his wife Angela puts as much care into making sure your stay is happy as he does into his menus.

Open all year except Christmas wk
Rooms: 10 with private facilities
Bed & Breakfast £30 - £70
Dinner B & B £55 - £95
Special Rates for 2+ to 7+ nights
Bar Lunch 12 - 3 pm (a)
Dining Room/Restaurant Lunch 12 - 3 pm (b)
Bar Supper 6 - 9.30 pm (b)
Dinner 7.30 - 9.30 pm (d)
Vegetarians welcome

Warm salad of wild mushrooms with balsamic dressing. Argyll smoked venison. Salmon en papillote. Roast gigot of lamb with garden mint sauce. Monkfish cooked in white wine and served with a green sauce.

STB Highly Commended 4 Crowns
Credit cards: 1, 3
Proprietors: David & Angela Wilson

Edinburgh

Atrium

10 Cambridge Street
Edinburgh EH1 2ED
Tel: 0131 228 8882

The Macallan Taste
of Scotland Award Winner 1994

Within Saltire Court, at entrance
to Traverse Theatre, adjacent to Usher Hall.

A flagship modern restaurant with an enviable
reputation.

- Stylish and much-lauded city restaurant.
- Outstanding modern Scottish cooking.
- "Chef/patron Andrew Radford's many awards
  have been richly deserved."

From its specially-designed oil-lamps to its overall
decor, the Atrium is a striking example of modern
Scottish design. Appropriately, the imaginative
cooking here is as distinctive as the restaurant it
serves. The restaurant's talented chef/proprietor,
Andrew Radford, has seen his success recognised
informally by a devoted clientele. He has won a
number of awards, including The Macallan
Personality of the Year 1994. The restaurant he
started offers an à la carte menu that is based on
fresh local produce and changes twice daily. The
Atrium also offers a snack menu available at
lunchtime and in the evening for pre-theatre meals
between 6 and 7 pm. Both menus are inspired,
creative and well-balanced, as befits the Atrium's
deserved reputation: one of Edinburgh's foremost
restaurants.

Open all year except 1 wk Christmas
Dining Room/Restaurant Lunch 12 - 2.30 pm
except Sun Sat (b)
Dinner 6 - 10.30 pm except Sun (d-e)
Closed Sun
Vegetarians welcome

Crabcake with frisee salad. Scallops, noodles,
asparagus and tomato. Grilled sea bream with leek
and a gratin of salsa parmesan. Pan-fried Guinea
fowl with root vegetables and black pepper. Baked
salmon with spinach, roquette and pesto oil. Tart of
raspberries with raspberry sorbet.

Credit cards: 1, 2, 3 + SWITCH, DELTA
Proprietors: Andrew & Lisa Radford

Hotel of the Year

The Balmoral Hotel Edinburgh

1 Princes Street,
Edinburgh EH2 2EQ
Tel: 0131 556 2414
Fax: 0131 557 3747

Princes Street at corner of North Bridge.

A grand and impressive city hotel that has long
been an important Edinburgh landmark.

- Sumptuous, elegant and distinguished hotel.
- Variety of impeccable cuisines .
- "A wonderful experience to eat here."

Since its opening as the North British Hotel in
1902, The Balmoral has maintained its
reputation as the embodiment of hospitality and
ease. Under Executive Chef Billy Campbell, the
hotel's principal restaurant - the spacious and
elegant No. 1 Princess St. - offers outstanding
classically-orientated cooking which is
exquisitely presented and served. Alternatively, the
hotel's Brasserie is designed along continental
lines, with an all day service of light meals and
snacks. Bar lunches are available in NB's Bar and
the Palm Court affords somewhere to sit and
drink coffee or tea while a harpist plays. For
food, ambience and service, this hotel deserves its
reputation for all round excellence. Member of
the Scotch Beef Club.

Open all year
Rooms: 189 with private facilities
Bed &Breakfast from £64
Dinner B & B from £89
Room Rate from £120
Special Rates available for Weekends / 2nts
Bar Lunch (NB's Bar) 12 - 2.30 pm (a)
Brasserie (Bridges) food served all day (b-d)
Dining Room/Restaurant Lunch (No 1
Princes St) 12 - 2.15 pm except Sun Sat (c-d)
Dinner (No 1 Princes St) 7 - 10.30 pm (f)
Vegetarians welcome
Facilities for disabled visitors
No smoking area in restaurants
Guide dogs only

No 1 Princes St: grilled Oban scallops served with
a broad bean salad and lardons of crispy bacon.
Noisettes of Scottish lamb with a Lanark Blue
cheese sauce. Suprême of River Tay salmon with
a sharp fresh rhubarb sauce.

STB Deluxe 5 Crowns
Credit cards: 1, 2, 3, 5, 6 + SWITCH, DELTA

Caledonian Hotel

Princes Street
Edinburgh EH1 2AB
Tel: 0131 459 9988
Fax: 0131 225 6632

Prestige Award Winner 1992

West end of Princes Street.

One of Scotland's best hotels.

- City centre grand hotel.
- Traditional/modern cooking with French
  influences.
- "La Pompadour is where anyone who aspires to
  run a restaurant goes to see how it should be
  done."

The 'Caley' has been a landmark and an
Edinburgh institution since it opened its doors in
1903. La Pompadour Restaurant, is situated
immediately above the hotel's front door, and
affords engaging views over the busy West End of
Princes Street. Chef de Cuisine Tony Binks has
combed old manuscripts and investigated how
Scottish cooks applied and adapted classic methods,
in order to compose a menu which he describes as
'Legends of the Scottish Table'. Service is state-of-
the-art; the wine list is exceptional; and the
flavours are out of this world. Downstairs there is
Carriages Restaurant. Member of the Scotch
Beef Club.

Open all year
Rooms: 241 with private facilities
Bed & Breakfast £142.25 - £169.75
Dinner B & B £167.25 - £194.75
Room Rate £155 - £255
Special Weekend Rates
Lunch (Carriages) 12 - 2.30 pm Mon to Fri:
12.30 - 2.30 Sun Sat (c)
Lunch (Pompadour) 12.30 - 2 pm except Sun
Sat (e)
Afternoon Tea (Lounge) 3 - 5.30 pm
Dinner (Carriages) 6.30 - 10 pm (d)
Dinner (Pompadour) 7.30 - 10.15 pm
except Sun (f)
Vegetarians welcome
No smoking area in restaurants

Carriages: collops of Aberdeen Angus fillet with
pickled walnuts and Madeira sauce. Pompadour:
pan-fried Dublin Bay prawns and collops of
monkfish served in a filo pastry basket with stir-
fried vegetables and grated horseradish and tomato
sauce.

STB Deluxe 5 Crowns
Credit cards: 1, 2, 3, 5, 6

Carlton Highland Hotel

North Bridge
Edinburgh EH1 1SD
Tel: 0131 556 7277
Fax: 0131 556 2691

City centre - North Bridge links the east end of Princes Street with the Royal Mile.

Standing on the North Bridge and High Street, with fine views across the New Town to the Forth.

■ Large city centre hotel.
■ Traditional cooking with European influences.
■ "The Carlton Highland has become one of Edinburgh's leading hotels."

The Carlton Highland rises massively above the North Bridge, a ponderously articulated Edwardian building, which nevertheless commands wonderful views. The decoration is tasteful and the furnishings comfortable throughout; the hotel has a leisure club, gift shop, beauty/hair salon, pâtissèrie and even a nightclub. It also has two restaurants: Quills and Carlton Court. The latter is an informal bistro and carvery, with a huge hors-d'oeuvres table; the former, under the direction of Chef de Cuisine Charles Price - one of Scotland's senior names - has the theme of a country house library with professional service. The cooking gives an imaginative modern twist to classic dishes.

Open all year
Rooms: 197 with private facilities
Bed & Breakfast £77 - £99
Dinner B & B £93 - £115
Special Rates for 2+ nights
Bar Lunch 12 - 2.30 pm except Sun (a)
Dining Room/Restaurant Lunch 12 - 5 pm (b)
Dinner 5 - 10.30 pm (c)
Vegetarians welcome
Facilities for disabled visitors

Warm lamb fillet and west coast scallops on a bed of crisp lettuce leaves flavoured with a hint of garlic. Fillet of Scottish salmon served on a tarragon and vermouth cream sauce with saffron noodles. Fillet of beef pan-fried with foie gras and brioche on a Madeira flavoured jus. Lemon tart served warm with a vanilla and citrus sauce.

STB Highly Commended 5 Crowns
Credit cards: 1, 2, 3, 5, 6 + SWITCH

Channings

South Learmonth Gardens
Edinburgh EH4 1EZ
Tel: 0131 315 2226
Fax: 0131 332 9631

South Learmonth Gardens is parallel to Queensferry Road, a few minutes walk from the west end of Edinburgh city centre.

A private hotel and brasserie in a quiet residential street.

■ Town hotel.
■ Innovative Scottish cooking.
■ "A charming basement restaurant, with an Edwardian atmosphere serving good food."

Originally five terraced townhouses in a smart Edwardian terrace, Channings is a privately owned hotel with the atmosphere of a gentleman's club. The attractive features of the buildings have been retained in the conversion, and furniture and fabrics are tasteful; bedrooms are individually designed. In the Brasserie, the interesting menus change with the seasons and draw inspiration from old classic European dishes. The ingredients are fresh, and the house 'specials' are original and delicious. Appropriate wines are suggested for each dish. The atmosphere of the Brasserie is relaxed and pleasant, and the garden adjacent to it is used in the summer. The bar offers a wide range of malt whiskies.

Open all year except 26 to 29 Dec: open Christmas Day for lunch
Rooms: 48 with private facilities
Bed & Breakfast £57.50 - £97
Dinner B & B £49.50 - £55
Special Weekend Rates available
Bar Lunch 12 - 2 pm except Sun (a)
Dining Room/Restaurant Lunch 12 - 2 pm except Sat (a)
Dinner 6.30 - 9.30 pm (c)
Vegetarians welcome

A chowder of fine Scottish seafood. Scotch rump steak garnished with sautéd onions and mushrooms enhanced with mustard and claret. Pot-roasted pheasant on a cabbage parcel with glazed apple and rowan jelly. Braised gigot of mutton with fresh root vegetables and butter beans. Grilled darne of salmon with a savoury dill butter. Caramelised orange and honey brose.

STB Highly Commended 4 Crowns
Credit cards: 1, 2, 3, 5, 6 + SWITCH
Proprietor: Peter Taylor

Cramond Gallery Bistro

4 Riverside Cramond, Cramond Village
Edinburgh EH4 6NY
Tel: 0131 312 6555

Follow Cramond Glebe Road down to harbour front.

A small restaurant by the sea.

■ Village restaurant with apartments.
■ Simple, fresh cooking.
■ "A fine old house, with a lovely situation close to the harbour."

Cramond Gallery Bistro overlooks Cramond Harbour, at the mouth of the River Almond, where it joins the Forth. It is a 16th century cottage, built on the site of a second century Roman boatshed (Cramond was an important Roman base: there are the remains of a fort alongside the church). A small low dining room with timber beams, astragal windows and a pleasant atmosphere. Changing exhibitions of pictures (for sale) decorate the walls of the restaurant - hence its name. Fish is something of a speciality, but game and other meats also feature on the short menus. The cooking is straightforward and well priced. Four luxury, self-catering cottage apartments are available, awarded Highly Commended 3 Crowns.

Open all year except Christmas Day
Dining Room/Restaurant Lunch 12 - 2.30 pm (a-b)
Afternoon Tea
Dinner 6.30 - 9.30 pm (d)
Note: closed Mon Tue from Oct to Jun
Unlicensed - guests welcome to take own wine
Vegetarians welcome
No smoking in restaurant

Hazelnut and mushroom loaf. Mussel bisque. Lobster bisque. Salmon in basil and tomato coulis. Grilled fresh lobster. Saddle of lamb in claret and mint jus. Suprême fillet of Aberdeen Angus with roasted garlic. Apple and blackberry pie. Chocolate rum fudge cake. Cream teas.

No credit cards
Proprietors: Alan & Evelyn Bogue

Crannog Scottish Seafood Restaurant

14 South St Andrew Street
Edinburgh EH2 2AZ
Tel: 0131 557 5589
Fax: 0131 558 3067

City centre between St Andrew Square and
Princes Street, opposite Waverley Market.

> The freshest seafood served with style.

- Informal, cheerful city centre restaurant.
- Modern British cuisine concentrating on seafood.
- "This shows what can be done with the best of Scottish produce."

Five years ago, a group of Scottish fishermen had the idea of opening their own restaurant and supplying it with the fish they caught. The first Crannog, in Fort William, was soon followed by one in Glasgow. The third, in Edinburgh, follows the same highly successful, award-winning formula: the finest and freshest seafood in simple, friendly surroundings. The restaurant is spacious and furnished in pine; candles enhance the homely atmosphere. A large blackboard announces each day's specials. Consistently good, the cuisine lives up to all expectations.

Open all year except Christmas Day
+ Sundays (winter)
Restaurant Lunch 12 - 2.30 pm (a-b)
Dinner 6 - 10 pm (c)
Vegetarians welcome

Langoustines with garlic butter. Salmon collops with fresh sorrel. Skate with dark vinegar butter and capers. Crannog special seafood platter. One meat dish and one vegetarian dish always available. Rich chocolate mousse. Scottish farmhouse cheeses.

Credit cards: 1, 2, 3 + SWITCH, DELTA

Creelers Seafood Wine Bar & Restaurant

3 Hunter Square
Edinburgh EH1 1QW
Tel: 0131 220 4447/4448
Fax: 0131 220 4149

The Square surrounds the back of the Tron Kirk on the Royal Mile.

> A recently opened establishment, bringing Arran's excellent seafood to Edinburgh.

- Predominantly fish restaurant in the heart of the Old Town.
- Modern Scottish cooking.
- "Unusual and confident combinations of flavour."

A sister establishment to Creelers in Brodick (Isle of Arran - see entry), Tim and Fran James bring fresh fish and home-smoked products from the island to their restaurant in the heart of Edinburgh, just off the High Street. The wine bar has a bistro atmosphere, with quiet decor and murals of Arran; the restaurant is more formal and exhibits the work of local artists (for sale). Downstairs is a private room, seating 12-15 people. Head Chef David Murray has an impressive pedigree (The Buttery and One Devonshire Gardens). He presents a light-weight table d'hôte menu and a lengthy à la carte menu, for lunch and dinner, featuring game and vegetarian dishes as well as seafood.

Open all year except Christmas Day + Boxing Days + New Year's Day + 2 Jan
closed Sun Oct to Apr
Bar Meals available 11 am - 10.30 pm Sun to Thu: 11 am - 11 pm Fri Sat (b)
Dining Room/Restaurant Lunch 12 - 2.30 pm (a-c)
Dinner 6.30 - 10.30 pm Sun to Thu: 6.30 - 11 pm Fri Sat (c-e)
Vegetarians welcome
No parking

Gâteaux of Creelers own smoked salmon with cream cheese layered between wholemeal crêpes with Arran mustard. Roasted monkfish tail coated in crushed hazelnuts on a duo of sauces. Raspberry and Drambuie iced soufflé with shortbread.

Credit cards: 1, 3 + SWITCH
Proprietors: Fran & Tim James & Co Ltd

Dalmahoy Hotel

Country Club Resort
Kirknewton nr Edinburgh EH27 8EB
Tel: 0131 333 1845
Fax: 0131 333 1433

On A71 Edinburgh-Kilmarnock, 7 miles from Edinburgh city centre. 3 miles from Edinburgh International Airport.

> A large hotel and country club with two golf courses, sophisticated leisure facilities and comfortable accommodation.

- Restored Georgian country house in well-landscaped grounds just outside Edinburgh.
- International hotel cuisine.
- "Excellent menu with many choices; all dishes cooked to order."

Dalmahoy is the family home of the Earl of Morton, who converted it into a luxurious hotel about five years ago. The building is a stately Georgian mansion, standing in its own park, contains two internationally acclaimed golf courses and a state of the art leisure complex. The formal Pentland Restaurant is an elegant Regency-style room, beautifully furnished, with splendid views towards the Pentland Hills. The menu is extensive, well-balanced and beautifully presented. Last year the hotel was awarded 3 Rosettes by the AA. Dalmahoy also has a bistro-style restaurant in the Leisure Centre. Member of the Scotch Beef Club.

Open all year
Rooms: 151 with private facilities
Bed & Breakfast £60 - £85
Dinner B & B from £75
Room Rate £109 - £184
Special Rates + Leisure Breaks available
Bar Meals (Terrace Restaurant) 9.30 am - 11.30 pm (a)
Dining Room/Restaurant Lunch 12 - 2 pm except Sat (b)
Dinner 7 - 9.30 pm (d)
Vegetarians welcome
Facilities for disabled visitors
No dogs

Terrine of marinated pork and smoked bacon served with a Cumberland sauce. Hot confit of Scotch salmon with creamed fennel and red wine butter sauce. Millefeuille of honey wafers and cranachan.

STB Highly Commended 5 Crowns
Credit cards: 1, 2, 3, 5, 6 + SWITCH

Dubh Prais Restaurant

123B High Street
Edinburgh EH1 1SG
Tel: 0131 557 5732
Fax: 0131 557 5732

Edinburgh Royal Mile.

> Small basement restaurant in the Old Town.

- City centre restaurant.
- Traditional Scottish cooking.
- "Good Scottish dishes in a convivial atmosphere."

Walking down the Royal Mile which leads from Edinburgh Castle to Holyrood Place, look out for the sign of the black pot (in Gaelic 'dubh prais') down a few steps on the right in the Canongate. Its imaginative chef/owner, James McWilliams, presents a well-balanced à la carte menu which devotes itself entirely to Scottish seasonal produce and regional recipes. The restaurant is popular with locals and tourists alike, and the dishes offered are described with patriotic fervour and are cooked using as simple methods as the freshest produce requires.

Open all year except 2 wks Christmas +
2 wks Easter
Dining Room/Restaurant Lunch 12 - 2 pm Tue
to Fri (a)
Dinner 6.30 - 10.30 pm Tue to Sat (c-d)
Closed Sun Mon
Vegetarians welcome

Thin slices of smoked venison served on oak leaf lettuce and apple tossed in apple liqueur dressing. Baked smoked haddock served on a traditional potato scone coated witth orkney cheese sauce. West coast scallops poached in white wine served on a grain mustard and lemon grass sauce.

Credit cards: 1, 2, 3, 6 + Switch
Proprietors: James & Heather McWilliams

(fitz) Henry

19 Shore Place, Leith
Edinburgh EH6 6SW
Tel: 0131 555 6625
Fax: 0131 554 6216

City end of 'the shore' in Leith.

> First class restaurant in a tastefully converted warehouse.

- Informal town restaurant.
- Modern Scottish (state-of-the-art).
- "(fitz)Henry's is a very new restaurant . An amazing find. Excellent quality preparation and presentation."

David Ramsden, the charismatic owner of (fitz)Henry, had a bistro in William Street ten years ago called 'Hoora Henry's'. Hence the name. He is a man of considerable panache, and this shows in his new venture. The venue is a beautifully restored old warehouse just off the shore in Leith: spacious, simply furnished, subtly lit. Head Chef Stephen Simpson is young and extremely talented. This is his first appointment as Chef de Cuisine, and his enthusiastic and unusual combinations demonstrate considerable flair. Presentation is well-considered and service attentive and friendly. The relaxed ambience of (fitz)Henry's communicates style, good taste and high standards. This restaurant deserves to do very well.

Open all year except Christmas Day, Boxing
Day lunch, New Year's Day lunch + 2 Jan
Dining Room/Restaurant Lunch 12.30 - 2 pm
except Mon (b)
Dinner 6.30 - 10 pm except Sun Mon (b)
Closed Mon
Vegetarians welcome - prior notice required
Facilities for disabled visitors

Tartare of smoked haddock with spring onions and aioli. Raw marinaded monkfish with lemon grass and ginger. Roast pigeon breasts on a rosti potato with lentil and shallot sauce. Lambs sweetbreads in puff pastry with port and thyme sauce and vegetable spaghetti. Grilled monkfish tail with roast tomatoes and a saffron beurre blanc. Strawberry baverois.

Credit cards: 1, 2, 3 + SWITCH
Proprietors: David Ramsden & Roz McKnight

George Inter-Continental Edinburgh

"Le Chambertin"
George Street
Edinburgh EH3 2PB
Tel: 0131 225 1251
Fax: 0131 226 5644

City centre of Edinburgh.

> A restaurant of distinction within one of Edinburgh's finest hotels.

- An elegant, gourmet restaurant with a relaxed ambience.
- Modern/traditional French cuisine with Scottish influence.
- "Where the 'Auld Alliance' becomes a reality."

Although within the highly regarded George Inter-Continental Hotel, Le Chambertin is fast developing a formidable reputation of its own, not least for its excellent and fairly priced business lunches. Restaurant Manager Barnaby Hawkes makes the most of the restaurant's grand and gracious ethos. Tables are well spaced out amid a splendid blue decor. The atmosphere is unhurried, calm. Menus are creative and well-balanced, with a good selection of game, fish, beef and lamb. The excellent value wine list reflects the range of such gourmet cuisine.

Open all year
Rooms: 195 with private facilities
Bed & Breakfast £45 - £90
Dinner B & B £60 - £105
Room Rate £130 - £180
Bar Meals 11 am - 10 pm (a)
Restaurant Lunch (Carvers Table) 12 -
2.30 pm (b)
Dining Room/Restaurant Lunch (Chambertin)
12.30 - 2 pm except Sun Sat (d)
Dinner (Carvers Table) 6.30 - 10 pm (b)
Dinner (Chambertin) 7 - 10 pm except Sun (c)
Note: Chambertin closed Sun
Vegetarians welcome
No smoking area in restaurant

Scottish salmon marinated with lime, peppers and coriander. Carpaccio of Highland venison with a whisky and onion chutney. Grilled peppered tuna steak with Pinot Noir, rainbow rice and plum tomato. Marinated sirloin steak of Aberdeen Angus beef with a ginger-garlic jus and potato gratin.

STB Commended 5 Crowns
Credit cards: 1, 2, 3, 5, 6

Henderson's Salad Table

94 Hanover Street
Edinburgh EH2 1DR
Tel: 0131 225 2131
Fax: 0131 220 3542

2 minutes from Princes Street under
Henderson's wholefood shop.

A popular city centre wholefood eating and
meeting place.

- Lively, informal, cosmopolitan basement bistro
  in New Town.
- Innovative and interesting vegetarian cuisine.
- "At the forefront of good eating and good
  company for over 30 years."

Henderson's was an established institution long
before wholefoods became popular and its enviable
reputation for excellent and inexpensive fare is as
well deserved now as in Janet Henderson's day. The
atmosphere here is always congenial and the
counter-served helpings generous. Vegetarian
salads, savouries, quiches and puddings are freshly
prepared and eagerly consumed throughout the day
with an unusual selection of real ales and wines,
some Scottish and many organic also on offer.
Henderson's still actively run by the family, appeals
to all ages proving that wholefoods can be fun,
especially Monday to Saturday nights when real
musicians enliven the wine bar.

Open all year except Christmas +
Boxing Days, 1 + 2 Jan
Hot meals served all day from 11.30 am:
open from 8 am
Breakfast 8 - 11.30 am except Sun (a)
Lunch 11.30 am - 3 pm except Sun (a)
Dinner 4.30 - 10.30 pm except Sun (a)
Bistro Bar 12 - 8 pm Mon to Sat: 12 -
8 pm Sun (a)
Closed Sun except during Edinburgh Festival
Vegans welcome
Main restaurant areas non-smoking

Wide selection of herb teas, wines from growers
using organic methods, hand-made bakery items
made with stoneground flour, free range eggs. Local
organic produce where possible.

Credit cards: 1, 2, 3 + SWITCH
Proprietors: The Henderson Family

The Howard

32/36 Great King Street
Edinburgh EH3 6QH
Tel: 0131 557 3500
Fax: 0131 557 6515

Great King Street is off Dundas Street, the
continuation of Hanover Street - 5 minutes
from Princes Street.

New Town hotel in Edinburgh.

- Elegant Georgian terrace house.
- Modern Scottish cooking.
- "A selection of original and inspired dishes."

The Howard is in one of Edinburgh New Town's
grandest and broadest streets. The Georgian
elegance of the buildings lends itself to this
unpretentious, discreet and luxurious hotel which
is only a few minutes walk (up-hill!) from many of
Edinburgh's main attractions. The restaurant in the
basement of the hotel, Number 36, is very elegantly
furnished and offers an innovative à la carte menu,
intelligently composed and elegantly executed by
the team of young chefs who work behind the
scenes. Cooking methods, sauces and presentation
reflect contemporary trends, as does the insistence
on fresh ingredients.

Open all year - please telephone if booking for
Christmas period
Rooms: 16 with private facilities
Bed & Breakfast £65 - £110
Dinner B & B - £80 - £105
Special Weekend Rates Oct to Apr
Dinner 7.30 - 9.30 pm (d)
Vegetarians welcome
Dogs by arrangement

Grilled escalope of wild salmon with a fennel,
creamed tomato and basil sauce. Roast 'best-end'
of Border lamb with skirlie and a port wine and
rosemary jus.

STB Commended 4 Crowns
Credit cards: 1, 2, 3, 5, 6 + SWITCH

Igg's Restaurant

15 Jeffrey Street
Edinburgh EH1 1DR
Tel: 0131 557 8184

Off the Royal Mile.

An attractive small restaurant off the Canongate.

- Elegant L-shaped restaurant with a continental
  style.
- Spanish and Scottish cuisine.
- "Charming service, good atmosphere and
  interesting food."

There is nothing of the 'Spanish-donkeys-with-
paniers, bandelleros and wrought-iron-Don-
Quixotes' about Igg's. Indeed, it is difficult to know
whether to describe it as a Scottish restaurant with
Spanish influences or vice versa. Its decoration,
pictures and furnishing are elegant and tasteful;
tables are attractively dressed with linen and
flowers; lighting is subtle. Ignacio Campos, is
enthusiastic, generous and laid back - an excellent
host who sets a relaxed tone in his stylish little
restaurant. At lunchtime and in the early evening a
tapas menu is available (delicious fresh Spanish
snacks) as well as a good priced three/four course
table d'hôte and à la carte menus.

Open all year
Dining Room/Restaurant Lunch 12 - 2.30 pm
except Sun Mon (a-b)
Dinner 6 - 10.30 pm except Sun Mon (c-d)
Closed Sun Mon
Vegetarians welcome
Wheelchair access
No smoking area in restaurant

Roulade of smoked salmon and crab mousse with a
watercress and lemon purée. Fillets of lemon sole
and queenie scallops poached in white wine with a
pink peppercorn and grapefruit sauce. Tournedos of
Scottish beef brushed with chopped rosemary and
mustard, served on a sweet pimento sauce.

Credit cards: 1, 2, 3, 5 + SWITCH
Proprietor: Ignacio Campos

Jackson's Restaurant

209-213 High Street
2 Jackson Close, Royal Mile
Edinburgh EH1 1PL
Tel: 0131 225 1793
Fax: 0131 220 0620

On the Royal Mile.

A restaurant in the heart of Edinburgh's Old Town.

- Cellar restaurant with more formal dining upstairs.
- Modern Scottish cooking.
- "The food is prepared and presented with flair - delightful combinations of flavours using herbs and delicate spices."

Jackson's is on the High Street, the original thoroughfare and market place of the ancient city of Edinburgh. The cellar restaurant is open for both lunch and dinner, offering table d'hôte and à la carte menus (à la carte only in the evenings during the Festival) and its location attracts many tourists in this busy area. There is a bistro-style feel to the cellar with alcoves, stone walls, pine tables, tapestries and discreet lighting. Upstairs there is a more formal dining room which can also be hired for private dinners. The table d'hôte 'business' lunch is creative and very well-priced; the à la carte majors on Scottish dishes, treated in unusual and original ways.

Open all year except Christmas + Boxing Days
Dining Room/Restaurant Lunch 12 - 2 pm
except Sun Sat (a)
Dinner 6 - 11 pm (d)
Extended hours during Edinburgh Festival
Vegetarians welcome

Breast of chicken poached with seasonal vegetables and topped with crème frâiche. Fillet of halibut braised with winkles and fresh tarragon finished in an oyster cream and lemon grass sauce. Aberdeen Angus steaks.

Credit cards: 1, 2, 3, + SWITCH, DELTA
Proprietor: Lyn MacKinnon

Keepers Restaurant

13B Dundas Street
Edinburgh EH3 6QG
Tel: 0131 556 5707/0831 185792

Dundas Street (continuation of Hanover Street) is to north of Princes Street.

A basement restaurant in the heart of the Georgian New Town.

- City centre restaurant.
- Traditional Scottish cooking.
- "Natural stone walls and stone-flagged floors make for an atmosphere of calm in this centrally located cellar restaurant."

As its name suggests, this well-established restaurant specialises in game - supported by fish, shellfish and prime meat. The cooking is traditional, with good sauces and rich gravies; the menus are both table d'hôte (four starters, four main courses) and à la carte and the dishes are simply presented. Although centrally located, just down the hill from George Street, Keepers has an attractive intimacy. The wine list is not extensive but is well-chosen and reasonably priced. The restaurant serves lunch and dinner on a table d'hôte and à la carte basis. Individual rooms (or, indeed, the entire place) can be booked for private or business functions.

Open all year except Boxing Day
Dining Room/Restaurant Lunch 12 - 2 pm
Tue to Fri (a-b)
Dinner 6 - 10 pm except Sun (b-e)
Pre-Theatre Meals 6 - 7 pm (a)
Note: Alternative times by arrangement
No smoking area in restaurant

Haggis and turnip tartlets with a rich onion. Squat lobster pan fried in garlic butter. Trio of Scottish medallions on a bed of leeks with a redcuurrant sauce (lamb, beef, venison), Scottish salmon served in a sauce of leeks and grapes.

Credit cards: 1, 2, 3, 5
Proprietor: Sheena Marshall

Le Café Saint-Honoré

34 North West Thistle Street Lane
Edinburgh
EH2 1EA
Tel: 0131 226 2211

Centre of Edinburgh, just off Frederick Street, 3 minutes from Princes Street.

A small French bistro, serving excellent Scottish food.

- Traditional Parisian cafe-style.
- Modern scottish cooking, with French influences.
- "A quaint little restaurant of great charm."

Cafe St Honore is located in a service street parallel to George street. It was formerly an authentic French restaurant, was decorated accordingly and still has a Gallic charm. Its new owners favour a more Scottish style of cooking, making good use of the produce available, although there are French influences in the preparation. The lunch and dinner menus change daily and are à la carte - realistically limited to about half a dozen starters and the same number of main courses, and very reasonably priced. The cooking is adventurous and highly professional; interesting combinations and fresh, innovative sources appear regularly. Chef Chris Colverson is an outstanding vegetarian cook, and is delighted to prepare vegetarian dishes if given notice (they don't generally appear on the menu).

Open all year except Christmas + Boxing Days,
24 Mar to 7 Apr + 13 to 20 Oct
Restaurant Lunch 12-2.30pm except Sun Sat (b)
Dinner 7-10.30 pm (unless by prior arrangement) except Sun (d)
Closed Sun
Vegetarians welcome
No parking
No smoking area in restaurant

Warm salad of squid, scallops and smoked haddock. Breast of pigeon with wild mushrooms. Roast haunch of venison with Puy lentils and juniper. Brandy snap basket with mixed berries and melon sorbet and crème brûlée.

Credit cards: 1, 2, 3, 5, 6 + SWITCH, DELTA
Proprietors: Jerry Mallet & Chris Colverson

Le Marché Noir

2/4 Eyre Place
Edinburgh EH3 5EP
Tel: 0131 558 1608
Fax: 0131 556 0798

Eyre Place is at northern end of Dundas Street (continuation of Hanover Street, north of Princes Street).

An excellent small French restaurant.

- Highly regarded, cosy and intimate.
- Outstanding modern French/Scottish cuisine.
- "A relaxed and delightful place to eat."

Proprietor Malcolm Duck established this friendly restaurant in what had been a shop. A third of the available space is given over, in the French style, to a bar and reception area. Tucked away in a quiet corner of the New Town, Le Marché Noir's ambience is relaxed and restful. Staff are cheerful, efficient and welcoming. The kitchen produces innovative and excellent French/Scottish à la carte cuisine that is always well-presented. Malcolm Duck takes justifiable pride in his extensive and interesting wine list.

Open all year except Christmas + Boxing Days
Dining Room/Restaurant Lunch 12 - 2.30 pm except Sun Sat (b-c)
Dinner 7 - 10 pm Mon to Thu: 7 - 10.30 pm Fri Sat: 6.30 - 9.30 pm Sun (c-d)
Vegetarians welcome
Facilities for disabled visitors

Terrine of salmon and prawns. Warm salad of goats cheese. Black pudding with red wine. Suprême of Guinea fowl with a Calvados sauce. Escalopes of venison with mint and redcurrants. Delice of salmon grilled with orange butter.

Credit card: 1
Proprietor: Malcolm Duck

Martins Restaurant

70 Rose Street North Lane
Edinburgh EH2 3DX
Tel: 0131 225 3106

In the north lane off Rose Street between Frederick Street and Castle Street.

A first class restaurant tucked away in a back street.

- Small city centre restaurant.
- Creative contemporary Scottish.
- "Many thoughtful and sensitive touches make Martins one of the best restaurants in Scotland."

Generally regarded as one of the best places to eat in Edinburgh, Martin and Gay Irons established their restaurant in 1983. It is small and discreet, tucked away in a cobbled service lane parallel to Princes Street, in the very heart of the city. Its modest exterior gives no clue to the excellence within: the interior is bright, fresh and pastel-hued, decorated with fresh flowers and good contemporary pictures, and cleverly lit; the dining room is a pleasure to behold. Chef Forbes Stott creates innovative dishes which allow the true flavours of the essential ingredients to come through (Martins buys its produce carefully, mainly from small producers). His menus are healthy and well-balanced, his style light; organic and wild foods are favoured. Service is good. Martins sets out to provide a 'total gourmet experience' - and succeeds.

Open all year except 23 Dec to 16 Jan, 26 May to 3 Jun + 28 Sep to 7 Oct
Dining Room Lunch 12 - 2 pm except Sun Mon Sat (b-e) - booking essential
Dinner 7 - 10 pm except Sun Mon (e-f) - booking essential
Closed Sun Mon
Vegetarians welcome - prior notice required
No smoking in dining areas

Home-made bread served with a daily changing fresh herb vinaigrette. Suprême of wild salmon baked with leeks and mustard. Grilled saddle of venison with beetroot and Puy lentils. Fillets of turbot and halibut pan-fried with chicory and a sweet pepper coulis. Whole roasted and boned quail stuffed with couscous, spinach and smoked bacon. Award-winning cheeseboard.

Credit cards: 1, 2, 3, 5, 6 + SWITCH, DELTA
Proprietors: Martin & Gay Irons

Norton House Hotel

Ingliston, Edinburgh
Midlothian EH28 8LX
Tel: 0131 333 1275
Fax: 0131 333 5305

Just off A8, 6 miles from Edinburgh city centre, ½ mile from airport, on the road to Glasgow.

A country house hotel just outside Edinburgh.

- Victorian mansion set in its own park.
- Gourmet/Scottish cooking.
- "Wide choice, high quality, creative presentation - and very reasonably priced."

Recently refurbished in luxurious style, this 19th century country house is a Listed building. The hotel is part of Richard Branson's Virgin Group. The hotel has two restaurants: the Norton Tavern, which offers a high quality family menu in a walled garden with a barbeque area, and the Conservatory Restaurant. This is an extremely elegant, flower filled glass-house, which has been awarded two AA Rosettes for the excellence of its cooking. An experienced team of chefs cook the food for both venues and in the Conservatory you will be treated to an extensive à la carte menu, a lunch/dinner table d'hôte menu and a short Taste of Scotland menu. The dishes are imaginative - a combination of the unusual and the traditional, but even the latter are given a creative twist.

Open all year
Rooms: 47 with private facilities
Bed & Breakfast £99 - £175
Dinner B & B £60 - £220
Bar Lunch 12 - 2.30 pm (b)
Dining Room/Restaurant Lunch 12 - 2.30 pm except Sat (c)
Bar Supper 5.30 - 10 pm (b)
Dinner 7 - 10 pm (d)
Vegetarians welcome
Facilities for disabled visitors
No smoking area in restaurant

A warm boudin of chicken, pine nuts, chives and mushrooms with a sesame seed dressing and onion marmalade. Fish and shellfish poached and presented between layers of puff pastry with a light lobster sauce. Apple and blackcurrant crumble with crème anglaise sauce.

STB Highly Commended 5 Crowns
Credit cards: 1, 2, 3, 5, 6 + SWITCH

Overtures Restaurant

18-22 Greenside Place, Edinburgh
Midlothian EH1 3AA
Tel: 0131 557 8339
Fax: 0131 557 6520

At top of Leith Walk, entrance adjacent to
Edinburgh Playhouse Theatre ticket office.

A city centre theatre restaurant of distinction
and style.

- A formal, opulent restaurant recalling high
  Victorian splendour.
- Classic French/Scottish cuisine with
  international flavours.
- "Only the best of cuisine and service."

Though part of the Playhouse Theatre and
therefore ideal for a pre- or post-theatre meal,
Overtures is also open to the public and has its own
entrance. Lavishly furnished in scarlets and golds,
with brocade curtains recapturing Victorian
opulence. Carefully considered and cosmopolitan,
the cuisine is no less stylish. The table d'hôte menu
changes each month and represents excellent
value, as does Overture's wine list. Two small suites
are available for private parties. Offering the same
menu as the main restaurant, they can
accommodate up to 16 guests.

Open all year except Christmas Eve,
Christmas + Boxing Days
Restaurant Lunch Matinee Days ie Wed Sat - or
by appointment, this incl private suites
Dinner 6 - 11 pm Tue to Sat: Mon - if a
performance is on or by appointment (c)
Closed Sun
Vegetarians welcome
No smoking in restaurant

Partan bree - crab soup. Roasted Guinea fowl served
with fried bread crumbs, redcurrants, jus and bread
sauce. Char-grilled rump steak glazed with Stilton-
garlic and Worcester sauce. Marinated salmon
grilled in oatmeal with an anchovy butter. Roasted
loin of lamb with a black pudding stuffing, roasted
garlic and burgundy sauce.

Credit cards: 1, 3, 6 + SWITCH, DELTA

Rock Cafe Restaurant

18 Howe Street
Edinburgh EH3 6TG
Tel: 0131 225 7225

Howe Street (continuation of Frederick Street)
is to north of Princes Street.

Situated in trendy Stockbridge the Rock Cafe
Restaurant is popular with all ages.

- Informal restaurant with American diner theme.
- American-style cooking with modern Scottish
  influence.
- "A cafe with a difference - very distinctive rock-
  inspired decor and an interesting, well-presented
  menu."

The Rock Cafe's decor is a real talking point for
guests over a meal in this fashionable informal
restaurant. Huge murals of rock stars dominate the
room and there is a relaxed, laid back atmosphere.
As well as excellent steaks and burgers the menu
features fish and shellfish and good local
vegetables. The dishes of the day are listed on a
blackboard and there is no shortage of choice.
When the food arrives, it does not disappoint. There
is a small selection of wines. An interesting venue
which promises excellent food.

Open all year except 24 Dec to 4 Jan incl
Open 12 - 11 pm Sat only
Dinner 5 - 11 pm except Sun Mon (b-c)
Closed Sun Mon
Vegetarians welcome

Smoked salmon. Aberdeen Angus beef steaks and
burgers. Char-grilled Scottish salmon with basil
butter. Baked chicken suprême with Stilton sauce.
King prawns meunière. Moules marinière. Fish of
the day. Fresh pasta.

Credit cards: 1, 2, 3 + SWITCH
Proprietor: John Mackay

The Round Table

31 Jeffrey Street
Edinburgh EH1 1DH
Tel: 0131 557 3032

Off the Royal Mile and less than
5 minutes walk from Waverley Station.

An ideally located city centre restaurant-bistro.

- Unpretentious, no frills, inexpensive eating.
- Good traditional cooking.
- "A cheerful place that is excellent value for
  money."

With its fine views over the city to the north, The
Round Table takes its name from the shape of the
tables on which it serves its simple, good fare. The
ambience is informal and fun. No money has been
wasted on creating a theme or pseudo-atmosphere:
what you see is what you get. The cooking is based
on fresh Scottish meats and fish. The lunch menu
is available from 12 - 5.30 pm and offers a fixed
price option of outstanding value. The simple, two
page wine list is well-chosen and fairly priced.
Downstairs is a small private, non-smoking room
available for private parties of up to 14.

Open all year except Christmas +
Boxing Days, 1 Jan
Open from 10 am
Dining Room/Restaurant Lunch 12 - 5.30 pm
except Sun (a)
Dinner 5.30 - 10 pm Tue to Sat (b)
Closed Sun except during Edinburgh Festival
Vegetarians welcome

Smoked salmon and avocado gratin. Cream dill
fish soup. Mignons of beef and venison with
Drambuie onion marmalade. Poached salmon.
Smoked haddock and trout fillet grilled and topped
with a leek cream sauce. Raspberry cranachan with
malt whisky.

Credit cards: 1, 3, 6
Proprietors: Anne & Robert Winter

Scandic Crown Hotel

80 High Street, The Royal Mile
Edinburgh EH1 1TH
Tel: 0131 557 9797
Fax: 0131 557 9789

Centre of the Royal Mile.

> A new building designed to look old on
> Edinburgh's High Street.

- ■ Large city centre hotel.
- ■ Modern/British cooking with Scandinavian overtones.
- ■ "A controversial and important building offering authentic smörgåsbord and an interesting menu."

The Scandic Crown occupies a large and important site on the High Street in Edinburgh's Old Town incorporating four historic closes. Its architects have strived to create a building which fits in with the mood of the street and have produced an outsized pastiche of an antique frontage, comprising five or six 'lands', close entrances and ground floor shops. Inside, the hotel is modern, although its main restaurant 'Carrubers' (named after one of the closes swallowed up) attempts to perpetuate a medieval theme in its murals and simulated eaves. The à la carte and table d'hôte menus are a sensible length and offer imaginative combinations and flavours. There is also an extensive smörgåsbord in the centre of the dining room, from which you can help yourself to as much as you want.

Open all year except 25 to 27 Dec
Rooms: 238 with private facilities
Bed & Breakfast £85.50 - £135.50
Special Weekend Rates available
Bar Meals available 12 - 9 pm (a)
Dining Room/Restaurant Lunch 12 - 2.30 pm
Mon to Fri: 12.30 - 2.30 pm Sun Sat (a-c)
Dinner 6 - 10 pm (c-e)
Vegetarians welcome
Facilities for disabled visitors

Venison liver parfait with a marinated sultana and apple chutney. Smoked fillet of lamb and summer vegetable salad with a tomato and olive oil vinaigrette. Char-grilled monkfish tail on an aubergine and basil provençal. Rosette of lamb with a crisp potato cage with baby vegetables and a mint-scented jus.

STB 4 Crowns
Credit cards: 1, 2, 3, 5, 6 + SWITCH, DELTA

Sheraton Grand Hotel

1 Festival Square
Edinburgh EH3 9SR
Tel: 0131 229 9131
Fax: 0131 229 6254

Lothian Road opposite Usher Hall and only 5 minutes from Princes Street.

> A 5 Star City centre hotel, with two high class restaurants. Winner 1993 Taste of Scotland Prestige Award

- ■ Although part of an international chain, the Sheraton Grand Hotel embodies the best of Scottish style.
- ■ Imaginative French cuisine, with a strong Scottish emphasis.
- ■ "A superbly trained restaurant staff led by a very talented chef, presents meals which are a gastronomic delight."

The Sheraton Grand Hotel is sumptuously appointed. It is a modern hotel, and no expense has been spared in its furnishing and decoration; there is also a 'Leisure Club'. The staff are extremely professional and well-trained, but they are also helpful and friendly - amongst all the grandeur they haven't lost the human touch. The hotel has two restaurants; the Grill Room and the Terrace. The latter overlooks Festival Square (and its fountain) and offers a sophisticated brasserie-style menu. The former is formal and intimate: Executive Chef, Jean-Michel Gauffre, brings his extensive experience of classic and modern French cuisine to bear on the best of Scottish raw materials. His creations are a hymn to the Auld Alliance. Member of the Scotch Beef Club.

Open all year
Rooms: 261 with private facilities
Bed & Breakfast £77 - £167
Dinner B & B £95 - £203
Room Rate £63 - £102.50
Special Rates available
Bar Meals 11 am - 11 pm (a)
Lunch (Terrace) 11am - 3 pm (b-c)
Lunch (Grill) 12 - 2.30 pm except Sun Sat (c-d)
Dinner (Terrace) 6 - 11 pm (b-c)
Dinner (Grill) 7 - 10.30 pm except Sun (d-f)
No smoking areas in restaurants + lounge
Vegetarians welcome

Stornoway black pudding with home-smoked bacon and mushroom salad. Roasted monkfish with wild mushrooms, thyme and potato scones. Munro of three chocolate mousses and orange sauce.

STB Deluxe 5 Crowns
Credit cards: 1, 2, 3, 5, 6

Stac Polly

8-10 Grindlay Street
Edinburgh EH3 9AS
Tel: 0131 229 5405
Fax: 0131 556 5331

Opposite Sheraton Hotel off Lothian Road, 100 yards from Usher Hall and Lyceum Theatre.

> A small and friendly city centre restaurant of character.

- ■ Informal and distinctively Scottish.
- ■ Modern/Scottish cuisine.
- ■ "A delightful ambience in which to enjoy good food."

Stac Polly, from which this restaurant takes its name, is a magnificent mountain on Scotland's west coast. Proprietor Roger Coulthard, who also runs the established restaurant of the same name in Dublin Street, has tastefully decorated Stac Polly to reflect the heather-clad hills, with tartan curtains to make for an air of cosiness. The strength of Stac Polly's menu is its originality. Chef Steven Harvey compiles menus which take full advantage of Scotland's glorious larder to provide exciting interpretations of modern and traditional Scottish cuisine. From a full to a light meal, choice and service are excellent. The wine list is small but selective and moderately priced and is complemented by a comprehensive malt whisky and Scottish beer list.

Open all year
Dining Room/Restaurant Lunch 12 - 2 pm (a)
Dinner 6 - 11 pm (c)
Vegetarians welcome
Smoking area in restaurant

Baked filo pastry parcels of haggis set on a sweet plum sauce. Saddle of venison with a herb crust set on pickled red cabbage with an orange and basil sauce. Poached escalopes of wild salmon set on green vegetables, ginger and woodland mushrooms. Rack of lamb with an oatmeal and mint crust with a tarragon and whisky sauce. Bread and butter pudding with vanilla custard.

Credit cards: 1, 2, 3, 5
Proprietor: Roger Coulthard

The Witchery by the Castle
Castlehill, Royal Mile
Edinburgh EH1 1NE
Tel: 0131 225 5613
Fax: 0131 220 4392

Situated at the entrance to Edinburgh Castle.

Unusual restaurant in the historic Old Town.

- Formal restaurant.
- Innovative Scottish cooking.
- "The Witchery is quite unique - absolutely first class food enhanced by fantastically baroque decor in a historic location."

The Witchery is situated right by the entrance to Edinburgh Castle on a site that was once the centre of witchcraft in the Old Town. It has been decorated with immense style and taste and The Secret Garden, converted from a former school playground, is one of the most romantic dining spots in the city. Lunch and dinner are table d'hôte and à la carte with a choice of stylish and interesting dishes. James Thomson's wine list is spectacular with a large selection of excellent wines from all the wine-growing countries. There is a private dining room, The Inner Sanctum suite has its own private dining room.

Open all year except Christmas Day
Rooms: 1 suite with private facilities
Room Rate from £120
Dining Room/Restaurant Lunch 12 - 4 pm (b)
Dinner 4 - 11.30 pm (e)
Reservations advisable

Mixed mushroom soup with walnut croûtons. Grilled escalope of salmon on a gooseberry and nutmeg cream. Loin of lamb cutlets en papillote with garlic potatoes and light pepper jus. Pan-fried scallops, cooked with mussels and shallots, topped with a pesto crust. Bitter chocolate cup filled with lavender ice cream on a purée of blueberries.

Credit cards: 1, 2, 3, 5 + SWITCH
Proprietor: James Thomson

Mansefield House Hotel
Mayne Road, Elgin
Moray IV30 1NY
Tel: 01343 540883
Fax: 01343 552491

Just off A96 in Elgin. From Inverness, drive towards town centre and turn right at first roundabout. At mini-roundabout, hotel on right.

A popular town hotel and restaurant.

- Town house hotel.
- Traditional Scottish cooking, with some French influences.
- "Imaginative use is made of local produce, particularly fish and shellfish."

Close to the centre of Elgin, this well-converted Georgian house provides a comfortable retreat. It has excellent facilities to suit the commercial and private guest and the restaurant is especially popular with the local business community. The chef presents a well-priced à la carte menu made up of classic Scottish dishes, using market-available fish, meat and vegetables. The quality of his cooking has been recognised by an AA Rosette and an RAC Merit Award.

Open all year
Rooms: 17 with private facilities
Bed & Breakfast from £30
Dinner B & B from £50
Dining Room/Restaurant Lunch 12 - 2 pm
Mon to Sat: 12.30 -2.30 pm Sun (a)
Dinner 6.30 - 9.30 pm Sun to Thu: 6.30 -
10 pm Fri Sat (c)
Vegetarians welcome
Facilities for disabled visitors
No smoking in restaurant
No dogs

Salmon and sole terrine studded with North Sea prawns presented with seasonal leaves and lemon dressing. Pan-roasted quail on a compote of plums and port. King scallops baked in a rich cheese sauce. Lobster, steamed, then grilled with garlic butter. Prime fillet steak topped with bread croûton and chicken liver parfait, finished in a rich Madeira sauce.

STB Highly Commended 4 Crowns
Credit cards: 1, 2, 3 + SWITCH
Proprietors: Ross & Kathleen Murray

Mansion House Hotel & Country Club
The Haugh, Elgin
Moray IV30 1AW
Tel: 01343 548811
Fax: 01343 547916

Turn off main A96 in Elgin into Haugh Road.

An imposing mansion on the River Lossie.

- Country house hotel.
- Classical cooking.
- "An interesting range of cooking styles, and a confident handling of texture and colour."

The baronial house was built by the Bibby Shipping Line and stands in beautifully landscaped grounds overlooking the River Lossie, only minutes from the centre of Elgin. The interior is opulent and High Victorian - with sumptuous detailing and individually styled four poster bedrooms. It also has a fully equipped Country Club (with swimming pool and gymnasium). Chef John Alexander presents daily changing table d'hôte and à la carte menus: the latter is comprehensive, the former combines fresh produce with unusual sauces and liaisons. The hotel also has a well-priced wine list.

Open all year
Rooms: 22 with private facilities
Bed & Breakfast £55 - £90
Dinner B & B £75 - £95
Special Rates available
Bar Lunch 12 - 2 pm (a)
Dining Room/Restaurant Lunch 12 - 2 pm (b)
Bar Supper 5 - 9 pm (a)
Dinner 7 - 9 pm (c)
Vegetarians welcome
No dogs
No smoking in restaurant

Light pastry pouch filled with a ragoût of local seafoods. Wild mushrooms in white wine and cream with home-made garlic bread. Smoked chicken and lemon soup. Loin of venison with a liver and blackcurrant mousse. Darne of salmon topped with a halibut and herb mousse and glazed with cheese sauce.

STB Highly Commended 5 Crowns
Credit cards: 1, 2, 3, 5 + SWITCH
Proprietors: Jim & Joan Stirrat

Erbusaig

Fairlie

Falkirk

The Old Schoolhouse Restaurant
"Tigh Fasgaidh," Erbusaig, Kyle
by Kyle of Lochalsh
Ross-shire IV40 8BB
Tel: 01599 534369

Outskirts of Erbusaig on Kyle-Plockton road.

A small restaurant with three bedrooms.

- A charming 19th century schoolhouse in its own grounds on the picturesque road between Kyle and Plockton.
- Imaginative modern cooking.
- "The excellent fresh fish and other dishes; the friendly owner and the tranquility of the place combine to create a wonderful experience."

This old school has been tastefully converted by the owners Calum and Joanne Cumine into a small restaurant with two bedrooms (soon to be three), each of which is restfully decorated and en suite. The conversion has been sensitively done, and retains the character of the place, and the feel of the past, while providing the level of comfort required by today's guests. The cooking is imaginative and versatile, and makes good use of the wonderful fish, shellfish, meat and game so readily available in this unspoiled corner of the West Highlands. The menu is reasonably priced and the owners are delighted to cater for vegetarians. It is no wonder that this small restaurant has such a big reputation locally.

Open 1 Apr to 30 Oct
Rooms: 2 with private facilities
Bed & Breakfast £18 - £30
Special Rates for 7+ nights
Dinner 7 - 10.30 pm (b-d)
Vegetarians welcome

Scallops marinaded in fresh herbs and citrus juices, sautéed in walnut oil. Prawns grilled with a fennel vinaigrette. Poached salmon served with elderflower wine and tarragon sauce. Monkfish braised in wine, finished with cream and fresh basil. Noisettes of lamb served with a mint and white wine sauce. Raspberry brûlée made with locally produced yoghurt.

STB Commended 3 Crowns
Credit cards: 1, 2, 3
Proprietors: Calum & Joanne Cumine

Fins Restaurant
Fencefoot Farm, Fairlie
Ayrshire KA29 0EG
Tel: 01475 568989
Fax: 01475 568921

On A78, 1 mile south of Fairlie near Largs.

Fish farm, smokehouse, farm shop and first-rate seafood restaurant.

- Fish restaurant.
- Innovative Scottish cooking.
- "An outstandingly good restaurant with an award-winning chef, serving the freshest possible seafood."

Fins is part of Fencebay Fisheries in Fairlie and fish of all kinds are cured and smoked by traditional methods; an agreement with the oyster farm across the way also provides them with scallops, prawns and other seafood (since they also have a fishing boat). The fish at Fins is landed daily. The enterprise, owned by Jill and Bernard Thain, won the Scottish Seafood Product of the Year Award 1995 at the Scottish Food Proms. Chef Gillian Dick's lunch and dinner menus are à la carte, supplemented by a blackboard 'catch of the day' (there is also a steak dish for non-'fishies'). The cooking is modern and accomplished. The restaurant itself is situated in an old barn, very tastefully decorated (with a fishy theme), bright, friendly and cheerful. Service is excellent. A thoroughly good fish restaurant.

Open all year except Christmas Days to New Year's Day
Dining Room/Restaurant Lunch 12 - 2 pm except Mon (b)
Dinner 6.30 - 9 pm except Sun Mon (d)
Closed Mon
Vegetarians welcome
Facilities for disabled visitors

Fresh lobsters, langoustines and oysters always available. Plaice fillets stuffed with squat lobster tails with a chardonnay sauce. Salmon Macallan peppered salmon fillet pan-fried with a whisky cream sauce. Fencebay smoked cod with spinach, sautéed potatoes and poached egg with a grain mustard beurre blanc. Summer pudding. Chocolate hazelnut and rum truffle. Own ice creams.

Credit cards: 1, 2, 3, 5, 6 + SWITCH, DELTA
Proprietors: Bernard & Jill Thain

Inchyra Grange Hotel
Grange Road, Polmont
Falkirk FK2 0YB
Tel: 01324 711911
Fax: 01324 716134

Junction 4 or 5, M9 motorway. Situated on border of Polmont/Grangemouth.

A country house hotel with gardens and full leisure facilities.

- Fully modernised and extended country house.
- Good hotel cooking.
- "One of the most popular restaurants in Falkirk District."

Inchyra Grange traces its origins to the 12th century, but its internal lay-out and furnishings are modern. It stands in five acres of garden and park, and has a popular leisure club with swimming pool, sauna and steam baths, multi-gym, solarium and resident beautician. Twenty five bedrooms have been added in the past year and more are planned. There are two restaurants: the first is in the Leisure Club, and features 'healthy meals and snacks'; the main restaurant specialises in classic Scottish cooking and offers extensive à la carte and table d'hôte menus. The hotel's central situation near Falkirk makes it popular as a business venue, for meetings and conferences, not to mention business lunches, and it also does a good trade in functions.

Open all year
Rooms: 43 with private facilities
Bed & Breakfast £50 - £90
Dinner B & B from £55
Room Rate from £85
Special Weekend Rates available
Bar Lunch 12 - 2 pm (a)
Dining Room/Restaurant Lunch 12.30 - 2.30 pm except Sat (a)
Bar Supper 6 - 10 pm (a)
Dinner 7 - 9.30 pm (c)
Vegetarians welcome

Rich game terrine wrapped in bacon and served with apple and red onion chutney. Sliced aubergine in breadcrumbs, deep-fried and served with a roasted red pepper sauce. Grilled fillet of beef with a braised oxtail and ale sauce, garnished with onions, bacon and mushrooms.

STB Commended 4 Crowns
Credit cards: 1, 2, 3, 5, 6 + SWITCH

Covenanter Hotel

The Square, Falkland
Fife KY7 7BU
Tel: 01337 857542/857224
Fax: 01337 857163

Centre of Falkland.

Small village inn looking on to Falkland Palace.

- 17th century coaching inn.
- Good hotel cooking.
- "Idiosyncratic traditional charm."

George and Margaret Menzies have run this hotel for nearly 20 years, during which time they have cultivated a reliable custom, through their honest no-nonsense approach to guests and emphasis on providing good food with few frills. The hotel has a real old-school Scottish resonance about it. There is a choice of eating either in the bistro which is ideal for the family - the food being familiar. For more substantial meals, the choices in the dining room have more of the Taste of Scotland about them. Lots of steaks as well as chicken, salmon and trout on offer.

Open all year
Rooms: 4 with private facilities
Bed & Breakfast £25 - £37.50
Dinner B & B £37.50 - £50
Bar Lunch 12 - 2 pm except Mon (a)
Dining Room/Restaurant Lunch 12 - 2 pm except Mon (a)
Bar Supper 6 - 9.30 pm except Mon (a)
Dinner 6 - 9.30 pm except Mon (c)
(table d'hôte + à la carte dinner menus available)
Restaurants closed Mon
Vegetarians welcome
No dogs

Scampi Falkland cooked in a cream sauce with sliced onions and mushrooms. Tay salmon steak grilled or poached. Sirloin steak Auld Alliance coated in French mustard, topped with soft brown sugar and grilled.

STB Commended 3 Crowns
Credit cards: 1, 2, 3, 5
Proprietors: George & Margaret Menzies

Kind Kyttock's Kitchen

Cross Wynd, Falkland
Fife KY7 7BE
Tel: 01337 857477

A912 to Falkland. Centre of Falkland near the Palace, turn up at the Square into Cross Wynd.

An outstanding tearoom in an historic setting.

- Traditional Scottish tearoom.
- Home cooking; home baking; home-made preserves.
- "A rare survivor. Do not go to Falkland without enjoying the good things on offer here."

Kind Kyttock's is situated in a charming 17th century terraced cottage overlooking the cobbled square in one of Scotland's most picturesque villages. Its two rooms are most attractive - comfortable, informal and cheerful, with a 'country tearoom' feel. And this is precisely what Kind Kyttock's is, but a tearoom of outstanding quality, which has frequently won the Tea Council's Award for Excellence. Bert Dalrymple is its owner/cook. His baking is divine - including soda scones, oatcakes, pancakes and other Scottish delicacies - and as well as this he preserves his own fruits, jams, pickles and chutneys, roasts his own meats for sandwiches, makes his own soups, etc. No wonder the place is so popular with locals, and you can buy baking to take away when it is available.

Open all year except Christmas Eve to 5 Jan
Food service 12 - 5.30 pm except Mon (a)
Closed Mon
Vegetarians welcome
No smoking throughout

Home-baked pancakes, scones, fruit squares, shortbread, wholemeal bread, stovies, cloutie dumpling. Locally grown vegetables used in Scotch broth and at salad table. Selection of teas available.

Credit cards: 1, 3
Proprietor: Bert Dalrymple

Baxters Visitor Centre

Fochabers
Moray IV32 7LD
Tel: 01343 820666
Fax: 01343 821790

Situated on A96 Aberdeen-Inverness, 1 mile west of Fochabers.

A quality and unique 'visitor experience' on the Spey.

- A well laid-out and interesting visitor centre.
- Home cooking and baking.
- "The Baxters story is fascinating, and the food in the tearoom delicious."

Baxters of Speyside dominate the quality soup market in the U.K. (75% share) and sell their products worldwide. They achieved such pre-eminence by recreating the taste of home cooking in a can. Every potato and carrot that goes into one of their soups is individually inspected, and at their Visitor Centre near Fochabers, you can see exactly how their famous preserves and tinned foods are prepared. The self-service Spey Restaurant there is spacious and attractive, furnished with pine. It features their own products, but also home baking (pancakes made to order are a speciality!) and daily changing hot lunch dishes.

Open all year
Open 9.30 am - 5 pm: 6 pm Jun to Sep)
Lunch 11 am - 2.30 pm: traditional roast Sun (a)
Table Licence
Vegetarians welcome
No smoking area in restaurant

A choice of Baxters famous soups. Rollmop herring with salad. Pâté and oatcakes. Highland cheeseboard. Two daily changing main meal dishes, one vegetarian. Filled baked potatoes. Salads and sandwiches. Selection of home baking. Pancakes cooked to order on open griddle.

Credit cards: 1, 3 + SWITCH, DELTA

Forfar

Forres

Chapelbank House Hotel

69 East High Street, Forfar
Angus DD8 2EP
Tel: 01307 463151
Fax: 01307 461922

Town centre - Forfar. 12 miles north of
Dundee.

> A family-run hotel with an emphasis on service.

■ Small, town centre hotel.
■ Good, traditional home cooking.
■ "Friendly and well-run, this is an excellent small hotel."

Built in 1865 on the main road leading through the market town of Forfar, Chapelbank was once the home of the town's doctor. The present owners, Duthie and Edith Douglas, have converted and furnished it well. Standards of fittings are high throughout and the Douglas' take a special pride in their cuisine. Calm and spacious, the dining room is popular with local non-residents as a place where fair prices and fresh, straightforward produce meet in both a table d'hôte and an extensive à la carte menu. A large dining room window overlooks the small but attractive front garden. Landscapes by local artists adorn the walls. From a warm welcome to a simple but varied wine list, from freshly-prepared porridge and cream among other things for breakfast to service that is friendly and capable, Duthie and Edith know what they are doing and do it well.

Open all year except first 2 wks Jan
Rooms: 4 with private facilities
Bed & Breakfast £35 - £48
Dinner B & B £51.50 - £64.50
Dining Room/Restaurant Lunch 12 - 2 pm
except Mon (b)
Dinner 6.30 - 8.30 pm except Sun Mon (c)
Restricted Hotel Licence
Vegetarians welcome
Facilities for disabled visitors
No smoking in dining room
Guide dogs only

Lunch: Arbroath smokie. Lamb cutlet. Dinner: Home-made pâté. Steak au poivre. Aberdeen Angus beef. Variety of home-made sweets.

STB Highly Commended 4 Crowns
Credit cards: 1, 3 + SWITCH, DELTA
Proprietors: Duthie & Edith Douglas

Knockomie Hotel

Grantown Road, Forres
Moray IV36 0SG
Tel: 01309 673146
Fax: 01309 673290

On A940 just south of Forres on Grantown road.

> A timeless and elegant hotel overlooking the Royal Burgh of Forres.

■ A rare example of Arts and Crafts Movement architecture - an elegant villa built in 1914 around an earlier building.
■ Modern Scottish cooking with French influences.
■ "Interesting and imaginative dishes with a wide variety of finishes and flavours."

Ideally placed for visiting the castles, stately homes and distilleries of the north-east, this gracious country house offers guests first-rate accommodation and dining facilities. Part of the hotel's landscaped gardens are set aside to supply herbs and salad leaves; vegetables are grown locally, to order. Knockomie's resident proprietor is Gavin Ellis, who is knowledgeable, courteous and hospitable, and his staff are smart and well trained. The daily changing table d'hôte menu is carefully selected; the food is all local and fresh; cooking is 'modern classic'. The wine list is of especial interest - very well-priced, with some wonderful rarities; over 80 whiskies are also listed. A bistro was opened at the hotel last summer.

Open all year except Christmas Day
Rooms: 14 with private facilities
Bar Lunch 12 - 2 pm (a)
Bed & Breakfast £37.50 - £75
Dinner B & B £61 - £98.50
Dining Room/Restaurant Lunch 12 - 2 pm (b)
Bistro Supper 5.30 - 9 pm (b)
Dinner 7 - 9 pm (d) 4 or 5 course menu
Vegetarians welcome

Moray Firth mussel and saffron bisque. Magret of duck served on a nest of red cabbage and glazed with a port sauce. Mille feuille of caramelised pear. A selection of Scottish cheeses served with home-made oatcakes.

STB Highly Commended 4 Crowns
Credit cards: 1, 2, 3, 5 + SWITCH, DELTA
Proprietor: Gavin Ellis

Ramnee Hotel

Victoria Road, Forres
Moray IV36 0BN
Tel: 01309 672410
Fax: 01309 673392

A96 Inverness-Aberdeen, off bypass at roundabout at eastern side of Forres - 500 yards on right.

> An attractive small hotel in the centre of Forres.

■ Turn of the century Edwardian private house.
■ A combination of classical French and modern Scottish cuisine immaculately served.
■ "Offers guests very high standards of accommodation and food at prices which represent real value for money".

The Ramnee Hotel was built in 1907 as a private residence for Richard Hamblin returning to Scotland after a long career in the Indian Civil Service. Set in two acres of carefully landscaped gardens, the hotel enjoys a central location in Forres, a charming Victorian spa town on the Morayshire and Nairnshire border. Each of the hotel's 20 bedrooms is individually furnished and fitted with all the extras you would expect in a first-rate establishment. Food in Hamblin's Restaurant is characterised by generous portions imaginatively presented. There is a choice of excellent value table d'hôte and à la carte menus at both lunch and dinner. The accompanying wine list is extensive and well chosen. Lighter, more informal meals are available in Tippling's cocktail lounge.

Open all year except Christmas Day +
1 to 3 Jan
Rooms: 20 with private facilities
Bed & Breakfast £37.50 - £57.50
Dinner B & B £55 - £80
Special Weekend Rates available
Bar Lunch 12 - 2 pm (a)
Dining Room/Restaurant Lunch 12 - 2 pm (a)
Bar Supper 6 - 9 pm (b)
Dinner 7 - 9 pm (c)
Vegetarians welcome

Smoked mackerel and creamed beetroot. Breast of Guinea fowl in apricot sauce. Medallions of beef fillet with shallots, mushrooms, tomato concassé, white wine and herbs. Escalope of pork with a heather honey and mead sauce.

STB Commended 4 Crowns
Credit cards: 1, 2, 3, 5 + SWITCH, DELTA

Fort Augustus

The Brae Hotel
Bunoich Brae, Fort Augustus
Inverness-shire PH32 4DG
Tel: 01320 366289
Fax: 01320 366702

200 yards off A82, overlooking the town.

In an elevated position overlooking Fort
Augustus this is a family run hotel with a period
atmosphere and a warm welcome.

- A Victorian manse with fine views.
- International modern cooking.
- "With no formal training Mrs Reive produces
  the highest standard of imaginative cuisine
  capitalizing on the bounty of local produce."

This restored Victorian building stands in its own
pretty grounds, looking out over Fort Augustus and
the Great Glen, with spectacular views of the
Caledonian Canal, River Oich and Loch Ness. The
resident owners, Andrew and Mari Reive want their
hotel to be a 'home from home' and go to great
lengths to put their guests at ease. An enclosed
verandah has been added recently in which to
lounge away wet days with a good book and the
dining room is light and airy. Mrs Reive does all
the cooking, including the preserves and
marmalades which are served for breakfast, and
heavenly after dinner chocolates. She describes her
style of cooking as 'international' and her eclectic
menus feature fresh fish, seafood and game from
nearby Loch Lochy.

Open Mar to 31 Oct
Rooms: 8 , 5 with private facilities
Bed & Breakfast £22 - £28
Dinner B & B £38 - £49
Special Rates available
Dinner 7 - 8.30 pm (d) 4 course menu
Children over 7 years welcome
No smoking in dining room
Vegetarians welcome - prior notice required

Prawns en croûte with a minted orange sauce.
Smoked and fresh salmon rillettes. Grilled duck
breast with plum and ginger, and an apple and
chive crêpe. Venison fillet with spiced cranberry
sauce and cumin rice timbale. Salmon baked with
ginger, garlic and lime. Fillet steak with red wine
and mushrooms. Home-made bread, ice creams
and desserts.

STB Highly Commended 3 Crowns
Credit cards: 1, 2, 3
Proprietors: Andrew & Mari Reive

Lovat Arms Hotel
Fort William Road, Fort Augustus
Inverness-shire PH32 4DU
Tel: 01320 366206/4
Fax: 01320 366677

A82 Fort William-Inverness.

A small and informal country hotel in an
excellent location.

- Friendly, unhurried and relaxed Highland
  hospitality.
- Traditional home cooking.
- "Assured of a warm welcome."

This spacious Victorian building stands in 2½ acres
of well-kept grounds overlooking the village of Fort
Augustus. Proprietors Hector and Mary MacLean are
welcoming hosts. High ceilinged and wood-
panelled, the dining room offers unpretentious
home cooking using a wide range of west coast fish
and shellfish together with local game and beef.
There is also a bar meal menu served in the
spacious lounge bar.

Open all year
Rooms: 21 with private facilities
Bed & Breakfast £26.50 - £33.50
Special Rates available
Bar Lunch 12.30 - 2 pm: 12.30 - 2.30 pm
Jun to Sep (a-b)
Dining Room/Restaurant Lunch - by
arrangement groups only
Bar Supper 6.30 - 8.30 pm: 6.30 - 9 pm
Jun to Sep (a-b)
Dinner 7 - 8.30 pm: 7 - 9 pm Jun to Sep (c)
Vegetarians welcome

Scallops in beurre blanc sauce. Mussels,
langoustines and salmon. Pâtés, fish and game
terrines. Saddle of venison. Noisettes of lamb. Angus
beef. Vegetarian dishes.

STB Commended 3 Crowns
Credit cards: 1, 3
Proprietors: Hector & Mary MacLean

Fort William

An Crann
Seangan Bridge, Muirshearlich
Fort William
Inverness-shire PH33 7PB
Tel: 01397 772077

From A830 at Banavie, take B8004 for 2½
miles. From A82 at Commando Memorial take
B8004 for 8 miles.

Original and interesting 30 seater restaurant.

- Converted steading.
- Imaginative Scottish cookery.
- "Salmon with lemon grass sauce is unique and
  justifiably the most popular dish served."

This little restaurant has been beautifully converted
from an old farm steading which was built for one
of Sine Ross's forbears in 1896. This was done three
years ago, retaining the original stone work and
adding large arched windows to allow in the light.
Home- made snacks and baking are available
throughout the day, as well as daily specials, soups
and vegetarian dishes. Sine is an original cook,
preferring to adapt her sauces and techniques to the
food she has available. Venison, lamb and salmon
are all readily obtainable locally and she tends to
concentrate her energies on creating interesting
combinations of flavours and textures according to
her mood and the seasonal produce. There is a
delightful honesty about the food at An Crann;
there are no aspirations to grandeur but the dishes
are the work of a dedicated and inspired cook.

Open Easter to end Oct
Soup, sandwiches + home baking available
11.30 am - 4 pm
Dining Room/Restaurant Lunch 12 - 3 pm
except Sat (a)
Dinner 6 - 9 pm (b-c)
Table Licence
Vegetarians welcome
Facilities for disabled visitors

Lunch: Home-made burgers, toasties, fresh salads
(salmon, tuna, ham, cheese, Brie etc), Marinated
salmon or herring in a dill or grain mustard sauce.
Local scallops with coriander and lentil sauce.
Venison with red wine and rowan jelly sauce.
Scottish lamb with rosemary and Madeira. Bread
and butter pudding with rum and raisin syrup.

Credit cards: 1, 3
Proprietor: Sine Ross

Crannog Seafood Restaurant

Town Pier, Fort William
Inverness-shire PH33 7NG
Tel: 01397 705589/703919
Fax: 01397 705026

Fort William town pier - off A82 Fort William town centre bypass.

> An award-winning seafood restaurant, established by fishermen.

- Seafood restaurant.
- Fresh seafood, cooked simply.
- "Excellent seafood."

The Fort William branch of Crannog is the original (there are now offshoots in Glasgow, Edinburgh and Oban): a small, octagonal, red-roofed building on the pier at Fort William. The decor is simple - white walls, varnished pine tables, comfortable chairs - and the room has splendid views over Loch Linnhe. When they are not admiring the view, diners can watch the catch being landed direct into the kitchen - and soon afterwards enjoy the freshest imaginable seafood. This is Crannog's philosophy: very fresh seafood in friendly surroundings. It works, and the restaurant is very popular, so it is advisable to book.

Open all year except Christmas Day + 1 Jan
Dining Room/Restaurant Lunch 12 - 2.30 pm (b-c)
Dinner 6 - 9.30 pm: 6 - 10.30 pm
May to Sep (c)
Note: opening times may vary in winter months
No smoking area in restaurant

Crannog bouillabaisse made from a variety of finfish and shellfish. Salmon fillet in filo pastry with a rich prawn sauce. Wing of skate in foamed lemon butter with capers. Langoustine prawns served cold with three mayonnaises - garlic, spicy and parsley rémoulade. Walnut tart and cream. Cranachan - whipped cream, raspberries, toasted oats and whisky.

Credit cards: 1, 3 + SWITCH, DELTA

The Moorings Hotel

Banavie, Fort William
Inverness-shire PH33 7LY
Tel: 01397 772797
Fax: 01397 772441

Situated off A830, 3 miles from Fort William at Banavie.

> A Highland hotel on the banks of the Caledonian Canal.

- A family-run hotel with a nautical theme.
- Modern Scottish cooking with unusual flair.
- "The hotel's theme sums up its atmosphere - clean, ship-shape, sparkling and very efficiently run."

Set against a backdrop of dramatic Highland scenery The Moorings Hotel deserves its Scottish Tourist Board's 4 Crowns status. Bedrooms are well appointed and comfortable with colour TV and satellite. Much of the charm of the public rooms derives from faithfulness to the hotel's nautical imagery and you can enjoy splendid views of Ben Nevis and Aonach Mhor while sipping a pre-dinner drink in the Upper Deck Lounge Bar. The highlight of a visit however is dinner in the hotel's Jacobean Restaurant with its cheerful and colourful atmosphere. Here you find modern Scottish cooking at its best with beautifully cooked food presented with an interesting choice of accompaniments and garnishes, and by a wine list with just the right balance between price and choice.

Open all year except Christmas
Rooms: 24 with private facilities
Bar Lunch 12 - 2 pm (a)
Dining Room Lunch - by prior arrangement
Bar Supper 6 - 9.30 pm (b)
Dinner 7 - 9.30 pm Mon to Sat: 7 - 8.30 Sun (d)
Bed & Breakfast £30 - £40
Dinner B & B £65 - £85
Special Rates for 3/7 nights
Vegetarians welcome

Saute of pigeon breast with a port and garlic sauce. Loin of Rannoch venison with chanterelles and a rich Madeira sauce. Platter of west coast seafood. Roast Mallaig monkfish tail with a tomato and herb crust and fresh lime butter.

STB Highly Commended 4 Crowns
Credit cards: 1, 2, 3, 5
Proprietor: Norman Sinclair

Torbeag House

Muirshearlich, Banavie
by Fort William
Inverness-shire
PH33 7PB
Tel: 01397 772412

Take A830 Mallaig road from Fort William. After 1 mile turn right into Banavie on B8004. Follow for 2½ miles.

> A modern country house converted into an outstanding guest house.

- Stylish modern guest house, with spectacular mountain views.
- Excellent home cooking.
- "The best salmon I have ever eaten...residents who had been there for 4 nights said the food was out of this world!"

Ken and Gladys Whyte bought Torbeag House in late 1992, and opened their doors in early 1994, with the intention of offering 'top quality accommodation and food in agreeable surroundings at sensible prices'. A well-designed 1960s building with large picture windows giving stunning views of the north face of Ben Nevis and Aonach Mor. The owners are warm and welcoming, and have decorated and appointed their home tastefully, with a mixture of modern and traditional furniture and some fine paintings. Ken was a farmer and is a self-taught chef; he serves a set four course menu for dinner (consulting guests about preferences). Baking, preserves, after-dinner fudge and breakfast muesli are all made in-house.

Open 1 Jan to 31 Oct
Rooms: 2 with private facilities
Bed & Breakfast £20 - £35
Dinner Bed & Breakfast £35 - £50
Special Rates for 3+ nights
Dinner at 7.30 pm (b) 4 course menu
Unlicensed - guests welcome to take own wine
Residents only
Vegetarians welcome
No smoking in dining room

Turnip, cashew and ginger soup. Wild Highland venison casseroled in apple juice. Rhubarb meringue pie. Home-made fudge. Home-made bread, oatcakes, bannocks and preserves. Home-grown vegetables and soft fruit in season.

STB Deluxe 3 Crowns
No credit cards
Proprietors: Ken & Gladys Whyte

Little Lodge

North Erradale, Gairloch
Wester Ross IV21 2DS
Tel: 01445 771237

Take B8021 from Gairloch towards Melvaig, situated ¼ mile beyond turning to North Erradale.

A charming converted crofthouse with lovely views.

- Small guest house.
- Traditional Scottish and innovative cooking.
- "Menus are planned with the guests, and the cooking is delicious."

Little Lodge stands on a heather-clad peninsula north of Gairloch, and the splendid views towards the Torridon Mountains and Skye are enjoyed to advantage from its conservatory dining room. Di Johnson and Inge Ford, its owners, are charming and welcoming hosts, and have restored their home in a way which best displays its original features. Outside, their own hens, sheep and goats roam; their garden provides vegetables and herbs. Di's imaginative marinades and sauces enhance the excellent seasonal local produce (especially freshly-landed fish from Gairloch itself), while Inge's home-made bread, oatcakes, yoghurt and preserves make breakfast a special treat. Little Lodge is an idyllic retreat with superb cuisine which has earned Di and Inge much praise.

Open Apr to Oct
Rooms: 3 with private facilities
Dinner B & B £37.50 - £42 (min stay 2 nights)
Dinner at 7 pm (b-c) 4 course menu
Residents only
Unlicensed - guests welcome to take own wine + spirits
Vegetarians welcome - by prior arrangement
No children
No smoking throughout
No dogs

Goujons of monkfish with garlic mayonnaise. Local smoked and poached salmon terrine. Little Lodge hot-pot of home-reared lamb and haggis. Breast of chicken marinated and baked with lime, fresh ginger root and sherry. Wild salmon with spinach and orange purée sauce. Pear and stem ginger custard tart. Highland raspberry brûlée.

STB Highly Commended 3 Crowns
No credit cards
Proprietors: Di Johnson & Inge Ford

Woodlands House Hotel & Restaurants

Windyknowe Road, Galashiels
Selkirkshire TD1 1RQ
Tel: 01896 754722
Fax: 01896 754722

Just off A7, take A72 towards Peebles. Turn left up Hall Street - Windyknowe Road is second on right.

A fine Victorian mansion in the heart of the Borders countryside.

- A country house-style hotel, yet close to the town centre.
- Bistro-style food in the bar and formal food in the restaurant.
- "A place of ambience and character."

A Victorian gothic mansion of wood panelling and marble fireplaces, Woodlands sits in two acres of its own grounds and has views over Galashiels and the surrounding countryside. Resident proprietors Kevin and Nicki Winsland have recently carried out major refurbishments which enhance the ambience of the house. The hotel's lounge bar meals are popular locally. The Winslands also offer straightforward menus in their formal dining room and informal meals in their steak-house restaurant.

Open all year except 26, 27 Dec
Rooms: 9 with private facilities
Bed & Breakfast £34 - £42
Dinner B & B £42 - £55
Special Rates for 5+ nights
Bar Lunch 12 - 2 pm (a)
Carvery 12 - 7 pm Sun (b)
Bar Supper 6 - 9.30 pm (a)
Dinner 6 - 9.30 pm (c)
Vegetarians welcome

Marinated duck with an apple and honey dressing. Lobster bisque. Smoked salmon layered over a bed of Waldorf salad with a lime dressing. Fillet of pork filled with apple and Stilton cheese served with a cider cream sauce. Lamb cutlets accompanied with a minted chasseur sauce. Prime sirloin steaks.

STB Highly Commended 4 Crowns
Credit cards: 1, 3 + SWITCH, DELTA
Proprietors: Kevin & Nicki Winsland

Inchbae Lodge Hotel

by Garve
Ross-shire
IV23 2PH
Tel: 01997 455269
Fax: 01997 455207

Situated on A835 Inverness-Ullapool road. 6 miles north west of Garve.

A small family-run hotel with a panoramic view of Ben Wyvis.

- Small country hotel.
- Home cooking.
- "A charming, friendly place offering good imaginative cooking."

A former Victorian hunting lodge. It stands in seven acres of lovely wild garden, including its own island with free trout fishing in the River Blackwater and clay pigeon shooting available, by arrangement. The lodge has an intimate cottage feel - reminiscent of its previous life as a Victorian hunting lodge. The 12 rooms are divided between the lodge itself and a cedar wood chalet nearby. The owners, Patrick and Judy Price, go to great lengths to make their guests comfortable: children are accommodated free of charge. Patrick's menus are inventive with a choice of two starters, main course and pudding and table d'hôte; produce is all fresh and imaginatively cooked.

Open all year except 25 to 29 Dec
Rooms: 12 with private facilities
Bed & Breakfast £30 - £35
Dinner B & B £50 - £55
Special Rates available for 2+ nights
Bar Lunch 12 - 2 pm Mon to Sat: 12.30 - 2 pm Sun (a)
Bar Supper 5 - 8.30 pm Mon to Sat: 6.30 - 8.30 pm Sun (a)
Dinner 7 - 8 pm (c) 4 course menu
Vegetarians welcome
No smoking in dining room

Venison medallions marinaded in port pan-fried pink, served with a blackcurrant and crème de cassis sauce. Monkfish topped with a herb Provençale crust, served with a red pepper sauce. Cider, orange and Calvados syllabub. Baked cheesecake with apricot and kirsh coulis.

STB Approved 4 Crowns
Credit cards: 1, 3
Proprietors: Patrick & Judy Price

Gatehouse-of-Fleet

Cally Palace Hotel
Gatehouse-of-Fleet
Dumfries & Galloway DG7 2DL
Tel: 01557 814341
Fax: 01557 814522

1 mile from Gatehouse-of-Fleet exit off A75
Dumfries-Stranraer, 30 miles west of Dumfries.

A country house hotel with a truly regal
appearance.

- ■ Palatial, 4 Star hotel overlooking its own loch
  and golf course
- ■ Fine traditional Scottish cooking.
- ■ "Few other hotels attract as much repeat
  business."

Approached by a long, sweeping drive through
beautiful woodland, this mansion stands in its own
100 acres of magnificent grounds. Its marble
pillars, floors and tables combine with gilt and fine
plasterwork to recall the grandeur of the 18th
century. The hotel's public rooms are elegant and
grand, with fine views over the landscaped grounds.
Bedrooms, suites and family rooms are all tastefully
appointed with every comfort. The traditional
dining room offers flowers, candles and silver
service. Menus concentrate on selecting and
presenting good, fresh, local produce with style.
Both the table d'hôte and à la carte menus change
daily. Manageress Jennifer Adams selects and trains
her staff to be alert and responsive. In addition to
the hotel's recently opened 18-hole, 70-par golf
course, there is putting, tennis and croquet outside
and a swimming pool and sauna inside.

Open 3 Mar to 3 Jan
Rooms: 56 with private facilities
Dinner B & B £58 - £98
Special Rates available
Snacks only 12.30 - 2 pm
Dining Room/Restaurant Lunch 12.30 -
2 pm (c)
Dinner 6.15 - 9.30 pm (d) - 4 course menu
No smoking in dining room

Prawn bisque. Roast sirloin of beef with baby
vegetables. Roast cannon of venison seasoned in
five spice with a juniper berry jus-lie. Steamed
suprême of salmon in a light saffron velouté served
with spinach flavoured noodles. Ecclefechan butter
tart with hazelnut sauce.

STB Deluxe 4 Crowns
Credit cards: 1, 3 + SWITCH

Glasgow

The Brasserie
176 West Regent Street
Glasgow G2 4RL
Tel: 0141 248 3801
Fax: 0141 248 8197

Approach via Bath Street from city centre; turn
left into Blythswood Street then left into West
Regent Street. From outwith city, follow one
way systems via Blythswood Square to West
Regent Street.

City centre restaurant and brasserie.

- ■ Restaurant in the heart of Glasgow.
- ■ Modern Scottish cooking.
- ■ "As well as familiar favourites and Scottish
  theme dishes, there are some real treats
  appearing on the menu here."

This elegant brasserie lies close to both Glasgow's
theatreland and its mercantile centre and is
popular both with businessmen at lunchtime and
theatre goers in the evening (they suggest a
delicious 'after-theatre supper' of warm duck salad
or scrambled eggs with smoked salmon). The
Brasserie has an impressive pillared facade, and
inside there is a horseshoe bar and dining area with
a Victorian atmosphere. It has an air of restrained
elegance and the à la carte menu reflects this, with
a good choice of freshly cooked dishes, both
brasserie-style and more substantial. A daily
changing plât du jour is also available. Flair,
continental influences and modern cooking styles
are evident, and the service is excellent.

Open all year except public holidays
Bar Meals 12 - 11 pm except Sun (a)
Dining Room/Restaurant Meals 12 - 11 pm
except Sun (b)
After-Theatre Supper until 11 pm
except Sun (a)
Dinner until 11 pm except Sun (c)
Closed Sun
Vegetarians welcome

Isle of Seil oysters. Smoked salmon and scrambled
egg. Warm salad of goats cheese with gooseberry
vinaigrette. Prime fillet Aberdeen Angus béarnaise.
Grilled salmon in pinhead oatmeal. Creme brûlée.
Dark chocolate cheesecake with banana sauce.

Credit cards: 1, 2, 3, 5 + SWITCH, DELTA

The Buttery
652 Argyle Street
Glasgow G3 8UF
Tel: 0141 221 8188
Fax: 0141 204 4639

Junction 19, M8 - approach by St Vincent
Street and Elderslie Street.

Gourmet restaurant in Glasgow.

- ■ Converted tenement building.
- ■ Innovative Scottish cooking.
- ■ "One of the best restaurants in Glasgow."

The Buttery is a perennial favourite and continues
to be one of Glasgow's premier restaurants. The
outside of this old tenement building gives no clues
to the interior, which has a unique character, with
bits of church furniture and Victoriana lending the
whole of the restaurant an air of comfort and
charm. Polite, well-informed and unobtrusive
service characterises The Buttery, which is
efficiently run by Jim Wilson, a man with a
reputation for high standards. Chef Stephen
Johnson's à la carte menus are an appetising
balance of traditional Scottish dishes treated in a
novel way and with unusual combinations,
exquisitely presented with lots of interesting textures
and flavours. He also presents outstanding
vegetarian and dessert menus.

Open all year except Christmas +
Boxing Days, 1 + 2 Jan
Bar Lunch 12 - 2.30 pm except Sun Sat (b)
Dining Room/Restaurant Lunch 12 - 2.30 pm
except Sun Sat (c-d)
Dinner 7 - 10.30 pm except Sun (e)
Closed Sun
Vegetarians welcome

Roast breast of Guinea fowl filled with rosemary
farce on honey-glazed pears with a roast garlic
essence. Fillets of sole rolled with banana and
prawns poached and set on a slightly curried
cream. Separate vegetarian menu.

Credit cards: 1, 2, 3, 5, 6 + SWITCH, DELTA

The Cabin Restaurant

996 Dumbarton Road, Whiteinch
Glasgow G14 9RR
Tel: 0141 954 7102

From Glasgow city take Clyde expressway, pass Scottish Exhibition & Conference Centre to Thornwood Roundabout. Follow sign to Whiteinch (½ mile). Restaurant on right hand side.

A Victorian 'front room' on Dumbarton Road.

- Small city restaurant.
- Modern Scottish, with continental influences.
- "A talented young chef, friendly service and Wilma make booking essential!"

The restaurant opened three years ago. It is the original front room of an Edwardian tenement building, and is decorated accordingly, with original Art Deco features, a sideboard with china ornaments, old pictures and mirrors. The atmosphere is informal and cheerful. Dishes from the table d'hôte menu (four starters, five main courses) are cooked to order; the cooking technique is creative, confident and to a very high standard; menus change daily, according to what is available in the market. About 9 pm, Wilma arrives with her toy microphone and sings. She is larger than life, first visited the restaurant shortly after it opened, and now returns nightly to encourage guests to sing along and let their hair down. The BBC made a half hour TV programme about her in Las Vegas!

Open 14 Jan to 31 Dec incl
Dining Room/Restaurant Lunch 12 - 2.30 pm except Sun Mon (a)
Dinner 7 - 10 pm except Sun Mon (d)
Closed Sun Mon
Vegetarians welcome
Facilities for disabled visitors

Wood pigeon, venison and rabbit fillet terrine with home-made rowanberry sauce and home-made soda bread. Fish and shellfish chowder. Sirloin beef olives filled with chicken and pork fillet with aromatic wild Arran herbs accompanied with root vegetables. Char-grilled vegetables wrapped in crisp filo with red pepper and basil coulis. Bread and butter pudding with vanilla custard. Caramel souffle with hazelnut praline.

No credit cards
Proprietors: Mohammad Abdulla & Denis Dwyer

The City Merchant Restaurant

97 Candleriggs
Glasgow G1 1NP
Tel: 0141 553 1577

Facing City Halls in Candleriggs, in Glasgow's Merchant City. Candleriggs on right going east along Ingram Street.

Post office converted into an oyster bar.

- City centre restaurant.
- International/Scottish cooking.
- "Really fresh fish, simply presented and reasonably priced."

Situated in a totally upgraded old cobbled street, in the heart of the Merchant City, this restaurant is not only popular with the business community but also shoppers and visitors. The restaurant specialises in seafood, but also offers game, Aberdeen Angus steaks and vegetarian dishes. Daily fish market 'extras' are offered on the blackboard: Isle of Seil oysters Loch Sween mussels, king scallops, lobster turbot as well as exotics such as red snapper. Shellfish on offer on any day. The wine list is extensive with a choice of over 60 bins, but a 'bin-end' blackboard offers excellent value.

Open all year except Christmas + Boxing Days, 1 to 7 Jan + 14 to 29 Jul
Dining Room/Restaurant Lunch 12 - 2.30 pm except Sun (a)
Dinner 5.30 - 10.30 pm except Sun (c) - booking advised
Closed Sun
Bookings advisable
Vegetarians welcome
Facilities for disabled visitors
Children over five years welcome

Partan bree - a creamy crab soup with anchovy essence and rice. Steamed Loch Sween mussels. King scallops baked in mild smoked Highland cheese and white wine sauce with duchess potato. Grand selection of fish and shellfish served hot or cold. Venison, pan-sealed with a game and wild chanterelle sauce. Blackened Aberdeen Angus sirloin - char-grilled in a Louisiana sauce.

Credit cards: 1, 2, 3, 5, 6 + SWITCH
Proprietors: Tony & Linda Matteo

Crannog Seafood Restaurant

28 Cheapside Street
Glasgow G3 8BH
Tel: 0141 221 1727
Fax: 0141 221 1727

Off Broomielaw by River Clyde. At north end of Kingston Bridge. Accessible from Clydeside expressway.

A small seafood restaurant in Finnieston.

- Away from the hustle and bustle of the city centre this restaurant is a joy to find.
- Fresh fish and shellfish plainly cooked.
- "An enthusiastic and capable chef, who knows about fish."

Crannog's Glasgow branch is tucked away in Cheapside Street, Finnieston - parking may be difficult during the day, although there is no problem in the evening. The address is somehow appropriate for a seafood restaurant, but the situation is very different from the original Crannog Restaurant in Fort William, which looks out over Loch Linnhe. Here the spartan interior - white-washed walls decorated with interesting pieces of driftwood, furnished with pine tables and chairs - complements the fresh fish and shellfish which are the restaurant's speciality. The à la carte menu is brief and to the point; smoked fish comes from Crannog's own smokery in Fort William (if you like the dishes, you can order them to take away); blackboard menu features specialities of the day.

Open all year except Christmas + New Year
Dining Room/Restaurant Lunch 12 - 2.30 pm except Sun Mon (b-d)
Dinner 6 - 9.30 pm Tue to Thu: 6 - 10.30 pm Fri Sat (d)
Note: Pre-theatre meals available 5.30 - 7 pm - booking essential
Closed Sun Mon
Vegetarians welcome

Crannog bouillabaise - a hearty soup made from a variety of finfish and shellfish. Salmon marinated in brandy and dill, with a mustard sauce. Langoustine prawns served cold with three mayonnaises - garlic, spicy and parsley rémoulade. Sole fillets rolled with smoked salmon, in a light sherry sauce. Walnut tart. Cranachan - whipped cream, raspberries, toasted oats and whisky.

Credit cards: 1, 3 + SWITCH, DELTA

Drum & Monkey

St Vincent Street
Glasgow
G2 5TL
Tel: 0141 221 6636

100 yards from Central Train Station. 200 yards from Queen Street.

A bar was named 'Pub of the Universe' in 1995.

- City centre pub with interesting bistro.
- Very atmospheric.
- "Modern Scottish cooking; unusual combinations."

The Drum and Monkey was originally a downtown bank but today it has a warm and comfortable ambience where shoppers rest on wicker chairs and leather couches. A fine selection of beers especially real ales and continental lagers is readily available. Bar food is served from 12 to 3 pm, with a simpler menu thereafter of freshly prepared filled sandwiches and wholesome salads. But for the real food experience the adjoining bistro provides more elaborate lunches and dinners in the most intimate of settings, combining modern dishes with the more traditional Scottish classics.

Open all year except Christmas, Boxing Days + 1, 2 Jan
Note: Open Sun from 6 pm
Food available 11 am - 11 pm except Sun (a)
Dining Room/Restaurant Lunch 12 - 3 pm except Sun (b-c)
Dinner 6 - 11 pm (b-c)
Vegetarians welcome
Facilities for disabled visitors
No parking

Haggis with clapshot (neeps and tatties). Baked fillet of cod with champ potatoes, tomato and leek butter sauce. Seared suprême of chicken with oyster mushroom and black pudding risotto. Hickory-smoked salmon. Selection of hearty home-made puddings.

Credit cards: 1, 2, 3, 5 + SWITCH, DELTA
Proprietor: Glyn McDonald

Fifty Five BC

128 Drymen Road
Bearsden
Glasgow G61 3RB
Tel: 0141 942 7272
Fax: 0141 942 9650

On the main Drymen Road in Bearsden village.

A bistro and wine bar with a growing reputation.

- Small restaurant attached to a large wine bar.
- Modern Scottish cooking, with French influences.
- "Meets the demands of the discerning connoisseur as expertly as those of the hungry reveller."

Fifty Five BC was, of course, the date that Julius Caesar first arrived in Britain: the restaurant has adopted this date as its name on account of the Roman remains that have been found nearby. Gary MacLean, head chef, is a talented young man - a runner up in the Young Chef of the Year Competition 1995 and recommended by Egon Ronay. His short à la carte menus are imaginative; his creations make ingenious use of fresh local produce, are beautifully presented and delicious. Robust bar meals (potato skins, burgers, pasta) are served in the bar. The style of the place is modern, light and airy. Service is casual. Fifty Five BC is particularly popular locally and deserves to be better known.

Open all year except New Year's Day
Bar Lunch 12 - 3 pm Mon to Fri: 12 - 3.30 pm
Sat: 12.30 - 4 pm Sun (b)
Dining Room/Restaurant Lunch 12 - 2 pm except Sun (b)
Bar Supper 5 - 6.30 except Sun (b)
Dinner 7 - 10 pm (c)
Vegetarians welcome

Chicken liver parfait with toasted brioche and cranberries. Steamed Loch Etive mussels flavoured with shallots, garlic, white wine and cream. Seared venison with fresh figs, glazed beetroot and rosemary flavoured jus. Suprême of chicken with nutmeg mousseline and creamed spinach. Honey ice cream in a tuille basket with raspberry coulis. Trio of soufflés.

Credit cards: 1, 2, 3 + SWITCH, DELTA
Proprietor: Hamish McLean

Froggies

53 West Regent Street
Glasgow G2 2AE
Tel: 0141 332 8790
Fax: 0141 332 8790

From George Square take St Vincent Street, turn third right into Hope Street, then first right into West Regent Street.

A French restaurant in the heart of Glasgow.

- A spacious, city centre bistro/restaurant.
- First class cuisine.
- "Delicious French regional cooking, at incredible prices!"

Froggies has the unforced style and vibrant atmosphere of a cafe/restaurant in Lyons (more friendly than Paris!). It first opened in 1990 and is so well supported by the local business community that it was substantially expanded in late 1992. Jean-Louis Turpin, its Toulouse-born proprietor, says that his goal is 'to de-mystify the forbidding atmosphere of some French restaurants, and to produce authentic French dishes, using fresh Scottish produce'. His chef, Philippe Avril (from Marseilles) presents a distinguished à la carte menu, two table d'hôte menus and a 'Repas d'Affaire'. All are very well-priced.

Open all year except Christmas + Boxing Days, 1 + 2 Jan
Dining Room / Restaurant Lunch 12 - 3 pm (a)
Dinner 5 - 12 pm (b)
Vegetarians welcome

Barbary duck breast cooked in its own juices with a raspberry sauce, cream and white wine. Pan-fried scallops with parsley and lemon. Grilled salmon steak with home-made tartare sauce. Fillet of beef in a red wine Bordelaise sauce.

Credit cards: 1, 2, 3, + Switch
Proprietor: Jean-Louis Turpin

Glasgow Hilton International
Camerons Restaurant

1 William Street
Glasgow G3 8HT
Tel: 0141 204 5555
Fax: 0141 204 5004

Access from M8 to hotel, or via Waterloo Street and Bishop Street from city centre.

> 20 storey landmark in central Glasgow.

- International luxury hotel.
- Grand hotel cooking.
- "Camerons is beautifully appointed, and the staff are courteous and professional. The meal I ate was faultless."

As befits a hotel of this size and reputation, the Glasgow Hilton has two restaurants and two bars, a substantial leisure centre. The main restaurant is 'Camerons' - named in honour of 'The Gentle Lochiel', Chief of Clan Cameron with waiting staff wearing Cameron tartan trews. The restaurant is divided up into dining room, library, etc. Executive chef Michael Mizzen presents a well priced table d'hôte menu and an à la carte menu which offers a comprehensive range of Scottish fish and shellfish (from Loch Fyne), game and meat, cooked lightly and accompanied by appropriate jus and sauces. Minsky's Deli and Restaurant adopts a 1900 New York theme and offers light meals and snacks all day long (including a traditional Japanese breakfast). Member of the Scotch Beef Club.

Open all year
Camerons Restaurant closed Boxing Day + New Years Day
Rooms: 319 with private facilities
Bed & Breakfast £127.50 - £362
Dinner B & B £132 - £367
Room Rate £115 - £350
Dining Room/Restaurant Lunch 12 - 2.30 pm except Sun Sat (c)
Dinner 7 - 10 pm except Sunday (e)
Facilities for disabled visitors
No smoking area in restaurant
No dogs

Light broth of Western Isles seafood and summer vegetables with pastry twists. Lightly smoked fillet of Borders lamb with polenta, charred aubergine and fresh vegetable dips. Medley of Highland game with forest mushrooms on a rich game jus.

STB Deluxe 5 Crowns
Credit cards: 1, 2, 3, 5, 6 + SWITCH

Glasgow Moat House

Congress Road
Glasgow G3 8QT
Tel: 0141 204 0733
Fax: 0141 221 2022

Prestige Award Winner 1992

Situated on the banks of the River Clyde, next to the SECC.

> A stylish city centre hotel on the bank of the River Clyde.

- Large, modern skyscraper hotel in the heart of Glasgow.
- Modern international cuisine.
- "The healthy style of cooking allows the true flavours of the meat and fish to come through."

The Glasgow Moat House takes its theme from its splendid position on a former wharf, close to the River Clyde: its fully equipped leisure area is the 'Waterside Club', its principal restaurant 'The Mariner', its carvery 'The Pointhouse', and its cocktail bar the 'Quarter Deck'. The hotel is recent (1990) and epitomises all the confidence and style of the City of Culture. Both its award-winning restaurants provide much better food than one often encounters in large 'international' hotels. The Pointhouse (open 6.30am to 10.45pm) is brasserie-style, The Mariner (which has two AA Rosettes) more formal. The style of cooking is modern, fresh and elegant: Scottish produce and international techniques.

Open all year
Rooms: 300 with private facilities
Bed & Breakfast from £40
Dinner B & B from £58.95
Room Rate from £60
All day dining (Pointhouse) 6.30 am - 10.45pm
Note: Buffet from 12 - 2 pm + 7 - 10.30pm
Dining Room/Restaurant Lunch (Mariner) 12 - 2.30pm except Sun Sat (c)
Dinner (Mariner) 7 - 11pm except Sun (c-d)
Vegetarians welcome
Facilities for disabled visitors
No smoking areas in restaurants

Smoked Salmon mille feuille with sour cream and chives. Seared red snapper on a fennel and apple compote, cream spinach sauce. Char-grilled duck breast with a plum confit and bramble jus. Warm brioche with strawberries and a vanilla parfait.

STB Highly Commended 5 Crowns
Credit cards: 1, 2, 3, 5

Rogano Restaurant & Cafe Rogano

11 Exchange Place
Glasgow G1 3AN
Tel: 0141 248 4055
Fax: 0141 248 2608

Glasgow city centre, near Buchanan Street precinct and Queen Street/George Square.

> Glasgow's most famous restaurant.

- City centre restaurant.
- Classic cooking, specialising in fish.
- "Wonderful Art Deco atmosphere; wonderful food. One of the most stylish restaurants in Scotland."

Really good restaurants survive, and Rogano has been around for generations. It was remodelled in the Art Deco style in 1935 - with mirrors, mermaids and seashell carvings - and was painstakingly restored about 12 years ago. A bistro, 'Cafe Rogano', opened downstairs. The atmosphere is authentically of that period and service is formal and stylish. The restaurant's reputation was built on seafood - and this is still a feature, delivered fresh every day - although at least as many meat alternatives are offered on the marvellous à la carte menu. The style of cooking in the main restaurant is modern with powerful classical influences. Downstairs is less formal and less expensive, and the cooking is simpler - but as delicious.

Open all year except 25, 26 Dec + 1 to 3 Jan
Bar Meals 12 - 6 pm Mon to Sat 12.30 - 6 pm Sun (a)
Cafe Rogano 12 - 11 pm Mon to Thu: 12 - 12 midnight Fri Sat: 12 - 10 pm Sun (b)
Dining Room/Restaurant Lunch 12 - 2.30 pm (f)
Dinner 7 - 10.30 pm Mon to Sat: 6.30 - 10 pm Sun (f)
Vegetarians welcome
No smoking requested before 2 pm (Lunch) and 9 pm (Dinner)

Crisp-fried salmon with redcurrants and coriander. Feuilleté of mussels and monkfish on a chive cream. Fillets of halibut with a Champagne and oyster broth. Iced caramel parfait. Mousse brûlée.

Credit cards: 1, 2, 3, 5 + SWITCH, DELTA

Two Fat Ladies Restaurant

88 Dumbarton Road
Glasgow
Strathclyde
G11 6NX
Tel: 0141 339 1944

In the heart of Glasgow's west end, 500 metres from Kelvingrove Museum/Park towards Byres Road.

> One of Glasgow's leading fish restaurants.

- Contemporary restaurant.
- Fish a speciality, but offers meat and vegetarian as well.
- "Flavours were all clean and fresh; seasoning and accompaniments did not distract from the main ingredients."

A small, busy, modern restaurant at 88 Dumbarton Road (hence the name), in the contemporary 'spartan/post-punk' style. The atmosphere is intimate, informal and cheerful. Chef/patron Calum Matheson's cooking is also very contemporary - 'Riverside Café-ish' - relying on utterly fresh ingredients, a searingly hot grill and the skilful use of fresh herbs. The results are extremely successful, the flavours of the fresh fish coming through well. The menu is table d'hote (six starters, six main courses) and includes poultry, meat and vegetarian dishes.

Open all year except 1 to 12 Jan + Bank Holidays
Dining Room/Restaurant Lunch 12 - 2 pm Fri Sat only (b)
Private Lunch Parties - by arrangement
Pre-Theatre Supper until 7 pm (b) Mon to Sat
Dinner 6 - 9.30 pm Mon to Thu: 6 - 10 pm Fri Sat (d)
Closed Sun
Table Licence
Vegetarians welcome
Facilities for disabled visitors

Grilled seabass with tomato and corriander salsa. Fillet of snapper teriyaki. Pan-fried fillet of turbot, with a brandy and green peppercorn sauce. Fillet of beef with Lochaber smoked cheese, red wine and shallot sauce. Cullen Skink. White and dark chocolate terrine with strawberry coulis.

Credit cards: 1, 3, + Switch, + Delta
Proprietor: Calum Matheson

The Ubiquitous Chip

12 Ashton Lane
Glasgow G12 8SJ
Tel: 0141 334 5007
Fax: 0141 337 1302

A secluded lane off Byres Road in the heart of Glasgow's West End.

> One of Scotland's very fine award-winning traditional Scottish restaurants.

- A spectacular covered courtyard in a mews lane behind busy Byres Road.
- Modern Scottish cooking.
- "The 'Chip' represents all that is great about Glasgow - it is modern and stylish and could not be found in any other city in the world."

The Ubiquitous Chip, known affectionately by its regulars as 'The Chip', was established in 1971 by Ron Clydesdale. The winner of 1991 Macallan/Decanter Scottish Restaurant of the Year, it has been described as a 'legend in its own lunchtime'. It has also received a Michelin Red M, an award never before bestowed upon a Glasgow restaurant. The cuisine marries the traditional and original in innovative recipes and this variety is complemented by a wine list rated among the top 10 in Britain for quality and value.

Open all year except Christmas Day, 31 Dec + 1 Jan
Upstairs Restaurant 12 - 11 pm Mon to Sat: 12.30 - 11 pm Sun
Downstairs Restaurant 12 - 2.30 pm + 5.30 - 11 pm Mon to Sat: 12.30 - 2.30 pm + 6.30 - 11 pm Sun
Vegetarians welcome

Credit cards: 1, 2, 3, 5
Proprietor: Ron Clydesdale

Victoria & Albert

159 Buchanan Street
Glasgow G1 2JX
Tel: 0141 248 6329

Approach via Buchanan Street pedestrian precinct towards St Vincent Street or from West George Street, short distance from George Square.

> A popular restaurant in the heart of Glasgow.

- Bar-restaurant situated underneath the City Stock Exchange.
- Scottish/continental cooking.
- "The thought of lunch keeps me going in the morning but it is difficult to return to work..."

This is a busy basement restaurant and bar patronised, during the day, by business people with offices in the area and at night by a livelier crowd. The building has a Victorian elegance about it, and this is reflected in the interior decor. The bar menu offers a range of lighter meals and sandwiches and the restaurant excels in its confident range of continental and Scottish influenced dishes, presented with a freshness of style and accompanied by flavoursome sauces.

Open all year except Christmas + Boxing Days, 1 + 2 Jan, public holidays
Coffee/Snacks from 10 am except Sun (a)
Restaurant/Bar Menu 11 am - 10.30 pm except Sun (a-c)
Closed Sun
Vegetarians welcome
Children welcome in restaurant only

Warm tartlet of ricotta cheese and spinach set on a chive cream. Pot-roasted breast of pheasant wrapped in streaky bacon served with château potatoes. Gratin of fresh fruits with kirsch.

Credit cards: 1, 2, 3, 5 + SWITCH

Yes Bar and Restaurant

22 West Nile Street
Glasgow G1 2PW
Tel: 0141 221 8044
Fax: 0141 248 9159

City centre between Gordon Street and St Vincent Street. 2 minutes from Central and Queen Street Stations.

Ultra stylish city centre restaurant.

■ Restaurant with public and private dining room, bar and brasserie.
■ Modern Scottish cooking.
■ "An exquisite meal which amply demonstrated the talents of one of our Scottish Master Chefs."

Among his many accolades including Master Chef, Ferrier Richardson has led both the Scottish and British national culinary teams to international success in prestigious events. This new restaurant in Glasgow's fashionable city centre bears his stamp both in the high standards of the food and wine served and the venue's stylishness and originality. As you would expect, food is outstandingly good, embodying the distinctive approach and innovative techniques that have established Ferrier Richardson as a master. The finest of Scottish dishes emerge beautifully presented to delight the taste buds. His wine list complements the menu with a balance and choice of wines to suit varied budgets. Given the quality of what is on offer here, prices are more than reasonable.

Open all year
Note: Bar and Brasserie closed Christmas + Boxing Days, 1 + 2 Jan
Restaurant closed all public holidays
Bar Meals 12 - 7 pm except Sun (a)
Dining Room/Restaurant Lunch 12 - 2.30 pm except Sun (b)
Dinner 7 - 11 pm (d)
Restaurant + Brasserie closed Sun
Vegetarians welcome
Facilities for disabled visitors in Brasserie
Guide dogs only

Warm smoked Otter Ferry salmon, with cucumber and orange salad and dill vinaigrette. Gâteau of haggis, neeps and tatties with whisky butter sauce. Roast salmon with cracked pepper and ginger, spring onions and saffron fumet. Honey, Glayva and hazelnut parfait. Caramel and pear soufflé with chocolate sauce.

Credit cards: 1, 2, 3, 5, 6 + SWITCH
Proprietors: Ferrier Richardson & CCG Services

Glenelg

Glenelg Inn

Glenelg Bay, Glenelg, nr Shiel Bridge
Ross-shire IV40 8AG
Tel: 01599 522273
Fax: 01599 522373

Access to Glenelg via unclassified road west of A87 at Shiel Bridge, 1 mile from Kylerhea-Skye ferry which runs April to October.

A small village inn with bedrooms.

■ Unpretentious hotel in the pretty, isolated village of Glenelg.
■ Home cooking.
■ "The informal approach here matches the food which is the unpretentious taste of Scotland."

The Glenelg Inn, an old coaching mews overlooking the sea, is run by Chris Main. The rooms are clean and comfortable and individually decorated and the whole atmosphere is in keeping with this lovely isolated West Highland hamlet. The inn justifies its widespread reputation for food and hospitality, and you are likely to meet all kinds of interesting people there, both locals and long-distance travellers, in the friendly bar. Open fires and ceilidh potential on any night of the week. The cooking is unfussy; the menu table d'hôte (three starters; three main courses); the food all fresh and seasonal, and freshly prepared. Weather permitting, boat trips can be arranged around the sea lochs to the unspoiled beaches and hidden coves of this area.

Open Easter to end Oct + New Year
Rooms: 6 with private facilities
Bed & Breakfast £28 - £58
Dinner B & B £47 - £77
Special Rates for 4+ nights
Bar Lunch 12 - 2 pm (a)
Bar Supper 7 - 9 pm except Sun (a)
Dinner 7.30 - 9 pm (c)
Vegetarians welcome
Facilities for disabled visitors
No smoking in dining room

Courgette and pickled ginger soup. Fillet of hill-bred lamb roasted in an aniseed glaze served with a blackcurrant scented jus. Brandy-soaked apples baked in sugar and oatmeal.

No credit cards
Proprietor: Christopher Main

Glenfinnan

The Prince's House

Glenfinnan
Inverness-shire PH37 4LT
Tel: 01397 722 246
Fax: 01397 722 307

15 miles west of Fort William on A830 'Road to the Isles' ½ mile on right past Glenfinnan Monument.

An old coaching inn with a lovely position, serving good traditional food.

■ A former 17th century coaching inn on the 'Road to the Isles' in Glenfinnan.
■ Scottish home cooking.
■ "Fresh and appetising food which complements the position and exterior charm of the building."

Formerly The Stage House, this inn was established well before Bonnie Prince Charlie raised his standard - just down the road - in 1745. It is claimed that he may even have taken a dram at the inn as it was the only building in the immediate vicinity at that time! Carole and Robert Hawkes bought the place in 1990 and have thoroughly modernised it, and changed its name. Log fires enhance the peaceful and relaxed atmosphere of the hotel in winter. Good bar lunches and suppers are available, and 'Flora's Restaurant' offers a well-priced à la carte dinner which features local smoked and fresh fish, Scottish beef, lamb and venison. A blackboard lists specialities of the day, depending upon the seasonal availability of fresh produce.

Open mid Mar to 30 Nov + 28 Dec to 2 Jan incl
Rooms: 8 with private facilities
Bed & Breakfast £28 - £40
Dinner B & B £45 - £58
Special Rates for 7+ nights
Bar Lunch 12.30 - 2.30 pm (a)
Bar Supper 5 - 9 pm (a)
Dinner 6.30 - 8.30 pm (c)
Vegetarians welcome
No smoking in restaurant + rooms

Locally smoked meats, thinly sliced. Pheasant braised in cider and cream with raisins and apples. Lamb cutlets char-grilled with a gooseberry and mint sauce. Cranachan. Scottish cheeses.

STB Commended 4 Crowns
Credit cards: 1, 2, 3, + SWITCH, DELTA
Proprietors: Robert & Carole Hawkes

The Glenisla Hotel
Kirkton of Glenisla
Alyth, Perthshire
PH11 8PH
Tel: 01575 582223
Fax: 01575 582223

Alyth to Glenisla take B954 to junction B951, turn left. Hotel opposite church in village.

A 17th century coaching inn in a pretty glen.

- Historic old stone country inn.
- Imaginative home cooking.
- "A friendly, sporting local, serving excellent food."

Kirkton of Glenisla is two-thirds of the way up the glen, on the old Perth-Braemar coach route. The current inn buildings have been standing since at least 1750, and the inn itself may be older. Today it is a friendly local, with an excellent pub, and a tastefully decorated small restaurant, with Georgian windows overlooking the glen. Simon and Lyndy Blake are justifiably proud hosts and welcome their guests warmly. Lyndy's cooking is unfussy, imaginative and robust; best local produce, skillfully handled. Vegetarian dishes are offered at every meal.

Open all year except Christmas + Boxing Days
Rooms : 6 with private facilities
Bed & Breakfast £30 - £35
Dinner B & B £40 - £45
Bar Lunch 12.30 - 2.30 pm (a)
Bar Supper 6.30 - 8.45 pm (b)
Dinner 6.30 - 8.45 pm (b)
Vegetarians welcome
Facilities for disabled visitors

Orkney scallops steamed in white wine and shallots. Mushrooms and bacon served in a smoked salmon cornet. Breast of duck with a morello sauce. Wild brown trout with lemon. Casserole of Glenisla venison with apricots. Fruit compote served in a brandy-snap basket.

STB Commended 3 Crowns
Credit cards: 1, 3 + Delta
Proprietors: Simon & Lyndy Blake

Minmore House
Glenlivet, Ballindalloch
Banffshire AB37 9DB
Tel: 01807 590 378
Fax: 01807 590 472

On B9136, off B9008, 9 miles from Tomintoul. Adjacent to The Glenlivet Distillery.

A country house hotel in the heart of whisky country.

- Converted Scottish country house with fine views over the River Livet.
- Imaginative Scottish traditional cooking.
- "Surrounded by spectacular countryside it is a grand place to stay, yet not intimidating."

The original home of the founder of The Glenlivet distillery and standing adjacent to it, Minmore House lies in its own grounds close by the River Livet. The house retains very much the feel of a Scottish country house thanks to period furnishings and atmospheric decor. Roaring log fires and comfortable armchairs are welcoming features of the hotel's public rooms. Owner Belinda Luxmoore has earned a well-deserved reputation for the quality of her cooking. She draws her inspiration from the abundance of fresh locally produced ingredients and serves a set menu that is changed daily. The cheeseboard is something of a speciality with a wide selection of Scottish cheeses attractively presented. To finish the evening, guests have the pleasure of choosing a night-cap from over 100 malt whiskies stocked at the bar.

Open 1 May to 25 Oct
Rooms: 10 with private facilities
Bed & Breakfast £37 - £40 (incl afternoon tea)
Dinner B & B £50 - £60 (incl afternoon tea)
Special Rates for 3+ nights
Bar + Picnic Lunches can be arranged for residents
Dinner at 8 pm (d) 5 course set menu
Vegetarians welcome
No smoking in dining room

Home-made soups e.g. pea and mint, Cullen skink. Grilled monkfish provençale. Aberdeen Angus chateaubriand. Roast rack of Highland lamb with fresh mint and honey glaze. Fresh raspberry pavlova. Lochinora sabayon. Scottish cheeses.

STB Highly Commended 4 Crowns
Credit cards: 1, 3
Proprietor: Belinda Luxmoore

Balbirnie House Hotel
Balbirnie Park, Markinch by Glenrothes
Fife KY7 6NE
Tel: 01592 610066
Fax: 01592 610529

Prestige Award Winner 1991

Off A92 on B9130, follow directions to village of Markinch and Balbirnie Park.

A much praised country house hotel in the grand manner.

- Georgian country house, converted to a splendid small luxury hotel. Balbirnie has been awarded the AA's supreme accolade of 4 Red Stars.
- Elegant Scottish cooking, with strong French and continental influences.
- "Exceptional quality is Balbirnie's hallmark."

Built in 1777 and standing in a beautiful estate of 400 acres, Balbirnie is a Grade A Listed Building of great architectural and historic importance. Now owned and run by the Russell family, the house and grounds have been immaculately and lovingly restored. The restaurant overlooks fine formal gardens and ancient yew hedges. Chef Robert Macpherson upholds the hotel's reputation for fine dining and interesting dishes that use fresh and local produce. Balbirnie has won STB 5 Crowns Deluxe rating and, for the fourth time, the AA's 2 Rosettes Award. "There is an air of quiet, friendly efficiency pervading the whole establishment - outstanding." Member of the Scotch Beef Club.

Open all year
Rooms: 30 with private facilities
Bed & Breakfast £62.50 - £112.50
Dinner B & B £87.50 - £137.50
Room Rate £90 - £225
Bar Lunch 12 - 2.30 pm (b)
Dining Room/Restaurant Lunch 12 - 2.30 pm (b)
Dinner 7 - 9.30 pm (e) 4 course menu
Special Rates available
Vegetarians welcome

Warm salad of monkfish with crisp shallot rings and sauce vierge. Vanilla and sloe gin sorbet. Rump of lamb roasted, served with a tartlet of spinach and a garlic, sorrel, mint and cream sauce. Crisp Gressingham duck with a blackcurrant and cassis sauce.

STB Deluxe 5 Crowns
Credit cards: 1, 2, 3, 5 , 6
Proprietors: The Russell Family

Rescobie Hotel & Restaurant
Valley Drive, Leslie, Glenrothes
Fife KY6 3BQ
Tel: 01592 742143
Fax: 01592 620231

8 miles from M90 - just off A911 at west end of the village of Leslie.

> A small country house with a family atmosphere.

- Country house hotel.
- Country house cooking.
- "Rescobie has a comfortable, homely atmosphere, friendly staff and impressive cooking."

Rescobie is an unpretentious and comfortable small Listed country house, built in the 1920s and retaining something of the feel of that era, with antique furniture, comfortable armchairs and an open fire in the lounge. It stands in two acres of secluded gardens on the edge of the village of Leslie and is personally run by its friendly owners Tony and Wendy Hughes-Lewis. The hotel is rated 2 Star and the cuisine merits a Rosette from the AA and a merit award from the RAC. Chef Ian McEwan specialises in unusual and appropriate sauces on his menus (table d'hôte, à la carte and vegetarian); the flavours are positive and delicious. All meals are very reasonably priced. French and German spoken.

Open all year except 24 to 26 Dec
Rooms: 10 with private facilities
Bed & Breakfast £34 - £52
Dinner B & B £44 - £58
Special Rates for 3+ nights
Dining Room/Restaurant Lunch 12 - 2 pm (a-b)
Dinner 7 - 9 pm (c-d)
Vegetarians welcome
No dogs

Crab bisque. Avocado tartlet. Monkfish tail wrapped in bacon, set on a bed of vegetables and coated with a tarragon butter sauce. Venison with home-made rowanberry jelly and pickled walnuts. Fruit tartlets. Deep-fried ice cream.

STB Commended 4 Crowns
Credit cards: 1, 2, 3, 5
Proprietors: Tony & Wendy Hughes-Lewis

Dalmunzie House Hotel
Spittal of Glenshee, Blairgowrie
Perthshire PH10 7QG
Tel: 01250 885224
Fax: 01250 885225

18 miles north of Blairgowrie on A93. Turn left at Spittal of Glenshee, hotel 400 yards on left.

> The hotel in the hills.

- Country house hotel.
- Traditional Scottish cooking.
- "A lovely place for all the family. Friendly family-run hotel, with unpretentious home cooking and magnificent surroundings."

Dalmunzie House Hotel is a substantial Victorian baronial mansion standing in its own 6,500 acre mountain estate. It has its own 9-hole golf course (every Sunday there is a 'Golf Marathon', where non-golfers are partnered with good golfers); fishing, stalking and grouse shooting are available, and the ski slopes of Glenshee are not far away. The Winton family who own the hotel have lived in the glen for decades and are genuine and experienced hosts. The house has a wonderfully friendly atmosphere, with log fires and comfy chairs and is hospitable and informal - the tone set by Simon and Alexandra Winton. The menu is table d'hôte (four-five choices) with a couple of à la carte supplements. The cooking is homestyle but imaginative; everything is fresh and cooked to order.

Open 27 Dec to first wk Nov
Rooms: 17, 16 with private facilities
Bed & Breakfast £25 - £54
Dinner B & B £40 - £74
Special Rates available
Bar Lunch 12.30 - 1.50pm (a)
Dinner 7 - 8.30 winter: 7.30 - 8.30 pm summer (c)
Vegetarians welcome
Facilities for disabled visitors

Roast beef with Yorkshire pudding. Haunch of venison with a port and juniper sauce. Fillet of pork stuffed with haggis with a whisky sauce. Dressed Orkney crab with lemon and dill mayonnaise. Fresh Tay salmon wrapped in pastry with a fresh tarragon sauce.

STB Commended 3 Crowns
Credit cards: 1, 3
Proprietors: Simon & Alexandra Winton

Waterybutts Lodge
Grange, by Errol
Perthshire PH2 7SZ
Tel: 01821 642894
Fax: 01821 642894

A85 Perth-Dundee, 9 miles out of Perth take road for Grange. Then after 1½ miles turn left, immediately before railway crossing.

> A sporting lodge of great character.

- Georgian country house.
- Country house cooking.
- "An unusual and attractive building with a terrific atmosphere."

A Georgian house (1802) on the site of a 15th century friary - the doocot and a turreted stair are all that remain of this - standing in lovely gardens. The brochure says: "We are not a hotel. At Waterybutts the atmosphere is definitely 'House Party'." Shooting, stalking, fishing and golf can be laid on; a pony and trap, limousine and landrover are all at your disposal; guests dine together, at a 16 foot Charles I refectory table. Game is a speciality - all kinds are offered in season - accompanied by vegetables and herbs from the kitchen garden (which was created from Dutch soil, brought over as ballast, and which supplies Scotherbs). The set menu is posted before dinner, and alternatives can be prepared. Sporting parties are especially welcome.

Open all year
Rooms: 8 with private facilities
Bed & Breakfast £27.50 - £32.50
Dinner B & B £42.50 - £47.50
Dinner 7 - 10 pm (b) 4 course menu
Non residents by prior arrangement
Restricted Licence
Vegetarians welcome
No children

Cullen skink. Fresh trout pâté. Moules marinière. Roast haunch of venison. Tay salmon poached in herbs. All game in season.

STB Commended 3 Crowns
Credit cards: 1, 2, 3
Proprietors: Barry & Rachel Allenby-Wilcox

Grantown-on-Spey

Ardconnel House

Woodlands Terrace, Grantown-on-Spey
Moray PH26 3JU
Tel: 01479 872104
Fax: 01479 872104

On A95, south-west entry to town.

> A family run guest house in Grantown-on-Spey.

- Victorian villa guest house/hotel.
- Home cooking.
- "Friendly, efficient, capable service - like being at a dinner party!"

Built in 1890, Ardconnel House is a typical example of a Victorian villa, and this combines with the high standard of renovation and interior design that Jim and Barbara Casey have achieved to make for an attractive and comfortable place to stay. Their attention to detail is apparent throughout the house and this care extends also to the food, wines and whiskies on offer. Dinner is a nightly changing, small set menu, cooked in traditional style by Barbara and drawing on the local seasonal availability of produce. With the Spey practically on the doorstep, salmon and trout make regular appearances. Booking for dinner is advisable.

Open New Year + Easter to Oct
Rooms: 7 with private facilities
Bed & Breakfast £25 - £32
Dinner B & B £40 - £47
Special Rates available
Dinner 7 - 7.30 pm (b)
Residents only
Restricted Licence
Children over 10 years welcome
No smoking throughout

Home-made soups e.g. wild mushroom; carrot, leek and ginger. Buckie haddock in a mornay sauce. Venison in a wine and cream sauce. Wild Spey salmon. Roasts of beef, lamb, pork. Chicken and herbs. Sticky toffee pudding. Raspberry meringue. Fudge cake with foaming orange sauce.

STB Deluxe 3 Crowns
Credit cards: 1, 3
Proprietors: James & Barbara Casey

Culdearn House

Woodlands Terrace, Grantown-on-Spey
Moray PH26 3JU
Tel: 01479 872106
Fax: 01479 873641

On A95, south-west entry to Grantown-on-Spey.

> A country house on the outskirts of Grantown; AA 'Guest House of the Year' 1994, Leading Guide 'Hotel of the Year for the Highlands 1995', 'AA Inspectors Choice' for 1995.

- Victorian country house.
- Traditional home cooking.
- "At the heart of Culdearn lies the hospitality of the convivial hosts, who provide a great dinner, as if you were just a friend staying the night."

This charming deluxe establishment has achieved many accolades for the style in which it is run. Alasdair and Isobel Little are enthusiastic hosts, and quickly put their guests at ease. Their house itself is elaborately and expensively furnished throughout (the dining room to be completely refurbished for 1996); service is professional and attention to detail meticulous. Isobel is a talented chef and prepares local produce in classic Scots ways. Fifty malt whiskies now on offer and an interesting new wine list.

Open 1 Mar to 30 Oct
Rooms: 9 with private facilities
Dinner B & B from £49.50
Special Rates for 3+/7+ nights
Picnic Lunches to order
Dinner 6.45 - 7.30 pm (c)
Residents only
Restricted Licence
No smoking in dining room
No dogs

Carrot and coriander soup. Roast Moray lamb served with redcurrant, mint and orange jelly. Poached fillets of Strathspey salmon in a butter sauce. Wild Highland venison gently cooked in red wine. Prime Angus fillet steak pan-fried with mushrooms in cream and Drambuie. Plum and cinnamon crumble. Chocolate roulade.

STB Deluxe 3 Crowns
Credit cards: 1, 3, 5, 6 + SWITCH, DELTA
Proprietors: Alasdair & Isobel Little

Ravenscourt House Hotel

Seafield Avenue, Grantown-on-Spey
Moray PH26 3JG
Tel: 01479 872286
Fax: 01479 873260

Just off main Square.

> A former manse now converted to an elegant town hotel.

- Country house atmosphere in a delightful 19th century house.
- Traditional Scottish ingredients prepared using classic European influences.
- "The menu offers the opportunity to experiment with interesting and unusual combinations expertly prepared and presented."

Elegance is the keynote of this tastefully modernised former manse just off the town square. The award-winning Orangery Restaurant undoubtedly sets the tone for the hotel. Located in an attractive conservatory, it is beautifully appointed and instantly welcoming. Dinner is à la carte. All dishes are freshly prepared with imagination and flair and there is a distinctive European feel to the menu. There are excellent value house wines in an extensive wine list that caters for all tastes and budgets. Bistro lunch is also served in the Orangery making it an ideal family venue. RAC Restaurant Award 1994/95.

Open 31 Dec + 1 Mar to 1 Nov
Rooms: 9 with private facilities
Bed & Breakfast £35 - £40
Special Rates on application
Dining Room Lunch 12.30 - 2 pm except Sun Mon (a)
Dinner 7 - 9.30 pm Mon to Sat: Sun residents only (d) 4 course set menu
Vegetarians welcome
No smoking area in restaurant
Dogs by arrangement

Marinated seafood brochettes with lime and ginger dressing. Mushrooms in garlic and bacon served with garlic rosti. Aberdeen Angus fillet served with sauce béarnaise. Whole Dover sole served with a light sauce Mêuniere. Fresh mushroom en croûte with tarragon crème frâiche. Cranachan. Dark chocolate roulade filled with white chocolate and orange mousse.

STB Deluxe 3 Crowns
Credit cards: 1, 3

Golf Inn Hotel
Main Street, Gullane
East Lothian EH31 2AB
Tel: 01620 843259
Fax: 01620 842066

18 miles east of Edinburgh, 4 miles west of North Berwick.

Village hotel in East Lothian golfing resort.

- Old coaching inn.
- Scottish hotel cooking.
- "The emphasis here is on sound food and good beer!"

The Golf was originally a coaching inn; it has been completely refurbished and modernised by Kathleen and Tom Saddler, who have been its proprietors for over 12 years. It is situated in Gullane, one of Scotland's prettiest villages, as well as having been a golfing resort for over 200 years. One of the village's five courses is the world famous Muirfield Course, over which the British Open is often played. The Golf is a sound pub in the traditional mould - with a convivial bar, good beers and a choice of eating: informally in the Carriage Lounge, where a range of light snacks and bar meals is available, and in Saddlers Restaurant where a reliable range of robust and traditional food is offered.

Open all year except Christmas Day
Rooms: 18, 11 with private facilities
Bed & Breakfast £32 - £42
Dinner B & B £45 - £55
Bar Meals 12 - 10 pm (a-b)
Dining Room/Restaurant Lunch 12 - 6 pm Sun only (c)
Dinner 6.30 - 10 pm (c)
Vegetarians welcome
Restricted parking
Dogs by arrangement

Trio of fillets, pork, beef and venison with a red wine, whisky and pink peppercorn sauce. Half rack of lamb roasted with honey, rosemary scented breadcrumbs, with a rich port sauce. Poached Scottish salmon garnished with smoked salmon in a lobster sauce.

STB Commended 2 Crowns
Credit cards: 1, 3, 5
Proprietors: Tom & Kathleen Saddler

Greywalls
Muirfield, Gullane
East Lothian EH31 2EG
Tel: 01620 842144
Fax: 01620 842241

At the eastern end of Gullane village (on the A198), signposted left as a historic building.

First-rate food and accommodation in a building of national importance on the edge of Muirfield. Just outside the golfing paradise of Gullane.

- An Edwardian architectural masterpiece.
- Refined country house cuisine.
- "A refreshing combination of well-chosen ingredients, interestingly blended with a deft hand and creative flair."

This charming, grand but understated house was designed at the turn of the century by Sir Edwin Lutyens and his collaborator Gertrude Jekyll to be a holiday home for the Hon Alfred Lyttelton. It was one of the architect's favourite buildings and is deservedly listed as being of national importance. It became an hotel in 1948, and is still family owned. Greywalls has a wonderful situation overlooking Muirfield Golf Course and the Firth of Forth. The hotel's lovely walled garden complements the serenity of the house itself, which still has the feel of a family home: relaxed, refined, elegant... a perfect backdrop for the discreetly attentive service one meets with in this distinguished hotel. Chef Paul Baron's menus are table d'hôte. His cooking is deft and light, with classical influences: "a refreshing combination of well-chosen ingredients, interestingly blended." The wine list is exceptional, since the present owner's father had the foresight to lay down some especially fine vintages.

Open mid Apr to mid Oct
Rooms: 22 with private facilities
Bed & Breakfast £75 - £95
Bar Lunch 12.30 - 2 pm except Sun (b)
Dining Room/Restaurant Lunch 12.30 - 2 pm (c)
Dinner 7.30 - 9.15 pm (f)
No smoking in dining room
Facilities for disabled visitors
Vegetarians welcome - prior notice required

Duck and green lentil terrine with Cumberland sauce and toasted brioche. Casserole of seafood with noodles and lime butter sauce. Hot passion fruit soufflé with blackcurrant sauce.

STB Highly Commended 4 Crowns
Credit cards: 1, 2, 3, 5 + SWITCH
Proprietors: Giles & Ros Weaver

Maitlandfield House Hotel
24 Sidegate, Haddington
East Lothian EH41 4BZ
Tel: 01620 826513
Fax: 01620 826713

Haddington on A1, take route to town centre. At east end of High Street take Sidegate (signposted Gifford and Lauder B6368) - about 300 yards - opposite St Mary's church.

Close to the centre of East Lothian's county town, this large modern hotel offers a high degree of comfort and two restaurants.

- A recently renovated and expanded large town house.
- Modern and classic Scottish cooking.
- "From bistro snacks to table d'hôte, familiar to original, formal or informal - all tastes are catered for."

Maitlandfield House Hotel is set in landscaped gardens within minutes of the centre of Haddington. The hotel has been completely refurbished in the last few years to provide high standards of accommodation and facilities. The 16 Kings Restaurant - named after the number of kings who have visited Haddington since 1124 - has a tent-like, canopied ceiling and offers candlelit dinner on polished wooden tables. The table d'hôte menus here use fresh local produce and are Scottish/French in style. Dishes are well-balanced and presented and avoid heavy sauces. The Conservatory Bistro is more informal. Bistro-style cooking 'for all the family,' the hotel also has a beer garden and children's play area.

Open all year
Rooms: 22 with private facilities
Bed & Breakfast £35 - £65
Dinner B & B £50 - £75
Special Breaks available
Conservatory Meals 12 - 9 pm Mon to Thurs: 12 - 9.30 pm Fri to Sun (a-b)
Dinner (16 Kings Restaurant) 7 - 9 pm Tue to Thu: 7 - 9.30 pm Fri Sat (d)
Facilities for disabled visitors
Vegetarians welcome

Fresh mussels cooked in elderflower Champagne and Cointreau, wrapped in smoked salmon with lemon dressing and seasonal leaves. Highland beef fillet cooked in truffle oil, topped with foie gras served with a Madeira sauce. Fresh berries and soft fruit glazed under a ginger wine sabayon.

Credit cards: 1, 2, 3, 6 + SWITCH, DELTA
Proprietor: Alan Berry

Mansfield House Hotel

Weensland Road, Hawick
Roxburghshire TD9 8LB
Tel: 01450 373988
Fax: 01450 372007

On the A698 Hawick to Kelso road. On the outskirts of the town.

An attractive mansion on the outskirts of Hawick.

- Family-run small country house hotel.
- Traditional Scottish cooking, using classical techniques.
- "Just within the town, but with a country house feel."

A Victorian mansion overlooking the River Teviot and the town itself and standing in 10 acres of well kept terraced lawns and mature shrubs and trees. Approached by a private drive, the hotel is secluded and quiet, yet it is within walking distance of the town centre. The building retains many of its original features - panelled doors, open fireplaces, ornate plasterwork - and a modern extension provides a large open bar and terrace. Chef David Tate presents well-priced à la carte and 'business lunch' menus in the formal dining room, and bar meals are also available. As well as the usual grills, the à la carte menu features some unusual combinations and meats (hare, kid, duck livers).

Open all year except Boxing Day + 1, 2 Jan
Rooms: 12 with private facilities
Bed & Breakfast £30 - £55
Dinner B & B £45 - £75
Special Weekend Rates available
Bar Lunch 12 - 2 pm (a)
Dining Room/Restaurant Lunch 12 - 1.45 pm (b)
Bar Supper 5.30 - 9 pm Mon to Sat: 5.30 - 8 pm Sun (a)
Dinner 7 - 9 pm Mon to Sat: 7 - 8 pm Sun (c)
Vegetarians welcome
No smoking area in restaurant

Loch Fyne smoked salmon. Haunch of venison. Salmon oven-poached in white wine with a cream butter sauce. Border beef steaks. Traditional puddings with a modern flair.

STB Commended 3 Crowns
Credit cards: 1, 2, 3, 5
Proprietors: Sheila & Ian MacKinnon

Whitchester Christian Guest House

Borthaugh, Hawick
Roxburghshire TD9 7LN
Tel: 01450 377477
Fax: 01450 371080

¼ mile off A7, 2 miles south of Hawick on B711 to Roberton.

A former Dower House on the Buccleuch Estate.

- Peaceful small country house in its own grounds.
- Home cooking.
- "Warm, charming and cheerful."

The circumstances which guided David Maybury, an Episcopal priest, and his wife Doreen (now a Deacon), to establish a place where 'people could go and feel loved...pampered' are extraordinary, but ten years ago they achieved their goal. Whitchester House was established as a Christian Centre with charitable status. Everything here - the growing of vegetables and fruit in the garden, the preparation of local game, the cooking and baking (by Doreen), the waiting (by David) - is done 'For the Greater Glory of God'. And it shows: the friendliness and thoughtfulness, cheerfulness and warmth, is palpable. And the cooking is blessed!

Open Feb to Dec
Rooms: 8, 4 with private facilities
Dinner B & B £27 - £36
Dining Room/Restaurant Lunch 12.30 - 1.30 pm (a)
Full Afternoon Tea 4.30 - 5 pm
Dinner 6.30 - 8 pm (b) 4 course menu
Unlicensed
Vegetarians welcome
No smoking in dining room, bedrooms + conservatory

Home-made soups, pâtés and bread. Salmon. Poached trout. Grouse, pheasant, venison. Local fruit cranachans, syllabubs. Original desserts. Vegetarian dishes a speciality, using home-grown vegetables.

STB Commended 3 Crowns
Credit cards: 1, 3
Proprietors: David & Doreen Maybury

Navidale House Hotel

Helmsdale
Sutherland KW8 6JS
Tel: 01431 821258
Fax: 01431 821531

On A9, ½ mile north of Helmsdale.

A country house hotel in its own gardens overlooking the Moray Firth.

- Comfortable and friendly small hotel in dramatic Sutherland.
- Excellent home cooking with flair.
- "The best of the old and the new."

Built as a shooting lodge for the Dukes of Sutherland in the 1830s, Navidale retains that atmosphere. Public rooms are elegant, spacious and well-appointed. Set in five acres of woodland and garden that lead down to the sea, the hotel affords dramatic views over the Moray Firth and the Ord of Caithness alongside modern comforts. Chef and co-proprietor Marcus Blackwell's menus make good use of the fine supply of local seafood, Highland lamb, beef and game. The hotel's own kitchen garden supplies fresh vegetables in season.

Open 1 Feb to 5 Nov
Rooms: 15 with private facilities
Bed & Breakfast £25 - £35
Dinner B & B £50 - £60
Special Rates for 3+ nights
Bar Lunch 12 - 2 pm (a)
Dining Room/Restaurant Lunch - by arrangement
Dinner 6.45 - 8.45 pm (d)
Vegetarians welcome
No smoking in restaurant

Wild mushrooms with smoked ham and leeks in a light cream and garlic sauce in a puff pasry case. Fresh local halibut with a red pepper, tomato and basil sauce. Roast loin of lamb in a herb crust served with a red wine jus.

STB Commended 3 Crowns
Credit cards: 1, 3
Proprietor: Marcus Blackwell

Humbie nr Edinburgh

Johnstounburn House Hotel
Humbie
East Lothian EH36 5PL
Tel: 01875 833696
Fax: 01875 833626

From A68 Edinburgh-Jedburgh 2 miles south
of Pathhead, turn at Fala (hotel is signposted) -
2 miles on right.

A peaceful, charming country house hotel only
15 miles from Edinburgh.

■ A beautifully restored and maintained Scottish
  baronial mansion
■ Scottish cuisine.
■ "A hotel of grace and courtesy."

Built below the rolling Lammermuir Hills in 1625,
Johnstounburn House stands in its own extensive,
lovely grounds. The staff are welcoming and
friendly, as is the ambience - open log fires,
panelled and comfortable rooms. The hotel is a
Thistle Country House Hotel. The table d'hôte
dishes are excellent, making the most of good, local
produce. The wine list is large - 70 bins - and
concentrates on French and European wines.

Open all year
Rooms: 20 with private facilities
Bed & Breakfast £47.50 - £110
Dinner B & B £75 - £137.50
Special Weekend Rates available
Bar Lunch 12 - 2 pm (a)
Dining Room/Restaurant Lunch 12 - 2 pm (b)
Dinner 7 - 9 pm (e)
Vegetarians welcome

Poached délice of Scottish salmon with a tomato
and dill cream sauce. Roast noisettes of Border
lamb with à mint and cucumber sauce. Pan-fried
medallions of prime Aberdeen Angus beef with a
coarse grain mustard sauce.

STB Commended 4 Crowns
Credit cards: 1, 2, 3, 5

by Huntly

The Old Manse of Marnoch
Bridge of Marnoch
by Huntly AB54 5RS
Tel: 01466 780873
Fax: 01466 780873

On B9117, 1 mile off A97 midway between
Huntly and Banff.

A small country house hotel on the river
Deveron in unspoilt Aberdeenshire.

■ Secluded and peaceful, a small hotel of rare
  distinction.
■ Outstanding creative cuisine.
■ "A destination for the discerning traveller."

Remarkable for its solitude and peace, this fine
Georgian house was built in the 1780s as the manse
for the ministers of Marnoch Old Church. Its
owners Patrick and Keren Carter have preserved the
Georgian elegance in a tasteful and sympathetic
conversion to an intimate country house hotel.
Using fresh local produce and, in season, herbs and
vegetables from their own four acre garden, Keren
Carter deserves her growing reputation for
imaginative, fine cooking. Her four course dinner
changes every day. Her breakfasts are unrivalled.
For a small establishment, the wine list is a
triumph, both familiar and adventurous and
always reasonably priced. Fluent German spoken.
Dogs welcome, but not in the dining room.

Open all year except 2 wks Oct/Nov
Rooms: 5 with private facilities
Bed & Breakfast £38.25 - £60
Dinner B & B £63.25 - £85
Special Rates available
Picnic lunch - as requested (a)
Dining Room/Restaurant Lunch - residents
only by request (b)
Afternoon Tea - residents only (a)
Dinner 7.30 for 8 pm (d) 4 course menu
Reservations essential for non-residents
Vegetarians welcome - prior notice required
No smoking in dining room

Meg Dods' 'high-flavoured onion soup'. Game
consommé. Home-cured gravlax. Galia melon with
smoked Argyll ham and red pepper mayonnaise.
Barbecued darne of Deveron salmon with
cucumber and crème fràiche. Fillet of Aberdeen
Angus with wild mushrooms. Bitter lemon tart.
Three-gooseberry pavlova.

STB Deluxe 3 Crowns
Credit cards: 1, 3
Proprietors: Patrick & Keren Carter

Innerleithen

Traquair Arms Hotel
Traquair Road, Innerleithen
Peeblesshire EH44 6PD
Tel: 01896 830229
Fax: 01896 830260

On A72 midway between Peebles and
Galashiels. Midway along Innerleithen High
Street take B709 Yarrow. Hotel 150 yards on left.

An attractive town house hotel in Innerleithen
in the Scottish Borders.

■ An attractive Victorian village inn.
■ Modern Scottish cooking
■ "Wonderfully cooked Angus steak washed down
  with a locally brewed ale."

A pleasant family-owned hotel close to the centre of
this small Borders town. It is a sturdy stone
building in a quiet street with a well-kept garden.
The town, made famous by Sir Walter Scott, is
popular with visitors, especially those looking for
the cashmeres and tweeds for which these parts are
renowned. Hugh and Marian Anderson run their
hotel in a relaxed and friendly manner with
genuine concern for the comfort of their guests.
Imaginative table d'hôte menus use fresh local
produce, and everything is cooked to order. You can
eat, depending on the weather, in the charming
secluded garden or beside the blazing fire in the
dining room. The bar prides itself in its real ales
and there is a range of lighter meals available all
day.

Open all year except Christmas + Boxing Days,
1 + 2 Jan
Rooms: 10 with private facilities
Bed & Breakfast £32 - £42
Dinner B & B £46 - £56
Special Rates for 2+ nights
All day menu 12 - 9 pm (a)
Dinner 7 - 9 pm except Mon Tue (c) - four
course menu
Vegetarians welcome

Hot smoked salmon with tomato and horseradish
sauce. Aberdeen Angus steaks. Salmon poached in
orange and lemon juice with tarragon and cream.
Scottish cheeseboard.

STB Commended 3 Crowns
Credit cards: 1, 2, 3, 5 + SWITCH, DELTA
Proprietors: Hugh & Marian Anderson

110

Inverkeilor

Gordon's Restaurant
Homewood House, Main Street
Inverkeilor, by Arbroath
Angus DD11 5RN
Tel: 01241 830364

Cottage-style restaurant with two rooms.

■ Victorian terrace house.
■ Classic/Scottish cooking.
■ "This is unashamed classic cooking at its best."

This small restaurant is run by Maria and Gordon Watson and their son Garry. They took it over as a bed and breakfast establishment and have now built up a reputation for excellent food. Gordon was a head waiter and manager in hotels before opening here and Maria is a trained pâtissèrie chef. He has a flair and a sound sense of showmanship, having trained classic flambé cooking at diner's tables. Being so close to Arbroath and Lunan Bay, Gordon's Restaurant has access to fresh catches; soft fruits come from the berry fields which surround them; herbs from their own herb garden. Everything is cooked from scratch, using the classic recipes which were familiar in large hotels 20 years ago. The à la carte menu changes regularly according to seasonal availablity and the range of dishes covers the spectrum of good Scottish foods.

Open all year except last 2 wks Jan
Rooms: 2 with private facilities
Bed & Breakfast £25 - £28
Dinner B & B £45 - £50
Room Rate £25 - £28
Bar Lunch 12 - 2.30 pm except Mon (a)
Dining Room/Restaurant Lunch 12 - 2.30 pm except Mon (a)
Bar Supper 6 - 9.15 pm except Mon Sat (a)
Dinner 7 - 9.15 pm except Mon (c)
Closed Mon - residents only
Vegetarians welcome
Facilities for disabled visitors
No smoking area in restaurant

King scallops served in shell with white wine sauce and sliced mushrooms. Scampi poached in Noilly Prat and cream sauce, served with pilaff rice. Chicken with cider, apples and cream flamed in Calvados. Sirloin steak grilled and served with wild rosemary butter.

STB Commended 2 Crowns
Credit cards: 1, 3
Proprietors: Gordon & Maria Watson

111

Invermoriston

Glenmoriston Arms Hotel
Invermoriston, Glenmoriston
Inverness-shire IV3 6YA
Tel: 01320 51206

At junction of A82 and A887 in Invermoriston.

A country hotel with a village inn atmosphere; ideal location for country sports and holidays.

■ A traditional coaching inn in Glenmoriston for over 200 years.
■ Traditional Scottish cooking.
■ "Confident use of the seasonally available game and fish from the area, cooked in interesting ways."

The Glenmoriston Arms is a modern hotel within a traditional coaching inn. It has a glorious situation - surrounded by the wonderful mountain scenery of the Glenmoriston Estate, at the junction of the main routes to Inverness and Kyle of Lochalsh, close to Loch Ness - and offers access to all the country pursuits for which this area is so popular. This is a family run hostelry, simply furnished, and having eight bedrooms (all equipped with en suite bathrooms, colour TV, direct dial telephones, etc). The restaurant serves a huge range of national and regional food on its seasonally changing menu. The Cocktail Bar offers around 100 malt whiskies.

Open all year except Christmas Day
Rooms: 8 with private facilities
Bed & Breakfast £30 - £45
Dinner B & B £47 - £62
Special Rates for 3/7 nights
Bar Lunch 12 - 2 pm (a)
Dining Room/Restaurant Lunch - prior booking required
Bar Supper 5.30 - 8.30 pm (a)
Dinner 6.30 - 8.30 pm (c)
Vegetarians welcome

Local haggis with a whisky and chive sauce. Roast rack of lamb with a rosemary and light port wine sauce. Grilled West Coast turbot with a light orange and watercress sauce.

STB Commended 4 Crowns
Credit cards: 1, 3
Proprietor: Alan Draper

112

Inverness

Bunchrew House Hotel
Bunchrew
Inverness IV3 6TA
Tel: 01463 234917
Fax: 01463 710620

On A862 Inverness-Beauly, c. 10 minutes from centre of Inverness.

A country house hotel on the Beauly Firth.

■ 17th century mansion.
■ Country house cooking.
■ "First rate menu. Not for the faint-hearted or culinarily-challenged!"

Bunchrew House is a short way out of Inverness nestling on the shores of the Beauly Firth, in 20 acres of woodland. The house dates back to 1621 when it was built by the 8th Lord Lovat, whose marriage the same year is commemorated by a stone fireplace lintel in the drawing room. Stewart and Lesley Dykes are continuing to renovate this lovely house and their painstaking attention to detail is apparent throughout the public and private rooms. Menus are innovative and interesting, and, like the rest of the house, the attention to detail is painstaking. Chef Walker's cooking embraces a variety of traditional and modern styles, with a penchant for deliciously complex sauces. Member of the Scotch Beef Club.

Open all year
Rooms: 11 with private facilities
Bed & Breakfast £40 - £70
Dinner B & B £65 - £95
Dining Room/Restaurant Lunch 12 - 2 pm (b)
Dinner 7 - 9 pm (d)
Vegetarians welcome
Facilities for disabled visitors
No smoking in dining room

Scallop terrine with lemon beurre blanc. Guinea fowl tourte with Madeira sauce. Black Isle lamb. Calamari filled with a langoustine mousseline. Praline cheesecake with honey ice cream. Spiced poached plums with a lime sorbet.

STB Highly Commended 4 Crowns
Credit cards: 1, 2, 3
Proprietors: Stewart & Lesley Dykes

Culloden House Hotel

Culloden
nr Inverness IV1 2NZ
Tel: 01463 790461
Fax: 01463 792181
Toll-free fax from USA: 1 800 373 7987

Take A96 from Inverness. In 1 mile take road signed to Culloden at Culloden House Avenue. 5 miles from Inverness Airport.

Historic and deluxe country house hotel.

- Georgian Palladian mansion.
- Country house cooking.
- "The hotel has been favourably compared to some of Europe's best and on the whole the food matches up to this claim."

This is an upmarket country house hotel with lovely grounds. The atmosphere is formal and there is a majestic splendour and romance about the place. For many years the house was the seat of the Forbes' of Culloden, a prominent Whig family, and it was occupied by the Jacobite army in 1745. Bonnie Prince Charlie buckled on his sword here before setting off to the battle which ruined his cause. The early 16th century house was later destroyed by fire, and was rebuilt according to designs by Robert Adam - evident in the restrained interior detailing, ornate ceilings and the neo-classical symmetry. Chef Michael Simpson unites classic and Scottish traditions in his cooking and presents opulent and original dishes created from fresh produce. Member of the Scotch Beef Club.

Open all year
Rooms: 23 with private facilities incl 4 non-smoking Garden Suites in the grounds
Dining Room/Restaurant Lunch 12.30 - 2 pm (c)
Dinner 7 - 9 pm (f)
Room Rate £125 - £220
Vegetarians welcome

Warm filo pastry parcel of scallops and smoked salmon served with a creamed dill sauce. Medallions of fillet of beef coated with a cheese sauce, topped with forestière mushrooms. Paupiettes of salmon with julienne of vegetables on a creamed chervil sauce. Baked hot sorrel and onion tart.

STB Deluxe 5 Crowns
Credit cards: 1, 2, 3, 5, 6 + SWITCH
Proprietors: Ian & Marjory McKenzie

Dunain Park Hotel

Dunain Park
Inverness IV3 6JN
Tel: 01463 230512
Fax: 01463 224532

A82, 1 mile west of Inverness.

A country house hotel in a beautiful setting, offering outstanding cuisine, cooked by a Master Chef.

- A handsome 19th century 'Georgian Italianate' hunting lodge, in six acres of parkland, overlooking the Caledonian Canal and the River Ness.
- First rate Scottish cooking, with assured French influences.
- "A true country house hotel: beautifully furnished without being oppressive, exceptionally good food and a warm welcome."

Dunain Park is a fine Georgian country house, standing in six acres of gardens and woodlands, overlooking the Caledonian Canal. The large kitchen garden supplies herbs, vegetables and soft fruit. Ann and Edward Nicoll have won a high reputation for their establishment and several awards. Public and private rooms are immaculately furnished - and there is an indoor swimming pool and sauna. But it is for its food that Dunain is particularly renowned. Ann Nicoll is self-taught, with spells of training in France and encouragement from the famous John Tovey of Miller Howe. She goes to great length to source top quality local produce - the only beef she will use is from Highland cattle - and her style of cooking brings out the flavour of fresh produce, and enhances it with wonderfully assured sauces.

Open all year except 3 wks Jan/Feb
Rooms: 14 with private facilities
Bed & Breakfast £55 - £75
Dinner B & B £75 - £99
Special Rates for 2+ nights Oct to Apr
Dining Room/Restaurant Lunch 12.30 - 1.30 pm (c) 5 course menu - booking essential
Dinner 7 - 9 pm (d) 5 course menu
Vegetarians welcome
No smoking in dining room

Turnip and pine kernel soup. Fillet of Lochinver halibut served on buttered spinach. Saddle of lamb cooked pink, topped with a mushroom duxcelle, wrapped in pastry and served with a mint bearnaise.

STB Deluxe 4 Crowns
Credit cards: 1, 2, 3, 5, 6 + SWITCH, DELTA
Proprietors: Ann & Edward Nicoll

Glen Mhor Hotel & Restaurant

Ness Bank
Inverness IV2 4SG
Tel: 01463 234308
Fax: 01463 713170

On river bank below castle.

Family-run hotel in Inverness.

- Victorian town house.
- Scottish cooking.
- "An elaborate menu prepared in a manner that obviously requires great professional culinary skills."

The family run Glen Mhor Hotel is situated in the centre of Inverness just below the castle. It is a large 19th century town house which offers full private facilities in its 30 bedrooms, which are chintzy and mellow, some with four posters. The public rooms are comfortable and furnished with a baronial Scottish theme. The Riverview Seafood Restaurant, overlooking the River Ness, offers an extensive à la carte menu (in French) stressing seafood, but with other meat and game choices. The Bistro, Nico's, which offers a less complex range of dishes, from char-grilled steaks to traditional Scottish dishes, vegetarian options available.

Open all year except 31 Dec to 3 Jan
Rooms: 30 with private facilities
Bed & Breakfast £35 - £65
Dinner B & B £49 - £85
Special Rates available Oct to Apr
Note: Restaurant closed Sun evenings Oct to Apr
Bistro Lunch (Nico's) 12 - 2.15 pm (a-b)
Lunch (Riverview Restaurant) 12.30 - 2 pm by prior arrangement
Bistro Supper (Nico's) 5 - 10.30 pm (a-c)
Dinner (Riverview Restaurant) 6.30 - 9 pm (d)
Vegetarians welcome

Seafood bistro. Haggis in a filo pouch with purée of carrots, neeps and a whisky and onion sauce. Pan-fried collops of venison with a sherry vinegar, red wine and juniper berry sauce. Grand cold seafood platter - 'House' speciality.

STB Commended 4 Crowns
Credit cards: 1, 2, 3, 5, + SWITCH
Proprietors: Nicol & Beverley Manson

Glendruidh House Hotel

by Castle Heather
Old Edinburgh Road South
Inverness IV1 2AA
Tel: 01463 226499
Fax: 01463 710745

2 miles from Inverness centre. ½ mile south of Sir Walter Scott Drive (formerly Inverness southern distributor road).

A quiet oasis two miles from Inverness, with extensive grounds, comfortably furnished bedrooms, and good quality cooking.

- A most unusual building, dating mainly from the 1850s.
- Traditional Scottish cooking.
- "Deceptively simple traditional fare using fresh local produce, well-presented with charming service."

This is an unusual and attractive small country house set in three acres of woodland and lawns overlooking the Moray Firth: seclusion and privacy within minutes of Inverness, and with two golf courses close by. This is a haven for non-smokers - smoking is prohibited even in the grounds. The Druid's Glen Bar provides an excellent range of whiskies and the relaxing sitting room has the unusual feature of being completely circular, its windows and doors shaped to the contour of the room. The elegant dining room (residents only) has an Italian marble fireplace and overlooks the tidy gardens. Christine Smith's simple table d'hôte menus change daily and offer classic dishes employing local game and fish.

Open all year
Rooms: 7 with private facilities
Bed & Breakfast £25 - £50
Dinner B & B £54.50 - £69.50
Special Rates available for 3/7 nights
Dining Room/Restaurant Lunch 12 - 2 pm (c)
Dinner 7 - 10.30 pm (c)
Residents only
Vegetarians welcome
Facilities for disabled visitors
No smoking throughout
No dogs

Chicken and spring onion soup. Baked rainbow trout filled with assorted wild mushrooms. Roast haunch of hill venison with wild rowan sauce. Strawberry flan and cream.

STB Highly Commended 3 Crowns
Credit cards: 1, 2, 3, 5
Proprietors: Christine & Michael Smith

Moyness House

6 Bruce Gardens
Inverness IV3 5EN
Tel: 01463 233836
Fax: 01463 233836

From A9 (north + south) and A862 Beauly, follow signs for A82 Fort William holiday route. Through Tomnahurich Street to Glenurquhart Road (A82), turn into Bruce Gardens diagonally opposite Highland Regional Council offices.

Lovely Victorian house in the centre of Inverness.

- A detached villa built in 1880, formerly the home of Neil Gunn, the celebrated Scottish author.
- First class home cooking.
- "Classic dishes treated with a deft, light touch by a talented cook."

Moyness House is situated in a quiet residential part of Inverness, within ten minutes walk of the town centre and Eden Court Theatre. It is tastefully decorated and appointed in a way which respects the Victorian nature of the house, and retains its elegance. The bedrooms are charmingly decorated and have en suite facilities; the principal rooms are smart and spacious. A large garden to the rear of the house is also available for guests to enjoy. Moyness is family-run by Nonna and Michael Jones. Nonna is responsible for the cooking and her daily changing menus show flair and imagination. She goes to great lengths to source high quality Scottish produce, and treats her ingredients imaginatively, within a classic context - just as her many regular guests like it!

Open all year except 23 Dec to 3 Jan
Rooms: 7 with private facilities
Bed & Breakfast £25 - £29
Dinner B & B £41 - £45
Special Rates available
Dinner 6.30 - 7.30 pm (b)
Residents only
Restricted Licence
Vegetarians welcome
No smoking in restaurant

Fillet of salmon with sun-dried tomato sauce and braised Puy lentils. Medallions of venison with red wine sauce and onion marmalade. Warm spicy apple cake with orange cream cheese sauce.

STB Deluxe 3 Crowns
Credit cards: 1, 2, 3 + DELTA
Proprietors: Nonna & Michael Jones

Restaurant No 1

Greig Street, Inverness
Inverness-shire IV3 5PC
Tel: 01463 716363
Fax: 01463 234125

Centrally situated on the corner of Greig Street/Huntly Street, on the banks of the Ness.

A small congenial restaurant on the banks of the Ness.

- Restaurant specialising in fish.
- Modern Scottish cooking.
- "It is not surprising the visitors book is so full of superlatives!"

This comfortable and intimate L-shaped restaurant is on the corner of Greig Street/Huntly Street, on the west bank of the River Ness in the capital of the Highlands. It was formerly a shop and has fine views of the river, the old town and the castle. Now it has been refurbished in a style in keeping with the building and has a cosy atmosphere, somewhat Victorian. Fergus and Avril Ewart specialise in fresh west coast seafood - lobsters, crabs and langoustines, crabs and scallops, halibut and turbot. Lamb and beef is also offered on the daily changing à la carte menu.

Open all year except 25, 26, 30, 31 Dec + 1, 2 Jan
Restaurant Lunch 12.30 - 2.30 pm except Sun (b)
Dinner 6.30 - 9.30 pm Mon to Thu: 6.30 - 10.15 pm Fri Sat (d)
Dinner earlier/later by arrangement
Closed Sun
Vegetarians welcome
Facilities for disabled visitors
No smoking in restaurant

Casserole of wild salmon, west coast scallops and halibut in a saffron and ginger cream. Sautéed shelled Lochinver lobster with a timbale of wild rice and a Madeira and shellfish reduction. Roast boneless quails with a shallot and woodland mushroom stuffing and port wine essence. Fillet of Sutherland lamb pan-fried in rosemary with a celeriac rosti and redcurrant and mint glaze. Toasted oatmeal and honey ice cream with raspberries and flavoured with The Macallan Malt.

Credit cards: 1, 3 + SWITCH
Proprietors: Fergus & Avril Ewart

Isle of Arran

Auchrannie Country House Hotel

Auchrannie Road, Brodick
Isle of Arran KA27 8BZ
Tel: 01770 302234
Fax: 01770 302812

One mile north of Brodick Ferry Terminal and 400 yards from Brodick Golf Club.

Country house hotel and leisure centre in Brodick.

- 19th century mansion, with substantial additions.
- Country house cooking.
- "Every choice of dining is catered for here and dinner in the conservatory restaurant is the perfect evening."

Auchrannie House is a pink sandstone Victorian country house, formerly the home of the Dowager Duchess of Hamilton. Today it has been fully refurbished in a reproduction period style with modern comforts. A number of self-catering 'lodges' have been built in the grounds, STB Deluxe 5 Crowns, (each accommodating up to six people), also a state-of-the-art leisure complex with 20m pool. Brambles Bistro is a popular venue for families and snacks, and the Garden Restaurant (which extends the original dining room with a conservatory) offers more formal dining. The sizeable table d'hôte menu offers a good range of local Scottish meat and fish dishes complemented by fresh vegetables and a daily vegetarian speciality.

Open all year
Rooms: 28 with private facilities
Bed & Breakfast £27 - £52.50
Dinner B & B £42.50 - £72
Lunch (Brambles Bistro) 12 - 2.30 pm (a)
Dinner (Brambles Bistro) 5 - 9.30 pm (b)
Dinner (Garden Restaurant) 6.30 - 9.30 pm (d)
Vegetarians welcome
No smoking in Garden Restaurant
No dogs except in lodges

Grilled suprême of turbot with a lobster ravioli on a basil and garlic sauce. Roast saddle of venison with a wild mushroom parfait set on a tarragon and port wine essence. Cutlet and loin of lamb topped with a spinach and basil mousse on a rosemary and garlic scented jus.

STB Highly Commended 5 Crowns
Credit cards: 1, 2, 3 + SWITCH
Proprietor: Iain Johnston

Creelers Seafood Restaurant

The Home Farm, Brodick
Isle of Arran KA27 8DD
Tel: 01770 302810
Fax: 01770 302797

Prestige Award Winner 1993

From Brodick Pier, go north following coast road towards Brodick Castle and Corrie for 1½ miles. Restaurant on right.

A fish restaurant within the Arran Visitors Centre.

- Sophisticated seafood bistro.
- Fish and Modern Scottish cooking.
- "The best restaurant I have been to this year."

Creelers Seafood Restaurant is based in the old bothy of the Brodick Castle home farm. Tim and Fran James have established it as an excellent seafood restaurant, where the decor is simple and colourful and the atmosphere has something continental about it. Tim once a trawlerman on the west coast still provides much of the shellfish through his own boat. The rest of the produce is either purchased on the quayside of Kintyre or carefully sourced on the island or the mainland. Daily changing menus appear on blackboards, and are extremely good value. Service is friendly and efficient. Chef Robin Gray, who also grows the vegetables for the restaurant, organically, is professional and enthusiastic, and the style of his cooking is minimalistic, with flashes of colour and fascinating textures.

Open mid Mar to 31 Oct
Restaurant Lunch 12.30 - 2.30 pm except Mon (b)
Dinner 7 - 10.30 pm except Mon (e)
Closed Mon except Bank Holidays
+ during Jul Aug
Vegetarians welcome
Facilities for disabled visitors

Rendezvous of local sea and shellfish with Pernod and dill sauce. Fillet of hake with fresh crab and fish mousse on chive bisque. Delice of Kintyre salmon with lemon and chive fumet. Tournedos of black Angus beef on celeriac and potato rosti with red wine jus. Sika venison steak on a light scented liquorice reduction. Cranachan cheese cake.

Credit cards: 1, 3
Proprietors: Tim & Fran James

Dunvegan House

Shore Road
Brodick
Isle of Arran KA27 8AJ
Tel: 01770 302811

Turn right from ferry into Brodick, c 500 yards - on sea front. Other option, ferry from Lochranza to Kintyre.

A small hotel run by Naomi and David Spencer who were the winners of the 1995 Booker Prize for Excellence 'Best Hotel/Guest House in the UK' Award.

- Traditional red sandstone seafront hotel overlooking Brodick Bay on the Isle of Arran.
- Daily changing table d'hôte menu offering good traditional cooking.
- "Good food at a good price, with friendly service."

Dunvegan House is set back from the village's waterfront promenade by its own garden, and affords good views across the bay to Brodick Castle and Goatfell. David and Naomi Spencer arrived here from England six years ago with no experience of the hotel business. They have learned fast, do all of the work with the help of a small dedicated team, and maintain a very high standard. The dinner menus offer seasonally available local produce in a small choice of familiar dishes. The breakfasts are memorable, especially the locally smoked kippers.

Open all year
Rooms: 10, 7 with private facilities
Bed & Breakfast £18.50 - £26
Dinner B & B £31 - £38.50
Room Rate £37 - £52
Dinner 7 - 7.30 pm (b)
Residents only
Restricted Licence
No dogs
No smoking in bedrooms

Home-made soups. Baked salmon in a prawn and lemon sauce. Arran lamb cutlets in rosemary gravy with fresh mint sauce. Guinness and steak pie with traditional suet crust. Baked trout stuffed with almonds and herbs. Traditional hot puddings with creamy custard. Breakfast - haggis or fruit pudding, locally smoked kippers.

STB Highly Commended 3 Crowns
No credit cards
Proprietors: David & Naomi Spencer

Glen Cloy Farmhouse

Glencloy, Brodick
Isle of Arran KA27 8DA
Tel: 01770 302351

1½ miles from Brodick Pier on road towards Brodick Castle. Sign at post box in wall.

A family-run farm guest house on Arran.

- Old farmhouse.
- Home cooking.
- "Everything here seems as if little has changed over the past 100 years."

This is a charming old sandstone building in a little glen on the road to Brodick Castle. The bedrooms have a very homely air about them and two have private facilities. Mark and Vicki Padfield run the house and cook themselves. They bake their own bread, and the vegetables and herbs come from the garden. The food is traditional fare, locally sourced and carefully prepared. It is served in the immaculate dining room overlooking the glen.

Open 1 Mar to 7 Nov
Rooms: 5, 2 with private facilities
Bed & Breakfast £20 - £27
Special Rates for 3 + nights
Dinner B & B £32 - £38
Dinner 7 - 7.30 pm (b)
Residents only 1 Mar to 7 Nov
Vegetarians welcome
Unlicensed - guests welcome to take own wine
No smoking in dining room

Home-made mushroom and Arran mustard soup. Roast Sannox pheasant with herb stuffing. Glen Cloy gooseberry pie. Steamed marmalade and ginger sponge.

STB Commended 2 Crowns
No credit cards
Proprietors: Mark & Vicki Padfield

Glenisle Hotel

Shore Road, Lamlash
Isle of Arran KA27 8LS
Tel: 01770 600 559/258

On main street of Lamlash. 17 miles to Lochranza, alternate ferry for Kintyre.

Quiet, island hotel of considerable charm, where you will encounter friendly hospitality and efficient service.

- Traditional white-washed hotel set in a neat garden overlooking Lamlash Bay.
- Home-cooking.
- "A broad choice of robust, familiar dishes."

This hotel on the main street of Lamlash has a clean, scrubbed look with hanging flower baskets and awnings. A programme of internal refurbishment has been carried out, and continues. The bedrooms are comfortably furnished, and those at the front have fine views of Lamlash Bay and Holy Isle (now a Buddhist retreat). There is a relaxed and friendly atmosphere about the place. In the cocktail lounge a feature has been made of wooden carvings from the famous old Clyde steamer, 'The Talisman'. The restaurant menu offers a decent range of dishes reflecting the Scottish and local Arran produce available.

Open 1 Feb to 1 Jan
Rooms: 13 with private facilities
Bed & Breakfast £24 - £48.50
Dinner B & B £35.50 - £60
Special Rates available
Bar Lunch: 12 - 2 pm (a)
Dining Room/Restaurant Lunch 12 - 2 pm (a)
Dinner 7 - 9 pm (b)
Vegetarians welcome

Home-made soups and pâtés. Trout grilled in lemon butter, served with a coating of flaked almonds. Chicken suprême stuffed with haggis, with a cream and whisky sauce. Prime Scotch fillet of beef in a Guinness and mussel sauce. Smoked fish layer - whiting, haddock and trout served with a lemon and lime glaze.

STB Commended 4 Crowns
Credit cards: 1, 3 + SWITCH
Proprietor: Fred Wood

Grange House Hotel

Whiting Bay, Isle of Arran
KA27 8QH
Tel: 01770 700263
Fax: 01770 700263

8 miles south of ferry terminal at Brodick, 1 mile past the centre of Whiting Bay village.

A traditional hotel with a pleasant situation.

- Turn-of-the-century hotel.
- Good home cooking.
- "Good food and attentive, efficient service."

Grange House Hotel was built in dressed stone in 1896 and retains many of its original features. It has been sensitively decorated and furnished, and has fine views over Whiting Bay. Within the acres of garden is a putting green, and the hotel has a sauna. Clive and Janet Hughes have many years experience in the catering trade in England and their experience is manifested by the efficient service and the well prepared and presented dinners they offer.

Open Christmas/New Year + 15 Mar to 30 Nov
Rooms : 9, 7 with private facilities
Bed & Breakfast from £35
Dinner B & B from £50
Special Rates available
Dinner 7 - 8.30 pm (c)
Non residents by arrangement
Vegetarians welcome
No dogs
Facilities for disabled visitors
No smoking throughout

Pladda fish pie. Venison, duck and beef available. Musselburgh pie. Bread and butter pudding with orange whisky cream.

STB Highly Commended 3 Crowns
Credit cards: 1, 3
Proprietors: Clive & Janet Hughes

Kilmichael Country House Hotel

Glen Cloy, by Brodick
Isle of Arran KA27 8BY
Tel: 01770 302219
Fax: 01770 302068

1½ miles from Brodick Pier, turning inland at golf course (signposted). In own grounds at end of long private drive.

A splendid hotel on the Isle of Arran.

- Historic house with great period character.
- Superb modern cooking.
- "There is a touch of the exquisite in everything here."

Kilmichael is believed to be the oldest house on Arran - the present building is late 17th century, but there was an early christian cell on the site. Described as a 'mansion' in the records, in fact it is an elegant and compact lodge, exquisitely furnished by its present owners (oriental antiques are a feature), who engagingly describe its attractions in order of importance as "...comfort, tranquility, books and home made ice-cream". It is the only hotel on Arran graded 'Deluxe' by the STB and has 2 red entries in Michelin. The menus presented in the dining room are very interesting and demonstrate French and Italian influences. Every dish has something unique and authentic about it, with piquant flavours and delicately spiced sauces.

Open all year except Christmas wk
Rooms: 6 with private facilities
Bed & Breakfast £34 - £50
Dinner B & B £56 - £75
Special Rates for 3+/7+ nights
Dinner 7.30 - 8.30 pm except Sun Wed (d) 5 course menu
Dinner for non residents booking essential
Vegetarians welcome
Children over 12 years welcome
No smoking in dining room + bedrooms

Salad of mixed leaves and flowers with sun-dried tomatoes and Arran goats cheese. Pea, pear and watercress soup. Arran king scallops and monkfish with fennel in a saffron cream sauce. Fillet of Scotch Beef Wellington with wild mushroom sauce. Plums baked in sloe gin with home-made cinnamon ice cream.

STB Deluxe 4 Crowns
Credit cards: 1, 3
Proprietors: Geoffrey Botterill & Antony Butterworth

Lilybank Hotel

Shore Road, Lamlash
Isle of Arran KA27 8LS
Tel: 01770 600230

On main street in Lamlash, 4 miles from ferry terminal (Brodick). 17 miles from Lochranza and the ferry to Kintyre.

A small family-run hotel in Lamlash on the Isle of Arran; with comfortable accommodation and excellent food.

- An 18th century house charmingly converted with views across the bay to Holy Isle.
- Modern Scottish cooking.
- "Such caring and attentive hosts make this a lovely place to stay."

Built in the late 18th century, Lilybank is a charming, white-washed, small, family-run hotel which has been lovingly restored and refurbished by its present owners, Clive and Carol Berry. The hotel has been tastefully renovated by the owners to a high standard to provide quality accommodation throughout with comfortable en suite bedrooms which are well-appointed and two cosy lounges where guests can take an aperitif before dinner. In this relaxed and comfortable atmosphere guests may experience some of the finest views over the bay to Holy Isle whilst enjoying the food prepared by Carol based on Arran's abundant local produce. The table d'hôte menu changes daily and represents excellent value for money.

Open 1 Mar to 31 Dec
Rooms: 6 , 5 with private facilities
Bed & Breakfast £20 - £27.50
Dinner B & B £32 - £40
Special Rates for 3+ nights
Dinner 7 - 8 pm (b)
Restricted Hotel Licence
Facilities for disabled visitors
No smoking in restaurant + bedrooms
Vegetarians welcome

Home-made bread, soups, pâtés and desserts. Smoked trout mousse. Collops of Arran lamb with a bramble sauce. Poached fillet of salmon with a lemon and chive sauce. Carbonnade of beef. Prime Arran sirloin steak. Apricot and Drambuie oaty crumble. Brodick Blue cheese and oatcakes.

STB Highly Commended 3 Crowns
No credit cards
Proprietors: Clive & Carol Berry

Dark Island Hotel

Liniclate, Isle of Benbecula
Western Isles PA88 5PJ
Tel: 01870 603030/602414
Fax: 01870 602347

Benbecula lies between North and South Uist (Western Isles). A865 to Liniclate. Hotel is c. 6 miles from the airport.

A modern, purpose built hotel in the Outer Hebrides.

- A motel with vivid antique red roof.
- Traditional Scottish cooking.
- "'Surf and Turf' emphasis on the wide ranging menu."

The Dark Island Hotel - the name comes from a well-known Hebridean song - is a surprising discovery in the Outer Hebrides. The Lace Restaurant - offering table d'hote and a la carte menus; a wonderful range of fresh local shellfish, cheeses and smoked produce including salmon, venison, chicken and eel which is equally matched by a lengthy list of steaks and grills with salad, chips or baked potato on offer. Flavours are fresh and positive. As an alternative for lunch, 'Carriages' carvery offers a selection of cold seafoods and hot roasts.

Open all year
Rooms: 42 with private facilities
Bed & Breakfast £35 - £65
Dinner B & B £51.50 - £81.50
Special rates available
Bar Meals 12 - 10 pm (a)
Dining Room/Restaurant Lunch 12.30 - 2 pm (b)
Dinner 6.30 - 9 pm (c)
Vegetarians welcome

Prime halibut steak served with king prawn, lobster and brandy sauce. A wing of fresh local skate, butter-baked and dressed with minced peat-smoked salmon and lumpfish caviar. Variety of seafood crepes. Sauted noisettes of lamb served with caramelised shallots with a rosemary and red wine sauce. Special diets catered for.

STB Commended 4 Crowns
Credit cards: 1, 3

Isle of Gigha

Isle of Harris

Gigha Hotel

Isle of Gigha
Argyll PA41 7AA
Tel: 01583 505 254
Fax: 01583 505 244

A83 Lochgilphead-Campbeltown, c. 18 miles south of Tarbert turn into Tayinloan. Follow Gigha ferry sign.

> A traditional, family-run hotel and island with glorious views.

■ An classic stone-built and white-painted 18th century hostelry.
■ Traditional Scottish home cooking.
■ "Comfort and friendliness in an simple setting."

Overlooking the Sound of Gigha towards the hills of Kintyre, Gigha Hotel is the island's original inn and traces its origins back two centuries. The island was described by our inspector "one of the wonders of our western seaboard", and although it is only 20 minutes ferry trip from Kintyre, you immediately step back a couple of decades. Life is gentle and slow-moving. The hotel combines old-world charm with modern comfort. The accommodation is cottage-style; and the friendly hotel bar is popular with locals and visiting yachtsmen. The hotel also has several cottages on the island if you wish to be more independent. The restaurant specialises in Scottish country cooking, and makes good use of the seafood landed by local fishing and lobster boats. Table d'hôte menus change daily. William and Sandra Howden, the resident owners of the hotel, are attentive and happy to accept any special requests.

Open Mar to Oct
Rooms: 13, 11 with private facilities
Bed & Breakfast £34 - £38
Dinner B & B £48.50 - £49.50
Special Rates for 3+ nights
Bar Lunch 12 - 3 pm (a)
Bar Supper 6 - 8.30 pm (a)
Dinner 7 - 9 pm (c) 4 course menu
Vegetarians welcome - prior notice required

Gigha scallops with garlic butter. Pan-fried duck with a peach sauce. Roast pheasant with a port wine and pink peppercorn sauce.

STB Commended 3 Crowns
Credit cards: 1, 3
Proprietors: William & Sandra Howden

Allan Cottage Guest House

Tarbert
Isle of Harris HS3 3DJ
Tel: 01859 50 2146

Upper road overlooking ferry road, c. 600 yards from ferry.

> An attractive family-run guest house in Harris' main village.

■ A converted telephone exchange on Tarbert's main street.
■ Traditional Scottish cooking.
■ "Homely atmosphere with excellent cuisine. Mrs Reed travels 80 miles a week in search of fresh produce."

This attractive old building has been interestingly converted maintaining many of the original features. It has been extended to form a house of unusual charm; quiet and homely. Rooms are all well furnished in cottage style and the bedrooms have private facilities. Bill and Evelyn Reed are wonderfully enthusiastic and look after guests with true island hospitality. The dinner menu is discussed with guests in the morning, so that individual preferences can be taken into account. The cooking is interesting and imaginative and always attracts favourable comment. A charming unpretentious establishment.

Open 1 Apr to 30 Sep
Rooms: 3 with private facilities
Bed & Breakfast from £25
Dinner B & B from £41
Dinner at 7 pm (c) 4 course menu
Residents only
Unlicensed
Vegetarians welcome
No smoking in dining room + bedrooms

Aberdeen Angus beef stuffed with smoked oysters served with cucumber sauce. Local venison in port and Guinness with cassis sauce. Wild salmon with prawns and dill sauce. Pheasant with claret and orange sauce. Harris lamb with apricot and walnut stuffing.

STB Highly Commended 3 Crowns
No credit cards
Proprietors: Bill & Evelyn Reed

Ardvourlie Castle

Aird A Mhulaidh
Isle of Harris HS3 3AB
Tel: 01859 50 2307

On A859, 10 miles north of Tarbert.

> A lovingly restored house run by Derek and Pamela Martin, with four elegant and comfortable bedrooms.

■ Recently restored 19th century hunting lodge on the island of Harris.
■ Traditional Scottish cooking.
■ "The food is unpretentious and delicious, and exceptionally good value. The house and its situation are breathtaking."

Ardvourlie stands on the shores of Loch Seaforth under the imposing crags of Clisham. It was built in 1863 by the Earl of Dunmore but fell into a semi-ruinous state in recent years - which makes the achievement of Derek and Pamela Martin all the more remarkable. They have restored the place magnificently, with sensitivity and outstandingly good taste. The castle is furnished in keeping with its period. The dining room offers views over the wilderness beyond and it uses designs and furniture from the Victorian and Art Noveau periods. Here you will encounter the Martins' fine cooking. Much of the raw materials that are unavailable locally are very carefully sourced on the mainland which comprises dishes to suit all tastes using as much local produce as is available on this remote island, and where necessary fresh foods are brought in by sea from the mainland.

Open all year except over Christmas period
Rooms: 4
Bed & Breakfast £45 - £50
Dinner B & B £70 - £75
Special Rates for 5+ nights
Dinner at 7.30 pm - earlier/later by arrangement (e)
4 course menu
Residents only
Restricted Licence
Vegetarians welcome - prior notice required

Monkfish kebab served on a spiced boiled rice decorated with fried apricots, nuts, sultanas and fried peppers. Half roast duck basted with honey and crisped, served with an orange liqueur sauce. Hazelnut meringues, whipped cream and hot fudge sauce.

No credit cards
Proprietor: Derek Martin

Isle of Islay

Two Waters Guest House

Lickisto, Isle of Harris HS3 3EL
Tel: 01859 530 246

From Tarbert take road signed to Roghadal (Rodel), then fourth road on left C79 single track. Between Stockinish and Geocrab.

> A wonderfully isolated house with a homely atmosphere created by John and Jill Barber.

- Modern bungalow set on the wild shores of the Isle of Harris.
- Scottish home cooking.
- "The home-smoked produce, and fish caught by John himself added a feeling of real rural relish to the meal."

This is a modern family bungalow set in the wild mountaineous countryside of Harris, just 15 yards from the sea. If you are lucky you may well spot otters and seals on this rugged coast as well as the host of other natural wildlife. The owners have made a point of creating a comfortable homely atmosphere and guests have much to look forward to in the imaginative dinners provided, which feature fresh local seafood and fish smoked by John himself. The four bedrooms are en suite, with attractive personal touches. Free trout fishing is close by and this is a lovely spot from which to enjoy bird-watching, sailing and hill-walking.

Open 1 May to 30 Sep
Rooms: 4 with private facilities
Bed & Breakfast £28 - £30
Dinner B & B £41 - £43
Dinner at 7 pm (b) 4 course menu
Residents only
Unlicensed
No children
No smoking in dining room

Hot smoked salmon roulade. Lamb with apricots and fresh herbs. Vegetable medley cake. Apple and pear tarte tatin with cinnamon yoghurt.

STB Highly Commended 3 Crowns
No credit cards
Proprietors: Jill & John Barber

Scarista House

Isle of Harris PA85 3HX
Tel: 01859 550 238
Fax: 01859 550 277

On A859, 15 miles south-west of Tarbert (Western Isles).

> Distinctive country house hotel in a peaceful island location.

- Converted Georgian mansion house with magnificent views.
- Modern Scottish country house cooking.
- "A beautiful house in a tranquil setting which provides excellent food and hospitality and a relaxing atmosphere."

Scarista House overlooks a three mile long shell sand beach on the dramatic Atlantic coast of Harris. The eight bedrooms all have views out to sea. This makes for an ever-changing panorama of scenery and atmosphere. The bedrooms are comfortably and traditionally furnished with bathrooms en suite. The public rooms which also include an extensive library are cheery and welcoming and the absence of radio and television is an asset not a liability. The hotel's dining room has featured in many guides worldwide and is known particularly for its superb fish and shellfish. There is a very decent wine list chosen to complement the dishes on offer.

Open May to Sep
Rooms: 8 with private facilities
Bed & Breakfast £45 - £65
Dinner B & B £70 - £85
Dinner at 8 pm (e)
Residents Licence
Vegetarians welcome
Children over eight years welcome
No smoking throughout

Razor-shell clams. Prawn soufflés. Fillet of wild venison with a blackcurrant and cassis sauce. Vegetables from the garden. Praline ice cream with raspberry and almond biscuits. Various Scottish cheeses. Home-made oatcakes, bread, scones etc.

No credit cards
Proprietors: Ian & Jane Callaghan

The Croft Kitchen

Port Charlotte
Isle of Islay
Argyll PA49 7UN
Tel: 01496 850230

On the main road into Port Charlotte opposite the Museum of Islay Life.

> A charming family restaurant, now offering full meals.

- Informal village bistro-style restaurant.
- Home cooking.
- "I had the most wonderful lobster."

Joy and Douglas Law took over the Croft Kitchen in 1995, having run a hotel on the island for ten years. The Croft Kitchen itself was established 17 years ago in a fine situation close to a sandy beach, with views of the Paps of Jura and Loch Indaal. As well as home baking, home-made soups, family snacks and sandwiches, the Kitchen now also offers a good range of daily 'specials', chosen from a blackboard, which features local scallops, mussels, lamb and so on - at incredibly reasonable prices. A friendly, informal place where the whole family is made welcome.

Open 22 Mar to 3 Nov except 8 Aug
Restaurant Lunch 11.30 am - 3 pm (a)
Dinner 6 - 8.30 pm except Wed (b)
Unlicensed
Vegetarians welcome

Home-made soups. Loch Gruinart oysters in oatmeal. Roast leg of Islay lamb with apricots and garlic. Roast haunch of Islay venison. Half lobster. Bread and butter pudding with nuts and honey. Fresh strawberry meringue. Rhubarb and ginger crumble with custard.

No credit cards
Proprietors: Joy & Douglas Law

Glenmachrie Farmhouse

Port Ellen, Isle of Islay
Argyll PA42 7AW
Tel: 01496 30 2560

Midway on A846 between Port Ellen and
Bowmore.

Farm guest house near Port Ellen.

- Traditional island farmhouse.
- Highland speciality table.
- "Pork, lamb, sausages, eggs, vegetables - all
  come from the farm itself."

Glenmachrie is a mixed farm of 450 acres, with
cattle, sheep, ponies, horses and a small fold of
Highland cattle. Rachel and Alasdair Whyte
welcome guests into their home with great warmth
and a genuine Hebridean hospitality. Generous
helpings of home cooking are cheerfully served in
the candlelit dining room. Rachel offers a choice of
dishes which include meat and game from the
farm and salmon and wild brown trout from their
own loch and river which overlooks the famous
Machrie golf links. With access to private fishing
guests are also offered the opportunity to make
their own catches.

Open all year
Rooms: 5 with private facilities
Bed & Breakfast £25 - £35
Dinner B & B £40 - £50
Dinner 6.30 - 7.30 pm
Residents only
Unlicensed - guests welcome to take own wine
Vegetarians welcome
Children over five years welcome
Facilities for disabled visitors (ground floor
bedroom)
Dogs accepted - by prior agreement only
No smoking throughout

Scotch tomatoes stuffed with home-made haggis
spiked with Islay malt whisky. Mussels and prawns
in an Islay cheese sauce. Collops of Glenmachrie
lamb in a rowan and rosemary sauce. Dunlossit
Estate venison and prune casserole. Glenmachrie
salmon poached in white wine and served with Islay
parsley butter. Glenmachrie beef casseroled with
home-made herb dumplings.

STB Highly Commended 3 Crowns
No credit cards
Proprietor: Rachel Whyte

Kilchoman House and Restaurant

by Bruichladdich, Isle of Islay
Argyll PA49 7UY
Tel: 0149 6850382
Fax: 0149 6850277

Take B8018 road signposted Kilchoman, off
A847. 6 miles from Bruichladdich.

A Georgian manse in rural Islay.

- Informal restaurant with rooms.
- Imaginative home cooking.
- "Fresh scallops and lobster, Islay beef and lamb;
  good value for money."

Kilchoman is a charming small 'A Listed' former
manse tucked away in a little hollow, well off the
beaten track on the Atlantic side of the Rhinns of
Islay. It is the home of Stuart and Lesley Taylor, who
have two rooms in the house itself and five self-
catering cottages nearby (minimum 3 nights stay,
early booking advised). Lesley's cooking is popular
locally (although the restaurant is closed to non-
residents Sunday and Monday, and reservations
must be made in advance); she uses local produce
to present a straightforward table d'hôte menu
offering a good choice of starters and main courses.

Open all year for accommodation
Restaurant open Apr to Oct + Christmas/
New Year
Rooms: 2, 1 with private facilities
Bed & Breakfast £20 - £35
Dinner B & B £35 - £50
Dinner 7.30 - 9 pm Tue to Sat - non-residents
by reservation only: Sun Mon residents
only (c)
Table Licence
Vegetarians welcome - prior notice required
No smoking in restaurant

Islay venison with a pureé of leek and parsnip and
port and blackcurrant sauce. Fillet steaks. Hot
smoked local salmon. Lobster. Kilchoman lamb
medallions pan-fried with mint and watercress
sauce.

No credit cards
Proprietors: Stuart & Lesley Taylor

Kilmeny Farmhouse

Ballygrant, Isle of Islay
Argyll PA45 7QW
Tel: 0149 684 0668

3 minute drive up private road, ½ mile south of
Ballygrant.

Isolated Islay guest house.

- 19th century farmhouse.
- Home cooking.
- "The beautiful surroundings and the Rozga's
  indulgent hospitality are second to none."

Kilmeny is a working farm of 300 acres, within easy
reach of Port Askaig. Margaret and Blair Rozga
have been running their guest house for over
twenty years and enjoy a loyal following of guests
from all over the world. The bedrooms and public
rooms are very elegantly decorated, with many fine
antiques and luxurious furnishings. Margaret is an
accomplished cook and uses some of the farm's
own beef and lamb as well as local venison and
seafood. There is a distinctly Scottish concentration
on substantial and unpretentious dishes which are
full of natural flavours.

Open all year except Christmas/New Year
Rooms: 3 with private facilities
Bed & Breakfast from £30
Dinner B & B £46 - £50
Dinner 6.30 - 8 pm (b)
Residents only
Unlicensed - guests welcome to take own wine
No smoking throughout
Dogs by arrangement

Home-made bread. Roast sirloin of Islay beef and
Yorkshire puddings. Islay scallops poached in white
wine and cream. Steak in a peppercorn sauce. Wild
rabbit and leek pie. Hot Islay cheese soufflé. Bread
and butter pudding.

STB Deluxe 3 Crowns
No credit cards
Proprietor: Margaret Rozga

Isle of Lewis

Eshcol Guest House

Breasclete, Callanish
Isle of Lewis HS2 9ED
Tel: 01851 621 357

On A858, 17 miles from Stornoway, 40 miles
from Tarbert.

> A guest house on the Isle of Lewis.

- A small croft in the weaving village of
  Breasclete.
- Home cooking.
- "Good food, lovely peat fire, great views."

Isobel and Neil Macarthur run this croft on the west
coast of Lewis, within walking distance of the
mysterious Stones of Callanish. There are
wonderful views across Loch Roag to the island of
Great Bernera and beyond, with the hills of Uig and
Harris in the distance. The three bedrooms all have
their own bathrooms and have a nice simple rustic
feel to them. This is a small establishment and Neil
will regale you for hours (in Gaelic if you desire)
with tales and folklore of the area and its past. The
food here is home cooking at its best with no
pretentions. Eshcol really does offer 'real island
hospitality'.

Open 1 Mar to 31 Oct
Rooms: 3 with private facilities
Bed & Breakfast £20 - £23
Dinner B & B £36 - £39
Special Rates available
Dinner 6.30 - 7 pm Mon to Sat: 6.30 - 8 pm
Sun (c) 4 course menu
Residents only
Unlicensed - guests welcome to take own wine
Vegetarians welcome
No smoking in dining room

Home-made soups. Local smoked salmon. Lamb
with rosemary. Cranachan (Eshcol-style). Lemon/
chocolate roulade. Fresh vegetables from garden.

STB Highly Commended 3 Crowns
No credit cards
Proprietors: Neil & Isobel Macarthur

The Macallan Personality of the Year

Handa

18 Keose Glebe (Ceos),
Lochs
Isle of Lewis PA86 9JX
Tel: 01851 830334

1½ miles off A859, 12 miles south of
Stornoway, 25 miles north of Tarbert, Harris:
last house in village of 'Ceos.

> A hilltop house on the Hebridean island of
> Lewis; a small family-run guest house which
> provides comfortable accommodation and good
> food.

- This is a newly built home, furnished in pine
  with all modern facilities.
- Traditional Scottish home-cooking.
- "Christine Morrison's cooking is excellent and
  she makes innovative use of herbs and
  vegetables from her northern kitchen
  garden."

This is the last house in the Hebridean haven of
Keose village. It is idyllically appointed on top of
a hill overlooking a private loch and ideally
positioned for exploring the island and nearby
Harris. Stepping from the house itself you can
follow a range of pursuits from bird-watching to
hill-walking and (if you are fortunate) otter
sighting. The loch provides brown trout fishing
and a boat and equipment can be hired. The
owner, Christine Morrison, runs the guest house
with genuine island hospitality. Alongside
traditional recipes, she does all of her own baking
and uses the best of local seafood and fresh
produce from her garden.

Open 2 May to 5 Oct
Rooms: 3, 1 with private facilities
Bed & Breakfast £16 - £22
Dinner B & B £29 - £35
Dinner at 7.30 pm Thu to Sat (b)
Unlicensed - guests welcome to take own
wine
Vegetarians welcome
No smoking in dining room

Home-made breads, soups. Scallops in brandy.
Baked turbot. Edwardian lovage syllabub.

STB Highly Commended 2 Crowns
No credit cards
Proprietors: Murdo & Christine Morrison

Park Guest House & Restaurant

30 James Street, Stornoway
Isle of Lewis HS1 2QN
Tel: 01851 70 2485

½ mile from ferry terminal. At junction of
Matheson Road, James Street and A866 to
airport and Eye peninsula.

> A traditional family-run guest house in the
> centre of town.

- A stone-built Victorian guest house.
- Traditional Scottish cooking.
- "Friendly hosts and substantial dinners."

A substantial stone-built B Listed building dating
from the 1880s, standing in the centre of
Stornoway, this house has a homely atmosphere
and Roddy and Catherine Afrin are friendly hosts.
Catherine was trained in interior design at the
Glasgow School of Art, and the house has benefited
from her skill and good taste. Note the original
Glasgow-style fireplace in the dining room. Roddy
was formerly head chef on an oil rig in the North
Sea, and his robust à la carte menus use local fresh
fish and meat and vegetables. Each dish is cooked
to order. The restaurant is popular with local
people.

Open all year except 24 Dec to 8 Jan
Rooms: 6, 2 with private facilities
Bed & Breakfast £20 - £45
Dinner B & B £34 - £59
Packed Lunches available (a)
Dinner 6 pm (table d'hôte) Tue to Sat: Sun Mon
residents only (b)
Dinner 7 - 8.30 pm (à la carte)
except Sun Mon (c-d)
Note: Dinner Sun Mon - residents only
Vegetarians welcome
No dogs

Home-made soups. Suprême of chicken with
ginger and leeks. Lobster thermidor. Grilled loin of
Lewis lamb with minted yoghurt. Steamed
chocolate sponge with orange marmalade sauce.
Scotch pancake with ice cream and butterscotch
sauce.

No credit cards
Proprietors: Catherine & Roddy Afrin

Isle of Mull

Ardfenaig House

by Bunessan, Isle of Mull
Argyll PA67 6DX
Tel: 01681 700210
Fax: 01681 700210

2 miles west of Bunessan on A849, turn right on private road to Ardfenaig House, ½ mile.

A lovely old country house hotel surrounded by woodland, sea and moorland on the Isle of Mull.

- Originally an estate factor's house then shooting lodge in a glorious position on the shores of Loch Caol on the Ross of Mull.
- Innovative use of traditional Scottish cooking.
- "Probably the best meal I have eaten this year."

Ardfenaig House stands in the southwest corner of Mull midway between Bunessan and Fionnphort. The house is now home to Malcolm and Jane Davidson, hospitable and welcoming hosts who look after you charmingly. It has five en suite bedrooms and the newly refurbished Coach House by a small burn 50 yards away provides additional self-catering accommodation for four to six people. In front of the house is a small jetty and Malcolm will be happy to take you for a sail in the bay or an early morning fishing trip. The dining room overlooks the garden and woods behind the house and the drawing room has magnificent views over Loch Caol. The excellent food is freshly prepared in the kitchen from fresh local produce and is beautifully presented. Menus are short but imaginative, and since the Davidsons have a share in a French vineyard, the wine list is rather special.

Open 1 Apr to 31 Oct + winter by arrangement
Rooms: 5 with private facilities
Dinner B & B from £85
Special Rates for 2+/6+ nights
Dinner at 8 pm (d) 4 course menu
Restricted Licence
Vegetarians welcome
No smoking in dining room + bedrooms

Home-made bread, soups and ice creams. Collops of venison pan-fried with lemon juice and port. Fresh home-grown vegetables. Fillet of salmon en crôute. Iced Grand Marnier nougat with apricot coulis. Chocolate roulade. Scottish cheeses.

STB Highly Commended 3 Crowns
Credit cards: 1, 3
Proprietors: Malcolm & Jane Davidson

Ardrioch

Ardrioch Farm, Dervaig
Isle of Mull PA75 6QR
Tel: 01688 400264

1 mile from Dervaig on Calgary road.

A delightful farm guest house with four bedrooms and pine-panelled annexe in an informal garden setting, with wonderful views.

- A modern bungalow/farmhouse on a working 70 acre farm.
- Scottish home cooking.
- "All of the dishes made by Jenny Matthew, are unpretentious but highly imaginative."

This cedar-built bungalow on the west coast of Mull can accommodate six guests. It is the pleasant, comfortable home of Jenny and Jeremy Matthew - tastefully furnished with antiques, good pictures and lots of books. It is redolent of cedar wood and you will find yourself living very much amongst the busy clutter of a warm family home. Jenny's meals are delicious and homely; all dishes use fresh local produce. The day's menu is fixed, according to what is available, but she is more than happy to accommodate any preferences or requests from her guests where possible, if you ask her in advance. The house is two miles from Croig Harbour, where Ardrioch's inter-island day cruises depart for wildlife and sightseeing trips.

Open Easter to mid Oct
Rooms: 5, 2 with private facilities
Bed & Breakfast £18 - £20.50
Dinner B & B £29.50 - £32
Special Rates available
Dinner 6.30 - 7.30 pm (b)
Unlicensed - guests welcome to take own wine
Vegetarians welcome
No smoking throughout
No dogs

Mull smoked mussels with avocado pâté. Crab tarts and Mull prawns. Local venison, salmon and trout. Chicken in a honey and pear marinade. Home-made ice creams: toffee and apple, apricot and almond, chocolate and ginger.

STB Commended 2 Crowns
No credit cards
Proprietors: Jenny & Jeremy Matthew

Assapol House Hotel

Bunessan
Isle of Mull, Argyll
PA67 6DW
Tel: 01681 700 258
Fax: 01681 700 445

From Craignure-A849 towards Fionnphort. When approaching Bunessan, pass village school on the right, take first left signed Assapol House.

A former manse with lovely views to the west.

- Small country house hotel.
- Good home cooking.
- "Wonderfully friendly, relaxing place; the delicious dinner carefully prepared."

The feature that immediately impresses the visitor to Assapol is the care and attention to detail that your hosts, Alex Robertson and his mother Onny, manifest in every department: fresh flowers in the bedrooms, beds turned down, sewing kits supplied, etc. Assapol House itself, a former manse, is 200 years old and overlooks the loch of the same name, with the Burg Peninsula, the Treshnish Isles and Staffa beyond. Wildlife, secluded beaches and historical sites abound in this delightful corner of Mull. The dinner menu offers a choice of starters and puddings and a set main course. The food is locally sourced and features local delicacies; it is sensitively cooked and imaginatively presented; and it is extremely good value.

Open 1 Apr to 31 Oct
Rooms: 6 with private facilities
Bed & Breakfast £30 - £35
Dinner B & B £45 - £50
Special Rates available for 3+ nights
Dinner at 7.45 pm (c)
Restricted Hotel Licence
Residents only
Vegetarians welcome - prior notice requried
Children over 10 years welcome
No smoking in dining room
Dogs by prior arrangement

Warm salad of bacon and avocado. Smoked salmon and buckwheat crêpe gâteau with cream cheese. Rosemary baked lamb cutlets with a redcurrant and vermouth sauce. Chocolate and raspberry meringue. Frosted fruit pudding.

STB Commended 3 Crowns
Credit cards: 1, 3, + Switch, Delta
Proprietors: Onny & Alex Robertson

Calgary Farmhouse Hotel
Calgary, nr Dervaig
Isle of Mull PA75 6QW
Tel: 01688 400256
Fax: 01688 400256

B8073 just up hill from Calgary beach.

A farm guest house with tearoom and gallery.

- Converted farm steadings.
- Home cooking.
- "The menu is very reasonably priced and prepared to order with plenty of local seafood evident."

Calgary Farmhouse is just up the hill from the beautiful white sands of Calgary Beach. The farm buildings and courtyard have recently been sensitively converted by Julia and Matthew Reade into nine bedrooms with private facilities, and two public rooms. Exposed stonework, wooden furniture and wood-burning stoves all contribute to a warm and cosy environment. The Dovecote Restaurant offers an à la carte menu which changes four times a week according to the seasonal produce available. The accent is on simple, home cooking in an informal atmosphere while family's fishing connections ensure a wonderful supply of Mull's bountiful catches. There is also a tearoom, The Carthouse Gallery, charmingly converted and open throughout the day for light lunches and home baking. A changing exhibition of pictures by local artists is displayed here, many of them for sale.

Open 1 Apr - 31 Oct
Rooms: 9 with private facilities
Bed & Breakfast £30 - £37.50
Dinner B & B from £45.80
Special Rates for 4 + nights
Light Lunch 12 - 2.30 pm (a)
Sun - Sat Carthouse Gallery
Dinner 6.30 - 9 pm (b - d)
Vegetarians welcome
No smoking in restaurant

Tartlet of Mull smoked mussels in tomato sauce. Chicken breast with Argyll smoked ham in creamy mushroom sauce. Locally caught crab, fish and shellfish. Home-made berry crumble. Selection of Isle of Mull cheeses.

STB Commended 3 Crowns
Credit cards: 1, 3 + Switch
Proprietors: Matthew & Julia Reade

Druimard Country House
Dervaig, by Tobermory
Isle of Mull PA75 6QW
Tel: 01688 400345/400291
Fax: 01688 400345

Situated adjacent to Mull Little Theatre, well signposted from Dervaig village.

A small country house hotel run by husband and wife.

- A restored Victorian manse.
- Modern Scottish cooking.
- " A strong emphasis on fresh local meat and fish."

Druimard is just on the outskirts of the pretty village of Dervaig, adjacent to the famous Mull Little Theatre and eight miles from Tobermory. The old house has been well restored by Haydn and Wendy Hubbard, who run their hotel with the standards of comfort one would expect from a country house: service is professional, the en suite bedrooms are very comfortable, the restaurant has a strong reputation, and has been recognised by the award of an AA Rosette. The table d'hôte menus have moved with the current eating trends towards a large choice of fish which is locally caught and meat which is traditionally reared. The cooking is assured and fresh. The cuisine is imaginative with unusual sauces and everything is prepared to order.

Open 1 Apr to 28 Oct
Rooms: 6, 4 with private facilities
Bed & Breakfast £30 - £49.50
Dinner B & B £46.50 - £66
Special Rates for 3+ nights
Dinner 6 - 8.30 pm Mon to Sat: Sun residents only (c)
N.B. Dinner 7 pm - if no theatre performance
Restaurant Licence only
Vegetarians welcome
No smoking in restaurant

Noisettes of Scottish lamb with a shallot and red wine essence served with deep-fried filo parcels of apricot marmalade. Medallions of Oban landed monkfish served on a pool of two pepper sauces topped with Provencal breadcrumbs. Suprême of chicken stuffed with Mull crab and fresh ginger with a brandy and cream sauce. Home-made desserts with wide selection of Scottish cheeses.

STB Highly Commended 3 Crowns
Credit cards: 1, 3
Proprietors: Haydn & Wendy Hubbard

The Old Byre Heritage Centre
by Dervaig
Isle of Mull PA75 6QR
Tel: 01688 400229

1½ miles from Dervaig. Take Calgary road for ¾ mile, turn left along Torloisk road for ¼ mile, then left down private road following signs.

A gift shop and small heritage centre on the Isle of Mull.

- Converted barn with self-service restaurant.
- Home cooking and baking.
- "There are two kinds of cloutie dumpling, large and enormous!"

A remotely situated, picturesque old cattle byre in Glen Bellart (near Dervaig) has been restored and converted into a heritage centre which explores the traditions and natural history of the Isle of Mull, from the first settlers to the present day. There are audio-visual displays and exhibits as well as a gift shop with souvenirs and crafts for sale. The licensed tea room offers a range of light meals and home baking and daily specials, using fresh Mull produce. By prior arrangement meals can be arranged for groups and vegetarians are well catered for.

Open 31 Mar to 25 Oct
Light Meals served throughout day 10.30 am - 6 pm (a)
Vegetarians welcome

Crofter's soup served with warm rolls. Ploughman's lunch with Mull cheese. Cloutie dumpling a speciality. Selection of home baking.

No credit cards
Proprietors: Michael & Ursula Bradley

Isles of Orkney

The Puffer Aground

Main Road
Salen, Aros
Isle of Mull PA72 6JB
Tel: 01680 300389

On A849 Craignure-Tobermory, at junction of road signed to the pier.

Small, family-run island restaurant.

■ Informal restaurant.
■ Scottish home cooking.
■ "A well-balanced menu which is very attractively priced makes a visit thoroughly worthwhile".

The unusual name for this restaurant derives from the days when the local steamboat - the 'puffer' - ran right on to the shore to unload its cargo. The interior is very comfortable and ship-shape with a strong nautical theme and attractive marine memorabilia on display. Menus offer excellent variety - home-made soups, salmon, seafood, lamb and an interesting 'vegetarian option' hot choice. On the three course menu there is a choice of four or five dishes for each course which is commendably ambitious for such a relatively small establishment.

Open 1 May to 30 Sep
Light Lunch 12 - 2.30 pm except Sun Mon (a-b)
Dinner 7 - 8.30 pm except Sun: 7 - 9 pm
Jul Aug except Sun (b-d)
Reservations advisable
Closed Sun
Vegetarians welcome and
special diets catered for

Scottish and Mull produce used whenever possible to create 'home-type' cooking in a friendly atmosphere.

Credit cards: 1, 3
Proprietors: Graham & Elizabeth Ellis

Western Isles Hotel

Tobermory
Isle of Mull PA75 6PR
Tel: 01688 302012
Fax: 01688 302297

Tobermory is a 40 minute drive from Oban/ Craignure ferry.

Island hotel in picturesque fishing village.

■ Town hotel of Scottish baronial architecture.
■ Traditional Scottish cooking.
■ "The kitchen at the Western Isles specialises in fresh, simple menus using ingredients which are island produced and island caught."

The hotel occupies one of the finest positions in the Western Isles set above the village of Tobermory with glorious views over the Sound of Mull. You can enjoy the ever-changing, dramatic scenery from all of the hotel's public rooms and many of the bedrooms. The newly built conservatory is a particularly delightful spot and is popular with guests and visitors to the island who drop in for lunch or even coffee. The bar lunch menu is extensive with a very wide choice, from soup of the day and filled sandwiches to a full three or four course meal of hot and cold dishes and salads. The dinner menu offers four courses on a table d'hôte menu of good, traditional Scottish cooking accompanied by a reasonably priced wine list.

Open 21 Jan to 3 Jan except 20 to 27 Dec
Rooms: 28 with private facilities
Bed & Breakfast £36 - £81
Dinner B & B £58 - £103
Special Rates for 3+ nights
Bar Lunch 12 - 1.45 pm (a)
Bar Supper 7 - 8 pm except Sun (a)
Dinner 7 - 8.30 pm: 7 - 8 pm winter (d)
Vegetarians welcome - prior notice preferred
No smoking in dining room
Dogs welcome by prior arrangement,
at a small charge

Lightly poached local scallops on saffron sauce with rice pilaff. Pan-fried slices of venison in a plum and walnut sauce. Grilled Aberdeen Angus steak with mushrooms and a light garlic cream sauce. Home-made rhubarb and apple strudel with a cinnamon egg custard. Strawberry and green peppercorn parfait with an orange coulis.

STB Highly Commended 4 Crowns
Credit cards: 1, 3 + SWITCH
Proprietors: Sue & Michael Fink

Albert Hotel

Mounthoolie Lane, Kirkwall
Orkney KW15 1JZ
Tel: 01856 876000
Fax: 01856 875397

50 yards from Harbour. Just off Junction Road (A963).

Old town hotel in Kirkwall.

■ Hotel at the hub of things in Old Kirkwall.
■ Wholesome traditional cooking.
■ "This is good honest island fare which has the accolade of being popular with the local farming population."

The Albert Hotel has played an important role in the life of Kirkwall for over a 100 years. It stands within the conservation area in the centre of the town, between the harbour and St Magnus Cathedral, and has recently been refurbished in a style which retains its character and atmosphere. Attached to the hotel is the intimate Stable's Restaurant, which offers table d'hôte and à la carte menus, featuring local seafood, beef and lamb, all prepared to order. Its personable owner, Anjo Casey, also runs a busy local 'both bar' (with a fine open fire) and a nightclub which is one of the most popular venues in Kirkwall, so you are never at a loss for entertainment at the Albert. Children's menu available.

Open all year except Christmas Day + New Year
Rooms: 19 with private facilities
Bed & Breakfast £23 - £48
Dinner B & B £37.50 - £62
Special Rates available
Bar Lunch 12 - 2 pm (a)
Dining Room/Restaurant Lunch 12 - 2 pm (b)
Bar Supper 5 - 9.30 pm (a)
Dinner 6 - 9.30 pm (d)
Vegetarians welcome
Facilities for disabled visitors in dining room + bar

Tranched fillet of Orkney beef layered with local scallops, in a mild creamy white wine sauce. Prime Orkney fillet stuffed with smoked cheese, wrapped in bacon, oven-roasted and served with a Madeira sauce.

STB Commended 3 Crowns
Credit cards: 1, 2, 3, 6 + SWITCH
Proprietors: Anjo & Paddy Casey

Cleaton House Hotel

Cleaton, Westray
Orkney KW17 2DB
Tel: 01857 677508

Signposted at Rapness (Westray) ferry terminal 5 miles. Signposted right, ¾ miles·at end of single track road.

A friendly, family-run hotel on the Island of Westray.

- Victorian manse of distinctive 'ink bottle' design.
- Traditional Orkney cooking.
- "The owners are local and buy almost all their fish, shellfish, meat and vegetables from relations on the island!"

A regular roll-on, roll-off ferry service connects Westray to Kirkwall, and Cleaton's owner, Malcolm Stout, is happy to meet you at the pier. Such personal concern for guests is manifested in every aspect of this delightful small hotel. Malcolm is helped in the kitchen by his mother, and their menu offers local dishes which make the most of the outstanding local produce, simply but effectively. The hotel is being sympathetically restored and refurbished and has splendid views. An excellent base from which to explore Westray's beaches, cliffs and coves - and the second largest sea-bird colony in Britain.

Open all year except New Year's Day
Rooms: 5 with private facilities
Bed & Breakfast £22.50 - £25
Dinner B & B £32.50 - £45
Special Rates available
Bar Lunch 12 - 2 pm (a)
Dining Room/Restaurant Lunch 12 - 2 pm (b)
Bar Supper 6 - 9 pm Sun to Thu: 6 - 10 pm Fri Sat
Dinner 7 - 9.30 pm (c)
Vegetarians welcome
Facilities for disabled visitors
No smoking in dining room

Mussels in garlic and cider. Prawns with melon in lightly curried mayonnaise. Poached halibut on a lime and coriander sauce. Local scallops in a prawn and cream sauce. Fillet steaks. Sticky toffee pudding.

STB Highly Commended 3 Crowns
Credit cards: 1, 3 + Delta
Proprietors: Malcolm, Timothy & Sheelagh Stout

Creel Restaurant & Rooms

Front Road, St Margaret's Hope
Orkney KW17 2SL
Tel: 01856 831 311

13 miles south of Kirkwall over Churchill Barriers, at seafront.

This delightful Orcadian restaurant received a 'Taste of Britain' Award in 1986 and its chef/owner Alan Craigie recently appeared in a television series.

- Historic seafront house, stark, white-washed and gabled, overlooking St Margaret's Hope.
- Innovative modern cooking with strong influences of traditional Orcadian recipes.
- "The reward you might hope to find at the end of a rainbow... magic on plates."

The clean white walls of the Creel shine out on the quayside; a small, family-run restaurant with an international reputation. Chef/owner Alan Craigie presents a short menu which changes daily according to the availability of local produce and features Orcadian specialities. He cooks with great skill, respecting textures and flavours, creating original and unusual sauces, and spectacular desserts. He is assisted in the restaurant by his wife, Joyce. The atmosphere of the place is informal and friendly; the restaurant has three spacious and comfortable bedrooms, with bathrooms en suite. Since Alan's television appearances (in Keith Floyd's Britain and Ireland, Scotland's Larder and Rhodes Around Britain) the Creel has become a place of pilgrimage for gourmets, but its cheerful understated ambience has not changed - nor have its incredibly reasonable prices.

Open weekends Oct to Mar: daily Apr to Sep - advisable to book, especially in low season
Closed Christmas + Boxing Days
Rooms: 3 with private facilities
Bed & Breakfast £27 - £30
Dining Room/Restaurant Lunch 12.30 - 2 pm Sun only - by arrangement (b)
Dinner 7 - 9 pm (d)
Vegetarians welcome

Chef's home-made fishcakes with lemon sauce. Roasted lamb with mustard and oatmeal crust, with baby haggis on a risotto of pearl barley. Layers of chocolate mousse, crème caramel, meringue in a brandy-snap basket with home-made butterscotch sauce.

Credit cards: 1, 3
Proprietors: Alan & Joyce Craigie

Foveran Hotel

nr Kirkwall, St Ola
Orkney KW15 1SF
Tel: 01856 872389
Fax: 01856 876430

On A964 Orphir road, 2½ miles from Kirkwall.

Rural modern hotel in the Isles of Orkney.

- Scandanavian style, purpose-built hotel.
- Traditional Scottish cooking.
- "Orkney Scallop Chowder could be the benchmark for the best Scottish foods!"

This is a modern Scandinavian bungalow, purpose built as an hotel, with views over Scapa Flow. The interior is warm and inviting, and the Corsies are happy and charming hosts. Their menus rely heavily on the outstanding fresh seafood and meat of the islands, and familiar dishes are given a local twist (rich sauce laced with Highland Park whisky, Orkney Raven Ale sauce, etc). There is a separate vegetarian menu with a delicious range of dishes: this in itself is indicative of the attention you will encounter here.

Open all year except Jan
Rooms: 8 with private facilities
Bed & Breakfast £35 - £45
Dinner 7 - 9 pm Mon to Sat: Sun residents only (c-d)
Vegetarians welcome

Arbroath smokies served hot with butter. Orkney salmon steak poached gently and served with a light Champagne sauce. King of scallops served with a cheese and garlic sauce. Orkney bouillabaisse. Pan-fried noisette of lamb served with a marinated minted pear and a light sauce. Breast of chicken in a light lemon and sage sauce.

STB Commended 4 Crowns
Credit cards: 1, 3 + SWITCH, DELTA
Proprietors: Ivy & Bobby Corsie

Isles of Shetland

Busta House Hotel
Busta, Brae
Shetland ZE2 9QN
Tel: 01806 522 506
Fax: 01806 522 588

On the Muckle Roe road, 1 mile off A970
Hillswick road.

A 16th century laird's house with wonderful
views.

- Historic Shetland house.
- Traditional Scottish, with modern influences.
- "Perfect hosts and an enthusiastic and talented young chef."

This important 16th century house is typically
austere from the outside, which belies the restrained
charm of the interior. Run by Judith and Peter Jones
it is reputedly the oldest inhabited house in
Shetland and enjoys a commanding site
overlooking Busta Voe. It was formerly the seat of
the local laird and abounds with tales of ghosts and
past events; your hosts quickly put you at ease with
their caring and friendly approach. The cooking is
by a young local chef, Robert Richardson, whose
basis of sound traditional dishes is now being
augmented by more adventurous creations, such as
fresh octopus 'Provençal'.

Open all year except 22 Dec to 3 Jan
Rooms: 20 with private facilities
Bed & Breakfast £42 - £63
Dinner B & B from £60 (min 3 nights stay)
Bar Lunch 12 - 2 pm Mon to Sat: 12.30 - 2 pm
Sun (a-c)
Bar Supper 6.30 - 9.30 pm (a-c)
Dinner 7 - 9 pm (d) 4 course menu
Vegetarians welcome
No smoking in dining room

Poached local turbot fillet with a fresh rosemary
and mushroom sauce. Roast sirloin of beef with a
wholegrain mustard sauce. Baked Shetland salmon
with a honey and sesame glaze. Roast breast of
duck with a peach and spring onion sauce. Home-
made orange and Cointreau ice cream. Separate
vegetarian menu.

STB Commended 4 Crowns
Credit cards: 1, 2, 3, 5 + SWITCH, DELTA
Proprietors: Peter & Judith Jones

Isle of Skye

Ardvasar Hotel
Ardvasar, Sleat
Isle of Skye IV45 8AS
Tel: 01471 844223

At roadside A851, close to Armadale pier
(Armadale-Mallaig ferry).

A small hotel in the 'Wild Garden of Skye'.

- Traditional white-washed coaching inn.
- Innovative home cooking.
- "Halibut is quite the best fish on the island, here served coated in a golden Glayva sauce of wonderful flavour and a tantalising aroma."

Ardvasar Hotel is situated at the south end of the
Sleat Peninsula, near Armadale (the ferry point for
Mallaig) and enjoys lovely views over the Sound of
Sleat to the mountains of Knoydart. The hotel is
run by Bill and Greta Fowler who show personal
concern over their guests' comfort and well-being,
and encourage many to become regular visitors.
Bill cooks imaginatively and with great attention to
detail, with local fresh produce complemented by
unusual sauces and accompaniments. An
appetising à la carte menu is presented in the
restaurant and bar food is also available.

Open Mar to Nov
Note: bar open all year except Christmas +
New Year
Rooms: 10 with private facilities
Bed & Breakfast £32 - £37
Dinner B & B £50 - £55
Bar Lunch 12 - 2.15 pm (a)
Dining Room/Restaurant Lunch 12 - 2.15 pm
Bar Supper 5 - 7 pm (b)
Dinner 7 - 8.30 pm (b-c)
Vegetarians welcome

Cullen skink. Ardvasar smoked salmon and seafood
platter with horseradish cream. Roast stuffed lamb
with plum and cranberry sauce. Sauté salmon steak
fillet with leeks and white wine. Pan-fried haddock
fillet and local scallops meunière. 'Daily'
vegetarian dish.

STB Commended 3 Crowns
Credit cards: 1, 3 + DELTA
Proprietors: Bill & Gretta Fowler

Bosville Hotel
Bosville Terrace, Portree
Isle of Skye IV51 9DG
Tel: 01478 612846
Fax: 01478 613434

Town centre overlooking Portree Harbour and
Cuillin Mountains.

A bustling hotel in the centre of Portree village.

- Town centre hotel.
- Traditional Scottish cooking.
- "This lively restaurant which fronts the harbour has a high local reputation."

Centrally situated on a busy corner in Portree, the
Bosville has old fashioned award-winning Highland
hospitality. The popular restaurant fronts the street;
diners come and go and locals drop in for a chat, or
to deliver goods and fresh produce. The hotel stands
on a brae and commands fine views across the
harbour, with the Cuillin Mountains beyond. Table
d'hôte lunch and dinner menus are presented,
using local produce wherever possible and
featuring a number of Scottish specialities.

Open all year
Rooms: 18 with private facilities
Bed & Breakfast £25 - £35
Dinner B & B £40 - £50
Special Rates available
Meals available all day:
Bar Lunch 11.30 am - 5 pm except Sun (a)
Dining Room/Restaurant Lunch 12 - 2 pm
except Sun (a)
Bar Supper 5 - 9 pm Jun to Sep except
Sun: 5 - 8 pm Oct to May except Sun (b)
Dinner 5 - 9 pm Jun to Sep except
Sun: 5 - 8 pm Oct to May except Sun (c)
Residents only - Sun
Vegetarians and children welcome
Facilities for disabled visitors
No smoking in dining room
No dogs

Darne of locally caught wild Skye salmon gently
baked in a golden pastry envelope with a
mushroom, prawn and herb sauce laced with
Drambuie liqueur. Oven-baked Skye strawberries
laced with Cognac and served with a light
meringue covering.

STB Commended 3 Crowns
Credit cards: 1, 2, 3 + Switch, Delta
Proprietors : Murdo & Marie MacLeod

Dunorin House Hotel

Herebost, Dunvegan
Isle of Skye IV55 8GZ
Tel: 01470 521488

From Kyleakin A850 to Sligachan, then A863 to Dunvegan. 2 miles south of Dunvegan turn left at Roag/Orbost junction, 200m on right.

A small and modern, family-run hotel in a beautiful corner of Skye.

- Purpose-built with modern comforts in mind.
- Scottish cooking with island recipes/hotel cooking.
- "Providing a truly Highland hospitality."

Dunorin House is the brainchild of Gaelic-speaking native islanders Joan and Alasdair MacLean. Built in 1989, it offers comfortable accommodation in ten en suite rooms. The hotel enjoys panoramic views across Loch Roag to the Cuillin Hills. All bedrooms and public rooms are on ground level with wide corridors and so are specially suitable for the disabled. In the evenings, Joan and Alasdair's son Darren, a Gaelic Festival winner, entertains guests with traditional Scottish music. With many local recipes, the hotel's à la carte menu seeks to make the most of fresh local produce such as scallops, venison and salmon. It also offers more routine hotel fare. The wine list is reasonably priced and varied.

Open Apr to Nov
Rooms: 10 with private facilities
Bed & Breakfast £29 - £38
Room Rate £47.50 - £54.50
Dinner 6.45 - 9 pm (c)
Restricted Hotel Licence
Vegetarians welcome
Facilities for disabled visitors
No smoking in dining room
No dogs

Scallops in garlic butter. Highland haggis laced with Talisker. Scottish lamb cutlets served with provençal sauce. Medallions of venison with a port and redcurrant sauce. Clootie dumpling. Atholl brose. Cranachan.

STB Highly Commended 3 Crowns
Credit cards: 1, 3
Proprietors: Joan & Alasdair MacLean

Hotel Eilean Iarmain

Sleat, Isle of Skye
Inverness-shire IV43 8QR
Tel: 01471 833332
Fax: 01471 833275

Barely 20 minutes drive on A851 Armadale-Kyleakin.

Gaelic charm at 'The Inn on the Sea'.

- Island hotel.
- Modern Scottish cooking.
- "Lovely welcome, gorgeous food. A great pleasure to stay here."

Hotel Eilean Iarmain (Isle Ornsay Hotel) stands on the small rocky bay of Isle Ornsay in the south of Skye, with expansive views over the Sound of Sleat to the hills of Knoydart. The hotel was built in 1888 and retains the charm and old-world character of a gentler age, with log fires in the public rooms and a panelled dining room. It is owned by Sir Iain Noble - who has done so much for Gaelic culture and language: staff and locals are all Gaelic speakers. The award-winning restaurant serves a four course table d'hôte menu (in Gaelic, but translated) which features local shellfish (landed only yards from the hotel), game and vegetables. AA 'Rosette for Restaurant'. RAC 'Restaurant Award'.

Open all year
Rooms: 12 with private facilities
Bed & Breakfast £42 - £60
Dinner B & B £68.50 - £86.50
Special Rates available
Bar Lunch 12.30 - 2.30 pm (a)
Dining Room/Restaurant Lunch 12.30 - 2 pm (c)
Bar Supper 6.30 - 9.30 pm (a)
Dinner 7.30 - 9 pm (e)
Vegetarians welcome
No smoking in restaurant

Eilean Iarmain oysters grilled with parmesan. Roast breast of duck with plum and port gravy. Salmon steaks with asparagus sauce. Herb pancakes with green pea pâté served with a creamy mushroom sauce. Chocolate and mint syllabub flan. Selection of cheeses with home-made oatcakes and biscuits.

STB Commended 3 Crowns
Credit cards: 1, 2, 3, 6
Proprietors: Sir Iain & Lady Noble

Flodigarry Country House Hotel & The Water Horse Restaurant

Staffin, Isle of Skye
Inverness-shire IV51 9HZ
Tel: 01470 552002
Fax: 01470 522301

A855 north from Portree to Staffin, 4 miles from Staffin to Flodigarry.

Country hotel at the north end of Skye.

- Unsurpassed views.
- Fine Scottish cuisine.
- "More like a home than an hotel."

This country house hotel crouches between the towering pinnacles of the Quiraing and has panoramic sea views over Flodigarry Island, and across Staffin Bay. Its 19th century castellate additions lend it the air of folklore, especially being so close to the mysterious 'Fairy Glen', and adjacent is Flora Macdonald's cottage (now converted to provide seven luxury en suite rooms, five with sea view). Adding to the interest is the ruin of a broch in the hotel gardens, inhabited around 500 BC. In the Water Horse Restaurant, residents and non-residents can enjoy a daily changing table d'hôte menu, featuring traditional dishes, or choose from an à la carte menu. Bar meals are served in the Conservatory.

Open all year
Rooms: 23, 18 with private facilities
Bed & Breakfast £23 - £49
Dinner B & B £40 - £69
Special Rates available
Bar Meals (Conservatory) 11 am - 10 pm (a)
Dining Room/Restaurant Lunch 12.30 - 2.30 pm Sun only (b) or by arrangement
Dinner 7 - 10 pm (c) 4 course menu
Vegetarians welcome

Baked avocado pear with prawns and walnut dressing. Grilled lamb cutlets with an apricot and mint glaze. Prime Scottish steak on a bed of puff pastry with a mushroom and red wine sauce. Mushroom and leek crêpes with elderflower wine sauce. Local king scallops with ginger and spring onions. Staffin Bay prawns.

STB Commended 3 Crowns
Credit cards: 1, 3 + SWITCH, DELTA
Proprietors: Andrew & Pamela Butler

The Glenview Inn & Restaurant

Culnacnoc, Staffin
Isle of Skye
IV51 9JH
Tel: 01470 562 248
Fax: 01470 562 211

12 miles from Portree on the Staffin road.

A friendly and conscientious inn near Staffin.

- Restaurant with rooms.
- Good home cooking.
- "The best food I ate in Skye during this visit."

The bedrooms have the usual extras, and more - a large bottle of shampoo, shower gel, sticking plasters, paracetamol, cotton buds (and cotton wool), alka selzer. This is an indication of how keen Paul and Cathy Booth are to make their guests feel at home! Their home is traditional and is ideally placed for exploring the northern part of Skye. Paul's cooking uses local produce and ecclectic techniques to produce well-priced and varied meals, selected from an à la carte blackboard menu. The restaurant won a Certificate of Commendation for 'Highest Quality Meal' in the Talisker Quality Awards.

Open mid Mar to early Jan
Rooms: 4 with private facilities
Bed & Breakfast £20 - £32
Dining Room / Restaurant
Lunch 12 - 2.30 pm (a)
Dinner 6 - 9.30 pm (b)
Vegetarians welcome
No smoking area in restaurant

Fresh squat lobster tails from Skye, sautéd in garlic and parsley butter. Skye scallops sautéd with wine, cream and fresh herbs served on a bed of green noodles. Aberdeen Angus steaks. Individual hot chocolate soufflé pudding with strawberry sauce and fresh cream.

STB Commended 3 Crowns
Credit cards: 1, 3
Proprietors: Paul & Cathie Booth

Harlosh House

by Dunvegan
Isle of Skye IV55 8ZG
Tel: 01470 521367

Off A863, 4 miles south of Dunvegan.

A small hotel in a remote setting on the shores of Loch Bracadale.

- Charming 18th century tacksman's house with six bedrooms.
- Modern restaurant cooking.
- "We saw the crabs being hauled out of the loch for dinner!"

This converted farmhouse is not far south of Dunvegan in the north-west of the island, and has splendid views of the Cuillins and the islands which speckle the sea loch it sits beside. It has a relaxed and homely atmosphere inspired by its owners, Peter and Lindsey Elford who also prepare and serve the dinners. Peter cooks, making use of the fresh seafood (which is predominant in the restaurant), venison and lamb he can buy. His attention to detail is meticulous (he also makes his own breads, desserts and chocolates) and the dishes on his simple table d'hôte menus are plain, fresh and delicious.

Open Easter to mid Oct
Rooms: 6, 5 with private facilities
Bed & Breakfast £34 - £45
Dinner B & B £58.50 - £69.50
Lunch - residents only
Dinner 7 - 8.30 pm (d)
Vegetarians welcome - prior notice required
No smoking in restaurant
No dogs

Warm salad of smoked sprats and avocado with a hazelnut dressing. Pan-fried monkfish tail with a mustard sauce and caramelised shallots. Wild apricot strudel with cinnamon ice cream. Scottish cheeses.

Credit cards: 1, 3 + SWITCH
Proprietors: Peter & Lindsey Elford

Kinloch Lodge

Sleat, Isle of Skye
IV43 8QY
Tel: 01471 833214
Fax: 01471 833277

8 miles south of Broadford on A851. 10 miles north of Armadale on A851. 1 mile off A851.

The home of the High Chief of Clan Donald and Lady Macdonald.

- Country house hotel in Sleat.
- Outstanding traditional cooking with innovative influences.
- "Lord and Lady Macdonald are welcoming hosts, their staff are friendly, and the cooking is delicious."

Kinloch was built in 1680, as a farmhouse, and was expanded into a sporting lodge in the 19th century. As the home of Lord Macdonald of Macdonald, it is full of portraits of ancestors, old furniture and family treasures. It is very much a family home, with two comfortable drawing rooms, log fires and a variety of bedrooms. Lady Claire Macdonald is one of the best known cooks in Scotland: an award-winning journalist and the author of 12 cookbooks. Assisted by a small team she presents a five course table d'hôte menu each night which uses only fresh seasonal produce. The breakfasts are a very special treat. Member of the Scotch Beef Club.

Open Mar to Nov incl
Rooms: 10 with private facilities
Bed & Breakfast £50 - £85
Dinner B & B £78 - £120
Special Rates available
Dinner at 8 pm or by arrangement (f)
5 course menu
Vegetarians welcome - prior notice required
Children welcome by arrangement
No smoking in dining room
Dogs welcome by arrangement

Scallop soufflé. Stir-fried monkfish with leeks, ginger and crème fraîche. Char-grilled venison fillet with port and redcurrant sauce. Locally grown strawberries with almond meringue.

STB Highly Commended 4 Crowns
Credit cards: 1, 3
Proprietors: Lord & Lady Macdonald

Lochbay Seafood Restaurant

1/2 Macleod's Terrace
Stein, Waternish
Isle of Skye IV55 8GA
Tel: 01470 592235

Situated 5 miles down the Waternish Peninsula, in Stein Village. Last house in the village.

A small fish restaurant in Waternish, with three bedrooms.

■ Two restored 18th century cottages with gorgeous views over to the Outer Isles.
■ Traditional Scottish home cooking with a strong emphasis on seafood.
■ "What could be healthier than plain grilled mullet straight from the sea? But then I simply couldn't resist Margaret Greenhalgh's delicious home-made chips!"

Situated in the old fishing village of Stein and located just 30 yards from the pier with some lovely unspoilt views, these fisherman's cottages have been restored rather than converted. The old black range is still there, (and working), the copper kettle on the hob; white-washed walls and original pine panelling. The place has great charm, and this is enhanced by the hospitality of its owners, Peter and Margaret Greenhalgh. The fish and shellfish is brought up from the pier and cooked simply and deliciously by Margaret - it simply could not be fresher.

Open Easter to 31 Oct
Rooms: 3
Bed & Breakfast £16.50 - £18.50
Dining Room/Restaurant Lunch 12 - 3 pm except Sat (a)
Dinner 6 - 8 30 pm except Sat (b)
Restaurant closed Sat except Easter Sat
No smoking in restaurant

Starters of squat lobster, princess scallops, oysters, mussels etc. Seafood platter, lobster, king prawns, scallop, various selection of fresh fish. Clootie dumpling etc.

Credit cards: 1, 3
Proprietors: Peter & Margaret Greenhalgh

Rosedale Hotel

Beaumont Crescent, Portree
Isle of Skye IV51 9DB
Tel: 01478 613131
Fax: 01478 612531

Harbourside location, 100 yards from village square.

A small hotel in Skye's principal village with views over the harbour.

■ Harbourside fisherman's cottages comfortably converted to accommodate this friendly hotel.
■ Modern Scottish cooking.
■ " Very interesting menus, with unusual - and most successful - combinations of ingredients and flavours."

The Rosedale was originally a row of William IV cottages adjacent to the harbour in the heart of old Portree. The hotel has now spread its wings in all directions so that it now occupies practically all of one side of the Portree waterfront. Growth was in response to demand and demand was created by satisfied guests returning yet again for another stay. There are many unique and interesting features - not least of which is finding your way to the first floor restaurant! - from which there are splendid views out over the bay. Chef Linda Thomson presents a daily changing table d'hôte dinner menu which offers a good choice of imaginative dishes (there is always a speciality vegetarian main course), based upon fresh local produce whenever it is available.

Open 11 May to 1 Oct
Rooms: 23 with private facilities
Bed & Breakfast £30 - £40
Dinner B & B £50 - £60
Special Rates for 3+ nights
Dinner 7 - 8.30 pm (d)
Vegetarians welcome
No smoking in restaurant

Chicken liver pârfait with whisky soaked raisins. Roast leg of lamb with tartlets of aubergines and lentils. Warm bittersweet chocolate cup cake with vanilla ice cream and a drizzle of caramel sauce.

STB Highly Commended 4 Crowns
Credit cards: 1, 3
Proprietor: Hugh Andrew

Skeabost House Hotel

Skeabost Bridge
Isle of Skye IV51 9NP
Tel: 0147 032 202
Fax: 0147 032 454

4 miles north of Portree on Dunvegan road.

An imposing family-run hotel on the shores of Loch Snizort.

■ A 19th century hunting lodge set in lovely grounds.
■ Modern Scottish cooking.
■ "The fish and game is skilfully cooked, and retains both delicacy and strength. Well-matched sauces."

Built in 1870 this former hunting lodge has been a family-run establishment for over 26 years. Three generations of McNabs have owned it (Granny, aged 83, still prepares the traditional afternoon teas) It is an oasis of cultivated serenity within the wild and rugged terrain of Skye. Positioned in 12 acres of lovely grounds which stretch down to the waterside, its well-kept gardens also incorporate a nine-hole golf course. During 1994 a period-conservatory overlooking the loch was added to the main building and extended the hotel's dining facilities. A buffet menu is avilable during the day and in the more formal surroundings of the elegant, wood-panelled dining room Angus McNab presents daily changing table d'hôte menus which demonstrate considerable flair and skill, particularly with fish and game. Member of the Scotch Beef Club.

Open 1 Apr to 24 Oct
Rooms: 26 with private facilities
Bed & Breakfast £41.50 - £65
Dinner B & B £65 - £88
Room Rate £83 - £112
Special Rates for 2/3 nights Apr + Oct
Bar Lunch/Buffet Table 12 - 1.30 pm (b)
Bar Supper 6.30 - 9 pm (b)
Dinner 7 - 8.30 pm (d-e)
Vegetarians welcome

Terrine of Highland pheasant served with a cranberry and onion confit. Fillets of lemon sole served with a mild lobster sauce and glaced cucumber. Rich dark chocolate terrine served with an orange crème anglaise. Selection of Scottish farmhouse cheeses.

STB Commended 4 Crowns
Credit cards: 1, 3 + SWITCH, DELTA
Proprietors: Stuart/McNab/Stuart

Three Chimneys Restaurant

Colbost, nr Dunvegan
Isle of Skye IV55 8ZT
Tel: 01470 511258 (Glendale)

Prestige Award Winner 1992

4 miles west of Dunvegan on B884 road to Glendale. Look out for Glendale Visitor Route signs.

> Island restaurant in a gem of a setting.

■ Informal restaurant in converted crofter's cottage.
■ Imaginative modern Scottish cooking.
■ "The Three Chimneys is rightly acclaimed by food writers and lives up to its reputation for interesting food of very high quality."

This restaurant is practically at the end of the road, right on the shore at Dunvegan, on the scenic Glendale Visitor Route which takes you to the most westerly point of Skye. It is open all day. Morning coffee, lunch and afternoon tea are served. Dinner is a really full blown occasion with a four course table d'hôte menu accompanied by a well-chosen wine list offering a good choice of New World and European wines. As you would expect, given its location, seafood is a speciality of the menu but fish, lamb, venison and an intriguing vegetarian choice are also on offer. This is Scottish cooking at its best - simple, imaginative, delicious. Leave room for chef Shirley Spear's desserts which are irresistible.

Open 31 Mar to 21 Oct
Daytime Menu 10.30 am - 12 noon: 2 - 4.30 pm except Sun (a)
Dining Room/Restaurant Lunch 12.30 - 2 pm except Sun (a-d)
Dinner 7 - 9 pm except Sun (e) 4 course menu
Closed Sun except Easter Sun + Whitsun
No smoking in restaurant

Home-baked bread. Home-made soups including fish brees and bisques. Skye seafood platter. Warm salad of scallops and monkfish with prawns and bacon. Hot lobster medley. Seafood treasure trove. Rabbit and hare terrine with walnut oil dressing. Fillet of venison with raspberry and bitter chocolate game sauce. Sirloin steak split and filled with peat-smoked salmon. Delicious puddings, hot and cold.

Credit cards: 1, 3 + SWITCH
Proprietors: Eddie & Shirley Spear

Uig Hotel

Uig, Portree
Isle of Skye IV51 9YE
Tel: 01470 542 205
Fax: 01470 542 308

Entering Uig from Portree on A856, hotel is halfway down hill on right.

> Former coaching inn in charming island location.

■ Popular family-run hotel.
■ Traditional Scottish cooking.
■ "Grace Graham has been at the helm of the Uig Hotel for almost 50 years and is an experienced and skilful hostess."

The hotel is blessed with an extremely attractive location on a hillside overlooking Uig Bay and Loch Snizort. It is a well-known and popular stopping off point to or from the Hebridean ferries and is also an ideal base from which to explore Skye. Grace Graham has owned the hotel since 1946 and her personal touch is everywhere. Bedrooms and public rooms are comfortable and tastefully furnished and some are also self-catering apartments, particularly attractive for those looking for a family break. The hotel also has its own pony-trekking centre. Food and standards of hospitality are good with simple Scottish fare on a reasonably priced table d'hôte menu.

Open 1 Apr to 15 Oct
Rooms: 17 with private facilities
Bed & Breakfast £30 - £43
Dinner B & B £48 - £59
Special Rates available
Coffee Shop serves morning coffee + afternoon tea
Buffet Lunch 12.15 - 1.45 pm (a)
Dinner 7.15 - 8.15 pm (d) 4 course menu
Dogs by arrangement only
No smoking in restaurant
Vegetarians welcome

Home-made fishcakes. Roast leg of Dornoch lamb with mint sauce and redcurrant jelly. Roast rib of Scottish beef. Sauté of chicken with oranges, lemons, tomatoes and cinnamon. Grilled salmon steaks with parsley butter. Home-made sweets.

STB Commended 4 Crowns
Credit cards: 1, 2, 3, 5 + SWITCH
Proprietors: Grace Graham & David Taylor

Ullinish Lodge Hotel

Struan
Isle of Skye IV56 8FD
Tel: 01470 572214

Off A863 between Sligachan and Dunvegan, along well signposted side road.

> A lovely house overlooking the Cuillins with comfortable accommodation and a restaurant.

■ A small country house with a lovely situation on Loch Bracadale.
■ Strong traditional Scottish emphasis.
■ "I had difficulty deciding between the beauty of the views and such good food."

Ullinish Lodge was built in the 18th century and is situated just south of Dunvegan Castle, the home of the Chiefs of Clan Macleod for the past 1,000 years. John and Claudia Mulford are welcoming hosts; their hotel has a large and inviting lounge, with antique furniture, comfortable sofas and an open fire. Bedrooms are comfortable, also furnished with antiques, and have stupendous views. In the restaurant you can choose from a wide range of classic Scottish dishes, cooked with care and attention to clear, fresh flavours. The owners offer a decent wine list, including a range of Scottish wines.

Open 25 Mar to 31 Oct
Rooms: 8 with private facilities
Bed & Breakfast £30 - £40
Dinner B & B £49 - £53
Room Rate £23.50 - £33.50
Special Rates for 3+/7+ nights
Bar Supper 6 - 9 pm (b)
Dinner 7 - 8 pm (or by arrangement) (c)
Vegetarians welcome
No smoking in restaurant

Black Isle pheasant casserole. Fillet of salmon in asparagus sauce. Highland venison in a red wine casserole. Cranachan. Home-made crumble.

STB Commended 3 Crowns
Credit cards: 1, 3 + SWITCH
Proprietors: John & Claudia Mulford

123
Isle of Tiree

The Glassary
Sandaig, Isle of Tiree
Argyll PA77 6XQ
Tel: 01879 220684
Fax: 01879 220684

On west coast of island. On leaving pier turn left through Scarinish to Heylipol, Middleton and Sandaig at west end of the island.

A restaurant and guest house on the beautiful Isle of Tiree.

- The restaurant is a pine-lined coverted byre.
- Home cooking.
- "Traditional surroundings."

The Glassary is situated on the picturesque west coast of the island, close to long stretches of unspoiled white sandy beaches. The name is taken from the nearby ruined kelp (seaweed) factory which operated during the last century. The house offers limited accommodation. All the beef, lamb and seafood are local and you can order lobster in advance. Home-made soups are excellent and a speciality is carageen pudding, made from kelp. The menu prices are very reasonable and the cooking is imaginative with some original and inventive touches, making eating here a most enjoyable experience.

Open Easter to Oct
Rooms: 3
Bed & Breakfast £18 - £20
Dinner B & B £28 - £32
Restaurant Lunch 12 - 2 pm (a)
Dinner 7 - 8.30 pm (b-d)
Vegetarians welcome

Scampi poached with green peppercorns, vermouth and cream served on a bed of rice. Breast of duck fillet, served in a honey, Drambuie and lemon sauce. Medallions of pork fillet, pan-fried and served in a wholegrain mustard and redcurrant sauce. Banoffee roulade.

No credit cards
Proprietors: Mabel & Donnie Macarthur

124
Jedburgh

Willow Court
The Friars, Jedburgh
Roxburghshire TD8 6BN
Tel: 01835 863702
Fax: 01835 864601

From Market Place, Jedburgh, take Exchange Street - The Friars is first road on right.

Family guest house in historic Border town.

- Small, friendly guest house.
- Scottish home cooking.
- "Jane McGovern is a lively and capable hostess who is intent on ensuring her guests enjoy their stay to the utmost."

This charming little guest house in the centre of Jedburgh epitomises all that is best about Scottish hospitality - a warm welcome, a cheerful atmosphere and unstinting attention to the comfort of guests. Bedrooms are pleasingly decorated and very comfortable. The bright dining conservatory at the front of the house has splendid views over Jedburgh, and here breakfast and dinner are served. Jane's food is good, old fashioned, home cooking at its best, making the most of local produce and using fruit, vegetables and herbs from her own garden. Jane takes endlesss trouble to make guests feel at home and to introduce them to all the attractions of the area.

Open all year except Christmas Eve
+ Christmas Day
Rooms: 4 with private facilities
Bed & Breakfast £14 - £22
Dinner B & B £24.50 - £32.50
Special rates available
Dinner at 6.30 pm (b) - guests are requested to select their menu by 5 pm
Restricted Licence
Vegetarians welcome
Facilities for disabled visitors
No smoking in restaurant + bedrooms

Home-made soups. Dill marinated Orkney herring with cucumber and yoghurt dip. Local roe venison braised in red wine with juniper berries. Border lamb chops with fruit jelly. Chicken fillet with honey and mustard sauce. Salmon steak poached in butter and dry cider. Home-grown fruit and vegetables. Speciality home-made ice creams e.g. Drambuie and lemon, garden strawberry.

STB Highly Commended 3 Crowns
No credit cards
Proprietor: Jane McGovern

125
Kelso

Ednam House Hotel
Bridge Street, Kelso
Roxburghshire TD5 7HT
Tel: 01573 224168
Fax: 01573 226319

Off town square of Kelso, on right hand side of street leading to the bridge.

Impressive family-run hotel in Borders country.

- Georgian mansion.
- Traditional and modern Scottish cooking.
- "If you are a fisherman the chef will prepare your catch for dinner or have it smoked to take home."

Standing on the banks of the Tweed in Kelso and enjoying wonderful views, this is considered to be the finest Georgian mansion in Roxburghshire. It was built in 1761 and its elegant facade is complemented by an interior with ornate ceilings, fireplaces and carved woodwork. In spite of this grandeur, Ednam is not a daunting house, and you are very warmly received. It has a homely, attractively 'old fashioned' feel, and a genuine country house atmosphere, encouraged by the numbers of salmon fishermen who stay here. The proprietor/chef Ralph Brookes describes his cooking as 'straightforward, but along classical lines' and creates original dishes using unusual ingredients such as oxtail and wood pigeon, preferring to fashion his menus from the fresh ingredients he can obtain locally and seasonally.

Open 10 Jan to 22 Dec
Rooms: 32 with private facilities
Bed & Breakfast £33 - £46.50
Dinner B & B £46.50 - £60 (min 2 nights)
Bar Lunch 12.30 - 2 pm except Sun (a)
Dining Room/Restaurant Lunch
12.30 - 2 pm Sun only (b)
Dinner 7 - 9 pm (a-c)
Vegetarians welcome - prior notice required

Smoked haddock baked in a cheese sauce. Border lamb chops with a thyme gravy. Pot-roasted Guinea fowl with a red wine gravy. Collops of wild venison served with a cranberry and honey sauce. Cloutie dumpling with whipped cream and toasted flaked almonds. Whisky shortcake with coffee sauce. Home-made ice creams. Scottish cheeseboard.

STB Commended 4 Crowns
Credit cards: 1, 3 + SWITCH
Proprietors: R Alastair Brooks & Ralph Brooks

Sunlaws House Hotel

Heiton, Kelso
Roxburghshire TD5 8JZ
Tel: 01573 450331
Fax: 01573 450611

Situated at the village of Heiton, on the A698 Kelso-Hawick road. Signposed at western end of village.

One of Scotland's leading country house hotels in a lovely secluded setting.

■ Country house hotel.
■ Traditional Scottish, with grand hotel touches.
■ " Everything about this hotel is of the highest standard."

The Duke of Roxburghe, who owns Sunlaws, turned it into a gracious hotel in the 1970s. The building is in the Scottish baronial style, and stands on the banks of the River Tweed in many hundreds of acres of park and woodland. The hotel offers a variety of country pursuits and in June 1997 its own golf course will open. Although it is an imposing mansion, Sunlaws retains the common touch. The welcome is genuinely hospitable; there are many thoughtful, cosy touches; the overall manner and atmosphere is unpretentious. Well constructed table d'hôte menus are offered for lunch and dinner (an à la carte menu is also available in the evening) - offering both light and complex dishes and a good range of meat, fish and poultry. Chef David Bates gives careful thought to combinations of flavour and presentation. The hotel has an extensive wine list (160 bins). Given the standard of cooking and service, his meals are extremely good value for money. Member of the Scotch Beef Club.

Open all year
Rooms: 22 with private facilities
Bed & Breakfast £70 - £95
Dinner B & B £100 - £125
Special Rates available
Bar Lunch 12.30 - 2 pm (b)
Dining Room Lunch 12.30 - 2 pm (b)
Dinner 7.30 - 9.30 pm (e)
No smoking in dining room
Vegetarians welcome

Venison broth with beetroot and root vegetables. Steamed brill with salmon soufflé and chervil butter sauce. Roast sirloin of beef, rosemary gravy and pickled walnuts. Brandy-snap basket filled with praline ice cream.

STB Highly Commended 5 Crowns
Credit cards: 1, 2, 3, 5 + SWITCH

Croft-na-Caber

Garden Restaurant, Kenmore
Perthshire PH15 2HW
Tel: 01887 830236
Fax: 01887 830649

A827 to Kenmore, then take unclassified road along south shore of the loch for ½ mile.

Rural hotel and restaurant with chalets.

■ Converted Manse.
■ Simple cooking with some classic influences.
■ "Dishes are prepared and cooked with care and the results were rather appetising."

This is an old presbyterian manse on the shores of Loch Tay which now lies at the heart of a busy water sports and Austrian chalet complex which offers a multitude of activity holidays for the energetic and adventurous. The impressive Garden Restaurant overlooking the loch is now under the direction of Master Chef Kenneth McPhee, one time head chef at Inverlochy Castle. The menu is imaginative and well-presented. Three course dinner with five choices in each.

Open all year
Rooms: 5 with private facilities plus 17 chalets
Bed & Breakfast £23 - £35
Dinner B & B £39.50 - £51.50
Licensed coffee shop 9 - 5 pm
Bar Meals 12 - 10 pm weekends: 12 - 2 pm mid week (a)
Restaurant Lunch 12 - 2 pm Mon to Fri: 12 - 4 pm Sun (b)
Bar Supper 5 - 10pm (a)
Dinner 7 - 9 pm (c)
Taste of Scotland applies to Garden Restaurant
Vegetarians welcome
Facilities for disabled visitors
No smoking in restaurant

Light dill flavoured salmon mousse with mild mustard sauce. Roast pheasant with apple and Calvados sauce. Raspberry and bramble cranachan.

Credit cards: 1, 3
Proprietor: A C Barratt

Ardsheal House

Kentallen of Appin
Argyll PA38 4BX
Tel: 01631 740227
Fax: 01631 740342

On A828 Oban road, 4 miles south of Ballachulish Bridge.

A luxurious country house hotel in an historic and romantic setting overlooking Loch Linnhe.

■ An oustanding country house hotel.
■ Modern Scottish cooking.
■ "The food was so fresh and summery, one felt that it must be straight from the garden and estate; and it was."

Everywhere you turn, as you travel up the mile-long drive, there are ancient trees, and between them glimpses of sea and mountains.The original house was built by the Stewarts of Appin in the 1500s. Today, Ardsheal is the home of George and Michelle Kelso, although ownership passed recently to Mr and Mrs Neil Sutherland. It is beautifully appointed, with a magnificent oak-panelled hall, a traditional billiards room and a dining room conservatory. Throughout it is furnished with fine antiques, and log fires burn in the sitting rooms on chilly days. The cooking is elegant and assured. Vegetables, fruits and herbs come from the two acre kitchen garden; meat, fish and shellfish is sourced locally; all preserves are made in the kitchen. The atmosphere of the place is very much that of an elegant private house, and to stay at Ardsheal is like joining a very select house party. A very special place.

Open all year
Rooms: 13 with private facilities
Special Winter Rates available
Dinner B & B £65 - £90
Light Lunch (a)
Dining Room/Restaurant Lunch 12 - 1.45 pm (c)
Dinner at 8.30 pm (f) 6 course menu
Vegetarians welcome
No smoking in restaurant

Warm tartlet of quail with buttered cabbage, kummel and blackcurrant sauce. Pan-fried west coast scallops with saffron and cucumber butter sauce. Caramelised lemon tart with raspberry coulis and crème Chantilly.

STB Highly Commended 3 Crowns
Credit cards: 1, 2, 3 + SWITCH

Kilchrenan

Ardanaiseig Hotel

Kilchrenan, by Taynuilt
Argyll PA35 1HE
Tel: 01866 833 333
Fax: 01866 833 222

A85 to Taynuilt, then B845. At Kilchrenan take road signed for hotel (3½ miles).

> A Scottish baronial mansion in a glorious setting.

■ Award-winning country house hotel.
■ Country house cooking.
■ "An elegant and spacious country house hotel which blends the traditional and the modern in the best country house style."

Ardanaiseig stands on a wooded promontory on Loch Awe, looking towards mighty Ben Cruachan. It is a truly idyllic setting: the dramatic West Highland scenery provides a magnificent backdrop for the house's renowned shrub and woodland garden which contains many rare species. The hotel is everything you would expect from a Highland country house - comfortable, relaxing and hospitable. Bedrooms are individually furnished and convey a sense of privacy and peace; public rooms have log fires, big comfy chairs and antique furniture. The kitchen lives up to the hotel's high standard, producing imaginative, well-prepared and deliciously presented dishes. The table d'hote menus are well-balanced and offer a good choice of fresh, exclusively home-made food.

Open 1 Apr to 21 Oct
Rooms: 14 with private facilities
Bed & Breakfast £48 - £110
Dinner B & B £81.50 - £143.50
Special Rates for 2+/7+ nights
Light Lunch 12.30 - 2 pm (a)
Dining Room/Restaurant Lunch 12.30 - 2 pm (c)
Dinner 7.30 - 9 pm (f)
Vegetarians welcome - prior notice required
No smoking in dining room

Smoked salmon salad with a dill and mustard dressing. Medallion of beef fillet on a light horseradish flavoured jus. Darnes of monkfish served under a brioche crust, set on a pimento vinaigrette. Grand Marnier savarin. Hot hazelnut soufflé with poached fig and ginger sorbet. Selection of Scottish cheeses.

STB Highly Commended 4 Crowns
Credit cards: 1, 2, 3, 5
Proprietor: James Smith

Taychreggan Hotel

Kilchrenan, by Taynuilt
Argyll PA35 1HQ
Tel: 01866 833 211/833 366
Fax: 01866 833 244

Leave A85 at Taynuilt on to B845 through village of Kilchrenan to the loch side.

> A beautiful small country hotel set in the grandeur of Argyll.

■ A highly regarded, award-winning hotel of great distinction.
■ Elegant British cuisine.
■ "It is rare to find a hotel of this standard."

There has been a hotel here, nestling on the shores of Loch Awe, for 300 years. Taychreggan was a drovers' inn. With its cobbled courtyard and great charm, it retains that sense of peace and history. But under proprietor Annie Paul no effort has been spared to restore and enhance the hotel's unique ambience. Her emphasis and that of her dedicated staff is to make visitors feel like house guests, even well-behaved canine ones. Award-winning chef Hugh Cocker presents imaginative fine cuisine in the hotel's dining room. Simpler bar lunches are no less carefully prepared. Euan Paul's wine list is a revelation. The hotel has 2 AA Rosettes - voted by AA inspectors 'One of the Most Romantic Hotels in the UK' 1995. AA Courtesy and Care Award 1995 - Scotland. Les Routiers 'Newcomer of the Year 1995 Award. Children over 12 years welcome.

Open all year
Rooms: 20 with private facilities
Bed & Breakfast £37 - £52
Dinner B & B £65 - £80
Special Spring/Autumn Rates
Bar Lunch 12.30 - 2 pm (b)
Dinner 7.30 - 8.45 pm (e) 5 course menu
Vegetarians welcome - prior notice advised

Confit of duck with a sun-dried tomato risotto. Minestrone of Loch Etive mussels with saffron. Light terrine of salmon, trout and grey mullet with Noilly Prat and chives. Fillets of lemon sole stuffed with a crab mousse served with an orange and basil sauce. Hot soufflé of Aberfeldy raspberries.

STB Highly Commended 4 Crowns
Credit cards: 1, 2, 3 + SWITCH, DELTA
Proprietors: Euan & Annie Paul

Kildrummy

Kildrummy Castle Hotel

Kildrummy, by Alford
Aberdeenshire AB33 8RA
Tel: 019755 71288
Fax: 019755 71345

On A97 Ballater-Huntly, 35 miles west of Aberdeen.

> A grand country house hotel on Donside amidst acres of gardens.

■ A very grand Victorian house converted into a luxurious hotel.
■ Good hotel cooking.
■ "Choice of all the fruits of land and sea."

Kildrummy is a magnificent house near Alford, deep in rural Aberdeenshire and standing in 12 acres of gardens - one of several splendid castles and country houses in the area, many of them open to the public. Having been lavishly appointed when it was built and well-maintained ever since, it has a wonderful period charm. Its sumptuous colour schemes and ornately panelled ceilings, walls and fire surrounds create an atmosphere of opulence, and the attention to detail in furnishing the public rooms complements this well. Upstairs, the 16 en suite bedrooms are equally tastefully furnished. The menu is heartily luxurious - fine country house cooking, substantial and locally sourced fish, game and meat - and professionally served.

Open 9 Feb to 3 Jan
Rooms: 16 with private facilities
Bed & Breakfast £55 - £72.50
Dinner B & B £59 - £99
Special Rates available
Dining Room/Restaurant Lunch 12.30 - 1.45 pm (b)
Dinner 7 - 9 pm (e) 4 course menu
Vegetarians welcome
No smoking in dining room

Salad of smoked chicken and king prawns with a hazelnut oil dressing. Grilled fillet of Aberdeen Angus steak on a wholemeal croûton topped with lobster and a garlic sauce. Crème brûlee. Orange and Cointreau soufflé.

STB Deluxe 4 Crowns
Credit cards: 1, 2, 3, 6 + SWITCH, DELTA
Proprietor: Thomas Hanna

Kilfinan

Kilfinan Hotel
Kilfinan, nr Tighnabruaich
Argyll PA21 2EP
Tel: 01700 821201
Fax: 01700 821205

On B8000 between Tighnabruaich and Otter Ferry on eastern side of Loch Fyne. Best access from north B886/B8003 via Tighnabruaich; from east - from Dunoon B836/A8003 via Tighnabruaich.

Delightful old coaching inn

- 17th century inn set in lovely west coast countryside
- Modern Scottish cooking
- "Joy to visit - wonderful food"

Kilfinan Hotel is set in lovely countryside on the eastern shore of Loch Fyne and is a real haven of relaxation. Lynne and Rolf Mueller make their guests feel specially welcome and their attitude of caring attention is reflected in other members of staff. The dining room is a timeless characterful room of dark wood and low ceilings set out with fine china, glassware, fresh flowers and good table linen. The food is first class as one would expect from chef Mueller who is a member of the Master Chefs of Great Britain. Member of the Scotch Beef Club.

Open 1 Mar to 31 Jan
Rooms: 11 with private facilities
Bed & Breakfast £58
Dinner B & B £61 - £71
Special Rates available
Bar Lunch 12 - 2 pm (b)
Dining Room/Restaurant Lunch 12 - 2 pm Sun only (b)
Bar Supper 6 - 7.30 pm (c)
Dinner 7.30 - 9 pm (d) 4 course menu
Vegetarians welcome - prior notice required

Hot-smoked Alba salmon with fennel and honey vinaigrette. Fish terrine wrapped in smoked halibut. Escalope of wild salmon with saffron and dill sauce and sea asparagus. Supreme of Guinea fowl with truffle sauce. Langoustine tails served in a lobster sauce. Raspberry and blueberry sablé. Atholl brose.

STB Highly Commended 3 Crowns
Credit cards: 1, 2, 3

Killiecrankie

Killiecrankie Hotel
Killiecrankie, by Pitlochry
Perthshire PH16 5LG
Tel: 01796 473220
Fax: 01796 472451

On old A9, 3 miles north of Pitlochry.

An attractive country house overlooking the River Garry.

- Small country house hotel.
- Modern Scottish cooking, with classic influences.
- "Well-composed menus with unusual and imaginative sauces."

This is a former manse and stands in four acres of well-kept gardens and woodland above the River Garry and the historic Pass of Killiecrankie, where a notable battle was fought in 1689. The surrounding country abounds in wildlife and the hotel has the atmosphere of a sporting lodge. Its resident owners, Colin and Carole Anderson, have decorated and furnished the house very tastefully; and have provided a high standard of comfort. Head chef John Ramsay was commended by the Scottish Chef's Association as 'Newcomer of the Year'. His cooking is highly professional and imaginative, and his table d'hôte menus (four starters, four main courses) are well-balanced and appetising. A most attractive and well-run establishment.

Open 11 Mar to 3 Jan
Rooms: 10 with private facilities
Bed & Breakfast £39 - £50
Dinner B & B £50 - £75
Special Rates available
Bar Lunch 12.30 - 2 pm (b)
Bar Supper 6.30 - 9.30 pm (b)
Dinner 7 - 8.30 pm (e) 5 course menu
Vegetarians welcome
No smoking in dining room

Terrine of rabbit and Guinea fowl served with a warm port sauce. Pan-fried fillet of Scotch lamb sliced on to a bed of roast vegetables with a lightly minted hollandaise sauce. Chocolate Marquise with caramel nut tart.

STB Commended 4 Crowns
Credit cards: 1, 3, 6 + SWITCH, DELTA
Proprietors: Colin & Carole Anderson

Kilmarnock

The Coffee Club
30 Bank Street, Kilmarnock
Ayrshire KA1 1HA
Tel: 01563 522048

In town centre.

Town centre restaurant.

- Popular and busy town restaurant.
- Home cooking.
- "Friendly and hospitable staff make your visit a happy experience."

Situated in one of the oldest streets in Kilmarnock opposite the Laigh Kirk, this cheerful cafe offers something for everyone. There is a large varied menu with lots of choice including grills and vegetarian dishes and a range of quick snack meals. Service is fast, friendly and efficient. All food is produced on the spot using fresh produce wherever possible and the home baking is a speciality. There is a welcoming atmosphere at The Coffee Club.

Open all year except 25, 26 Dec + 1, 2 Jan
Coffee + meals served 9.30 am - 10 pm except Sun (a-b)
Closed Sun for meals but coffee lounge open 12 - 5 pm
Unlicensed - guests welcome to take own wine
Vegetarians welcome
No smoking area in air-conditioned restaurant

Sandwiches, salads, omelettes etc. Children's menu. Vegetarian dishes. Grilled salmon steak with hollandaise sauce. Sole with almonds in a rich cream sauce. Steaks with a variety of sauces.

Credit cards: 1, 2, 3
Proprietors: Svend Kamming & William MacDonald

Kilmelford

Cuilfail Hotel
Kilmelford
Argyll PA34 4XA
Tel: 01852 200 274
Fax: 01852 200 264

A816 midway between Oban and Lochgilphead, at top of Loch Melfort.

An old drover's inn of character and charm.

■ A relaxed and cosy small west coast hotel.
■ Good fresh pub food.
■ "Popular West Highland hotel to eat or stay."

There has been an inn here on the Oban-Lochgilphead road for centuries. The present Cuilfail Hotel, built in Victorian times, continues to offer traditional West Highland hospitality - down to an enormous choice of single malt whiskies. Service is relaxed and friendly. Proprietor/chef David Birrell has carried out major refurbishments while retaining the full character of the hotel. In each of the three dining areas - the bar, the bistro or the restaurant - he offers a good selection of simple, local produce that is reasonably priced, freshly prepared and well presented. His clientele - people of all ages - who are travelling, walking or holidaying in the area - clearly appreciate the Cuilfail Hotel's obvious charms.

Open all year
Rooms: 12 with private facilities
Bed & Breakfast £30 - £40
Dinner B & B £42.50 - £52.50
Special Rates for 3+ nights
Bar Lunch 12 - 2.30 pm (a)
Bar Supper 6.30 - 9.30 pm (a-b)
Dinner 6.30 - 9.30 pm (b)
Vegetarians welcome

Home-made pies with crisp puff pastry. Chicken in pastry with various fillings and sauces. Local salmon. Prawns.

STB Commended 3 Crowns
Credit cards: 1, 3 + SWITCH, DELTA
Proprietor: David Birrell

Kilmun

Bistro at Fern Grove
Kilmun
Argyll PA23 8SB
Tel: 01369 840 334
Fax: 01369 840 334

6 miles from Dunoon on A880 on the side of the Holy Loch.

Restaurant with rooms.

■ Victorian house.
■ Home cooking.
■ "Tender lambs kidneys cooked in stout - excellent fare."

This 19th century house was at one time the home of the Campbells of Kilmun overlooking Holy Loch. The hospitable hosts Ian and Estralita Murray have built up a strong reputation for their little bistro over the years. Simple cooking is their forte. A daily changing blackboard menu of chef's specials is supplemented by an à la carte menu of snacks. Accommodation is limited to two rooms at the moment, and plays a secondary role to the restaurant.

Open all year except Nov, weekends only Dec to Mar
Rooms: 3 with private facilities
Bed & Breakfast £18 - £22
Dinner B & B £33 - £38
Bistro Menu 11 am - 9 pm (a)
Restaurant (à la carte) 11 am - 9 pm (b-c)
Vegetarians welcome
No smoking in restaurant + bedrooms
No dogs

Home-baked breads. Carrot and ginger soup. Spinach mousse with spicy tomato sauce. Local wild venison steak in a mustard sauce. Lemon sole in a goat cheese and cream sauce. Loin of lamb in a red wine gravy. Baked Argyll ham with orange and honey sauce. Monkfish tails in Pernod. Apple and almond tarts with home-made honey ice cream. Crème brûlée. Sticky toffee pudding.

Credit cards: 1, 3
Proprietors: Ian & Estralita Murray

Kilwinning

Montgreenan Mansion House Hotel
Montgreenan Estate, Torranyard
Kilwinning
Ayrshire KA13 7QZ
Tel: 01294 557733
Fax: 01294 850397

On A736 4 miles north of Irvine.

A luxury country house hotel in its own grounds.

■ An impeccably restored and maintained Georgian mansion.
■ Fine modern/traditional Scottish cuisine.
■ "The elegance of a bygone age."

Although there has been a house here since the 14th century, the present Montgreenan was built in 1817. Under its owners, the Dobson family, it retains the elegance and graciousness of the past, down to white-aproned helpful staff. Yet the hotel offers every possible modern comfort: it even has a heliport. Based on the finest raw materials, the hotel offers excellent and imaginative cuisine. Its wine list is unusually comprehensive, and will satisfy the most demanding connoisseur. Guests can also enjoy horse-riding, clay pigeon shooting and fishing. AA 3 Star, one rosette, RAC 3 Star, H & R Award.

Open all year
Rooms: 21 with private facilities
Bed & Breakfast £46 - £73
Dinner B & B £56 - £98
Room Rate £60 - £146
Bar Lunch 12 - 2.30 pm (a)
Dining Room/Restaurant Lunch 12 - 2.30 pm (b)
Dinner 7 - 9.30 pm (d)
Vegetarians welcome

Poached fillet of sole with mushroom and Champagne sauce. Haunch of venison in a port, redcurrant and pickled walnut sauce. Baked salmon stuffed with crab in a light mustard sauce. Poached chicken stuffed with sweet chestnuts and tarragon cream.

STB Highly Commended 4 Crowns
Credit cards: 1, 2, 3, 5, 6
Host: Mr. Darren Dobson

Kincraig

March House Guest House

Feshiebridge, Kincraig
Kingussie, Inverness-shire PH21 1NG
Tel: 01540 651 388
Fax: 01540 651 388

Off A9 at Kincraig. Follow B970 for 2 miles to Feshiebridge. Past red telephone box, turn right. ½ mile on left down gravel drive.

A family-run guest house with six en suite bedrooms, beautifully situated in Glenfeshie.

■ Alpine style house secluded in a pine forest.
■ Traditional Scottish cooking with European overtones.
■ "Distinctly fresh, using local produce and home-grown herbs."

Standing in a glade of mature pines at the mouth of lovely Glenfeshie, March House enjoys wonderful views of the Cairngorm Mountains and is an ideal base for the many outdoor pursuits that Speyside offers, such as skiing, gliding, bird-watching, mountain-biking, watersports and golf. The house is modern and Alpine in style - with timber cladding, a large wood-burning stove and old stripped pine furniture. It has six bedrooms, all en suite and the spacious conservatory overlooking the mountains provides an idyllic setting for dinner (non-residents are welcome, but should telephone). It is owned and enthusiastically run by Caroline and Ernie Hayes, whose cooking and baking matches the clean, fresh atmosphere of March House itself. They use fresh local produce and present a very well-priced table d'hôte menu. The house is unlicensed and guests are encouraged to bring their own wine.

Open all year
Rooms: 6 with private facilities
Bed & Breakfast from £18
Dinner B & B from £30
Room Rate £15 - £45
Special Rates for 3+/5+ nights + weekends
Dinner at 7 pm (b)
Reservations essential for non-residents
Unlicensed - guests welcome to take own wine
Vegetarians welcome

Cauliflower and cumin soup. Wholemeal soda bread rolls with walnuts. Venison with pickled walnuts and red wine. Local trout, grilled and served with cucumber and yoghurt. Carbonnade of beef. Spinach roulade with tomato purée. Raspberry and apple pie.

STB Commended 3 Crowns
No credit cards
Proprietors: Caroline & Ernie Hayes

Kingussie

Columba House Hotel & Restaurant

Manse Road, Kingussie
Inverness-shire PH21 1JF
Tel: 01540 661402

Turn off A9 Kingussie/Kincraig. Manse Road second on left on B9152 (High Street).

An attractive house in a large garden on the edge of the village.

■ Victorian manse converted into a hotel.
■ Home cooking.
■ " A friendly, homely place."

The house stands in its own large garden and grounds, on a small hill, which gives it terrific views towards the Monadhliath and Cairngorm Mountains. It is family-run, and Myra Shearer provides a warm welcome to her home. She also cooks good homely fare, presenting table d'hôte menu (six starters, six main courses) which uses vegetables and herbs from her garden and local meat and fish. Four poster bedroom available.

Open all year
Rooms: 7 with private facilities
Bed & Breakfast £19 - £28
Dinner B & B £34 - £43
Special Rates for 3/5 nights
Bar Lunch 11.30 am - 3.30 pm (a)
Dining Room/Restaurant Lunch 11.30 am - 3.30 pm (a)
Bar Supper 5 - 9 pm (a)
Dinner 7 - 9 pm (c)
Vegetarians welcome
Facilities for disabled visitors - ground floor rooms
No smoking in restaurant

A rich coarse pâté marinated in wine and brandy served with warm brown toast. Chunks of tender local venison cooked in a fruity sauce. Roast leg of lamb with Cumberland sauce. Ecclefechan butter tart. Home-made petit fours.

STB Commended 3 Crowns
Credit cards: 1, 3
Proprietor: Myra Shearer

The Cross

Tweed Mill Brae, Ardbroilach Road
Kingussie PH21 1TC
Tel: 01540 661166
Fax: 01540 661080

From traffic lights in centre of village, travel uphill along Ardbroilach Road for c. 200 yards, then turn left down private drive (Tweed Mill Brae).

An outstanding restaurant, winner of Macallan Decanter 'Scottish Restaurant of the Year' 1994, and Egon Ronay Wine List Award 1992.

■ Restaurant with rooms.
■ Innovative Scottish cooking.
■ "Dining here is a marvellous experience: the food is sublime and the service unique!"

The Cross was built as a tweed mill in the late 19th century and is situated in a wonderful waterside setting. The original "Cross" was at a cross-roads in the middle of the town. Here they have also retained some nice features including the exposed original beams in the dining room and the upstairs lounge with its coombed ceilings. Ruth Hadley is a member of the Master Chefs of Great Britain. Egon Ronay has said her "love and passion for food shines through". She treats her ingredients deftly and there is an experimental energy behind some dishes. Where she can, she uses less common produce such as wild mushrooms, mountain hare, pike or fresh turbot, and she grows her own herbs in the restaurant's four acre garden. Tony Hadley's waiting style is renowned; he also makes a nightly selection of wines which will complement the menu. The Cross has one of the best cellars in Scotland.

Open 1 Mar to 1 Dec + 27 Dec to 5 Jan
Rooms: 9 with private facilities
Dinner B & B from £85
Special Rates for 3+ nights
Dinner 7 - 9 pm except Tue (e-f)
Closed Tue
Vegetarians welcome - prior notice required
No smoking in bedrooms

Home hot-smoked salmon accompanied by a tomato and basil pesto. Loin of Highland spring lamb, roasted pink with rosemary and red wine. Chocolate Drambuie tart served with Blairgowrie raspberries.

Credit cards: 1, 3 + SWITCH, DELTA
Proprietors: Tony & Ruth Hadley

The Osprey Hotel

Ruthven Road, Kingussie
Inverness-shire PH21 1EN
Tel: 01540 661510
Fax: 01540 661510

In Kingussie village, on corner of main road.

> An attractive small hotel in a quiet Highland town.

- A stone-built town house.
- Traditional Scottish cooking with French influences.
- "Imaginative, assured and delicious cooking. Exceptionally fine baking and desserts."

Conveniently situated in the centre of Kingussie, overlooking the memorial gardens, The Osprey Hotel is an excellent base from which to explore this part of the Highlands. Robert and Aileen Burrow are friendly, caring and attentive hosts, and these qualities, alongside Aileen's considerable culinary skills have earned them both an AA Rosette and a large number of returning guests each year. Our inspector met one 'regular' from London who returns every year and has done so for a long time; she is now 100 years old! Aileen is a talented cook; her menus, which are table d'hôte, are appetising and offer only freshly prepared dishes, carefully and imaginatively cooked. The home baking is a very special treat; the bread is fresh each day - and be sure to leave some space for a pudding.

Open all year
Rooms: 8 with private facilities
Bed & Breakfast £22 - £36
Dinner B & B £39 - £54
Special Rates for 3+ nights
Dinner 7.30 - 8.30 pm (c) 4 course menu
No smoking in dining room
Vegetarians welcome

Smoked salmon with apple, horseradish cream. Venison cooked slowly in red wine with bacon, mushrooms and redcurrant. Iced white chocolate terrine with mocha sauce.

STB Commended 3 Crowns
Credit cards: 1, 2, 3, 5
Proprietors: Robert & Aileen Burrow

Scot House Hotel

Newtonmore Road, Kingussie
Inverness-shire PH21 1HE
Tel: 01540 661351
Fax: 01540 661111

South end of main road through village of Kingussie (B9152 off A9 trunk road).

> An attractive, well-appointed hotel set amid the unique natural splendour of the Highlands.

- A friendly, comfortable and relaxing village hotel.
- Outstanding home cooking.
- "Where a Highland welcome awaits you."

George MacKenzie was a local man who made his fortune in Canada by founding the Singer Sewing Machine Company. In 1884 he provided the funds to build the village's Free Presbyterian Church manse. Converted in the 1960s, it is now the Scot House Hotel. Its present owners have recently restored and refurbished the entire building. With both table d'hôte and à la carte menus, the dining room makes the most of the area's excellent beef, fish and game yet also offers a vegetarian menu. Unpretentious and good, the hotel's cooking is matched by a varied and affordable wine list. Bar lunches and suppers are distinguished by wholesome ingredients, freshly prepared.

Open all year except Christmas + Boxing Days
Rooms: 9 with private facilities
Bed & Breakfast £25 - £38
Dinner B & B £45 - £55
Special Rates available for 2+/4+ nights
Bar Lunch 12 - 2 pm (b)
Bar Supper 6 - 9 pm (b)
Dinner 7 - 9 pm (c-d) 4 course menu
Vegetarians welcome
Entry ramp and toilets for the disabled visitor
No smoking in dining room

Smoked Scottish salmon and prawns Marie Rose. Chilled honeydew melon with Argyll ham. Scot House fillet steak in a Drambuie sauce. Venison cutlets au poivre. Spey salmon with white wine, mushroom, tomato and cream sauce. Medallions of venison with green peppercorns, Dalwhinnie whisky and cream sauce.

STB Highly Commended 3 Crowns
Credit cards: 1, 3 + SWITCH, DELTA
Proprietors: Bill & Morag Gilbert, Nigel & Val McConachie

Skiary

Loch Hourn, Invergarry
Inverness-shire PH35 4HD
Tel: 01809 511214

From Invergarry (on A82 Fort William-Inverness road) take A87 Invergarry-Kyle road. After 5 miles turn left to Kinlochourn. Proceed for 22 miles to end of single track road. You will then be met by boat by arrangement.

> Remote, small guest house accessible only by boat or on foot.

- A unique guest house on the very shore of a dramatic West Highland sea-loch.
- Home cooking.
- "On the shores of Loch Hourn, this century old fisherman's cottage offers simple, traditional Highland hospitality."

This must be the most remote guest house in Scotland but the journey is worth it. Christina's cooking is miraculous, she uses excellent fresh local game, meat and fish. Vegetables, herbs and soft fruit come from the garden and bread, scones and pastry are baked daily. The bedrooms are small but charming. Views from the house are truly spectacular with an abundance of wild life to be seen. A fantastic experience, not for the faint-hearted

Open 1 Apr to 31 Oct (Note: Skiary will be open before 1 Apr or after 31 Oct for a full week's booking of at least 4 - by arrangement only)
Rooms: 3
Full board £300 per wk
Dinner B & B £45 per night - shorter stays, with lunch on intervening days
Special Rates for flexible singles
Unlicensed - guests welcome to take own wine
Residents only
Meals are served at times to suit guests' requirements (within reason)
Vegetarians welcome
Downstairs bedroom suitable for mildly disabled persons

Salmon and sour cream pie. Casserole of local venison with red wine and orange. Roast gigot of Scotch lamb with home-made mint jelly. Steak and kidney pudding. Rhubarb and orange meringue pie. Chocolate Marquise. Home-made ice creams and parfaits.

No credit cards
Proprietors: John & Christina Everett

Kinloch Rannoch

Bunrannoch House

Kinloch Rannoch
Perthshire PH16 5QB
Tel: 01882 632407

Turn right after 500 yards on Schiehallion road, just outside Kinloch Rannoch off B846.

A family-run country hotel in Highland Perthshire.

- An old hunting lodge in lovely surroundings.
- Traditional cooking.
- "The menu is imaginative but simply served."

Set amidst mature trees, Bunrannoch is a Listed building and stands on the site of a medieval settlement, in the shadow of the 'sleeping giant' mountain, close to Loch Rannoch. There is an easy informality within this comfortable family home, making guests feel completely at ease and totally relaxed. The cosy lounge, log fires and uninterrupted Highland views complement the delicious aromas from the kitchen. Jennifer Skeaping is the chef/proprietor and her good cooking and friendly manner assure you of an enjoyable stay. The menus (a choice of two main courses) change daily, fresh food is sourced locally and tastefully prepared.

Open all year except Christmas + New Year
Rooms: 7, 5 with private facilities
Bed & Breakfast £16 - £18
Dinner B & B £30 - £32
Special Family Rates available
Dinner 7 - 9 pm (b-c)
Vegetarians welcome - prior notice required
No smoking in dining room

Spicy avocado soup. Warm salad of smoked venison with a walnut oil and sherry dressing. Fillet of Scottish lamb pan-fried and served with a Madeira sauce. Chocolate truffle cake with Cointreau strawberries.

STB Commended 2 Crowns
Credit cards: 1, 3
Proprietor: Jennifer Skeaping

Cuilmore Cottage

Kinloch Rannoch
Perthshire PH16 5QB
Tel: 01882 632218
Fax: 01882 632218

From Kinloch Rannoch take unclassified road signed Rannoch School on south side of Loch. Pass war memorial. Cuilmore Cottage 100 yards along first road on left.

This small restaurant with rooms won the 1992 Glenturret Award for 'The Best Restaurant Meal in Perthshire.'

- An 18th century converted croft house.
- Fresh home cooking.
- "The immaculate cottage decor was the ideal environment in which to enjoy this fine Scottish fare."

Anita Steffen has made a tremendous success of this cosy little croft house overlooking Loch Rannoch and the standard and style of her food has been lauded and publicised to a degree that is remarkable for so small an establishment. Much of her produce is grown in the cottage garden and the rest is locally sourced to ensure freshness and quality. Thereafter Anita displays her own culinary skill and flair to the great satisfaction of her diners. Dinners are served at the candlelit table in the intimate dining room of the cottage. Cuilmore is delightfully secluded and guests have the complimentary use of mountain bikes, a dinghy and canoe to explore the beautiful countryside.

Open Feb Oct incl
Rooms: 2 with private facilities
Bed & Breakfast from £20
Dinner B & B £45 - £50
Dinner 7 - 9 pm (c-e) Prior booking essential
Unlicensed - guests welcome to take own wine
Vegetarians welcome
No children
No smoking throughout

Pan-fried quail breasts on puy lentils and chorizo. Home-made soups. Char-grilled fillets of market fish served on a bed of nut mushrooms. Noisettes of lamb inlaid with rosemary mint mousse. Scottish cheeses.

STB Deluxe 3 Crowns
Credit cards: 1, 3
Proprietor: Anita Steffen

West Tempar House

Kinloch Rannoch, by Pitlochry
Perthshire PH16 5QE
Tel: 01882 632338
Fax: 01882 632338

1½ miles from Kinloch Rannoch village, on unclassified road to Schiehallion and Aberfeldy.

A private family-run country house.

- Edwardian shooting lodge with three bedrooms.
- Traditional/Cordon Bleu game and fish.
- "Mr Mineyko shoots or catches most of the delicious meat and fish which appear on the plate."

West Tempar House is an early 20th century hunting lodge. Tempar is an anglicisation of Teamhar - a Gaelic word meaning an eminence with a wide view. The house is peacefully isolated, and has all the charm of a tiny Loire chateau. It was designed as the 'the smallest possible grand house', able to accommodate shooting parties and servants. The Mineykos are the first year-round owners of over ten years' standing. There are no pretentions at West Tempar: you will find yourself comfortably accommodated in one of the three bedrooms and served dinner and coffee with the family in the dining and drawing rooms which retain the original pine panelling. Most of the food is freshly cooked by Janet, the rest by Andrew, and the emphasis is on fish and game with inventive accompaniments. Andrew can also take people on guided tours of the small estate. Spanish, French and Italian spoken.

Open 16 Mar to 10 Dec
Rooms: 3 with private facilities
Bed & Breakfast from £16
Dinner B & B £35 - £40
Special Rates for 4+ nights
Dinner at 8 pm (c)
Packed lunches available
Residents only
Unlicensed - guests welcome to take own wine + spirits
No smoking in dining room

Home-made soups. Pan-fried venison fillet with herbs, served with rowan jelly and coarse grain mustard. Various game and fish dishes. Chocolate brandy cake. Upside-down gingerbread.

No credit cards
Proprietors: Andrew & Janet Mineyko

Kinnesswood

The Lomond Country Inn
Kinnesswood, by Loch Leven
Perthshire KY13 7HN
Tel: 01592 840253
Fax: 01592 840693

4 miles from Kinross. From south, M90
Junction 5, B9097 via Scotlandwell. From
north, M90 Junction 7, A911 via Milnathort.

Family-run hotel overlooking Loch Leven.

- Hotel in an historic village.
- Scottish/home cooking.
- "For a good cheap lunch with no frills, this place is hard to beat."

This is an honest and unpretentious country hotel in the village of Kinnesswood. People come here for the food and the fine views as the inn is conveniently situated just minutes off the motorway. The food is freshly prepared and the dishes have a traditional Scottish character. A good wine list and some interesting real ales complement the menus and food available throughout the day.

Open all year
Rooms: 12 with private facilities
Bed & Breakfast £28.50 - £35
Dinner B & B £35 - £40
Special Rates available
Light snacks (scones, sandwiches and tea) served all day
Bar Lunch 12 - 2.30 pm (a)
Dining Room/Restaurant Lunch 12 - 2.30 pm (b)
Bar Supper 6 - 9 pm (a)
Dinner 6 - 9 pm (c)
Vegetarians welcome
Facilities for disabled visitors

Terrine of Perthshire game with orange, whisky and onion marmalade. Pan-fried Highland venison with rich beer sauce. Puff pastry parcel of wild salmon with vermouth sauce. Roast local pheasant with red wine and rosemary. East Neuk seafood pancake. Beef steak pie. Sticky ginger pudding. Raspberry cranachan. Summer fruit pudding.

STB Commended 3 Crowns
Credit cards: 1, 2, 3, 5, 6 + SWITCH
Proprietors: David Adams & Neil Hunter

Kinross

Croftbank House Hotel & Restaurant
30 Station Road, Kinross
Fife KY13 7TG
Tel: 01577 863819

Junction 6, M90 on approach to Kinross.

Family-run town hotel on the edge of Kinross.

- Converted Victorian house.
- Modern Scottish cooking.
- "Delicious scallops served with fennel and chives followed by pigeon breast which was very good."

This popular small hotel, not far off the motorway is owned by Bill Kerr and his wife. The hotel's reputation is based upon Bill's cooking, for which he has 2 AA Rosettes, but the overall ambience is relaxed and the rooms are comfortable: Diane Kerr, who looks after the house, does so with an understated efficiency and a winning smile. The cooking is assured, the menus imaginative. The style of cooking and presentation is contemporary - letting the natural flavour of the ingredients emerge. Member of the Scotch Beef Club.

Open all year except Christmas Day
+ 1 to 3 Jan
Rooms: 5 with private facilities
Bed & Breakfast £25 - £28
Dinner B & B £45 - £48
Bar Lunch 12 - 2 pm except Mon (a)
Dining Room/Restaurant Lunch 12 - 1.45 pm
except Mon (b)
Supper 6.30 - 9 pm except Mon (a)
Dinner 6.30 - 9 pm except Mon (d)
Closed Mon
Vegetarians welcome
No smoking in restaurant

A warm salad of seared west coast scallops and langoustines with toasted pine nuts and a fresh herb dressing. Breast of woodland pigeon cooked pink and served with braised brown lentils and a port wine jus-lie. Biscuit basket with Drambuie ice cream and a compote of warm fresh summer fruits.

Credit cards: 1, 3
Proprietors: Bill & Diane Kerr

The Grouse & Claret Restaurant
Heatheryford
by Kinross KY13 7NQ
Tel: 01577 864212
Fax: 01577 864920

Junction 6, M90, opposite the Granada Services.

Restaurant with rooms.

- Converted farm.
- Home/traditional cooking.
- "Conrad Wilson, food critic, says this is exactly what a country restaurant should be."

This restaurant is part of the Heatheryford Country Centre - a rural complex with facilities for functions, exhibitions, fishing, accommodation and dining. The old buildings have been attractively converted and The Grouse and Claret (named after a fishing fly) offers good home cooking, with many traditional dishes appearing on the menus. Seasonal game and fresh shellfish are a speciality and vegetarians are well catered for. Meriel Cairns and her sister Vicki take great pride in their successful establishment, always ensuring it looks appealing with fresh flowers and garlands around the beams. The detached accommodation has comfortable ground floor rooms overlooking the fishing lochans. French, Italian and German spoken.

Open all year except Boxing Day +
New Year's Day
Note: Oct to Apr closed pm Sun Mon
Rooms: 3 with private facilities
Bed & Breakfast from £22.50 - £29.50
Dinner B & B from £37.50
Special rates available
Bar Lunch 12 - 2 pm (a-b)
Dining Room/Restaurant Lunch
12 - 2 pm (b)
Dinner 7 - 9 pm (c)
Table Licence
Vegetarians welcome
Facilities for disabled visitors
No smoking in restaurant

Salmon and chervil fish cakes. Breast of Barbary duck with a Grand Marnier and orange sauce. Fresh west coast scallops. Pan-fried fillet of roe deer with a claret and juniper berry sauce.

STB Commended 3 Crowns
Credit cards: 1, 3, 6
Proprietors: John & Meriel Cairns

The Muirs Inn Kinross
49 Muirs, Kinross
Perthshire KY13 7AU
Tel: 01577 862270

M90 exit Junction 6 and follow A922
Milnathort for a short distance. At 'T' junction,
Inn is diagonally opposite to right.

An attractive and deservedly popular village inn.

■ Good, fresh, honest food at sensible prices.
■ The best of straightforward home cooking - and more.
■ "A village inn as it should be."

Built in the early 19th century as a farmhouse. The Muirs Inn is near the shores of Loch Leven. Mary, Queen of Scots, was imprisoned on an island there in 1567. The inn merits its excellent and growing reputation for attention to detail and care for guests' comfort in its five bedrooms, all with private facilities. The same care is evident in the inn's food and ethos. The Maltings restaurant has a warm, homely feel and offers a vast menu from traditional pub food to Caribbean and Chinese. All are freshly prepared and well-presented. This is an establishment run by and for people who care.

Open all year
Rooms: 5 with private facilities
Bed & Breakfast £27.50 - £35
Dinner B & B £37.50 - £45
Special Rates available
Bar Lunch 12 - 2 pm (a)
Dining Room/Restaurant Lunch 12 - 2 pm (a)
Traditional High Tea 5 - 6 pm
Bar Supper 5 - 9 pm (a)
Dinner 7 - 9 pm (b)
Vegetarians welcome
Smoking discouraged
No dogs

Canapé Carsgore - creamed smoked haddock with cheese, glazed and served on toast. Muirs fish brose. Prime Scottish venison with a bitter-sweet honey and hazelnut sauce. Tripe Threapmuir - cooked in traditional way, served with a creamed onion sauce. Smoked trout served with a Mull whisky dressing. Prime Scottish steaks. Separate vegetarian menu.

STB Commended 3 Crowns
Credit cards: 1, 3,
Proprietors: Gordon Westwood & Graham Philip

Cross Keys Hotel
Main Street, Kippen
by Stirling FK8 3DN
Tel: 01786 870293

On B822 Callander-Fintry and just off A811 Stirling-Erskine Bridge, only 8 miles west of Stirling.

Small family-run village inn.

■ 18th century droving inn.
■ Traditional home cooking.
■ "A very warm and friendly atmosphere and good plain fare."

This is a traditional village inn in the centre of the peaceful and picturesque village of Kippen: hospitable and unpretentious, with a warm and friendly atmosphere, old beams, stone walls, log fires and artifacts. It is owned and very efficiently run by Angus and Sandra Watt; this accounts for its popularity amongst both locals and visitors, who mingle in the delightful bar, perhaps eating one of Sandra's excellent, home-made bar meals (these can be eaten outside in the newly landscaped garden, which also has a children's play area). In addition to informal meals in the bar and family room, there is also a small restaurant where the interesting menu offers a good selection of freshly prepared dishes.

Open all year except Christmas Night + 1 Jan
Rooms: 3
Bed & Breakfast from £19.50
Bar Lunch 12 - 2 pm Mon to Sat: 12.30 - 2 pm Sun (a)
Dining Room/Restaurant Lunch 12 - 2 pm Mon to Sat: 12.30 - 2 pm Sun (a)
Bar Supper 5.30 - 9.30 pm (a)
Dinner 7 - 8.45 pm (c)
Vegetarians welcome

Home-made soup. Humble haddie pancakes. Medallions of fillet of beef with a peppered brandy and cream sauce. Scottish salmon poached with a ginger and lime sauce. Cloutie dumpling. Home-made meringues served with home-made chocolate sauce and dairy ice cream.

Credit cards: 1, 3
Proprietors: Angus & Sandra Watt

Auld Alliance Restaurant
5 Castle Street
Kirkcudbright DG6 4JA
Tel: 01557 330569

Kirkcudbright town, opposite the castle.

Small restaurant in Kirkcudbright.

■ A Listed stone cottage.
■ French/Scottish cooking.
■ "All dishes are cooked to order; Scottish produce prepared with French flair."

This is a converted tradesman's cottage built from stones quarried from Kirkcudbright Castle on the other side of the street. The restaurant is unfussy, plain and simple inside which is just as well for the dishes cooked by Alistair Crawford will focus your attention. They are a wonderful mixture of fresh local foods cooked in opulent, classical French style - the style in which Alistair was trained. The spirit of the establishment echoes the ancient union between Scotland and France - and what better way to express the bond than through the confluence of technique and supply.

Open Easter to 31 Oct
Dining Room/Restaurant Lunch 12.30 - 2 pm Sun only (a)
Dinner 6.30 - 9.30 pm (c)
Vegetarians welcome

Home-made chicken, garlic and brandy pâté, baked in pastry with redcurrant and port wine sauce. Pan-fried Scotch sirloin steak with heather honey mustard and Drambuie liqueur. Kirkcudbright Bay queen scallops in garlic butter with smoked Ayrshire bacon in Galloway cream.

No credit cards
Proprietors: Alistair & Anne Crawford

Selkirk Arms Hotel
High Street, Kirkcudbright
Kirkcudbrightshire DG6 4JG
Tel: 01557 330402
Fax: 01557 331639

Off A75, 27 miles west of Dumfries, between
Castle Douglas and Gatehouse-of-Fleet.

Town hotel with historic associations.

- Small, friendly hotel in pretty fishing village.
- Traditional Scottish cooking.
- "A very pleasant family-run hotel with lots of atmosphere and an innovative attitude towards food."

The hotel was built in 1770 in the then busy little port of Kircudbright. In 1794 Robert Burns was a guest and it is believed that he wrote 'The Selkirk Grace' during his stay. He would certainly find a warm welcome here today as the hotel has retained much of its character, despite modernisation and refurbishment. Bedrooms are tastefully decorated and comfortable and the standard of food is high. There are extensive à la carte and daily changing table d'hôte menus which offer extremely good value for money. Portions are generous and the menu displays an imaginative approach with interesting combinations of flavours. A recent extension has added a new lounge bar with real ales, and a charming patio restaurant.

Open all year
Rooms: 16 with private facilities
Bed & Breakfast £37.50 - £47
Bar Lunch 12 - 2 pm (a)
Dining Room/Restaurant Lunch
12 - 2 pm (a) - booking essential
Bar Supper 6 - 9.30 pm (b)
Dinner 7 - 9.30 pm (c)
Vegetarians welcome

Poached salmon with white wine, orange and grapefruit segments and dill. Chicken sautéed with juniper berries and gin. Local lamb cutlets with rosemary and mint sauce. Fillet steak coated in crushed black pepper with red wine, brandy, red and green peppers and cream.

STB Highly Commended 4 Crowns
Credit cards: 1, 2, 3, 5
Proprietor: John Morris

The Log Cabin Hotel
Kirkmichael, by Blairgowrie
Perthshire PH10 7NB
Tel: 01250 881288
Fax: 01250 881402

Signposted off A924 in Kirkmichael.

An informal country hotel in a beautiful setting.

- A friendly and unpretentious place to eat or stay.
- Good traditional cooking.
- "No stay is long enough."

Built entirely of Norwegian pine, the unique Log Cabin Hotel enjoys a dramatic setting, 900 feet above sea-level in Glen Derby, and offers panoramic views over the surrounding countryside. Both in its award-winning Edelweiss restaurant and its Maltings Bistro, the hotel uses fresh local produce for imaginative and inexpensive menus that change daily. The whole establishment is efficiently run by its proprietor, Alan Finch. Staff are warm and welcoming, as are the 120 different malt whiskies in the hotel's well-stocked bar.

Open all year except Christmas + Boxing Days
Rooms: 13 with private facilities
Bed & Breakfast £25 - £32
Dinner B & B £35 - £47
Tea/coffee, home made cakes etc served all day
Bar Lunch 12 - 1.45 pm (a)
Bar Supper 6 - 8.45 pm (a-b)
Dinner 7.30 - 8.45 pm (c) 4 course menu
Vegetarians welcome

Smoked Drumore rainbow trout on a passion fruit coulis with salad garnish. Chicken breast poached in flavoured stock served on a bed of fresh leeks. Medallions of local venison sautéed in butter and served with a Madeira sauce. Angus sirloin steak flamed in brandy with a pink peppercorn cream sauce.

STB Commended 3 Crowns
Credit cards: 1, 2, 3, 5
Proprietor: A F Finch

Conchra House Hotel
Sallachy Road, Ardelve
Ross-shire IV40 8DZ
Tel: 01599 555 233
Fax: 01599 555 433

From south continue westwards on A87 past Dornie/Eilean Donan Castle. Follow hotel signposts turn right for 3/4 mile (Sallachy/Killilan road).

An historic 18th century mansion in a picturesque setting.

- A family-run country house hotel.
- Home cooking.
- "A house of great character, offering genuine hospitality and good cooking."

Conchra House was built in the 1760s to house the government's agent in Kintail, following the seizure of Jacobite estates after the '45 Rising. The house is most attractive, fits into the landscape well and enjoys a lovely situation overlooking Loch Long. It is full of interesting antiques and period details. Conchra means 'a fold' or 'haven', and the stated aim of Colin and Mary Deans, the hotel's resident owners, is to provide just this for their guests. They succeed in full measure. The place is wonderfully peaceful; guests are made to feel very much at home; the food is simple but intelligently cooked and appetising. A gem of a place.

Open all year except Christmas + Boxing Days
Rooms : 6, 3 with private facilities
Bed & breakfast £22 - £35
Dinner B & B £34 - £50
Special Rates available
Dinner 7 - 9 pm (c)
Non-residents - advance booking required
Restricted Licence
Vegetarians welcome
No smoking throughout
Dogs by arrangement

Home-made leek and butterbean broth. Medallions of Killilan venison marinated in red wine and herbs. Broccoli and local curd cheese bake. Home-made shortcake biscuit toppped with local ice cream, and fruit in season.

STB Highly Commended 3 Crowns
Credit cards: 1, 3
Proprietors: Colin & Mary Deans

The Seafood Restaurant (Biadh Math)
Railway Platform, Kyle of Lochalsh
Ross-shire IV40 8XX
Tel: 01599 4813

At Kyle of Lochalsh railway station on platform 1. Parking on slipway to station.

An informal bistro and café in scenic location.

- Converted station waiting room.
- Modern Scottish home cooking.
- "An unusual location on a railway platform at Kyle gives the restaurant added appeal for lovers of good, homely Scottish cooking."

A railway platform is not the obvious choice of location for a restaurant but it is worth taking the trouble to track down The Seafood Restaurant for you will not be disappointed. The station is right next to the harbour in Kyle of Lochalsh close to the ferry terminal which, until the recently opened bridge, was the main crossing point to Skye. From your table in the converted waiting room you can look out over the Cuillins as you enjoy the abundance of fresh local seafood, langoustine, scallops and monkfish. The menu offers a variety of dishes cooked in interesting ways. In the peak season there is a breakfast and lunch menu with a selection of simple, home-cooked fare which changes to give a more sophisticated à la carte choice in the evening. You are advised to check opening hours as they vary depending on the time of year.

Open Easter to Oct
Breakfast served 10 - 11.30 am
Dining Room/Restaurant Lunch 12 - 2.45 pm
Mon to Fri (a)
Dinner 6.30 - 9 pm Mon to Sat: Sun to Sat Jul + Aug (c)
Table Licence
Vegetarians welcome
No smoking in restaurant

Langoustines in garlic butter. King scallops with white wine sauce and crunchy garlic and herb topping. Monkfish with home-made tartar sauce. Flambéd Drambuie and mushroom steaks. Spinach and crowdie pancakes. Raspberry cranachan. Brown sugar and hazelnut meringues.

Credit cards: 1, 3
Proprietors: Andrea Matheson & Jann Macrae

Seagreen Restaurant & Bookshop
Plockton Road
Kyle of Lochalsh IV40 8DA
Tel: 01599 4388

North of Kyle of Lochalsh, on road to Plockton.

A relaxed, informal bistro combined with bookshop and gallery.

- Charming stone-built schoolhouse conversion.
- Modern Scottish cooking.
- "Its pleasant laid-back atmosphere plus the outdoor terrace where you can enjoy a cup of coffee or a full a la carte evening meal are major attractions."

Situated on the outskirts of Kyle of Lochalsh this is a very attractive complex of an open plan kitchen and large, spacious restaurant area with a bookshop at one end which sells literature and traditional music CDs and cassettes. The dining room exhibits shows of local painters and photographers. Outside there is a sheltered sunny garden and terrace, popular with guests. From 10 am until 7 pm an all day counter-service offers delicious salads, soups, home baking, etc all made on the premises from fresh local ingredients. The restaurant does do very good wholefood but the emphasis is increasingly on fish and shellfish. From 6.30 to 9 pm a full à la carte menu is served in a separate dining room. The style of the food is different from that served during the day with a more sophisticated continental European influenced menu.

Open all year except 25, 26 Dec + 1 Jan, 6 Jan + end Feb
Lunch 12 - 5.30 pm (a)
Dinner 6.30 - 8.30 pm spring autumn:
6.30 - 9 pm 7 days summer (b): winter - advance booking only (b-c)
Reservations essential for dinner
Vegetarians welcome
No smoking in restaurant

Green pea and leek soup. Local oysters, raw or baked with garlic butter. Monkfish and mussel kebabs served on a bed of cous-cous with watercress sauce. Roasted Mediterranean vegetables on a potato pancake served with a red wine sauce. Duo of ice cream: caramelised oatmeal and Amaretto served on a mango and apricot coulis. Hand-made chocolates.

Credit cards: 1, 3
Proprietor: Fiona Begg

Linne Mhuirich
Unapool Croft Road, Kylesku
by Lairg, Sutherland
IV27 4HW
Tel: 01971 502227

½ mile south of the new Kylesku Bridge on A894, last house in a cul-de-sac road.

Lochside bed and breakfast in Assynt.

- Modern shoreside crofthouse.
- Home cooking.
- "Take the ecstatic comments in the visitors book as your guide!"

Fiona and Diarmid MacAulay welcome guests to their home close to the Kylesku Bridge which links Assynt to Scourie and the far north-west. A modern house of traditional design, it is peacefully positioned overlooking Loch Glencoul. The Handa Island Nature/Bird Reserve and lovely, lonely sandy beaches are nearby. Directions and maps for many local walks are provided. The dinner menus change daily and they are discussed with you after breakfast. Vegetarians are extremely well catered for and all the dishes are prepared in a homely style, using fresh local ingredients and taking account of guests' preferences. The food is unpretentious and wholesome. At 10 pm guests are offered supper. The house proudly proclaims itself to be a 'Non-smokers' Sanctuary'; guests are invited to bring their own wine. French and German spoken.

Open Easter to 30 Oct
Rooms: 2 , 1 with private facilities
Bed & Breakfast £17.50 - £20.50
Dinner B & B £27.50 - £30.50
Dinner at 7.30 pm except Sun Sat (b)
Residents only
Vegetarians welcome
No smoking throughout

Local fish and seafood - Kylesku prawn vol-au-vents; smoked haddock au gratin; fisherman's pie. Celtic salmon medallions with lime and almonds. Loch Beag mussels and Ullapool prawns in garlic butter. Pork, pepper and apple casserole. Home-made quiches and pâtés. Vegetarian dishes. Unusual salads. Tempting desserts and home-baking. Filter coffee. Scottish honey and cheeses.

STB Commended 2 Crowns
No credit cards
Proprietors: Fiona & Diarmid MacAulay

147

Laide

The Old Smiddy
Laide
Ross-shire IV22 2NB
Tel: 01445 731425
Fax: 01445 731425

A835 Inverness-Ullapool. At Braemore junction (44 miles north-west of Inverness) take A832 via Dundonnell to Laide (29 miles).

Unique cottage guest house with small restaurant in the tiny village of Laide.

- Converted white cottage
- Imaginative home cooking, beautifully presented.
- "Kate's cooking is justifiably famous locally."

Following the coastal road to Poolewe you arrive at Laide, a little south of the famous Inverewe Gardens. Opposite the church sits The Old Smiddy, an attractive and well-converted white cottage (formerly the village's blacksmith shop). The two bedrooms are very comfortable and the house itself is strewn with family treasures and fascinating objects collected by Steve Macdonald and his wife, Kate, who are both Highlanders. Old family photographs adorn the walls. The menus are compiled daily after careful consultation with guests, and depending upon what is available. Lunches and home-baked teas are also served. The restaurant specialises in local seafoods, venison and Highland lamb.

Open 1 Mar to 14 Nov
Rooms: 2 with private facilities
Bed & Breakfast £19 - £22
Dinner B & B £37 - £40
Tea Room 12 - 4.30 pm Mon to Fri - Easter to end Sep (a)
Restaurant Lunch 12 - 3 pm Mon to Fri (a)
Dinner at 7.30 pm Mon to Sat - booking essential (c)
Unlicensed - guests welcome to take own wine
Vegetarians welcome
Facilities for disabled visitors
No smoking throughout

Game soup with crofters oatmeal bread. Gairloch monkfish roasted with lemon, topped with a crunchy garlic coating and crisp courgettes and tomatoes. Home-made ice creams made with Highland cream. Chocolate Marquise.

No credit cards
Proprietor: Kate Macdonald

148

Langbank

Gleddoch House Hotel & Country Estate
Langbank
Renfrewshire PA14 6YE
Tel: 01475 540711
Fax: 01475 540201

Off M8/A8 Glasgow-Greenock at Langbank (B789).

Country house hotel in its own sporting estate overlooking the Clyde.

- First class country house hotel in lovely grounds.
- Modern Scottish cooking.
- "The interesting and appetizing descriptions made for a difficult choice which was justified as the food was inventive and professional."

Gleddoch House Hotel was once the home of the shipping baron, Sir James Lithgow, built as a wedding present for his wife. It stands in a 360 acre estate, on a hill looking across the River Clyde to the Lomond Hills. The estate allows the hotel to offer a variety of outdoor pursuits including an 18-hole golf course, horse-riding, clay pigeon shooting and off-road driving. Public and private rooms are all decorated and furnished to a very high standard. The restaurant is spacious and gracious; the four course, table d'hôte menu is succinct (three choices per course) superbly cooked and presented by a highly professional chef. Member of the Scotch Beef Club.

Open all year
Rooms: 39 with private facilities
Bed & Breakfast £70 - £97
Dinner B & B £70 - £75 Fri to Sun only
Special Rates available
Bar Lunch (Clubhouse) 12 - 2.30 pm (a)
Dining Room/Restaurant
Lunch 12.30 - 2 pm (c)
Bar Supper (Clubhouse) 7 - 9 pm (a)
Dinner 7 - 9 pm (e)
Vegetarians welcome

Fillet of Shetland salmon with cumin and black pepper on spinach leaves with vermouth, passion fruit and chive cream sauce. Roast medallions of prime beef fillet with hollandaise sauce on a tomato, courgette and aubergine ragoût. Heart shaped shortbread layers with a white chocolate mousse on a strawberry coulis.

STB Highly Commended 4 Crowns
Credit cards: 1, 2, 3, 5 + SWITCH

149

Letham

Fernie Castle Hotel
Letham, Cupar
Fife KY7 7RU
Tel: 01337 810381
Fax: 01337 810422

Off A914 Glenrothes-Tay Bridge/Dundee, 1 mile north of A91/A914 Melville roundabout.

A splendid 16th century tower house close to Cupar.

- Lochside Castle
- Innovative country house cooking.
- "Fine, fresh food with a good eye for presentation."

Fernie Castle is a 14th century foundation, but the heart of the existing building is an' L' plan tower house, raised in the 16th century. Additions were made during the 17th and 18th centuries by the Balfours of Burleigh. The house has been tastefully and sensitively converted to its current use. The Castle Restaurant, on the first floor, is a charming room, with large marble fireplaces, elegant chandeliers, white napery and a charming view over the garden. The majority of the bedrooms were refurbished in 1995, and it is planned to refurbish the remaining bedrooms in 1996. The young and talented head chef, Craig Millar - who was a regional finalist in the Young Chef of the Year Award 1995, presents a carefully thought out menu and imaginatively prepared food. The unique circular ballroom, overlooks a small loch which is floodlit at night.

Open all year
Rooms: 15 with private facilities
Bed & Breakfast £45 - £95
Dinner B & B £60 - £125
Special Mid Season Breaks available
Bar Lunch 12 - 2.30 pm (a)
Lunch (Castle Restaurant) 12.30 - 2.30 pm
Sun Sat (b)
Bar Supper 6 - 9.30 pm (a)
Dinner 7 - 9.30 pm (c)
Vegetarians welcome

Pan-fried breast of local pigeon set on a pearl barley and pine kernel risotto surrounded by a rosemary scented jus. Grilled fillet of turbot on a mussel and tomato ragoût topped with a confit of garlic, served with a white wine and chervil sauce. White peach mousse centred with a peach and brandy ice cream and a raspberry coulis.

STB Commended 3 Crowns
Credit cards: 1, 2, 3 + SWITCH, DELTA
Proprietor: Norman Smith

Little Loch Broom nr Ullapool

Loch Earn St Fillans

Dundonnell Hotel

Little Loch Broom, nr Ullapool
Ross-shire IV23 2QR
Tel: 01854 633204
Fax: 01854 633366

On A832 south of Ullapool.

A traditional family-run hotel.

- Converted coaching inn.
- Good hotel catering.
- "An unpretentious and balanced menu with some nice original touches."

There has been an inn on this site for over a century, and for the last 32 years it has been owned by the Florence family who have modernised it and built on two self-contained apartments. It stands between Ullapool and Gairloch, on the shore of Little Loch Broom. There is not a lot of local business in this sparsely populated corner of Scotland however the efficient attentiveness displayed by all the staff towards their guests is notable. The low-ceilinged dining room has a comfortable, chintzy feel and pleasant views over the loch. The table d'hôte menus are restrained, fresh and well-balanced, and an à la carte menu available during the high season when the hotel is at its busiest. The cooking is straightforward and professional. The hotel has been awarded AA/RAC 3 Star and Rosette for food. Member of Scotland's Commended Hotels.

Open Mar to Nov + Christmas/New Year
Rooms: 24 with private facilities
Bed & Breakfast £27.50 - £47
Dinner B & B £52 - £69.50
Special Rates for 2/3+ nights
Bar Lunch 12 - 2.15 pm (b)
Bar Supper 6 - 9 pm (b)
Dinner 7 - 8.30 pm (d)
Vegetarians welcome

Crab and scallop patties rolled in sesame seeds on an Arran mustard sauce. Poached escalope of Ardessie salmon topped by a vermouth sorrel sauce and garnished with a julienne of cucumber and trout caviar. Tenderloin of lamb marinated with fresh thyme and garlic, sautéed and presented with a provençal tartlet. Sirloin steak with a wholegrain mustard sauce.

STB Highly Commended 4 Crowns
Credit cards: 1, 2, 3, 6 + SWITCH, DELTA
Proprietors: Selbie & Flora Florence

Achray House Hotel

St Fillans, Loch Earn
Perthshire PH6 2NF
Tel: 01764 685 231
Fax: 01764 685 320

A85 lochside in village of St Fillans, 12 miles west of Crieff.

Family-run rural hotel beside Loch Earn.

- Traditional white-painted hotel.
- Traditional cooking based on quality produce.
- "Jane's desserts and puddings are renowned far and wide - leave room for one."

Owned and run by Jane and Tony Ross for over 12 years, this popular and well-established hotel has a stunning lochside position with its own foreshore and jetty, in this area of outstanding natural beauty. The Ross's have set themselves impressively high standards and it is little wonder that their guests keep coming back year after year. The food, for which the hotel has been awarded an AA Rosette for the last four years, is offered across a range of menus in both bar and restaurant and provides an excellent choice. Jane's freshly made, extensive selection of sweets are not to be missed. The dining room was recently extended and is tastefully appointed. The hotel has been awarded 2 Stars and Rosette from the AA, 'Best Loved Hotels of the World' recommended, and Michelin.

Open 1 Mar to 31 Oct
Rooms: 9 with private facilities
Bed & Breakfast from £29.50
Dinner B & B from £44.50
Special Rates available
Bar Lunch 12 - 2 pm Mon to Sat (a)
Bar/Restaurant Lunch 12.15 - 2 pm Sun (b)
Bar Supper 6.15 - 9.30 pm (b)
Dinner 7 - 9 pm (c)
Vegetarians welcome

Wide choice of Scottish produce - salmon, lamb, beef, venison, seafood. Good choice of freshly made vegetarian dishes always available. Large selection of desserts (the house speciality).

STB Highly Commended 3 Crowns
Credit cards: 1, 2, 3 + SWITCH
Proprietors: Tony & Jane Ross

The Four Seasons Hotel

St Fillans, Loch Earn
Perthshire PH6 2NF
Tel: 01764 685 333
Fax: 01764 685 333

On A85, 12 miles west of Crieff, at west end of St Fillans overlooking Loch Earn.

Rural hotel in charming village of St Fillans.

- Modern purpose-built hotel.
- Traditional/modern Scottish cooking.
- "A lunch of Skye mussels and Guinea fowl terrine kept me very happy."

Loch Earn is one of the most beautiful Perthshire lochs, surrounded by woods and hills. The Four Seasons has a wonderful unspoiled vista from where the seasons can truly be seen to change over the year. This is a modern building but what you may lose in period elegance you certainly gain in well-maintained bedrooms and rather quaint public rooms and bar. The Scott family run the hotel very efficiently and Chef Andrew Scott produces menus which have a strong emphasis on seafood and game in the best traditions of the Taste of Scotland. He tends to keep things simple, not using over-fussy sauces but highlighting flavours and textures where necessary.

Open Mar to 24 Dec
Note: Open only Fri to Sun mid Nov to 24 Dec
Rooms: 18 with private facilities
Bed & Breakfast £30 - £42.50
Dinner B & B £50 - £62.50
Bar Lunch 12.15 - 2.15 pm (b)
Dining Room/Restaurant Lunch 12.15 - 2.15 pm Sun only (b)
Bar Supper 6.30 - 9.30 pm (c)
Dinner 7.15 - 9.45 pm (d)
Vegetarians welcome
Facilities for disabled visitors
No smoking in dining room

Loch Sween oysters. Steamed fillet of lemon sole, with halibut mousse and tomato and lemon butter. Skye scallops and mussels with basil and tomato. Fillet of beef. Saddle of lamb with rosemary and mushrooms.

STB Commended 4 Crowns
Credit cards: 1, 2, 3, 5 + SWITCH
Proprietors: Allan & Barbara Scott

Cameron House Hotel

Loch Lomond, Alexandria
Dunbartonshire G83 8QZ
Tel: 01389 755565
Fax: 01389 759522

Prestige Award Winner 1991

On A82 near Balloch, on the banks of Loch
Lomond.

> Luxury hotel and leisure complex on the shores
> of Loch Lomond.

- ■ Converted baronial mansion with time-shared
  lodges and a state-of-the-art leisure complex.
- ■ Award-winning grand hotel cuisine.
- ■ "The Brasserie is a sunny, all-purpose restaurant
  with wonderful views of the loch."

A luxury hotel resort on the southern shore of Loch
Lomond, standing in 108 acres of parkland. It was
completely restored by the Craigendarroch Group in
1989. Executive Chef Jeff Bland has a Michelin Star
and presents a highly sophisticated and
imaginative menu in the hotel's main restaurant,
the elegant Georgian Room. The bright and airy
Brasserie has a more informal atmosphere and
offers grill/brasserie style of dishes from an à la
carte menu; bar snacks are available in the Marina
Clubhouse. Member of the Scotch Beef Club.

Open all year
Bed & Breakfast £125 - £295
Dinner B & B £150 - £325
Rooms: 68 with private facilities
Bar Meals (Marina Clubhouse) 12 - 9 pm (a)
Lunch (Brasserie) 12.30 - 2.30 pm
except Sat (c)
Dining Room/Restaurant Lunch (Georgian
Room) 12 - 2 pm except Sun Sat (c)
Dinner (Brasserie) 6.30 - 10 pm (c)
Dinner (Georgian Room) 7 - 10 pm (f)
Vegetarians welcome
Facilities for disabled visitors
No smoking area in Brasserie
No smoking in Georgian Room - jacket + tie
requested
No dogs

Warm timbale of salmon mousse with grilled
scallops on a silver birch and herb sauce. Grilled
suprême of halibut resting on lemon noodles with
glazed vegetables and crispy fried celeriac. Hot pear
soufflé infused with dark chocolate served with eau
de vie ice cream.

STB Deluxe 5 Crowns
Credit cards: 1, 2, 3, 5 + SWITCH, DELTA

Carron Restaurant

Cam-Allt, Strathcarron
Ross-shire IV54 8YX
Tel: 01520 722488

Lochcarron to Kyle of Lochalsh road.

> Restaurant overlooking Loch Carron.

- ■ Quaint purpose-built restaurant.
- ■ Home cooking.
- ■ "A familiar, no-frills menu with well-cooked,
  home-made dishes."

This restaurant lies at the side of Loch Carron and it
is most attractively positioned. Its appeal is
enhanced by the clean-cut exterior adorned with
hanging flower baskets and tubs of flowers. It is
adjacent to the Carron Pottery which makes the
charming hand-thrown crockery used in the
restaurant. The restaurant itself is furnished in
pine, and paintings for sale by local Highland
artists line the walls. Apart from the daily specials
which depend on local catches and seasonal
produce, the range of dishes is standard grills/
salads/chips/baked potatoes but the food is well-
presented and served.

Open 1 Apr to 26 Oct
Food available 10.30 am - 9.15 pm except
Sun (a-c)
Closed Sun
Vegetarians welcome
Facilities for disabled visitors
No smoking throughout

Home-made soup, pâté and desserts. Sea grown
smoked trout with salad. Prime Scottish beef, lamb,
venison, salmon and trout cooked on the chargrill.
Lochcarron whole prawns and scallops when
available.

Credit cards : 1, 2, 3
Proprietors : Seamus & Sarah Doyle

Lochcarron Hotel

Lochcarron
Ross-shire IV54 8YS
Tel: 015202 226
Fax: 015202 612

At east end of village, facing the loch.

> A small hotel with comfortable en suite
> bedrooms, bar and restaurant.

- ■ A 19th century Highland hostelry on the shores
  of Lochcarron amidst the rugged grandeur of
  Wester Ross.
- ■ Good hotel cooking, using local ingredients
  where possible.
- ■ "Catering to very wide clientele - local and
  touring - and providing them with what they
  want."

This family-run establishment has been modernised
to provide the facilities expected of an AA 2 Star hotel.
The majority of the accommodation, which includes
two suites with their own sitting rooms, has
wonderful views over the sea loch. The view is also
shared by the lounge bar and restaurant, where fish
and shellfish from local boats, and game from
nearby sporting estates, feature highly on both the
lengthy à la carte and table d'hôte menus (lunch
and dinner) which cater for every taste.

Open all year
Rooms: 10 with private facilities
Bed & Breakfast £29.50 - £45
Dinner B & B £45 - £58.50
Special Rates for 3/5 nights
Bar Meals 12 - 9 pm (b)
Dining Room/Restaurant Lunch 12 -
2.30 pm (b)
Dinner 5.30 - 9 pm (c) - 4 course menu
Vegetarians welcome

Crêpes filled with sole, salmon, prawns and
scallops. Prime Scottish steaks. Marinaded
venison, casseroled with seasonal vegetables.
Clootie dumpling.

STB Commended 4 Crowns
Credit cards: 1, 3
Proprietors: Pam & Tony Wilkinson

Rockvilla Hotel & Restaurant

Main Street, Lochcarron
Ross-shire IV54 8YB
Tel: 01520 722379

Situated in centre of village, c. 20 miles north of Kyle of Lochalsh.

Highland hotel in picturesque location.

- Small family-run hotel.
- Traditional Scottish cooking.
- "The hotel boasts a small but comprehensive menu featuring local produce and giving good value for money."

This is a charming little hotel right on the main street of a beautiful West Highland village with a cheerful air of informality guests find appealing. The dining room has a relaxed bistro feel and marvellous views out over the loch. An à la carte dinner menu offers excellent value and gives a good choice of starters, main courses and puddings. Local specialities and traditional favourites mean that there is something for everyone. After a hearty breakfast guests are well set up for a day's walking, fishing or exploring the West Highlands with its dramatic scenery.

Open all year except Christmas + Boxing Days + 1 Jan
Rooms: 4, 2 with private facilities
Bed & Breakfast £25 - £30
Special Rates for 3+ nights
Bar Lunch 12 - 2 pm (a)
Bar Supper 6 - 9.30 pm (b)
Dinner 6.30 - 9.30 pm (c)
Vegetarians welcome
No smoking in restaurant
No dogs

Cullen skink. Smoked venison with juniper chutney. Poached halibut steak with hollandaise sauce. Lamb cutlets with gooseberry and mint jelly. Prime beef steaks.

STB Commended 3 Crowns
Credit cards: 1, 3
Proprietors: Lorna & Kenneth Wheelan

Clachan Cottage Restaurant

Clachan Cottage Hotel
Lochside, Lochearnhead
Perthshire FK19 8PU
Tel: 01567 830247
Fax: 01567 830300

Lochearnhead is on A85 Crieff-Crianlarich.

Converted lochside cottages at Lochearnhead.

- Small country hotel.
- Scottish hotel cooking.
- "A wide choice in the bar but smaller in the dining room, accommodates all desires and appetites."

The hotel's brochure says that "Clachan is a Celtic word meaning a row of cottages housing, the Butcher, Baker and Candlestick-maker", and explains that these cottages have now been modernised and converted, in a way which retains a feel for the past. The range of food on the bar menu is large, offering something for everyone. In the dining room - which is on the first floor and enjoys splendid views over the loch - a smaller menu offers Scottish dishes with creative sauces: interesting descriptions and intriguing combinations. Golfing breaks a speciality..

Open 29 Mar to 3 Nov + Christmas/New Year
Note: Open Nov + early Dec for group bookings only
Rooms: 21 with private facilities
Bed & Breakfast £27 - £37
Dinner B & B £43 - £53
Special Rates for 3+/7+ nights
Food available all day Sun
Bar Lunch 12 - 2.30 pm (a)
Dining Room/Restaurant Lunch (a-c) pre-booked groups
Bar Supper 6 - 9 pm (a-c)
Dinner 7 - 9 pm (c)
Taste of Scotland applies to restaurant only
Vegetarians welcome
Smoking not encouraged in restaurant

Terrine of salmon with Drambuie and fresh tarragon. Aberdeen Angus steak with vegetable stuffing, grilled with a grain mustard crust. Chocolate and coconut cheesecake with a trio of sauces. Apple and ginger steamed pudding with rummed cream.

STB Commended 3 Crowns
No credit cards
Proprietor: Andrew Low

The Albannach

Baddidarroch, Lochinver
Sutherland IV27 4LP
Tel: 01571 844407

From Lochinver follow signs for Baddidarroch. After ½ mile, pass turning for Highland Stoneware, turn left for the Albannach.

An excellent small restaurant overlooking Lochinver.

- Restaurant with rooms.
- Contemporary Scottish cooking.
- "A talented cook, fresh produce and no shortcuts."

The Albannach is a 19th century house of considerable architectural character standing in a small glen overlooking Lochinver and the wild country beyond. It has been tastefully decorated by Colin Craig and has a Victorian feel and a cosy atmosphere. During 1996, an original outbuilding will be converted to two further en suite bedrooms. Seafood lunches are available in the conservatory, which has a paved patio and stone ballustrade beyond it. Dinner is served in the wood-panelled, candlelit dining room. Lesley Crosfield presents a set, four course dinner menu which relies entirely on the availability of fresh, free-range produce, her cooking is creative and assured. Colin Craig serves at table, resplendent in kilt and Jacobean shirt and some nights a piper plays outside before dinner.

Open 1 Mar to 31 Dec
Rooms: 4 with private facilities
Dinner B & B £44 - £49
Dining Room/Restaurant Lunch 12.30 - 2 pm except Mon (b)
Dinner at 8 pm (d) 4 course menu
Non-residents welcome by prior arrangement
Table Licence
Vegetarians welcome
Children over five years welcome
Facilities for disabled visitors
No smoking throughout
No dogs

Herb crêpes filled with local seafood in a brandy, cream and tarrgon sauce. Wild River Shin salmon with a dill hollandaise. Warm tart of apple and cinnamon topped with a layer of Calvados custard.

STB Highly Commended 3 Crowns
Credit cards: 1, 3
Proprietors: Colin Craig & Lesley Crosfield

Inver Lodge Hotel

Lochinver, Sutherland
IV27 4LU
Tel: 01571 844496
Fax: 01571 844395

A837 to Lochinver, first turn on left after village hall. ½ mile up private road to hotel.

A new West Highland hotel in the 'grand hotel' tradition.

- A modern luxury hotel with outstanding views.
- Modern Scottish cooking, with classic/grand hotel influences.
- "Very professional service; stunning views; one of the best meals I have eaten this season."

Inver Lodge was opened in 1988. It stands on the hill above Lochinver village and bay, and enjoys panoramic views across the Minch and the wild country of Assynt. The building itself is long, low and plain - even spartan. Inside, however, it is comfortably and tastefully appointed, with a 'highland shooting lodge' theme (it has good private fishing for salmon and trout); public rooms and bedrooms are spacious and airy, and all share the terrific view. It has a snooker room, solarium and sauna. Members of staff are uniformed in tartan, well trained and courteous. A la carte and table d'hôte menus feature Lochinver-landed fish and shelfish and Assynt venison. The cooking is highly professional, and the presentation and service is in the 'grand hotel' style. Great care and effort goes into every aspect of Inver Lodge's hospitality.

Open 15 Apr to 15 Oct
Rooms: 20 with private facilities
Bed & Breakfast £60 - £70
Dinner B & B £87 - £97
Bar Lunch 12 - 2 pm (b)
Dinner 7 - 9 pm (e)
Vegetarians welcome
No smoking in dining room

Lochinver-landed Minch turbot and halibut. Assynt venison. Sautéd mushrooms and butterbeans served with a mustard sauce.

STB Highly Commended 4 Crowns
Credit cards: 1, 2, 3 + Switch, Delta
Proprietor: Nicholas Gorton

Lochinver Larder's Riverside Bistro

Main Street, Lochinver
Sutherland IV27 4JY
Tel: 01571 844356

A837 to Lochinver, second property on right as enter village.

A fresh, restaurant on the banks of the River Inver.

- Bistro and restaurant.
- Home cooking.
- "One can find a wholesome range of dishes to eat in the bistro or take away ready prepared to eat in the holday home."

Ian and Debra Stewart runs this delicatessen shop with a restaurant in Lochinver. The dining room is situated behind the shop, next to the river, and looks out to where the River Inver flows into the bay. The emphasis here is on the delicious selection of sturdy home-made pies with a large variety of fillings. A selection of freshly cooked steaks and seafood is also offered every night given the easy access of excellent seasonal produce. During the day there is a self-service policy although at night the atmosphere is less informal. Another of the booming areas of business here is the take away food to heat at home, which is similar to that offered on the menu.

Open 1 Apr to 31 Oct
Food service 9 am - 9 pm
Snacks available 9 am - 5.30 pm (a)
Dinner 6.30 - 9 pm (b-c)
Vegetarians welcome
Facilities for disabled visitors
No smoking in restaurant

Locally cured smoked salmon. Noisettes of minted lamb with bacon and tomatoes in red wine. Halibut in lime and ginger butter with chopped chives. Cauliflower, broccoli and cheese bake served with puff pastry crowns. Prime cut sirloin steak.

Credit cards: 1, 3, 6 + SWITCH, DELTA
Proprietors: Ian & Debra Stewart

Old Manor Hotel

Lundin Links, nr St Andrews
Fife KY8 6AJ
Tel: 01333 320368
Fax: 01333 320911

On A915 Kirkcaldy-St Andrews, 1 mile east of Leven, on right overlooking Largo Bay.

An excellent small country hotel in a golfer's paradise.

- An award-winning informal restaurant and pub.
- Good Scottish cuisine in the restaurant; pub grub in the bar.
- "Dedicated to good food and fine wine."

Owned and run by the Clark family, their commitment to what they do here is obvious. As is appropriate to this area, the Clarks are a mine of information and advice on the game of golf. Their Aithernie Restaurant serves both à la carte and table d'hôte dishes, based on fresh local meat and fish, imaginatively prepared and presented. The wine list is sound and reasonably priced. The restaurant's success has been reflected in a number of awards for chef Alan Brunt. The hotel's Coachman's Grill caters for a different market, serving upmarket, inexpensive food simply and unpretentiously.

Open all year
Rooms: 19 with private facilities
Bed & Breakfast £42.50 - £65
Dinner B & B £58.50 - £81.50
Special Weekend Rates available
Bar Lunch 12 - 2.30 pm (a)
Dining Room/Restaurant Lunch 12 - 2 pm (b)
Bar Supper 5 - 9.30 pm (b)
Dinner 7 - 9.30 pm (d)
Vegetarians welcome
Facilities for disabled visitors
No smoking in restaurant

Poached delice of brill, white wine and dill sauce accompanied by queen scallops. Noisettes of Border lamb on a redcurrant jus with rosemary scented vegetables.

STB Commended 4 Crowns
Credit cards: 1, 2, 3, 6 + SWITCH, DELTA
Proprietors: The Clark Family

Lybster

Portland Arms Hotel
Lybster
Caithness KW3 6BS
Tel: 01593 721208
Fax: 01593 721446

On A9, 12 miles south of Wick.

A small, family-run hotel in a beautiful
Caithness village.

- ■ A peaceful, homely atmosphere with every
  modern comfort.
- ■ Unpretentious cooking.
- ■ "Good ingredients cooked well."

This hotel was built as a staging post for the
turnpike roads in the 19th century. Today, it makes
for an excellent base from which to explore the
charms of the surrounding countryside. The
emphasis now is on attentive, cheerful service. All
bedrooms are comfortable and well-equipped.
Some even have jacuzzi baths en suite. Local
weddings and small conferences enjoy the hotel's
new function room. The menus are
straightforward, using local produce when
available, and represent good value for money.

Open all year
Rooms: 20 with private facilities
Bed & Breakfast £38.50 - £55
Dinner B & B £55 - £70
Special Weekend Breaks available
Bar Lunch 12 - 2.30 pm (a)
Dining Room/Restaurant Lunch 12 - 2.30 pm
Sun only (a)
Bar Supper 5 - 9.30 pm (a)
Dinner 7 - 9.30 pm (c)

Oak-smoked salmon with dill sauce. Fillet of beef
Wellington with Madeira sauce. Baked fillet of
lemon sole with cream and grapes.

STB Commended 4 Crowns
Credit cards: 1, 2, 3, 6 + SWITCH
Proprietors: Gerald & Helen Henderson

Mallaig

Marine Hotel
Station Road, Mallaig
Inverness-shire PH41 4PY
Tel: 01687 462217
Fax: 01687 462821

Adjacent to railway station. First hotel on right
off A82, and a 5 minute walk from ferry
terminal.

A family-run hotel in the fishing port of Mallaig.

- ■ Hotel close to the harbour.
- ■ Hotel catering.
- ■ "Excellent local seafood, simply cooked."

Mallaig is at the end of the famous West Highland
Railway Line and also marks the termination of
The Road to the Isles. Once the busiest herring port
in Britain, the town has still a busy fishing harbour
and is the main ferry terminal to the Hebrides. The
hotel, which overlooks the harbour, has well-
appointed bedrooms most of which are en suite.
The menus take full advantage of freshly landed
fish and shellfish and is offered in both lounge bar
and restaurant. Cooking is simple and wholesome.
Good selection of malt whiskies available.

Open all year except 25, 26 Dec + 31 Dec
to 7 Jan
Note: Restricted served Nov to Mar
Rooms: 21, 16 with private facilities
Bed & Breakfast £26 - £35
Dinner B & B £43 - £48
Special Rates for 3 nights
Bar Lunch 12 - 2 pm (b)
Dining Room/Restaurant Lunch on request (b)
Bar Supper 6 - 9 pm (b)
Dinner 6 - 8.30 pm winter: 7 - 9 pm rest
of year (c)
Vegetarians welcome

Local seafood platter. Scampi tails in a butter
sauce. Venison in a port sauce. Home-made
gâteaux, pavlovas and clootie dumpling.

STB Commended 3 Crowns
Credit cards: 1, 3
Proprietors: Elliot & Dalla Ironside

by Maybole

Ladyburn
by Maybole
Ayrshire KA19 7SG
Tel: 01655 740 585
Fax: 01655 740 580

A77 (Glasgow-Stranraer) to Maybole then
B7023 to Crosshill. Turn right at War Memorial
(Dailly-Girvan). After exactly 2 miles, turn left
and follow signs. 5 miles south of Maybole.

Country house hotel.

- ■ 17th century country house.
- ■ Home cooking.
- ■ "Jane Hepburn is an exceptionally good cook. I
  found the whole experience a joy."

Ladyburn is an historic house set deep in 'the most
beautiful valley in Ayrshire' and is the family home
of Jane and David Hepburn. You are surrounded by
family heirlooms and portraits, and comfortable
old furniture. There is a homely authenticity about
the food served in the dining room, reflecting Jane
Hepburn's commitment to produce genuine dishes
cooked with original touches of flavours and
textures; neither overbearing nor trendily
understated. Substantial well-tried recipes cooked
with care are the order of the day. Dining room
open at all times for residents. Italian, French,
German and Russian spoken.

Open all year except 2 wks Nov + 4 wks
during Jan to Mar
Rooms: 8 with private facilities
Bed & Breakfast £70 - £80
Dinner B & B £95 - £105
Special Rates for 3+ nights
Dining Room/Restaurant Lunch 12.30 -
1.30 pm except Mon (b)
Dinner 7.30 - 8.15 pm except Sun Mon (d)
Reservations essential for non-residents
Restricted Licence
Vegetarians welcome
Children over 16 years welcome.
No smoking in dining room, bedrooms
+ drawing room
No dogs

Home-made soups. Oxtail and grape casserole.
Vicarage fish pie. Roast sirloin and Yorkshire
pudding. Aunt Ella's traditional chicken and
mushroom pie. Strawberry pavlova. 'Boozy'
chocolate mousse. Ladyburn tart.

STB Deluxe 3 Crowns
Credit cards: 1, 2, 3
Proprietors: Jane & David Hepburn

Melrose

Burts Hotel
Market Square, Melrose
Roxburghshire TD6 9PN
Tel: 01896 822285
Fax: 01896 822870

A6091, 2 miles from A68, 38 miles south of Edinburgh.

A family-run 18th century hostelry.

- Delightful 18th century inn.
- Modern Scottish cooking.
- "Creative and confident dishes presented with enthusiasm."

Burts Hotel, is a delightful 18th century Scottish inn. It stands in the centre of the square of this Borders market town, and is always bustling with activity. It is run by Graham, Anne and Nicholas Henderson, professional and friendly hosts, who make their guests feel very welcome. Their restaurant has a good local reputation. The à la carte menu is extensive and displays a thorough familiarity with contemporary eating fashions. Both it and the weekly changing table d'hôte menu are ambitious and display imaginative combinations, creative confidence and a sound appreciation of appropriate flavours. The cooking and presentation is akin to that you would expect to find in a refined country house. Member of the Scotch Beef Club.

Open all year except 24 to 27 Dec
Rooms: 21 with private facilities
Bed & Breakfast £38 - £45
Dinner B & B £60 - £68
Special Rates for 2+ nights
Bar Lunch 12 - 2 pm (b)
Dining Room/Restaurant Lunch 12.30 - 1.45 pm (b)
Bar Supper 6 - 9.30 pm Sun to Thu: 6 - 10 pm Fri Sat (c)
Dinner 7 - 9 pm Sun to Thu: 7 - 9.30 pm Fri Sat (d)
Vegetarians welcome

Home-smoked collops of monkfish. Gallantine of quail. Baked fillet of halibut with shellfish mousse. Seared Barbary duck breast with a home-made onion marmalade. Canon of lamb centred with haggis accompanied with a tartlet of kidneys.

STB Highly Commended 4 Crowns
Credit cards: 1, 2, 3, 5, 6 + SWITCH
Proprietors: Graham, Anne & Nicholas Henderson

Melrose Station Restaurant
Palma Place, Melrose
Roxburghshire TD6 9PR
Tel: 01896 822546

100 yards from Market Square. Take Dingleton Road singposted B6359 to Lilliesleaf - first right just before bridge.

An important building converted into a stylish, modern restaurant.

- Converted 19th century station-master's house.
- Modern Scottish, with international influences.
- "Inspired cooking, using produce mainly from Melrose itself and local farms."

Close to the Market Square at the centre of the town, Melrose station is one of the very few notable pre-1850 Scottish railway stations to have survived. It was closed in 1969, lay derelict until 1985 and has now been completely renovated as a Grade A Listed building. The restaurant is situated in what used to be the station-master's house and overlooks the leafy town and famous abbey. The style is modern and tasteful, simple and elegant, friendly and informal - the approach is bistro-style. Ian and Claire Paris gained hotel experience in Australia and their excellent small restaurant is much patronised by locals. A blackboard menu is presented at lunchtime and a very well priced table d'hôte menu for dinner.

Open all year except 25 to 28 Dec incl
+ 5 Feb to 26 Feb
Morning coffee 10 am - 12 noon except Mon
Dining Room/Restaurant Lunch 12 - 2 pm except Mon (b)
Dinner 6.45 to 9 pm Thu to Sat only (d)
Closed Mon

Lightly spiced tomato soup served with avocado cream. Tender beef steak rolled and stuffed with wild rice and pecans in an orange and cranberry sauce. Oven-baked avocado stuffed with mushrooms, sweet peppers and toasted pinenuts in a rich cheese sauce.

Credit cards: 1, 3 + DELTA
Proprietors: Ian & Claire Paris

Melvich by Thurso

The Sheiling Guest House
Melvich, by Thurso
Caithness KW14 7YJ
Tel: 01641 531 256
Fax: 01641 531 356

Melvich on A836, 18 miles west of Thurso.

Comfortable family home in beautiful countryside.

- Small guest house known for its hospitality.
- Scottish home cooking at its best.
- "Joan Campbell is a perfectionist and her influence is seen throughout her house and in the quality of the food served."

The Sheiling is a family-run guest house in an outstanding location, blessed with wonderful views over the Halladale River and Melvich Bay. The Campbells open their home to visitors between April and October and guests return year after year to enjoy their unfailing hospitality. Food is home-cooked and based on local produce, the set menu changing daily, using a variety of fresh vegetables. Breakfast is a special treat, with home-made porridge and home-made jams and marmalade as real treats.

Open 1 Apr to mid Oct
Rooms: 3 with private facilities
Bed & Breakfast £21 - £23
Dinner B & B £33 - £35
Special Rates for 7+ nights
Dinner 6.30 - 7 pm (b)
Residents only
Unlicensed - guests welcome to take own wine
Vegetarians welcome
No smoking in dining room

Baked Atlantic salmon. Grilled halibut. Local smoked haddock. Caithness beef and Sutherland lamb. Steamed with interesting sauces. Gooseberry and rhubarb meringue pie.

STB Highly Commended 3 Crowns
No credit cards
Proprietor: Joan Campbell

Moffat

Auchen Castle Hotel & Restaurant

Beattock, Moffat
Dumfriesshire DG10 9SH
Tel: 01683 300407
Fax: 01683 300667

Direct access from A74, 1 mile north of
Beattock village, 55 miles south of Edinburgh
and Glasgow.

A country house hotel near Beattock village.

- High-Victorian country villa.
- Traditional Scottish cooking.
- "A charming, old fashioned country house
  hotel in a lovely setting."

This exuberant 19th century country house stands
back from the A74 in 50 acres of land and gardens,
and has lovely views over Annandale. The house
was built in 1849 and later became the home of the
famous brewing family, the Youngers. Many of the
early features remain and the interiors have wood
panelling, parquet floors and a spectacular gilded
staircase. Ten of the 25 bedrooms are in a modern
wing of the hotel. The dining room has
magnificent, full-length bay windows and a classic
country house hotel atmosphere; the table d'hôte
menu is lengthy (nine starters, six main courses)
and well-priced. The desserts are a triumph and are
all fresh and home-made. A very good snacks and
sandwiches menu is also available in the bar. A
little French and Italian spoken.

Open all year except 3 wks Christmas/New Year
Rooms: 25 with private facilities
Bed & Breakfast £33 - £49.50
Dinner B & B £43.50 - £63.25 (min 2 nights
stay)
Special Rates available
Bar Lunch 12 - 2 pm (a)
Dinner 7 - 9 pm (c)
Vegetarians welcome

Tartlets of west coast crab. Arbroath smokie and
salmon terrine. Galloway beefsteak braisd with
vegetables and barley wine. Sea trout gravadlax.
Annandale lamb chops roasted with coriander and
served with bramble jelly.

STB Commended 4 Crowns
Credit cards: 1, 2, 3, 5
Proprietor: Hazel Beckh

The Buccleuch Arms Hotel and Restaurant

High Street, Moffat
Dumfriesshire DG10 9ET
Tel: 01683 220003
Fax: 01683 221291

Leave A74(M) for Moffat on A701. Hotel is first
on left as you reach main High Street.

A Georgian coaching inn in the centre of a
pretty town.

- Town hotel and restaurant.
- Home cooking and hotel catering.
- "Good, well-prepared food - most enjoyable."

'The Bucc', as it is known locally, was built in 1760
and retains some original features. The restaurant
is on the first floor, with long windows to the main
square and the hills beyond the town, - a pretty
room. A very extensive à la carte menu is presented
(combining some unusual dishes with pub grub),
supplemented by blackboard 'specials'. Service is
friendly and discreet; portions are large, and
everything is good value. The home cooking is
above the average standard. The hotel is featured
in the Michelin Guide and 'Best Eating Out Place'
in Dumfries and Galloway 1994.

Open all year except Christmas + Boxing Days
Rooms: 11 with private facilities
Bed & Breakfast £29 - £39
Dinner B & B £35 - £45
Bar Lunch 12 - 2.30 pm (a)
Dining Room/Restaurant Lunch 12 - 2.30 pm (b)
Bar Supper 6 - 9.30 pm (a)
Dinner 6 - 9.30 pm (b)
Vegetarians welcome

Home-made soups. Hot garlic greenlipped mussels.
Suprême of chicken in lemon, tarragon and mint.
Pork cooked in cider, bramley apples and cream.
Steak au poivre. Local trout with almonds. Poached
salmon.

Credit cards: 1, 2, 3
Proprietors: Bill & Hilary Jordon-White

Well View Hotel

Ballplay Road, Moffat
Dumfriesshire DG10 9JU
Tel: 01683 220184

At south end of Moffat take A708 (Selkirk). At
crossroads, left into Ballplay Road - hotel on
right.

A small town hotel in the Border's town of
Moffat.

- Victorian town house with gardens.
- Modern Scottish home cooking.
- "Interesting combinations and ideas - plenty of
  creative flair."

Janet and John Schuckardt run this traditional
hotel, which has a peaceful garden and stands on
the outskirts of Moffat. It is within easy walking
distance of the centre of this charming town which
sits in a fertile plain below the dramatic Devil's Beef
Tub. John has a good knowledge of wine and has
over a hundred bins available. The menus offer a
choice, which demonstrate an inventive approach
to more familiar dishes, accompanied by light
fruity sauces and dressings. The meat is served pink
and the vegetables al dente, which is a good sign of
use of fresh produce. The owners go out of their way
to look after their guests every need. German and a
little French spoken.

Open all year
Rooms: 6 with private facilities
Bed & Breakfast £26 - £44
Dinner B & B £49 - £69
Special Rates for 3+ nights
Dining Room/Restaurant Lunch 12.15 -
1.30 pm except Sat (b)
Dinner 7 - 8.30 pm (d) 5 course menu
Prior reservation essential for both
lunch + dinner
Vegetarians welcome
Facilities for disabled visitors
No smoking in dining room

Broccoli and spiced lentil soup with hand-made
rolls. Fillet of Barony venison carved and presented
with a wild cherry wine sauce and topped with sweet
potato crisps. Lemon mousse with lacy oatmeal
tuilles served with a raspberry sauce and crème
anglaise.

STB Deluxe 3 Crowns
Credit cards: 1, 2, 3
Proprietors: Janet & John Schuckardt

Moniaive nr Thornhill

Maxwelton House
Moniaive, nr Thornhill
Dumfriesshire DG3 4DX
Tel: 01848 200385

Entrance on B729, off A76 Dumfries-Thornhill,
or A702 New Galloway-Thornhill.

A historic and fascinating house in a beautiful
setting.

- Tearoom serving light meals and snacks.
- Good home cooking.
- "Well worth visiting."

Maxwelton's fame as the birthplace of Annie Laurie,
immortalised in the ballad, is sufficient reason to
visit. The house's original owners carefully restored
the house to its former glory. and a chapel and
small museum of agricultural and domestic tools
are further reasons to spend a few hours here. In a
Pavilion attached to the house, the tearoom serves
inexpensive, good, plain home cooking. Its proper
afternoon teas, with freshly-made home baking, are
a particular attraction.

Open 1 Jun to 30 Sep Public
Book Parties - Easter - 30 Sep
Closed Fri & Sat
Tearoom 10.30 am - 5 pm except Fri Sat (a)
Unlicensed
Vegetarians welcome

Variety of home-made items. Afternoon teas.

No credit cards
Proprietors: Maxwelton House Trust

Mossblown by Ayr

Scoulars Restaurant (Drumley Inn)
76-78 Mauchline Road
Mossblown, by Ayr
KA6 5DL
Tel: 01292 521100

3 miles east of Whitletts roundabout at Ayr.

Restaurant within traditional coaching inn.

- Informal restaurant/lounge bar.
- Modern Scottish cooking.
- "Very creative ideas which are put to good use."

Scoulars Restaurant (within the Drumley Inn) is
situated amidst the beautiful Ayrshire countryside.
The inn, which was formerly miners' cottages has
recently been refurbished to a modern bistro-style
with white-painted walls and dark wood panelling.
Scoulars is only in its first year of business but
already chef-proprietor John Fisher's imaginative
flair is evident in the à la carte and bar snack
menus.

Open all year - Except New Years Day
Note: open 12 - 9.30 pm Sat Sun
Bar Lunch 12 - 2.30 pm (a)
Restaurant Lunch 12 - 2.30 pm (a)
Bar Supper 6 - 9.30 pm (b)
Dinner 6 - 9.30 pm (b-c)
Vegetarians welcome

Home-made chicken liver pâté flavoured with
garlic and peppercorns accompanied with home-
made grape chutney. Salmon and plaice rolled
together, poached in white wine, cream and lemon
thyme. Grilled halibut steak with a light lime and
stem ginger sauce. Roast leg of lamb topped with
herb breadcrumbs and served with a reducrrant and
port sauce.

Credit cards: 1, 3, 6
Proprietor: John Fisher

Muir of Ord

Ord House Hotel
Muir of Ord
Ross-shire IV6 7UH
Tel: 01463 870492
Fax: 01463 870492

On A832 Ullapool-Marybank, ½ mile west of
Muir of Ord.

A relaxed and friendly small country house hotel
in beautiful surroundings.

- Comfortable and homely living.
- Good country cooking.
- "A place of peaceful pleasure."

John and Eliza Allen offer their guests the
unhurried peace of a bygone age in this 17th
century laird's house. Open fires and an elegant
drawing room match the calm beauty of the hotel's
50 acres of grounds. Bedrooms are tastefully and
well-appointed. The dining room offers
unpretentious and reasonably-priced honest
country cooking that uses fresh meat, game and
fish and vegetables, in season, from the hotel's own
garden. Service is attentive without being fussy. The
wine list is sound and inexpensive. Fluent French is
spoken. Children and dogs are welcome.

Open 5 May to 20 Oct
Rooms: 12 with private facilities
Bed & Breakfast £34 - £49
Dinner B & B £54 - £69
Special Rates for 7+ nights
Bar Lunch 12.30 - 2 pm (b)
Dining Room/Restaurant Lunch - by request
Dinner 7.30 - 9 pm (c) 4 course menu
Vegetarians welcome

Scottish prawn mousse. Home-made soups e.g.
courgette and Brie, Highland smoked chicken.
Poached wild salmon with hollandaise sauce. Roast
breast of duck with a peppercorn sauce. Chicken
with sherry vinegar and tarragon sauce. Pan-fried
quail with grapes in Madeira.

STB Commended 3 Crowns
Credit cards: 1, 2, 3
Proprietors: John & Eliza Allen

Nairn

The Golf View Hotel
& Leisure Club
Seabank Road
Nairn IV12 4HD
Tel: 01667 452301
Fax: 01667 455267

At west end of Nairn. Seaward side of A96. Turn off at large Parish Church.

> A large sporting hotel with a leisure club.

- 19th century seafront house in Nairn converted into a modern hotel with leisure club.
- Modern Scottish cooking.
- "Difficult to choose from the menus, and the quality of the cooking matches the descriptions."

Adjacent to the Nairn Golf Club, the appropriately named 'Golf View' is also within an hour's drive of 25 further courses, and when golfing palls, the hotel's fully equipped leisure club has a magnificent swimming pool and multi-gym, and splended views. The restaurant offers a nightly changing, invitingly descriptive, table d'hote menu. Fish and shellfish are featured strongly, and locally sourced meat and game. Creative and well-made sauces complement the dishes and demonstrate the chef's expertise; he does not need to resort to over-garnishing to achieve his effects. Vegetarian dishes show skill and imagination, and delicious fresh bread is baked every day.

Open all year
Rooms: 48 with private facilities
Bed & Breakfast £40 - £79
Dinner B & B £40 - £85 (min 2 nights stay)
Bar Lunch 12 - 2 pm (a)
Dining Room/Restaurant Lunch 12 - 2 pm (a)
Bar Supper 6.30 - 9 pm (b)
Dinner 7 - 9.15 pm (d) 4 course menu
Vegetarians welcome

Parcels of smoked haddock, bacon, Mozzarella cheese and basil baked in filo pastry served with a lime and ginger butter sauce. Loin of lamb roasted with a rosemary and mint crust served with sautéd lamb kidneys in a Burgundy red wine sauce. Crème brûlée. Poached peaches served with a red berry sauce in a brandy basket.

STB Commended 5 Crowns
Credit cards: 1, 2, 3, 5, 6 + SWITCH

Newbigging

Nestlers Hotel
Dunsyre Road, Newbigging
Lanark ML11 8NA
Tel: 01555 840 680

Equidistant between Glasgow and Edinburgh. On A721 midway between Carnwath and Elsrickle, 18 miles north of Peebles.

> A happy and welcoming small village hotel, with comfortable accommodation.

- Well-planned menu featuring traditional home cooking.
- Guests enjoy warm hospitality from attentive staff.
- "Good family food, with daily changing special dishes. A warm welcome."

Newbigging is an unpretentious village in rural Lanarkshire. The old stone-built house which is Nestlers doubles as a tourist information bureau; the intimate restaurant opens off the bar. Elaine and Nick Anderson ensure that their guests are well looked after. Better than average bar food is available throughout the day based on home cooking with broad appeal. Daily 'specials' feature local seasonal produce and the puddings are renowned locally.

Open all year
Rooms: 3 with private facilities
Bed & Breakfast £23.50 - £27.50
Dinner B & B £35 - £37.50
Special Rates available
Bar Lunch 12 - 5 pm (a)
Dining Room/Restaurant Lunch 12 - 2.30 pm (a)
Bar Supper 5 - 9.30 pm (b)
Dinner 6 - 9 pm (c) 4 course house menu with coffee
Vegetarians welcome
No smoking in restaurant

Venison steak slowly braised and served with a port and lemon sauce. Ham oven-baked with local Pentland honey and cloves, served with fresh parsley sauce. Scottish salmon coated in oatmeal with a Drambuie sauce.

STB Commended 3 Crowns
Credit cards: 1, 3, 5
Proprietors: Elaine & Nick Anderson

Newburgh

Udny Arms Hotel, Aberdeenshire
Main Street, Newburgh
Aberdeenshire AB41 0BL
Tel: 01358 789444
Fax: 01358 789012

On A975, 2½ miles off A92 Aberdeen-Peterhead, 15 minutes from Aberdeen.

> A hotel situated in the centre of Newburgh village, overlooking the golf course, it has a function suite and café bar.

- A traditional Victorian stone-built house with the style and character of an old village inn.
- Creative Scottish cooking.
- "My meal was a credit to the hotel as was the excellent and friendly service."

The Udny Arms Hotel overlooks the Ythan Estuary and has attracted sportsmen, nature lovers and tourists to the Aberdeenshire village of Newburgh for over 100 years. It is an unpretentious and intimate hotel, run by the Craig family, and the service is cheerful and efficient. Some recent changes to the building have made room for a cosy residents lounge. Dining is in the Forvie Room, a split-level restaurant overlooking the lovely Sands of Forvie. The extensive à la carte menu changes every six weeks, and includes a handful of 'specials' which change daily. Meat and game come from the famous Bain of Tarves. The hotel also has a brasserie-style restaurant, in the Parlour, with daily changing specials.

Open all year
Rooms: 26 with private facilities
Bed & Breakfast £38 - £58
Dinner B & B £48 - £58
Special Rates available
Bar Lunch (Bar + Parlour) 12 - 2 pm (a)
Dining Room Lunch (Forvie Room) 12 - 2 pm (d)
Bar Supper (Cafe Bar) 5 - 9.30 pm (a)
Dinner (Parlour) 6.30 - 9.30 pm (d)
Vegetarians welcome

Oysters served with shallot vinegar. Fricassé of mixed wild mushrooms wrapped in cabbage. Seared escalope of salmon, leek and potato pancake, red onion and fresh anchovy salsa. Breast of duck with orange and Grand Marnier sauce and mixed wild rice.

STB Commended 4 Crowns
Credit cards: 1, 2, 3, 5, 6 + SWITCH, DELTA
Proprietors: Denis & Jennifer Craig

Newton Stewart

Creebridge House Hotel

Minnigaff, Newton Stewart
Wigtownshire DG8 6NP
Tel: 01671 402121
Fax: 01671 403258

From roundabout signposted Newton Stewart on A75, through the town, cross bridge over river to Minnigaff. 250 yards - hotel on left.

An attractive country house hotel on the outskirts of Newton Stewart; winners of the 1993 'Scotch Lamb Challenge'.

■ An old Galloway family house with character and charm.
■ Imaginative country house cooking.
■ "A delicious lunch...altogether a good feel about this place."

Creebridge House Hotel was formerly owned by the Earls of Galloway and its present resident owners, Chris and Sue Walker, have made sure that it retains an atmosphere of unhurried elegance, peace and tranquility. The drawing room has an ornate ceiling and period fireplace, not to mention a baby grand piano. There is a choice of eating during the day, either in the bar or in the main restaurant. Chef/proprietor Chris Walker and chef Jim Gibson present imaginative table d'hôte menus for the Garden Restaurant. An outstanding à la carte bar menu is produced by chef Paul Sommerville. They have a deserved reputation.

Open all year
Note: accommodation closed over Christmas
Rooms: 18 with private facilities
Bed & Breakfast £27.50 - £37.50
Dinner B & B £45 - £55
Special Rates for 3+ nights
Bar Lunch 12.30 - 2 pm Mon to Sat: 12.30 - 2 pm Carvery Sun (a)
Bar Supper 6 - 9 pm (b)
Dinner 7 - 8.30 pm: Garden Restaurant closed Nov to Mar (c)
Vegetarians welcome
No smoking in restaurant

Scallop and mussel salad with a hazelnut dressing and chive cream sauce. Pan-fried escalope of pork fillet with a garlic, tomato and lovage sauce. Roast duck with a fresh herb and sloeberry sauce.

STB Commended 4 Crowns
Credit cards: 1, 2, 3
Proprietors: Chris & Sue Walker

The Kirroughtree Hotel

Newton Stewart
Wigtownshire DG8 6AN
Tel: 01671 402141
Fax: 01671 402425

Prestige Award Winner 1993

Signposted 1 mile outside Newton Stewart on A75.

A much-lauded country house hotel in the grand style, offering exceptional cuisine.

■ 18th century mansion converted into a stylish, family-run country house hotel.
■ Gourmet Scottish cooking.
■ "Every aspect of the hotel is of the highest standard. If a single feature must be highlighted, it is the food - superb in variety and cooking."

Kirroughtree has all the grandeur and opulence of an historical mansion, it is sumptuously furnished and elegantly decorated, yet it has an atmosphere which is welcoming and considerate rather than over-formal. There are two dining rooms, reached from the panelled lounge. Head Chef, Ian Bennett, was trained by the celebrated Michel Roux, and his cooking is highly accomplished. The menus are short (three main courses at dinner, two at lunch), creative and well balanced. Special golfing packages at sister hotel, Cally Palace. Member of the Scotch Beef Club.

Open 16 Feb to 3 Jan
Rooms: 17 with private facilities
Bed & Breakfast £45 - £70
Dinner B & B £60 - £85
Special Rates for Weekends, 3+ nights + over 60s
Snack Lunch 12 - 1.30 pm (a)
Dining Room/Restaurant Lunch 12 - 1.30 pm (c) - booking essential
Dinner 7 - 9 pm (e) 4 course menu
Vegetarians welcome - prior notice required
No smoking in dining rooms

Warm sliced breast of local wood pigeon on a carrot, lemon and garlic salad. Tournedos of venison on a bed of red cabbage and fondant potato with a Madeira sauce. Crème brûlée with rhubarb compote.

STB Deluxe 4 Crowns
Credit cards: 1, 3 + SWITCH
Proprietors: The McMillan Family

North Berwick

MacFarlane's Restaurant

2 Station Road, North Berwick
East Lothian EH39 4AU
Tel: 01620 894737

Next to North Berwick railway station.

A small and intimate restaurant in one of Scotland's oldest seaside resorts.

■ A pretty little white-painted building, originally an Edwardian tearoom.
■ Modern Scottish cuisine with French influence.
■ "The food here is of excellent quality and simply cooked."

Next to North Berwick's railway station and looking towards North Berwick Law, this is a charming small restaurant offering a good menu based on quality Scottish produce. The simple interior is light and airy with oak furniture and well-chosen local paintings decorating the walls. The atmosphere is intimate (nine tables), welcoming and informal. Michael and Kate French took over the restaurant in 1994 and their philosophy is to present high quality local produce, simply cooked. The short menus are à la carte; morning coffee (with home-made baking) and lunch are offered as well as dinner. Everything is home-cooked, and fish is something of a speciality, and there is always a 'fresh fish of the day'.

Open 17 Jan to 20 Dec except 9 to 19 Oct
Dining Room/Restaurant Lunch 12.15 - 2 pm except Mon Tue (b)
Dinner 6.30 - 9 pm except Mon Tue (d)
Closed Mon Tue
Smoking is discouraged until after 2 pm (lunchtime), after 9 pm (dinner)
Facilities for disabled visitors
Vegetarians welcome - by prior arrangement

Salad of feta cheese, sun-dried tomatoes, basil, bacon and finished with toasted pinenuts. Grilled Scottish lamb cutlets served with a redcurrant and mint sauce. Casserole of rabbit with red wine, garlic, mushrooms, sweetcorn and cream.

Credit cards: 1, 3
Proprietors: Michael & Kate French

North Middleton

Borthwick Castle Hotel & Restaurant

North Middleton, nr Edinburgh
Midlothian EH23 4QY
Tel: 01875 820514
Fax: 01875 821702

A7 to North Middleton, 12 miles south of Edinburgh, then follow signs for Borthwick. A private road leads to the Castle.

Medieval castle near Edinburgh.

■ Historic castle with hotel facilities.
■ Modern Scottish cooking.
■ "Powerfully atmospheric and with accomplished modern cooking. The highlight of dinner was an unusual grey mullet delicately cooked with salsify and coriander served in regal splendour."

Borthwick Castle was built in 1430 and it was here that Mary Queen of Scots sought refuge after her secret marriage to the Earl of Bothwell. The exterior of the castle has changed little, and, although it has been modernised, the rooms retain the character and atmosphere of the renaissance. You dine in the Great Hall, with suits of armour and appropriate weaponry around you. Chef Martin Russell is energetic and genuinely excited about food. His philosophy is to source the best ingredients from local game dealers and farms then cook them simply, concentrating on bringing out the natural flavours. With confidence and an undaunted enthusiasm he produces adventurous set menus according to what he has in his larder, accompanying his dishes with carefully made sauces and suggestions as to appropriate wines.

Open 15 Mar to 2 Jan
Rooms: 10 with private facilities
Room Rate £95 - £180 (incl b/fast)
Restaurant/Dining Room Lunch - booked parties + functions only
Dinner at 8 pm (e-f) 4 course set menu - reservations essential
Table Licence
Vegetarians welcome

Honey-roast quail with lentil du Puys and soft egg ravioli. Terrine of salmon and monkfish with baby leeks and a balsamic vinaigrette. Roast saddle of lamb with wild mushrooms and a rich basil jus. Caramelised lemon tart. Hot Valrhona chocolate souffle pudding with ginger syrup.

STB Commended 3 Crowns
Credit cards: 1, 2, 3, 5, 6 + SWITCH, DELTA

Oban

Ards House

Connel, by Oban
Argyll PA37 1PT
Tel: 01631 710255

On main A85 Oban-Tyndrum, 4 miles north of Oban.

Family-run guest house overlooking Loch Etive.

■ Victorian villa.
■ Home cooking.
■ "Imaginative cooking using good ingredients."

This is a comfortable guest house standing on the shores of a loch, with views over the Firth of Lorn and the Morvern Hills. All the bedrooms have private facilities and there is a happy air of the family home here, encouraged by the owners John and Jean Bowman, who take great trouble over their guests. The daily changing set menu is displayed in the afternoon and any special requirements are easily catered for. The dishes rely on local produce where possible, combining a taste for detail and fresh home cooking.

Open 7 Feb to 30 Nov
Rooms: 6 with private facilities
Bed & Breakfast £21 - £37
Dinner B & B £36.50 - £40.50
Special Rates available
Dinner at 7.30 pm - later by arrangement (c)
4 course menu
Dinner for non-residents by arrangement
Restricted Licence
Vegetarians welcome
No children
No smoking throughout
No dogs

Haggis en croûte with a creamy mustard sauce. Courgette and blue cheese soup with home-baked bread. Lamb and Scottish oatmeal stout ragoût with citrus and herb dumplings. Loch Feochan wild salmon. Breast of chicken with tarragon and white wine. Ruby fruits roulade.

STB Commended 3 Crowns
Credit cards: 1, 3 + DELTA
Proprietors: John & Jean Bowman

Dungallan House Hotel

Gallanach Road, Oban
Argyllshire PA34 4PD
Tel: 01631 563799
Fax: 01631 566711

In Oban, at Argyll Square, follow signs for Gallanach. ½ mile from Square.

A fine old Victorian house offering a tranquil, country atmosphere.

■ A small and friendly country house hotel.
■ Traditional fresh Scottish/home cooking.
■ "A country hotel in the town."

Set in its own five acres of mature woodland yet close to Oban's bustling centre, Dungallan House was built in 1870 by the Campbell family. It was used as a hospital in the First World War and as HQ for the Flying Boat Squadrons in the Second. Now owned and refurbished by George and Janice Stewart, Dungallan House enjoys magnificent panoramic views over Oban Bay to the Island of Mull, Lismore and the Hills of Morvern. As is appropriate for this prime west coast port, menus take full advantage of the range of fresh fish and shellfish available locally. Janice Stewart does the cooking in person. The well-balanced table d'hote menu offers four-five choices for each course. Though short, the wine list offers something to match each dish on Dungallan's rounded menu.

Open all year except part of Nov + Feb (please phone)
Rooms: 13, 9 with private facilities
Bed & Breakfast £28 - £36
Dinner B & B £49.50 - £57.50
Bar Lunch 12.30 - 2 pm (a)
Dining Room/Restaurant Lunch 12.30 - 2 pm (b)
Bar Supper 6 - 7 pm (b)
Dinner 7.30 - 8.30 pm (d)
Vegetarians welcome
Facilities for the disabled
No smoking in dining room

Vol-au-vent filled with prawns, scallops, salmon, squat lobster. Game soup. Fillet of beef with mushroom sauce. Terrines of monkfish; prawns; scallops. Meringue roulade. Cranachan.

Credit cards: 1, 3
Proprietors: George & Janice Stewart

The Gathering Scottish Restaurant & Ceilidh Bar

Breadalbane Street, Oban
Argyll PA34 5NZ
Tel: 01631 565421/564849/566159

Entering Oban from A85 (Glasgow) into Dunollie Road and one-way system, then first left. On foot from town centre - just past cinema leads to Breadalbane Street.

An informal, distinctive town restaurant.

- An unpretentious restaurant and bar with a Scottish theme.
- Good, plain cooking.
- "Serving the best of Scottish food for over a hundred years."

First opened in 1882 as a supper room for the famous annual Gathering Ball, The Gathering has a distinguished pedigree and is rightly popular with Oban's many tourists. With antlers and targes on the walls, the restaurant's ambience is decidedly and memorably Scottish. The menu offers first class, straightforward dishes made from local meat and seafood, as well as a range of imaginative starters and popular 'lighter bites'. The wine list is predictable but dependable. Portions are generous, prices modest and service cheerful. During July to September live music is available every night e.g. ceilidhs, folk music and local musicians. Live music at weekends off season.

Open Easter to 1 Jan: weekends (Thu to Sat)
Oct to Jan
Note: closed to public last Thu in Aug
Bar Lunch (Jul to Sep) 12.30 - 3 pm
reservation only (a)
Dining Room/Restaurant Lunch 12.30 - 3 pm
reservation only (b)
Bar Supper 5 - 11 pm (b)
Dinner 5 - 11 pm (d)
Vegetarians welcome
Facilities for disabled visitors
No smoking area in restaurant

Crofters chowder - seafood soup with scallops and mussels. Inverawe trout with pan-fried prawns, capers and parsley. Char-grilled prime steaks. Oban Bay seafood platter. Poached scallops in Islay cheese sauce. Roast Scottish lamb. Game dishes: pheasant, venison.

Credit cards: 1, 3 + SWITCH
Proprietor: Elaine Cameron

Isle of Eriska Hotel

Ledaig, by Oban
Argyll PA37 1SD
Tel: 01631 720371
Fax: 01631 720531

A85 north of Oban, at Connel Bridge take A828 for 4 miles. North of Benderloch village follow signs to Isle of Eriska.

This hotel, exceptional by any standards, was the 1994 winner of The Macallan/Taste of Scotland 'Hotel of the Year' Award.

- An impressive, grey granite Scottish Baronial house built in 1884, romantically situated on an island reached by a short road bridge.
- Gourmet country house cuisine.
- "The food here is superb - as is the warmth of hospitality, a most memorable stay."

Robin and Sheena Buchanan-Smith have run their home on the island of Eriska as a hotel for over 20 years and manage to combine the intimate atmosphere of a family-run country house with the highest standard of professional service. Although their affable son Beppo is now taking over much of the management, Robin remains the caring attentive host who will greet your arrival with the charm of a Scottish laird. Isle of Eriska is one of the best hotels on the west coast and its 300 acre grounds offer golf, tennis, putting, croquet, water-sports, clay pigeon shooting and magnificent gardens. The hotel also has a new leisure complex with swimming pool etc. Member of the Scotch Beef Club.

Open all year
Rooms: 17 with private facilities
Bed & Breakfast £175 - £205
Dinner B & B £122.50 - £175
Special Rates for 3+ nights
Bar Lunch - residents only
Dinner 8 - 9 pm (f) 7 course menu
Open to non-residents for dinner only
Vegetarians welcome
Facilities for disabled visitors
Children over 10 years welcome
No dogs in public rooms

Queen scallop with a cider and cream sauce. Pan-fried duck with potato rosti served with a seasonal fruit and honey sauce. Brandy-snap basket filled with a trio of home-made ice cream. Rosemary chocolate cassis.

STB Deluxe 5 Crowns
Credit cards: 1, 3, 6 + SWITCH
Proprietors: The Buchanan-Smith Family

Manor House Hotel

Gallanach Road, Oban
Argyll PA34 4LS
Tel: 01631 62087
Fax: 01631 63053

From south side of Oban follow signs to car ferry. At ferry entrance continue along main road for further ½ mile.

An historic house overlooking Oban Bay.

- Country hotel.
- Scottish cooking with French influences.
- "Lovely views, a pleasant atmosphere and a very attractive menu."

Situated on the southern tip of Oban Bay, the Manor House was built in 1780 by the Duke of Argyll, and was first a factor's residence and then a Dower House. In 1826 Oban's first bank, 'The National' opened here, and in 1845 Admiral Otter used it as his base which conducted hydrographic surveys on the west coast. Latterly it was the home of the MacLeans of Drimnin. The house retains much of the charm and atmosphere of the past. The five course table d'hôte dinner menu (three-four starters, three-four main courses) changes every day, according to what is available and seasonal. The cooking is fresh and creative.

Open 1 Feb to 2 Jan
Rooms: 11 with private facilities
Bar Lunch 12 - 2 pm (a)
Dining Room/Restaurant Lunch 12 - 2 pm
by arrangement
Dinner 7 - 9 pm except Sat (d) 5 course menu
No smoking in dining room
Dinner B & B £44 - £79
Special Rates for 2+ nights
Vegetarians welcome

Steamed finnan haddock mousse with a chive and horseradish butter sauce. Marinated beef fillet with Drambuie and pink peppercorns. Isle of Mull venison with roast swedes and bramble dressing. Baked west coast scallops with Arran mustard, Gigha cheese and rosemary. Parfait Flora MacDonald. Steamed raspberry pudding with a tayberry compot.

STB Highly Commended 4 Crowns
Credit cards: 1, 2, 3 + SWITCH, DELTA
Proprietor: J L Leroy

Sea Life Centre - Shoreline Restaurant

Barcaldine, Oban
Argyll PA37 1SE
Tel: 01631 720 386

On A828 Oban-Fort William, 10 miles north of Oban.

> A bright and modern self-service restaurant within Oban's Sea Life Centre.

- A splendidly-situated establishment to suit all tastes.
- Wide range of good home cooking.
- "Something for everyone, all day long."

With large picture windows looking onto Loch Creran and the majestic mountains beyond, this is an informal and welcoming place with menus to suit all tastes. Impeccably organised, the restaurant's dishes change daily and are written out on a blackboard. The ambience is relaxed and the prices inexpensive. The Shoreline is rightly popular with families on a day out.

Open mid Feb to end Nov + weekends
only Dec to mid Feb
Note: closed Christmas Day + 1 Jan
Coffee Shop open 10 am - 5.30 pm: 9.30 am - 4.30 pm Jul Aug
Meals available 12 - 4.30 pm: 10 am - 6.30 pm Jul Aug (a)
Table Licence only
Vegetarians welcome
No smoking area in restaurant

Fisherman's pie. Chicken, ham and mushroom pie. Vegetarian special - 'harvester's pie'. Local oysters with Scottish wine. Coffee shop has fresh ground coffee.

Credit cards: 1, 3 + SWITCH, DELTA

Soroba House Hotel

Soroba Road, Oban
Argyll PA34 4SB
Tel: 01631 62628

A816 to Oban.

> A small, family-run town hotel.

- Just on the outskirts of Oban, yet close enough to enjoy the town.
- Straightforward good British cooking.
- "A friendly atmosphere and a warm welcome."

A Georgian building set in its own nine acres of grounds, Soroba enjoys a fine outlook over Oban to the Hills of Morven. David and Edyth Hutchison offer a warm welcome to all guests, whether they've come for the hotel's proximity to the ferry terminal or to make the hotel their holiday base. Modern self-catering flats and suites dot the hotel's grounds. The hotel's dining room offers a good range of local meat, game and seafood, unpretentiously presented.

Open all year except 23 Dec to 5 Jan
Rooms: 25 with private facilities
Bed & Breakfast £28 - £48
Dinner B & B £40 - £62
Room Rate £35 - £60
Bar Lunch 12 - 2.30 pm (a)
Dining Room/Restaurant Lunch 12 - 2.30 pm (b)
Bar Supper 7 - 9.30 pm (a)
Dinner 7 - 9.30 pm (c)

Cullen skink. Local salmon served with a sauce of white wine, leeks, orange and cream. Pan-fried Rannoch venison steak flamed with port, served with cranberry jelly. Grilled Appin lamb cutlets served with onions, mushrooms and mint sauce. Local scallops pan-fried in butter and garlic.

Credit cards: 1, 2, 3 + DELTA
Proprietor: David Hutchison

The Waterfront Restaurant

No 1 The Waterfront
The Pier, Oban
Argyll PA34
Tel: 01631 63110

The waterfront, Oban.

> On the pier, with a fish shop below, the seafood couldn't be fresher.

- Seafood restaurant .
- Plain cooking.
- "The best fish and chips I have eaten all year."

'From the pier to the pan as fast as we can' reads the Waterfront's slogan. The restaurant is on the first floor, with Creel's Coffee Shop below (specialises in home baking and sandwiches with seafood fillings). The à la carte menus are supported by daily blackboard specials: although predominantly fish and shellfish, meat dishes are also offered. The cooking is straightforward and the treatments uncomplicated in the main, as befits the quality of the seafood. Service is friendly and obliging. The overall atmosphere is cheerful and unpretentious - including the price.

Open all year
Creel's Coffee Shop 8.30 am - 6 pm (a)
Dining Room/Restaurant Lunch 12 - 3 pm (a)
Dinner 6 - 10 pm (b)

Home-made soup. Balvicar Bay oysters. Tobermory scallops and prawns in a cream sauce. Loch Feochan salmon with hollandaise sauce. Fresh seafood platter of the day. Fillet steaks.

Credit cards: 1, 3
Proprietor: Stuart Walker

Willowburn Hotel

Clachan Seil, Isle of Seil
by Oban PA34 4TJ
Tel: 01852 300276

11 miles south of Oban, via A816 and B844,
signposted Easdale, over Atlantic Bridge.

A small privately owned hotel on the Isle of Seil standing in two acres of ground with fine views.

- A modern hotel, with fully equipped bedrooms, a dining room and bar.
- Excellent home cooking.
- "Carefully prepared fish and shellfish straight from the sea."

The lovely little island of Seil is noted for its wildlife, and for being connected to the mainland by 'the bridge over the Atlantic' (built in 1792). Willowburn is a modern family-owned hotel; guests are made very welcome. The dining room has stunning views across the Sound of Seil, and the à la carte and table d'hôte menus are especially strong on local seafood. The cooking is skilled and assured. The six bedrooms are all very comfortable and have their own bathrooms. The hotel has an AA Rosette.

Open Easter to end Oct: 3 day New Year break
Rooms: 6 with private facilities
Dinner B & B £44 - £48
Special Rates for 3+ nights
Bar Lunch: 12.30 - 2 pm (a)
Bar Supper: 6 - 8pm (c)
Dinner 7 - 8pm (c)
Vegetarians welcome

Venison steak with citrus and red wine juices. Paupiette of steak with wild mushrooms, with red wine and redcurrant juices. Pan-roasted monkfish with leek and ginger sauce. Raspberry soufflé.

STB Highly Commended 3 Crowns
Credit cards: 1, 3
Proprietors: Archie & Maureen Todd

Yacht Corryvreckan

Dal an Eas
Kilmore nr Oban
Argyll PA34 4XU
Tel: 01631 770246
Fax: 01631 770246

A yacht purpose-built for west coast cruising in comfort.

- Charter yacht.
- Home cooking.
- "Enter a gorgeous remote anchorage after an exciting day's sailing and sit down to a superb dinner party. This is Corryvreckan."

Douglas and Mary Lindsay have been offering chartered cruises on the west coast for many years and brought all their experience to bear when they designed Corryvreckan (strictly speaking Corryvreckan II, since their earlier vessel had the same name). She is 65 feet overall, 16 feet in the beam and has a wonderfully spacious feel - standing room is available throughout. There are five double guest cabins, and the dining table seats 12 comfortably. Mary's cooking is wonderful: everything (even baking and canapés) is cooked fresh; the galley is full of potted herbs; every night is a dinner party. Guests are members of the crew and help with washing up as well as actually sailing the ship.

Open Apr to Oct
Cabins: 5
1 wk cruises £410 - £440 (all incl)
No smoking below deck
Parking available
No dogs

Baked Scottish salmon with sorrel sauce. Roast leg of venison with rowan jelly. Pheasant casserole with stir-fry local vegetables. Gooseberry and elderflower suédoise.

No credit cards
Proprietors: Douglas & Mary Lindsay

Meldrum House

Oldmeldrum
Aberdeenshire AB51 0AE
Tel: 01651 872294
Fax: 01651 872464

A947 Aberdeen to Oldmeldrum (15 miles). 13 miles north of Aberdeen airport.

An historic house in rural Aberdeenshire.

- Scottish baronial mansion, now a country house hotel.
- Traditional Scottish cooking, with flair.
- "A delightfully faded and atmospheric baronial house and an appetising menu."

The nucleus of the building is a 13th century Z-Plan tower house, with charming baronial additions over the centuries - the old stone bar is within the original part of the house. Local tradition maintains that King Charles I spent part of his childhood here, when a ward of the Seton family of nearby Fyvie Castle. The historic atmosphere of the house is enhanced by antiques, portraits and faded furniture. The house stands in 15 acres of lawns and woodland, with its own small loch. The hotel's resident proprietors are Douglas and Eileen Pearson, attentive and courteous hosts who make you very welcome to their home. Eileen presents an imaginative and well constructed four course table d'hôte menu which changes every month.

Open all year
Rooms: 9 with private facilities
Bed & Breakfast £37.50 - £52.50
Dinner B & B £55 - £78
Special Weekend Rates available
Bar Lunch 12 - 2 pm (b)
Dining Room/Restaurant Lunch 12 - 2 pm (b)
Dinner 7 - 9.30 pm (d)
Restricted Licence
Vegetarians welcome
Facilities for disabled visitors
Children welcome
No smoking in restaurant
Dogs welcome

Crayfish bisque flavoured with Pernod. Slices of Scotch salmon with quenelles of Arbroath smokie mousse. Medallions of fillet steak topped with cèpe mushrooms on a peppercorn sauce. Rhubarb crumble ice cream in a tulip basket with a Champagne sauce.

STB Commended 4 Crowns
Credit cards: 1, 3 + Switch
Proprietors : Douglas & Eileen Pearson

Onich by Fort William

Allt-nan-Ros Hotel

Onich, by Fort William
Inverness-shire PH33 6RY
Tel: 0185 582 1210
Fax: 0185 582 1462

On A82, 10 miles south of Fort William.

Highland country hotel.

- Victorian house on the shores of Loch Linnhe.
- Country house cooking.
- "The dishes are of a modern style complemented by appropriate traditional sauces."

Situated halfway between Ben Nevis and Glencoe, Allt-nan-Ros is an attractive 19th century shooting lodge standing in an elevated position above the loch and commanding spectacular views: a most picturesque situation. The Gaelic name means Burn of the Roses, and derives from the cascading stream which passes through the gardens of the hotel. The decoration is modern, rooms are comfortably furnished, service is personal and dinner is served in a new conservatory. The menus offer a range of familiar Scottish dishes, prepared from locally sourced ingredients, and the style of the cooking has French influences. An accordionist serenades guests in the dining room from time to time!

Open 1 Jan to 10 Nov
Rooms: 21 with private facilities
Dinner B & B £55 - £75
Special Rates for 3 nights
Bar Lunch 12.30 - 2 pm (b)
Dining Room/Restaurant Lunch 12.30 - 2 pm (b)
Dinner 7 - 8.30 pm (d) 5 course menu
Vegetarians welcome
No smoking in dining room
No dogs

Ravioli of monkfish flavoured with chives and a cream sauce infused with coriander. Pan-fried breast of duck glazed with honey and served on an orange sauce. Fillet of salmon grilled with garlic butter on a bed of spinach. Prune and Armagnac ice cream. Baked apple strudel with crème anglaise. Selection of cheeses with walnut and rosemary bread.

STB Highly Commended 4 Crowns
Credit cards: 1, 2, 3, 5, 6 + SWITCH
Proprietor: James Macleod

Cuilcheanna House Hotel

Onich by Fort William
Inverness-shire
PH33 6SD
Tel: 01855 821226

250 yards off A82 in village of Onich.

An attractive and welcoming West Highland hotel.

- A small country house hotel with a warm welcome and peaceful setting.
- Quality home cooking.
- "I don't have a sweet tooth, but the chocolate marshmallow pie was wonderful!"

This is an old farmhouse (17th century foundation) now a traditional family hotel run by Russell and Linda Scott, who are most welcoming hosts. It stands in its own grounds overlooking Loch Linnhe, peacefully situated with views towards Glencoe and the Isle of Mull, and is pleasantly furnished - with piles of books of local interest and a cosy log fire in the lounge. The set four course dinner menu changes daily, and is complemented by a well thought out wine list, as well as a fine selection of quality malt whiskies. The emphasis is on genuine home cooking and Linda makes good use of prime local produce and fresh Scottish-grown herbs. The comprehensive breakfast choice includes local favourites such as venison sausage, haggis, herring in oatmeal and Mallaig kippers.

Open 1 Apr to 31 Oct
Rooms: 7 with private facilities
Bed & Breakfast £19 - £33
Dinner Bed & Breakfast £32.50 - £47.50
Special Rates for 7+ nights
Dinner at 7 pm (b) 4 course menu
Non-residents by arrangement
Vegetarians welcome
No smoking throughout
Dogs by arrangement

Cream of celery and walnut soup. Locally smoked duck breast served on a leaf and herb salad with a warm Inverness sauce. Shoulder of Lochaber venison casseroled with chocolate and almonds. Mallaig haddock and prawn pie. Blackberry and pear fudge crumble. Scottish farmhouse cheeses with Orkney oatcakes.

STB Commended 3 Crowns
Credit cards: 1, 3 + DELTA
Proprietors: Russell & Linda Scott

The Lodge On The Loch Hotel

Onich, by Fort William
Inverness-shire PH33 6RY
Tel: 0185 582 1237
Fax: 0185 582 1463

On A82, 1 mile north of the Ballachulish Bridge.

A comfortable hotel with good views.

- Victorian country hotel, with modern additions.
- Traditional Scottish cooking.
- "Good Scottish produce, interestingly served."

The Lodge on The Loch hotel is a granite Victorian villa connected to a new and rather severe looking block by a lobby and conservatory. It stands within yards of Loch Linnhe and enjoys good views towards the hills of Morvern. Guests of the Lodge on The Loch have automatic membership of a sister hotel's swimming pool, sauna, steam room, turbo pool, solarium and multi-gym. The bedrooms are comfortable and the dining room has recently been refurbished and redecorated. The table d'hôte menus feature several Scottish dishes.

Open Feb to Nov + Christmas/New Year
Rooms: 20, 18 with private facilities
Bed & Breakfast £39.50 - £52
Dinner B & B £62.50 - £75
Special Rates for 3+/7+ nights
Bar Lunch 12.30 - 2.30 pm (a)
Dining Room/Restaurant Lunch 12.30 - 2.30 pm (a)
Dinner 7 - 9.30 pm (d) 4 course menu
Vegetarians welcome
Facilities for disabled visitors
No smoking in dining room

Sauté wild mushrooms with fine herbs served on a puff pastry case, set on a Moniack Castle wine and cream sauce. Baked suprême of Loch Linnhe salmon on a cucumber and ginger butter. Grilled Glencoe lamb cutlets coated with a gooseberry and mint glaze. Blackcurrant and whisky charlotte set on a lime crème anglaise.

STB Highly Commended 4 Crowns
Credit cards: 1, 3
Proprietors: The Young Family

Peat Inn

The Peat Inn
Peat Inn
Fife KY15 5LH
Tel: 01334 840 206
Fax: 01334 840 530

A superb country restaurant now firmly established in a class of its own.

- ■ Restaurant with rooms in a converted village inn.
- ■ Innovative Scottish cooking which has won many awards for chef David Wilson.
- ■ "There are no superlatives that can do full justice to this establishment."

Food and style writers have waxed lyrical about The Peat Inn almost since the day it opened its doors. Chef and owner David Wilson has literally re-written the rule book on Scottish cooking and has created a world class restaurant whose name is synonymous with good food. His bold imaginative cooking style has gained him all the top food and wine awards including his most recent - the Scottish Chef Achievement Award. All ingredients are of the utmost freshness and quality and, with tremendous flair, they are transformed into truly memorable dishes. His wine list is formidable but provides great choice even in the lowest price range. Menus are table d'hôte, à la carte and a tasting menu of six or seven courses which must be ordered for a complete table. Member of the Scotch Beef Club.

Open all year except Christmas Day + New Year's Day, Sun + Mon
Rooms: 8 all with sitting room + private facilities
Bed & Breakfast £67.50 - £95
Dinner B & B £93 - £123
Room Rate £135 - £140
Dining Room/Restaurant Lunch 12.30 for 1 pm except Sun Mon (c) 4 course menu
Dinner 7 - 9.30 pm except Sun Mon (e) 4 course menu
Vegetarians welcome
No smoking in dining rooms

Sauté of scallops, monkfish and pork with spiced apple. Grilled fillet of beef with roasted shallots and a meat juice. Whole local lobster poached in a vegetable and herb broth. Selection of fish from the market. Little pot of chocolate and rosemary.

Credit cards: 1, 2, 3, 5 + SWITCH
Proprietors: David & Patricia Wilson

Peebles

Cringletie House Hotel
nr Peebles EH45 8PL
Tel: 01721 730 233
Fax: 01721 730 244

Off A703 Edinburgh-Peebles, 2½ miles north of Peebles.

Family-run hotel in the Borders, winners of 1990 Les Routiers 'Casserole' Award.

- ■ 19th century baronial mansion.
- ■ Home cooking.
- ■ "The dishes display a thoughtful dedication to blending colours, textures and flavours with happy results."

A charming Victorian baronial house designed for the Wolfe Murray family by the famous Scottish architect David Bryce. It stands in beautifully kept gardens, amidst the gentle Tweedsmuir countryside, with rolling hills and glens all about. The exterior of the house has an understated dignity which is echoed in the tasteful decor of public and private rooms. There is a two acre walled garden and some beehives which supply the kitchen; as far as possible fresh local meat and fish is used, and the table d'hôte menu changes every day. The dishes created by chef/owner Aileen Maguire use positively flavoured sauces and dressings and draw inspiration from continental and Eastern traditions.

Open 11 Mar to 1 Jan
Rooms: 13 with private facilities
Bed & Breakfast £49 - £62.50
Light Lunch except Sun (a)
Dining Room/Restaurant Lunch 1 - 1.45 pm Mon to Sat (a): Sun (b)
Afternoon Tea 3.30 - 4.30 pm
Dinner 7.30 - 8.30 pm (d) 4 course menu
No smoking in restaurant

Haggis stuffed mushrooms with whisky sauce. Rack of local lamb with mustard and peppers. Avocado, Inverloch and smoked Cumberland ham with fresh basil dressing. Baked rock turbot with lentil and mustard sauce. Cranachan ice cream with Drambuie served in an oatmeal basket.

STB Highly Commended 4 Crowns
Credit cards: 1, 3
Proprietors: Stanley & Aileen Maguire

Park Hotel
Innerleithen Road, Peebles
Tweeddale EH45 8BA
Tel: 01721 720451
Fax: 01721 723510

At eastern end of High Street (A72).

A peaceful country house hotel with good accommodation and food.

- ■ Attractive baronial-style country house set in parkland with views over the River Tweed.
- ■ Traditional hotel cuisine.
- ■ "The many dishes on the menu represent the best of local produce and there are some nice examples of Scottish specialities."

An attractive mansion standing in its own grounds on the outskirts of Peebles, on the banks of the River Tweed. It has a peaceful and relaxing atmosphere and caters primarily for the older visitor. The hotel is surrounded by well-tended gardens and lawns. The comfortable public rooms are on the ground floor, as are a number of en suite bedrooms. The leisure and sporting facilities of the Hydro are available to the Park's guests, who are then able to retreat from the family bustle of the larger hotel! The oak-panelled restaurant has splendid views of the Tweed and the rolling Border hills beyond, you will find a wide choice of familiar and more unusual dishes, plainly cooked and nicely presented.

Open all year
Rooms: 24 with private facilities
Bed & Breakfast £37 - £57
Dinner B & B £47 - £67
Bar Lunch 12 - .2 pm (a)
Dining Room/Restaurant Lunch 12 - 2 pm (a)
Bar Supper 6.30 - 9.30 pm (a)
Dinner 7 - 9 pm (c) 4 course menu
Vegetarians welcome

Leg of Border lamb roasted with rosemary, served with redcurrant jelly. Barbary duck breast sliced over diced pears, coated in a sharp orange sauce. Scottish cheeseboard.

STB Commended 4 Crowns
Credit cards: 1, 2, 3, 5, 6 + SWITCH

Peebles Hotel Hydro

Innerleithen Road
Peebles EH45 8LX
Tel: 01721 720602
Fax: 01721 722999

On A72, eastern outskirts of Peebles on
Innerleithen Road.

A distinguished resort hotel in the beautiful
Scottish borders.

- A château-style hotel with holidaymakers in mind.
- Traditional cooking.
- "More than just a hotel."

Opened in 1907 as a hydropathic spa, Peebles Hotel
Hydro retains an atmosphere of Edwardian
graciousness. It prides itself on warm, friendly
service. Surrounded by 30 acres of gardens and
grounds, this is an all-year resort hotel which
overlooks the valley of the River Tweed and the
rolling Border hills. Tennis, squash and horse-
riding are available and the hotel has its own
hairdresser and beautician. There is an excellent
leisure centre. Accommodation ranges from
executive suites to family rooms, all with the
facilities you would expect. Cuisine in the elegant
dining room reflects the demands of a wide
clientele which includes conferences. At its best, it
makes the most of fresh Scottish produce.

Open all year
Rooms: 137 with private facilities
Bed & Breakfast £39 - £65
Dinner B & B £55.50 - £80
Bar Lunch 12.30 - 3.30 pm (a)
Dining Room/Restaurant Lunch 12.45 - 2 pm (b)
Dinner 7.30 - 9 pm (c)
Vegetarians welcome

Achiltibuie oak-smoked salmon. Eyemouth seafood
platter of fresh and marinated fish with a dill and
lemon dressing. Braised escalope of Highland
venison on a bed of apples and berries with a rich
red wine sauce. Sliced loin of Border lamb with a
light coriander gravy, garnished with raspberries.
Cranachan. Blairgowrie cheesecake.

STB Highly Commended 5 Crowns
Credit cards: 1, 2, 3, 5, 6

Ballathie House Hotel

Kinclaven, by Stanley
Perthshire PH1 4QN
Tel: 01250 883268
Fax: 01250 883396

The Macallan Taste
of Scotland Award Winner 1994

Off A9, 2 miles north of Perth - turn off at
Stanley and turn right at sign to Kinclaven.
Or off A93 south of Blairgowrie to Kinclaven.

Overall winner of The Taste of Scotland Scotch
Lamb Challenge 1995. Ballathie is a country
house hotel with a great reputation.

- A Victorian baronial house overlooking the River Tay, standing in its own 1500 acre sporting estate.
- Award winning modern and classic Scottish cooking.
- "Elegant Scottish cooking served in superior surroundings."

An elegant turreted mansion, well seated in superb
shooting country on one of the best salmon beats on
the mighty River Tay. The hotel itself is furnished
and decorated in keeping with its age and station as
a top-flight country house hotel: the public rooms
are graciously proportioned and comfortably chintzy,
the bedrooms well-appointed. Chris Longden,
Ballathie's manager, is very experienced, and his
chef, Kevin McGillivray, presents lunches and dinners
which one inspector described as 'exciting'. His
menus change daily, use local produce and offer
subtle variations on classic Scottish dishes. Member
of the Scotch Beef Club.

Open all year
Rooms: 27 with private facilities
Bed & Breakfast £57.50 - £95
Dinner B & B £72.50 - £110
Special Rates available
Bar Lunch 12 - 2 pm except Sun (a-b)
Dining Room/Restaurant Lunch 12.30 - 2 pm
Easter to Nov: 12.30 - 2 pm Sun Fri Sat only
Nov to Easter (b)
Dinner 7 - 9 pm (e)
Vegetarians welcome
No smoking in dining rooms

Crisp seasonal salad of home-smoked chicken with
avocado, watercress and blue cheese. Roast leg of
Perthshire lamb with rosemary, garlic, oyster
mushrooms and Madeira jus.

STB Deluxe 4 Crowns
Credit cards: 1, 2, 3, 5, 6 + SWITCH, DELTA

Huntingtower Hotel

Crieff Road
Perth PH1 3JT
Tel: 01738 83771
Fax: 01738 83777

Signposted off A85, 1 mile west of Perth,
towards Crieff.

An elegant mansion in its own garden a mile
outside Perth.

- Country house hotel.
- Country house cooking, with French influences.
- "A good base from which to explore Perthshire."

Huntingtower is a half-timbered Edwardian
mansion standing in a four acre garden, with a
pretty little stream meandering through it. Both the
spacious conservatory and the dining room
overlook the garden. The former offers unusual bar
meals - including Mexican Fajitas, pasta, omelettes
and filled croissants, as well as substantial meat
and fish dishes. The latter is an elegant room,
panelled from ceiling to floor, with crystal
chandeliers, ornate cornices and a very handsome
inglenook fireplace. Both à la carte and table d'hôte
menus are offered. The latter is reasonably priced
and offers some unusual dishes and classic sauces.
Huntingtower is a popular venue for weddings and
business meetings.

Open all year
Rooms: 25 with private facilities
Bed & Breakfast from £41
Dinner B & B from £62
Special Rates for 2+ nights
Bar Lunch 12 - 2.30 pm except Sun (a)
Bar Meals available all day Sun (a)
Dining Room/Restaurant Lunch 12 - 2.30 pm (b)
Bar Supper 6 - 10 pm (a)
Dinner 7 - 9.30 pm (c)

Peppered roast sirloin of beef with a red wine sauce.
Collops of venison with spring onion cream sauce.
Seafood casserole bound in a saffron sauce served
in a puff pastry case. Oven-baked salmon with
creamed leeks and a herb crust.

STB Commended 4 Crowns
Credit cards: 1, 2, 3, 5, 6 + SWITCH

The Lang Bar & Restaurant

Perth Theatre, 185 High Street
Perth PH1 5UW
Tel: 01738 639136
Fax: 01738 624576

Perth city centre in pedestrian zone at middle
section of High Street.

> Restaurant and bar which is part of Perth
> Theatre.

- Theatre restaurant.
- Innovative/traditional Scottish cooking.
- "Suprême of Salmon cooked in peanut oil; a
  most imaginative recipe and cooked to
  perfection."

Perth Theatre was built in 1900, and has recently
been beautifully restored. The bar, restaurant and
coffee bar benefits both from its situation and the
refurbishment. The menus are changed to suit the
current production (a novel touch!). However
being theatrical, when the stage is 'dark' so is the
restaurant. The food is of a high standard and
covers the range of Scottish meat, fish and game in
really rather interesting dishes with continental
touches. For instance it is rare that gnocchi appears
as a prologue to dinner, let alone baked kippers as a
finale. There is a creative touch in the more
traditional dishes which demonstrates chef Colin
Potter's culinary energy. During the summer the
restaurant is open Thursday to Saturday evening
with live music adding to the atmosphere.

Open all year except Christmas/New Year +
Public Holidays
Bar Lunch 10 am - 4.30 pm except Sun (a)
Dining Room/Restaurant Lunch
11.45 am - 2 pm except Sun (a)
Bar Supper 6 - 7 pm except Sun (a)
Dinner 6 - 10 pm except Sun (b) - booking
advised
Note: Please telephone to ensure that
Restaurant is open
Closed Sun
Vegetarians welcome
Facilities for disabled visitors

Seafood chowder with saffron and tomato served
with a flaky pastry crust. Roast loin of pork stuffed
with apples and prunes, roasted with honey, brown
sugar and lemon. Deep-fried kiwi fruit coated in
almond batter served with butterscotch.

Credit cards: 1, 2, 3 + SWITCH

Murrayshall Country House Hotel

Scone, nr Perth
Perthshire PH2 7PH
Tel: 01738 551171
Fax: 01738 552595

4 miles out of Perth, 1 mile off A94.

> A country house hotel with its own golf course.

- Set in its own peaceful gardens and parkland.
- Elegant scottish cuisine.
- "The peace of the country, minutes from the
  town."

Golfers will feel particularly at home in this small,
grey-stoned mansion house, surrounded by its own
300 acres and private, 18-hole golf course. Tennis,
bowls, croquet and clay pigeon shooting are also
available in the hotel's grounds. The Old Masters
Restaurant is an elegant, spacious and well-
furnished room, its menus based on the best of
seasonally-available produce. Many of the herbs
and vegetables are grown in the hotel's own kitchen
garden. Service is polished and friendly. The wine
list is extensive, and in accord with the menus.
French spoken. Dogs welcome.

Open all year
Rooms: 19 with private facilities
Bed & Breakfast £125 - £140
Dinner B & B £85 - £105
Special Rates available
Bar Meals (Club House) 12 - 9 pm (a)
Dining Room/Restaurant Lunch (Club House)
12 - 2.30 pm (b)
Dinner (Old Masters) 7 - 9.30 pm (c)
Vegetarians welcome

Fillet of Scotch beef topped with a tarragon and
mushroom duxelle accompanied with a whisky and
pickled walnut sauce. Fillet of North Sea turbot and
scallops topped with a creamed leek sauce. Rack of
new season lamb carved and presented with a mint
and rosemary jus.

STB Highly Commended 4 Crowns
Credit cards: 1, 2, 3, 5 + SWITCH

Newmiln Country House Hotel

Guildtown
Perth PH2 6AE
Tel: 01738 552364
Fax: 01738 553505

4 miles north of Perth on A93 Blairgowrie road.
Follow signs for Scone Palace. 3 miles after
Scone Palace, Newmiln driveway on left.

> A country house and sporting estate just outside
> Perth.

- Country house hotel.
- British/Scottish cooking.
- "Little known at the moment, I forcast that this
  hotel - and its talented young chef - will be
  winning awards before too long."

Standing within its own 700 acre estate - pheasant,
duck and trap shooting are available to guests - the
house itself is Edwardian in character, although it
dates from the 17th century. Its owners, James and
Elaine McFarlane, succeed in making Newmiln a
'home from home' for guests; although imposing
and beautifully appointed, the house is cosy and the
welcome warm. Their young and talented chef,
Paul Burns (ex Auchterarder House, and The Cellar
Restaurant, Anstruther) presents a sophisticated set
menu in the handsome dining room, where guests
sit around a single oval polished mahogany table.
Altogether a delightful experience.

Open all year
Rooms: 8 with private facilities
Bed & Breakfast from £45
Dinner B & B from £70
Dining Room/Restaurant Lunch 12 - 2 pm (c)
Dinner 7 - 9.30 pm (e)
Reservations essential for non-residents
Vegetarians welcome
Facilities for disabled visitors
No smoking in dining room
Dogs accepted by prior arrangement

Home-made brioche crustade centred with west
coast mussel stew with cream and garden chives.
Warm Tay salmon with pepper and coriander
dressing. Char-grilled fillet of Perthshire beef
resting on a beef and potato oatmeal cake.
Medallions of estate-shot venison with onion
marmalade. Iced hazelnut praline and apricot
parfait with Amaretto ice cream. Tuille cup with
vanilla crème with seasonal fruits and coulis.

Credit cards: 1, 3
Proprietors: James & Elaine McFarlane

Number Thirty Three Seafood Restaurant

33 George Street
Perth PH1 5LA
Tel: 01738 633771

Perth city centre.

A stylish city centre restaurant.

- Well established and popular seafood restaurant in Perth.
- Formal Scottish cooking with a choice of eating styles.
- "The chef's dedication to his art is apparent in the simple elegance of the food and the quality of accompanying dishes."

Number Thirty Three is now an established presence on George Street, easily identified by its distinctive seahorse sign. The theme is Art Deco in muted tones of pink and grey with a clever use of sea imagery creates a stylish atmosphere, the perfect setting for an extremely good meal. The menu is based principally on fish and seafood balanced by interesting and original starters and puddings. The chef's own home-made gravadlax with dill mayonnaise is something of a house speciality. There is a choice of menu with light meals available in the Oyster Bar and more formal dining in the restaurant. Whichever option you choose, the food and wine list are impressive, confirming Number Thirty Three's well-earned reputation for quality.

Open all year except Christmas + Boxing Days
+ 9 Jan to 30 Jan
Light Lunch 12.30 - 2.30 pm except
Sun Mon (b)
Dining Room/Restaurant Lunch 12.30 -
2.30 pm except Sun Mon (c)
Light Supper 6.30 - 9.30 pm except
Sun Mon (b)
Dinner 7 - 9.30 pm except Sun Mon (c)
Closed Sun Mon
Vegetarians welcome

Parcel of monkfish cooked with fennel and garlic. Baked fillets of halibut with a sesame seed crust and sorrel butter sauce. Roast breast of duckling with Marsala sauce. Home-made elderflower ice cream with brown sugar meringue. Mary's seafood soup.

Credit cards: 1, 2, 3
Proprietors: Gavin & Mary Billinghurst

Parklands Hotel & Restaurant

St Leonards Bank
Perth PH2 8EB
Tel: 01738 622451
Fax: 01738 622046

Junction of St Leonards Bank and Marshall Place in centre of Perth adjoining South Inch Park.

Classical town house, city centre hotel.

- Well-restored town house with parkland views.
- Modern Scottish quality cooking.
- "Good food, freshly prepared and highly presented."

Formerly the home of the Lord Provost of Perth, Parklands Hotel has been luxuriously refurbished maintaining original features whilst offering the comforts expected of a city centre hotel. Every effort is made by the chefs to ensure the finest produce is cooked and presented with care and attention. Lunch is particularly suited to the business user with an inviting table d'hôte menu or as an alternative the bar snacks in the Conservatory are worth a visit. At dinner both à la carte and table d'hôte menus are offered. With its own small car park and central location Parklands is deservedly popular with business and leisure visitors alike.

Open 8 Jan to 22 Dec
Rooms: 14 with private facilities
Bed & Breakfast £40 - £65
Dinner B & B £47.50 - £60
Special Rates available
Bar Lunch 12 - 2 pm (a)
Dining Room/Restaurant Lunch 12 - 2 pm (c)
Dinner 7 - 9 pm (d)
Vegetarians welcome

Roulade of halibut lined with smoked salmon presented on a light tomato sauce. Choux pastry cups filled with smoked chicken and lime cream with a hazelnut dressing. Grilled fillet of cod with a fresh herb butter. Roast rack of lamb studded with orange and garlic with a sherry sauce.

STB Highly Commended 4 Crowns
Credit cards: 1, 2, 3, 5, + SWITCH, DELTA
Proprietor: Allan Deeson

Scone Palace

Perth PH2 6BD
Tel: 01738 552300

On A93 Braemar road, 2 miles out of Perth. Well signposted.

An informal restaurant in the old kitchens of a magnificent historic building.

- 14th century palace kitchens, refurbished as a charming restaurant.
- Home cooking.
- "The ancient character of this place adds relish to the food."

Scone Palace, just outside Perth, is the home of the Earl of Mansfield and a leading visitor attraction. Scone was the capital of Pictavia in the 6th century and the centre of the Culdee church. Here Kenneth MacAlpine united Scotland and, in 838AD, placed the Stone of Scone upon the ancient Moot Hill which thus became the crowning place of subsequent Scottish monarchs. The Old Kitchen Restaurant is below-stairs in an early part of the palace (it was substantially enlarged in 1804) and is decorated with gleaming copper pots and pans. This is a licensed self-service restaurant offering soup, salads and a 'hot dish of the day'. There is also a coffee shop offering home baking.

Open 5 Apr to 14 Oct
Food Service 9.30 am - 5 pm (a)
Dining Room/Restaurant Lunch 11.30 am -
2.30 pm (a)
Dinner 7 - 8 pm (f) - by arrangement only
Vegetarians welcome

Fresh Tay salmon, home-made soup always available on the lunch menu. Home baking, chutney and marmalade a speciality.

Credit cards: 1, 2, 3

Pitlochry

Auchnahyle Farm
Tomcroy, Pitlochry
Perthshire PH16 5JA
Tel: 01796 472318
Fax: 01796 473657

Off East Moulin Road, at end of Tomcroy
Terrace.

An unusual private house, in the heart of rural
Perthshire.

■ An 18th century farmhouse and steading with a
self-catering cottage.
■ Scottish home cooking.
■ "In the care of Penny and Alastair Howman,
we wanted for nothing."

This charming farm dates from the 16th century,
when the land was owned by the monks of
Dunfermline Abbey, one of the richest monasteries
in Scotland. In the house itself there are three en
uite bedrooms two of them overlook the garden and
the Tummel Valley. The comfortable family dining
room has Victorian mahogany chairs and table. It
is the epitome of home comfort, and here you will
be served by your attentive host, Alastair Howman.
Penny, his wife, works hard in the kitchen to
prepare excellent and imaginative dishes which
feature local seasonal ingredients, including those
from the farm itself.

Open Mar to mid Oct - other times by
arrangement
Rooms: 3 with private facilities
Bed & Breakfast £29 - £34
Dinner B & B £44 - £53
Special Rates available
Picnic Lunches on request
Pre-Theatre Supper at 6.45 pm (b) 2 course
menu
Dinner at 7.30 pm (c) 4 course menu
Unlicensed - guests welcome to take own wine
Vegetarians welcome
No children under 12 years
No smoking in dining room

Smoked trout mousse. Wild duck paprika. Scallops
with a white wine and cheese sauce. Pan-fried fillet
of venison with plums and ginger. Rhubarb and
orange meringue pie. Chocolate Drambuie
Marquise. Scottish cheeseboard with home-made
oatcakes.

Credit cards: 1, 3
Proprietors: Penny & Alastair Howman

Birchwood Hotel
East Moulin Road, Pitlochry
Perthshire PH16 5DW
Tel: 01796 472477
Fax: 01796 473951

200 yards off Atholl Road on Perth side of
Pitlochry.

A homely hotel with attractive accommodation
and sound menus.

■ An old stone Victorian mansion set on a wooded
knoll with four acres of grounds and gardens.
■ Traditional Scottish cooking.
■ "We had to force ourselves out of the restaurant
to get to the theatre on time."

Birchwood is a grand country villa built in the
1870s on the south side of Pitlochry surrounded by
four acres of woodland gardens. Unpretentious and
welcoming. It is managed by the resident
proprietors, Brian and Ovidia Harmon, who are
committed to making their guests welcome and
providing every comfort. Hospitality is allied to
good food and spacious bedrooms, all with private
facilities. The pleasant restaurant overlooks the
garden and the chef uses the fresh produce to create
table d'hôte and à la carte menus with a strong
Scottish flavour, at a reasonable price. The chef is
happy to cater for personal dietary preferences.
There is a modern bungalow adjacent to the hotel
which has five bedrooms with full facilities.

Open Mar to Nov
Rooms: 16 with private facilities
Bed & Breakfast £28 - £35
Dinner B & B £40 - £52
Special Rates for 2+ nights
Dining Room/Restaurant Lunch 12 -
1.30 pm (a-b)
Dinner 6.30 - 8.15 pm (c-d)
Vegetarians welcome
No smoking in restaurant

Fillet of pork Edradour. Baked wild salmon with
fennel. Loin of lamb with Highland stuffing.
Aberdeen Angus steaks with Drambuie haggis
stuffing. Chicken with skirlie and leek sauce.

STB Highly Commended 3 Crowns
Credit cards: 1, 3
Proprietors: Brian & Ovidia Harmon

Dunfallandy House
Logierait Road, Pitlochry
Perthshire PH16 5NA
Tel: 01796 472648
Fax: 01796 472017

On south side of Pitlochry, signposted off road
leading to Festival Theatre.

A country house hotel just outside Pitlochry.

■ Attractive Georgian house in stunning gardens
and woodland.
■ Country house cooking.
■ "Imaginative, flavoursome cooking without
over-fussy sauces."

Dunfallandy House is approached up a hill through
magnificent mature trees and rhododendrons. The
view is spectacular. The three-storey stone mansion
was built in 1790 for General Archibald Fergusson,
Chief of Clan McFergus of Atholl. There has been a
settlement on this site for centuries and the famous
Dunfallandy Stone, a 9th century Pictish monolith
stands close by. The house has been sensitively
restored and retains its period character in the clean
lines of the exterior and the extremely tasteful
interior decorations and antique furniture. Public
rooms and bedrooms are comfortable and very well
appointed. The Georgian Dining Room retains its
original black slate fireplace, the furniture is Louis
XV and it sparkles with crystal, silver and cut
flowers. Jane and Michael Bardsley are the resident
owners, and present a short but creative table d'hôte
menu (two main courses), with dishes made from
absolutely fresh local ingredients.

Open 1 Feb to 31 Oct
Rooms: 9 with private facilities
Bed & Breakfast £25 - £35
Dinner B & B £40 - £50
Bar Lunch 12 - 2 pm (a)
Dinner 6 - 8 pm (c)
Vegetarians welcome
No children
No smoking in dining room
No dogs

Locally smoked duck breast and kumquat sauce.
Monkfish with a celeriac and Dijon sauce.
Chocolate and Cointreau truffle tarte.

STB Highly Commended 3 Crowns
Credit cards: 1, 2, 3
Proprietors: Jane & Michael Bardsley

East Haugh Country House Hotel & Restaurant

East Haugh, by Pitlochry
Perthshire PH16 5JS
Tel: 01796 473121
Fax: 01796 472473

On old A9 road, 1 mile south of Pitlochry.

Small country house hotel.

- 17th century house.
- Traditional Scottish cooking.
- "Imaginative accompaniments to fish and game dishes."

Built originally as part of the Atholl Estate around 300 years ago, East Haugh is a turreted stone house, standing in its own gardens. It is run by Neil and Lesley McGown who bought the property in 1989 and have converted it sympathetically. Neil is a keen fisherman, and also shoots and stalks - encouraging pastimes for a chef, since the bag or catch appears on the menu. There is a great deal of food on offer at East Haugh, with children's menus, lunchtime bistro-style menus and those offered in The Gamekeeper's Restaurant for dinner. The lunch dishes are very wide ranging and are prepared to order; dinner is a more formal affair, with a well-composed menu which changes every two days and features local produce.

Open all year except Christmas Day
Rooms: 8 with private facilities
Bed & Breakfast £25 - £48
Dinner B & B £45 - £67
Special Rates for 2+ nights
Bar Lunch 12 - 2 pm Mon to Sat: 12 - 2.30 pm
Sun 'family lunch' (c)
Dining Room/Restaurant Lunch - party bookings + functions by arrangement (d)
Bar Supper 6 - 10 pm
Pre/After Theatre Supper - bookings only (c)
Dinner (Game Keeper's Restaurant)
7 - 10 pm (d)
Vegetarians welcome
No smoking in restaurant

Terrine of pheasant, duck and rabbit studded with pistachio nuts, served with wild rowan jelly and toasted fruit bread. Prawn and mushroom parcels on a lobster and brandy sauce. Home-made desserts.

STB Commended 3 Crowns
Credit cards: 1, 3
Proprietors: Neil & Lesley McGown

The House of Bruar

by Blair Atholl
Perthshire
PH18 5TW
Tel: 01796 483236
Fax: 01796 483218

7 miles north of Pitlochry on the side of A9 at Bruar. Restaurant services A9.

An astonishing new emporium of the 'best of Scottish'.

- Self-service restaurant.
- Home cooking and baking.
- "A remarkable showcase for Scottish goods, and a great place to break a journey."

The House of Bruar is a large, splendidly designed (inspired by Victorian hunting lodges) and expensively built (dressed stone, slate roof, astragal windows, etc) 'emporium' selling the very best of Scottish country products. It includes a cashmere hall, a cloth room, a wildflower nursery, country wear hall, food hall and 200 seater café/restaurant. Play and picnic areas are also provided. The lengthy blackboard menus offer snacks and full meals, with many classic Scottish dishes; the cooking is fresh and accomplished; breads, cakes and scones are freshly baked. A cheerful place for the whole family to break a journey.

Open all year except Christmas Day
Meals available 8.30 am - 6 pm incl
all day breakfast (a)
Vegetarians welcome
Facilities for disabled visitors
No smoking in restaurant
Dogs welcome outside

Aberdeen Angus sirloin steak. Venison stew. Ploughman's lunch. Freshly baked baguettes, various fillings. Home-made cakes and scones.

Credit cards: 1, 2, 3 + SWITCH, DELTA
Proprietors: Mark and Linda Birkbeck

Knockendarroch House Hotel

Higher Oakfield, Pitlochry
Perthshire PH16 5HT
Tel: 01796 473473
Fax: 01796 474068

High on a hill overlooking village - just off main road in the centre of town, up Bonnethill Road and take first right turn.

An imposing Victorian villa with a period atmosphere.

- Victorian mansion in Pitlochry.
- Good home cooking.
- "Well-run by enthusiastic and experienced hosts."

Knockendarroch is a sturdy villa, built in 1880 on a steep hillock in Pitlochry, and accordingly enjoying wonderful views up the Tummel Valley to the south and of Ben Vrackie to the north. The house is well-proportioned; the public rooms well-appointed and comfortable; the 11 bedrooms individually furnished. It was opened as an hotel in 1985 by its current owners, John and Mary McMenemie - courteous and enthusiastic hosts. The home cooking is of a high standard, and has earned Knockendarroch a Red Rosette from the AA. Booking is essential for non-residents.

Open 1 Mar to 31 Oct
Rooms: 12 with private facilities
Bed & Breakfast £30 - £45
Dinner B & B £45 - £60
Special Rates available
Dinner 6.15 - 7.45 pm (c)
Vegetarians welcome
No smoking throughout

Cream of courgette and rosemary soup. Smoked salmon quiche. Roast leg of Perthshire lamb with minted pears. Sole, salmon, trout and prawn in a parcel of puff pastry. Hazelnut and carrot burger in tomato and orange sauce. Collops of venison with cranberry and port sauce. Strawberry shortcake. Summer pudding.

STB Highly Commended 3 Crowns
Credit cards: 1, 2, 3, 5
Proprietors: John & Mary McMenemie

Pitlochry Festival Theatre Restaurant

Port-na-Craig, Pitlochry
Perthshire PH16 5DR
Tel: 01796 473054
Fax: 01796 473054

On south bank of the River Tummel, approx ¼ mile from centre of town. Clearly signposted.

An informal restaurant for theatre goers with a relaxed atmosphere.

- Restaurant and coffee bar.
- Modern Scottish cooking enlivened with imaginative touches.
- "Dinner at the Brown Trout Restaurant before a performance is always a treat - the quality of the meal is enhanced by wonderful views."

The Pitlochry Festival Theatre is beautifully situated on the banks of the River Tummel at the gateway to the Highlands. The theatre's restaurant and coffee bar are a boon to theatre patrons as well as Pitlochry locals who drop in regularly to enjoy the home baking which is such a feature of the coffee bar in the foyer. At lunchtime the restaurant is buffet-style with a choice of hot and cold dishes including local fish from the 'Summer Festival Buffet'. Portions are generous with lots of healthy eating options and staff are helpful. In the evening table d'hôte dinner is served at 6.30 pm to accommodate theatre goers. Booking is essential. French spoken.

Open 26 Apr to 5 Oct
Note: open early Apr for Coffee + Lunch only
Dining Room/Restaurant Lunch 12 - 2 pm
except Sun (a)
Dinner 6.30 pm except Sun * (c) - booking essential
* If theatre performance Sun, buffet served - booking essential
Vegetarians welcome
Facilities for disabled visitors
No smoking in restaurant during dinner
Smoking area in Coffee Bar

Scampi, scallops, salmon and prawns in a cream and dill sauce. Poached fillet of Scottish salmon with spinach and leek sauces. Loin of lamb filled with apricots, herbs and walnuts. Mincemeat roulade filled with a Glayva flavoured cream.

Credit cards: 1, 2, 3, 5, 6 + SWITCH

Torrdarach Hotel

Golf Course Road, Pitlochry
Perthshire PH16 5AU
Tel: 01796 472136

On road signposted to golf course at north end of town.

A small hotel offering comfortable accommodation and good value food.

- A red-painted house set in a pleasant garden near the golf course.
- Unpretentious home cooking.
- "Unpretentious home-cooked dishes, nicely presented."

This is an immaculately kept guest house-type hotel in a woodland setting on the north side of Pitlochry. Richard and Vivienne Cale are attentive hosts who cherish their home and make their guests welcome. Six of the seven bedrooms are en suite. Good value, simple fare is on offer in the evenings; the menu changes daily and the wine list is growing. This is a quiet spot from which to explore the town and its attractions as well as the glorious Perthshire countryside which surrounds it.

Open Easter to mid Oct
Rooms: 7 with private facilities
Bed & Breakfast £20 - £27
Dinner B & B £35 - £42
Special Rates for 3+ nights
Dinner 6.30 - 7 pm (c)
Residents only
Vegetarians welcome
No smoking throughout
No dogs

Home-made soups. Smoked salmon pâté. Poached salmon steak served with Drambuie sauce. Home-roast Perthshire turkey with cranberry sauce. Aberdeen Angus beef.

STB Highly Commended 3 Crowns
No credit cards
Proprietors: Richard & Vivienne Cale

Westlands of Pitlochry

160 Atholl Road, Pitlochry
Perthshire PH16 5AR
Tel: 01796 472266
Fax: 01796 473994

On old A9 north of town centre.

Attractive stone-built hotel.

- Country town hotel.
- Traditional cooking.
- "A comfortable base from which to explore Highland Perthshire."

An attractive stone building with an extension, built in keeping with the rest. The lawn, which is bordered by mature trees, slopes down to the main road, and Westlands has attractive views. The hotel is personally run by its resident proprietors, Andrew and Sue Mathieson, supported by their manager and chef. There is a straightforward table d'hôte menu and an à la carte menu which offers a wide range of Scottish dishes. Both are reasonably priced. Meals are served in the Garden Room Restaurant, which has pleasant views of the Vale of Atholl.

Open all year except Christmas Eve, Christmas Day + Boxing Day
Rooms: 15 with private facilities
Bed & Breakfast £30 - £48
Dinner B & B £46 - £54
Special Spring/Autumn Rates available
Bar Lunch 12 - 2 pm (a)
Bar Supper 6.15 - 9.30 pm (b)
Dinner 6.15 - 9 pm (c)
Vegetarians welcome

Orkney herring and cucumber terrine with crisp salad leaves. Roast gigot of Scottish lamb cooked with fresh herbs and garlic, served with a mint and redcurrant jelly. Poached fillets of sole with tomato, shallots, cream and white wine sauce. Tender beef in puff pastry set on a smooth tomato sauce.

STB Commended 4 Crowns
Credit cards: 1, 3
Proprietors: Andrew & Sue Mathieson

The Haven Hotel

Innes Street, Plockton
Ross-shire IV52 8TW
Tel: 01599 544223
Fax: 01599 544467

In the village of Plockton.

A small West Highland hotel.

- Stone-built, water-front hotel.
- Modern Scottish cooking.
- "Good food, creatively presented."

The Haven was built for a Victorian merchant and has a pleasing simplicity in its architecture, pink sandstone-fronted and harled sides and rear. Although detatched, it stands in the terrace of traditional houses overlooking the pretty bay at Plockton, only yards from the beach. The hotel continues to offer the same high standard of cooking for which it has long had such a good reputation. Dinner menus are table d'hôte (six choices of main course) and combine fresh local produce with interesting sauces.

Open 1 Feb to 20 Dec incl
Rooms: 13 with private facilities
Bed & Breakfast £33 - £35
Dinner B & B £45 - £54
Special Rates available
Dining Room/Restaurant Lunch 12.30 - 1.30 pm (a-c) - 24 hour notice required
Dinner 7 - 8.30 pm (d) 5 course menu
Restricted Licence
Vegetarians welcome
Children over seven years welcome
No smoking in restaurant

Crisp filo basket filled with wild mushrooms and garlic. Warm layered terrine of venison with an apple and honey sauce. Lightly steamed collops of Mallaig monkfish on a lime, ginger and coriander butter sauce. Chocolate mint cheesecake. Cranachan with raspberries.

STB Highly Commended 4 Crowns
Credit cards: 1, 3
Proprietors: Annan & Jill Dryburgh

Off The Rails

The Station, Plockton
Ross-shire IV52 8TN
Tel: 01599 554423/554306

On platform of Plockton railway station - ½ mile from centre of village and lochside.

Delightful themed restaurant in beautiful West Highland village.

- Small restaurant of character in an unusual setting.
- Informal modern Scottish cooking .
- "A bistro-type restaurant whose menu offers an interesting balance of traditional ingredients enhanced with interesting and subtle flavours."

A recent television series set in Plockton has made this particular West Highland village a star in its own right. You will find Off the Rails in a converted railway platform at Plockton Station through which pass the trains travelling the famous Kyle Line. The restaurant makes the most of its unusual location in a converted waiting room with its original timber panelling and black iron fireplaces. Here, owners Calum and Jane Mackenzie serve good quality, home-cooked food combining fresh local produce with an interesting use of spices and herbs from their own herb garden. You can also potter in the gift shop housed in the old ticket office. It has an interesting selection of crafts from all over Scotland. Drop in for a morning coffee and delicious home-baked goodies or a full three course candlelit dinner.

Open Easter to Oct
Food service 10.30 am - 9.30 pm over Easter + from late May
Dining Room/Restaurant Lunch 11.30 am - 5 pm (a)
Dinner 6.30 - 9.30 pm (b-c)
Note: Easter to late May open Thu Fri Sat Sun evenings only
No smoking in restaurant
Smoking at outside tables only

Local prawns in garlic butter. Skate wing with mustard and lime sauce. Roast leg of lamb with rosemary and anchovy. Haunch of venison with juniper berries and red wine. Sirloin steak with garlic whisky cream. Sticky toffee pudding. Oatcakes with a selection of local cheese.

Credit card: 1
Proprietor: Jane Mackenzie

The Pierhouse Hotel

Port Appin
Argyll PA38 4DA
Tel: 01631 730302
Fax: 01631 730521

Fort William-Oban on Argyll tourist route. Enter village of Appin, take road signed for Lismore ferry. Situated at pier.

An outstanding seafood restaurant and small hotel in an area of great beauty and interest.

- On the edge of Loch Linnhe, an informal family-run establishment.
- The best of fresh seafood cuisine with a Mediterranean influence.
- "Where seafood comes naturally."

Owned and run by the MacLeod family, the Pierhouse was originally the village post office and then the waiting room for the ferry. With fine views over Lismore to Mull and the Morven Hills, it is primarily a seafood restaurant to which 11 bedrooms were added in 1993. The restaurant's reputation rests on the outstanding quality of local seafood, landed almost at the door of the Pierhouse. Guests can see fresh oysters and lobsters in holding creels just off the jetty, in sight of the restaurant. Chef Sheila MacLeod lets such quality speak for itself, serving such bounty simply and effectively in her à la carte dinner menu. A daytime menu, served from 12 - 4 pm, also offers fresh sandwiches in addition to good, home-made soups and, of course, seafood.

Open all year except Christmas Day
Rooms: 11 with private facilities
Bed & Breakfast from £35
Room Rate £70 - £85
Bar Lunch 12 - 3.30 pm (a)
Dining Room/Restaurant Lunch 12 - 3.30 pm (a)
Dinner 6.30 - 9.30 pm (d)
No dogs

The Pierhouse Giant Platter: ½ lobster, mussels, prawns, oysters, scallops (2 persons). Loch Linnhe scallops cooked on a ribbed grill dry heat served with lemon butter. Fillet of salmon and langoustine Mornay served with fresh potatoes and vegetables. Lunch speciality: fresh salmon and potatoes bound together and covered in breadcrumbs.

STB Commended 3 Crowns
Credit cards: 1, 3
Proprietors: Sheila & Alan MacLeod

Port of Menteith

Lake Hotel
Port of Menteith
Perthshire FK8 3RA
Tel: 01877 385 258
Fax: 01877 385 671

On A81 - at Port of Menteith - 200 yards on road south to Arnprior.

> An Art Deco country hotel overlooking Lake Menteith.

- A well-established, comfortable and recently refurbished country hotel.
- Excellent cooking. Imaginative use of the best of Scottish produce.
- "Some of the dishes offered were most unusual, and when they arrived they were delicious."

Standing on the southern shore of Scotland's only 'lake', the hotel enjoys splendid views towards the Trossachs. The heart of the building was a 19th century manse, but it became an hotel over 50 years ago, with many well-integrated additions, and from the outside it is a classic example of a traditional Scottish country hotel. The interior provides a surprise: the theme is Art Deco, well executed, with may original pieces of furniture. The Conservatory Restaurant is on the lakeside, entered from the spacious lounge. Like all the other rooms, it is pleasantly appointed. The table d'hôte menus (lunch and dinner) are very well-priced and offer some unusual traditional dishes which have all but disappeared from more 'precious' restaurants. The excellence of the cooking has been recognised with 2 Rosettes from the AA.

Open all year
Rooms: 14 with private facilities
Bed & Breakfast £35 - £60
Dinner B & B £44 - £80
Dining Room/Restaurant Lunch 12 - 2 pm (c) - booking essential
Dinner 7 - 8.30 pm (d) 4 course menu
Vegetarians welcome
No smoking in restaurant

Puff pastry case filled with lambs sweetbreads and button mushrooms with a creamy garlic sauce. Loin of venison with braised red cabbage and apple chutney. Strawberry mille feuille.

STB Highly Commended 4 Crowns
Credit cards: 1, 2, 3 + SWITCH, DELTA
Proprietor: J L Leroy

Portpatrick

The Fernhill Hotel
Heugh Road, Portpatrick
nr Stranraer DG9 8TD
Tel: 01776 810220
Fax: 01776 810596

Just off main road into Portpatrick.

> A rural seaside hotel near Stranraer.

- Victorian house with modern conservatory extension.
- Modern Scottish cooking.
- "A talented new chef, who makes good use of local produce."

Set above the harbour of the beautiful, unspoiled fishing village of Portpatrick, The Fernhill Hotel has been family-run by Anne and Hugh Harvie for over 30 years. It began as a single Victorian villa-boarding house, and has gradually expanded in all directions, so that it now has 20 bedrooms and a sizeable conservatory restaurant with splendid views over the village to the sea. The chef, John Henry, uses locally landed fish and shellfish and Galloway beef and lamb. His cooking is fresh and healthy and his menus sensible and well-priced.

Open all year except Christmas
Eve + Christmas Day
Rooms: 20 with private facilities
Bed & Breakfast £39.50 - £85
Dinner B & B £50 - £104.50
Special Rates available
Bar Lunch 12 - 2 pm (a)
Dining Room/Restaurant
Lunch 12 - 2 pm (b-c)
Bar Restaurant Meals 6 - 10 pm (a)
Dinner 6.30 - 9.30 pm (c)
Vegetarians welcome
No smoking in restaurant + conservatory
No dogs in public rooms

Local crab and smoked salmon terrine set on a selection of crisp lettuce leaves with lemon. Strips of monkfish tails in a brandy and mustard sauce topped with cheese and grilled. Pan-fried breast of duck set on a bed of spinach served with a light orange sauce. Grilled Galloway fillet steak with queen scallops in a red wine sauce. Chocolate roulade with a fresh raspberry coulis.

STB Highly Commended 4 Crowns
Credit cards: 1, 2, 3, 5, 6 + SWITCH, DELTA
Proprietors: Anne & Hugh Harvie

Knockinaam Lodge
Portpatrick, Wigtownshire
DG9 9AD
Tel: 01776 810471
Fax: 01776 810435

Take A77 towards Portpatrick. 2 miles west of Lochans, Knockinaam sign on right. Take first left turning, past smokehouse. Follow signs for 3 miles to lodge.

> Outstanding cuisine in a remote corner of Galloway.

- A 19th century hunting lodge converted into a first class country house hotel.
- Contemporary haute cuisine.
- "The very talented chef conjures flavours which are outstanding and memorable."

Knockinaam was built in 1869 and was described 'as delightful a maritime residence as is anywhere to be seen'. It is remotely situated on the Galloway coast, close to the shore and facing toward the sunset (with Ireland on the horizon), surrounded on three sides by cliffs: tranquil and timeless. The public rooms are small and cosy, with open log fires in winter; the bedrooms, varying in size, are superbly appointed. The lodge's resident owners, Michael Bricker and Pauline Ashworth, are attentive and hospitable hosts, and their head chef Stuart Muir and second chef Tony Pierce prepare dishes which are both contemporary, unusual and outstandingly successful. A memorable place.

Open all year
Rooms: 10 with private facilities
Bed & Breakfast £50 - £80
Dinner B & B £93 - £115
Special Rates for 3/4 nights, 5+ nights
Bar Lunch 12 - 2 pm (b)
Dining Room/Restaurant Lunch 12 - 2 pm (e)
Dinner 7.30 - 9.30 pm (f)
Vegetarians welcome
No smoking in dining room

Grilled fillet of local turbot with Dijon mustard and herb brioche crust. Ravioli of forest mushrooms with a spaghetti of vegetables and a truffle oil dressing. Layered white, milk and dark chocolate terrine with a passion fruit sauce.

Credit cards: 1, 2, 3, 5 + Switch, Delta
Proprietors: Michael Bricker & Pauline Ashworth

Powmill by Dollar

Whinsmuir Country Inn & Restaurants
Powmill, by Dollar
Clackmannanshire FK14 7NW
Tel: 01577 840595
Fax: 01577 840595

On A977 Kincardine Bridge-Kinross.

Country inn surrounded by pretty landscape.

- Restaurant with accommodation.
- Modern Scottish bistro-style cooking.
- "A very convenient central location and experienced chef makes this an ideal venue for large functions."

Formerly the Gartwhinzean Hotel, it has now been taken over by the Brown family who are real experts in running hotels demonstrated by the success they have achieved at Auchterarder House, Auchterarder and Roman Camp, Callander. Many changes have been introduced including a recently completed new dining room with a large open fireplace and beautiful views. The bedroom accommodation is in the process of complete modernisation. Menus offer something for everyone and cater for all tastes and budgets with a good choice of lunch and snack dishes as well as a more sophisticated à la carte dinner menu giving five-six choices per course. Accompanying wine lists are well chosen and relatively competitively priced.

Open all year
Rooms: 13 with private facilities
Bed & Breakfast £22.50 - £40
Dinner B & B £32.50 - £50
Room Rate £45 - £65
Meals available 11 am - 10 pm (b)
Vegetarians welcome
Facilities for disabled visitors
No smoking area in restaurant

Scallop shell of puff pastry filled with langoustines served with a chive and beurre blanc sauce. Darne of poached Tay salmon with a light orange and ginger sauce. Noisettes of new season lamb with celeriac and rosemary crust on a Madeira and plum purée. Pan-fried sirloin steak glazed with oyster mushrooms, shallots and red wine. Honey, apple and raspberry charlotte with brandy and cinnamon crème fraîche.

Credit cards: 1, 2, 3
Proprietor: Paul M Brown

Rockcliffe

Torbay Farmhouse
Rockcliffe by Dalbeattie
Kirkcudbrightshire DG5 4QE
Tel: 01556 630403
Fax: 01556 630403

2½ miles south of Dalbeattie. Leave A710 Solway Coast road at Colvend for Rockcliffe, continue for 400 yards after church.

18th century farmhouse in tranquil setting.

- Thoughtfully refurbished farmhouse.
- Excellent home cooking.
- "The welcome, comfort and food here is exceptional."

Torbay Farmhouse is on the edge of the pretty Solway village of Rockcliffe, standing in a beautiful garden, surrounded by pastures and enjoying lovely southern views towards the Irish Sea and the Lakeland fells. Brenda Taylor is a charming and interesting host. The 18th century house has been thoughtfully refurbished and carefully extended; public rooms and bedrooms are all delightfully, even luxuriously, furnished. The dining room is in the modern extension - an attractive room with picture windows overlooking the garden: clean, bright and airy. The set menu of three courses is extremely good value. The food is all home-made (including bread and preserves) and much of it is home-grown. French, German and a little Italian and Spanish spoken.

Open 23 Mar to 21 Oct
Rooms: 3 with private facilities
Bed & Breakfast £19 - £24
Dinner B & B £29 - £34
Special Weekly Rates
Unlicensed - guests welcome to take own wine
Dinner 6.30 - 7.30 pm (b)
Vegetarians welcome
No smoking throughout

Smoked salmon pâté and Scottish oatcakes. Pheasant pâté with redcurrant jelly. Haddock and scrambled egg in toast baskets. Tomato and vodka sorbet. Beef with stir-fry celery and walnuts. Fish crumble. Galloway Forest venison pie and red cabbage. Chocolate and rum mousse. Pear and ginger crumble. Wide selection of Scottish cheeses.

STB Deluxe 3 crowns
No credit cards
Proprietor: Brenda Taylor

Rogart

Sciberscross Lodge
Strath Brora, Rogart
Sutherland IV28 3YQ
Tel: 01408 641 246
Fax: 01408 641 465

A9 over Dornoch Firth Bridge for c. 10 miles, then A839 for 4 miles. In Rogart turn right onto single-track road (Balnacoil) for 7 miles, lodge on left.

An attractive fishing lodge, well off the beaten track.

- Country house hotel.
- Country house cooking.
- "A marvellous place to get away from it all. You are made to feel very much a part of the family."

Sciberscross is the home of Peter and Kate Hammond, and this classic Victorian sporting lodge (built for the Duke of Sutherland in 1876) is full of homely touches - masses of fresh cut flowers, framed photographs and oil portraits, antiques. Peter dines with his guests, and the lodge offers fishing for salmon, sea trout, brown trout and char. It stands in spectacular scenery just across the Dornoch Firth, down a seven mile single-track road. Kate uses whatever can be sourced locally. Her five course dinners have set menus (choices for starter and dessert), and her cooking is delicious.

Open 1 Feb to 30 Nov
Rooms: 5 with private facilities
Dinner at 8 pm or by arrangement (f)
5 course menu
Dinners for non-residents by prior booking only
Bed & Breakfast from £40
Dinner B & B from £85 (fully incl)
Vegetarians welcome

Home-made soups. Wild venison pâté. Roast leg of Rogart lamb with redcurrant sauce. Fillet of fresh wild salmon with hollandaise sauce. Chocolate truffle torte. Selection of cheeses.

Credit cards: 1, 3
Proprietors: Peter & Kate Hammond

St Andrews

The Old Course Hotel, Golf Resort & Spa

St Andrews
Fife KY16 9SP
Tel: 01334 474371
Fax: 01334 477668

A91 to St Andrews.

A large modern hotel standing on the edge of the most famous golf course in the world.

- Grand resort hotel .
- Modern Scottish/grills.
- "Deserves its reputation as one of Scotland's leading resort hotels."

The hotel is set in a spectacular location overlooking the infamous 17th Road Hole and the historic Royal and Ancient clubhouse. All 125 bedrooms, including 17 suites, have unrivalled views, some looking over the Old Course to the sea, others towards the hotel's own Duke's Course and the surrounding countryside. The hotel offers its guests (residents and non-residents) a unique choice of dining experiences - the Road Hole Grill, with its open kitchen and rotisserie, the Conservatory - serving light meals throughout the day in summer, and the Jigger Inn, originally a 19th century cottage, now a popular golfing pub serving real ale and good wholesome food. The hotel has been awarded 5 Stars by the AA.

Open all year
Rooms: 125 with private facilities
Room Rate £176 - £295
Special short break rates available
Bar Lunch 11 am - 4 pm (a)
Dining Room/Restaurant Lunch 11.30 am -
7 pm (b)
Afternoon Tea available
Dinner 7 - 10 pm (e)
Vegetarians welcome
Facilities for disabled visitors

Salad of Comrie goats cheese with green beans and walnut vinaigrette. Shellfish cappuccino. Darne of Orkney salmon with fettucine and cherry tomato salsa. Hot-grilled Scotch sirloin with ratatouille of vegetables cooked in a red wine sauce. Pan-fried loin of Ayrshire lamb with a parsley and onion flan, herb potato scone and basil jus. Crème brûlée with minted raspberries.

STB Deluxe 5 Crowns

Credit cards: 1, 2, 3, 5

The Grange Inn

Grange Road, St Andrews
Fife KY16 8LJ
Tel: 01334 472670

From centre of town follow A917 signs to Crail/Anstruther. At edge of St Andrews take right fork signposted Grange, c. 3/4 mile to Inn.

A charming inn with a lovely view towards the harbour.

- Country inn with rooms.
- Traditional Scottish cooking.
- "The Grange has maintained its reputation for good food, attractive surroundings and excellent service."

This very attractive traditional country inn stands on the high ground to the south of the town and enjoys lovely views over St Andrews Bay. Under the capable management of proprietor Peter Aretz, The Grange has prospered and grown busy yet still managed to retain much of its old fashioned charm and atmosphere. There are three separate dining areas and two, simply furnished cottage-style bedrooms with private facilities. You'll find high standards of hospitality with uncomplicated, tasty, home-cooked food. A range of draught and bottled beers, spirits and liqueurs are available in the cosy, well-stocked, stone-flagged Ploughman's Bar and there is also a good well-priced wine list.

Open all year but closed Mon Tue Nov to Apr
Rooms: 2 with private facilities
Bed & Breakfast from £35
Dinner B & B from £45
Restaurant Lunch 12.30 - 2 pm (a-b)
Dinner 7.30 - 9.15 pm (a-c)
Vegetarians welcome
No smoking area available

Home-made soups. Loin of spring lamb wrapped in pastry lattice with Madeira sauce. Escalope of salmon with prawns and herb butter. Fillet steaks. Rhubarb in a pastry case with a vanilla cream. Caramel and pistachio cream served with home-made chocolate shortbread.

Credit cards: 1, 2, 3, 5, 6 + SWITCH, DELTA
Proprietor: Peter Aretz

Rufflets Country House & Garden Restaurant

Strathkinness Low Road, St Andrews
Fife KY16 9TX
Tel: 01334 472594
Fax: 01334 478703

On B939, 1½ miles west of St Andrews.

A most attractive country house near St Andrews.

- Country house hotel.
- Country house cooking.
- "The experience upon which Rufflets has buit its reputation over very many years shows in the attention to detail."

Rufflets is one of the oldest established country house hotels in Scotland, and has the distinction of being privately owned and managed by the same family since 1952. The house itself was built in 1924 in the elegant Lutyens-esque style and stands in formal gardens; furnishings are extremely tasteful (a mix of antique and contemporary country house); bedrooms are all individually designed and furnished. The attractive Garden Restaurant has an AA Rosette, among other awards. The daily changing menus are table d'hôte (six main courses) and the cooking combines the fresh seafood available from the East Neuk and good local meats and vegetables with imaginative sauces and stuffings. Service is smart and professional under the guidance of manager, John Angus.

Open all year
Rooms: 25 with private facilities
Bed & Breakfast £69 - £79
Dinner B & B £79 - £89
Special Rates available Nov to Apr
Bar Lunch 12.30 - 2 pm (a)
Dining Room/Restaurant Lunch 12.30 - 2 pm:
1 Nov to 30 Apr Sun Sat only (c)
Dinner 7 - 9 pm (e)
Vegetarians welcome

Light mousse of fresh salmon with fan of avocado pear and Orkney oatcakes. Fillet of North Sea halibut baked with lemon butter. Collops of Scottish beef fillet grilled with Stilton cheese and chives. Medallions of Rannoch venison on a garden beetroot, port wine and ginger sauce. Warm cloutie dumpling with coddled cream. Bramble shortcake.

STB Highly Commended 4 Crowns
Credit cards: 1, 2, 3, 5, 6 + SWITCH
Proprietor: Ann Russell

Rusacks Hotel

Pilmour Links
St Andrews
Fife KY16 9JQ
Tel: 01334 474321
Fax: 01334 477896

Situated on left as you enter St Andrews via M90-A91.

A famous golfing hotel overlooking the Old Course.

- Large town hotel.
- Elegant cooking with prime Scottish ingredients.
- "Recently redecorated most tastefully. The bedrooms are delightful and breakfast was of the highest calibre."

Founded in 1887 by Wilhelm Rusack (an Austro-Prussian who farmed near St Andrews) and a group of local businessmen, the hotel overlooks the first tee and 18th green of the Old Course - the most famous golf course in the world. Its stylish, comfortable furnishing and decoration are in keeping with its origins and enhance its Victorian atmosphere. The dining room continues the mood. Table d'hôte and à la carte menus are offered for lunch and dinner. The food is stylish, elegant and well-presented, cooked to bring out its fresh flavours.

Open all year
Rooms: 50 with private facilities
Bed & Breakfast £65 - £95
Dinner B & B £79 - £85
Room Rate £90 - £250
Special Rates available
Bar Food available 11 am - 9 pm (a)
Dining Room/Restaurant Lunch 12.30 - 2 pm (b)
Dinner 7 - 10 pm (d)
Vegetarians welcome
No smoking in dining room

Oak-smoked and home-cured salmon with caper dressing. Fillet of Dover sole with a lemon and chive butter. Fillet of beef pan-fried, topped with fois gras and served with a rich wine sauce. Collops of venison pan-fried in walnut oil with caramelised oranges and a whisky sauce. Breast of chicken set on a bed of sweet peppers and forest mushrooms served with a light tarragon cream.

STB Commended 4 Crowns
Credit cards: 1, 2, 3, 5, 6 + SWITCH, DELTA

St Andrews Golf Hotel

40 The Scores, St Andrews
Fife KY16 9AS
Tel: 01334 472611
Fax: 01334 472188

A91 to St Andrews, turn left at Golf Place then follow round to right to The Scores.

A golfing hotel close to the links with splendid views.

- Town hotel.
- Traditional Scottish cooking.
- "A traditional Scottish family-owned hotel, personally run by Maureen, Brian and Justin Hughes."

The Golf is a family-run hotel with fine views over St Andrews Bay to the distant Highlands, a mere 200 yards from the famous Royal and Ancient Golf Club and the championship courses. It is a Victorian terraced house, tastefully modernised and decorated with quality prints. The restaurant is oak-panelled and candlelit; à la carte and table d'hôte menus feature locally sourced Scottish fish, game and meat. In the basement is the convivial 'Ma Bells' pub, where bar food is served all day. Children welcome. Dogs accepted - small charge. Italian and some French spoken.

Open all year except 3 days Christmas
Rooms: 23 with private facilities
Bed & Breakfast £61 - £74
Dinner B & B £78.50 - £91.50
Bar Lunch 12 - 3 pm (a)
Dining Room/Restaurant Lunch 12.30 - 2.30 pm (a-b)
Bar Supper 5.30 - 9 pm (a-b)
Dinner 7 - 9.30 pm (c-d)
Vegetarians welcome
No smoking in restaurant

Roulade of smoked salmon and lemon sole with a light dill sauce. Fresh Tay salmon grilled with julienne of crisp vegetables and lemon butter. Noisettes of Perthshire lamb with garden rosemary served with pan juices. Prime Scottish sirloin with wholegrain Arran mustard. Vegetable strudel with a watercress and red pepper sauce.

STB Highly Commended 4 Crowns
Credit cards: 1, 2, 3, 5, 6 + SWITCH, DELTA
Proprietors: Maureen & Brian Hughes

Buccleuch Arms Hotel

The Green, St Boswells
Roxburghshire TD6 0EW
Tel: 01835 822243
Fax: 01835 823965

Situated on the main A68, 60 miles north of Newcastle. 40 miles south of Edinburgh.

An historic coaching inn, once a hunting lodge.

- Large village hall.
- Contemporary hotel cooking
- "A good tradtitional hotel, with cooking which is more than this"

The Buccleuch Arms dates from the 16th century, when it was a hunting lodge for the Dukes of Buccleuch. Situated on one of the main roads into Scotland (now the A68), beside the pretty village cricket pitch and green in the old village of St Boswells (established in the 11th century by a French monk, Boisil). A coaching inn now it is a popular base from which to tour the Tweed valley, fish, shoot or golf (there are 14 golf courses within a 20 mile radius). Lunch and suppers/dinners are served in the bar and in the restaurant. The cooking is adventurous, uses as much local produce as possible and favours aromatic sauces and combinations.

Open all year except Christmas Day
Rooms: 18, 17 with private facilities
Bed & Breakfast £34 - £37.50
Dinner B & B £42 - £52
Bar Lunch 12 - 1.55 pm (a)
Dining Room/Restaurant Lunch 12 - 1.55 pm (b)
Bar Lunch 6 - 8.55pm Sun to Thu: 6 - 9.55 pm Fri Sat (c)
Vegetarians welcome
No smoking in dining room

Scottish smoked pheasant with home-made gooseberry chutney. Suprême of Craufurdland guinea-fowl with a sharp lime sauce. Collops of Highland venison with pickled walnuts and brandy sauce. Eyemouth monktail kebab with wild rice, tomato and pineapple sauce. Home-made strawberry shortcake.

STB Commended 4 Crowns
Credit cards: 1,3
Proprietors: Louise Buchan / Bill & Sue Dodds

South Queensferry

by Spean Bridge

Dryburgh Abbey Hotel
St Boswells
Roxburghshire TD6 0RQ
Tel: 01835 822261
Fax: 01835 823945

Off A68 at St Boswells onto B6404. 2 miles turn left onto B6356. Continue for 1½ miles, hotel signposted.

A splendid luxury hotel, in the Scottish Borders, popular with anglers and country sportsmen with leisure facilities and comfortable accommodation.

- Scottish baronial red sandstone mansion on the banks of the River Tweed.
- International and modern Scottish cuisine.
- "From simple fare to the more complex dishes in the Tweed Restaurant, the chef utilises a good range of local fresh produce."

In a tranquil setting on the banks of the River Tweed, not far from the ruins of the historic Abbey, this mansion has been restored and converted into a first class hotel. The public rooms, bedrooms and suites are grand, comfortably appointed and maintained to high standards. The Tweed Restaurant is situated on the first floor, with views over the lawns and gardens to the river: a spacious, elegant room with decorative cornicing and ornate chandeliers. The Head Chef, Patrick Ruse, offers a table d'hote menu (lunch and dinner) which changes daily, and uses only fresh local produce. During the day a range of light meals is also available, served in the lounge or bar. A new indoor heated swimming pool was added in 1994.

Open all year
Rooms: 26 with private facilities
Bed & Breakfast £40 - £75
Dinner B & B £45 - £95
Special Rates for 2+/5+ nights
Bar Lunch 12 - 2.30 pm except Sun (b)
Dining Room/Restaurant Lunch 12 - 2.30 pm (b)
Dinner 7.30 - 9.15 pm (d)
Facilities for disabled visitors
No smoking in restaurant
Vegetarians welcome

Highland venison terrine with pine kernels, served with oatcakes. Medallion of halibut poached in white wine with lobster and tarragon essence. Quenelles of chocolate and Grand Marnier mousse set on lime caramel cream. Scottish cheeseboard.

STB Highly Commended 5 Crowns
Credit cards: 1, 3 + SWITCH, DELTA
Proprietors: David & Graham Grose

The Hawes Inn
Newhalls Road, South Queensferry
West Lothian EH30 9TA
Tel: 0131 331 1990
Fax: 0131 319 1120

At east end of the village, under the Forth Rail Bridge.

A quaint and charming 16th century inn, steeped in Scotland's history.

- A village inn of rare character.
- High quality pub food.
- "A memorable place for any meal and any occasion."

Splendidly situated, with fine views across the Forth and an outlook onto the Forth Railway Bridge, this is a justly popular establishment, much loved by both Sir Walter Scott and R L Stevenson. Among others, the novel Kidnapped was conceived here. As well as serving home-made, no-nonsense bar meals in generous portions, the inn has a traditional, fairly priced Scottish restaurant and a large beer garden with a children's play area.

Open all year except Christmas Day + 1 Jan
Rooms: 8
Bed & Breakfast £27.50 - £50
Dinner B & B £35 - £67
Room Rate £34 - £55
Special Rates available
Bar Meals 12 - 10 pm (a)
Dining Room/Restaurant Lunch 12 - 2 pm except Sat (a)
Dinner 6 - 10 pm (c)
Vegetarians welcome

Fresh mussels poached in white wine, orange, cream, leeks and herbs. Smoked seafood crêpes. Char-grilled steaks. Vegetarian strudel. Fillet of salmon baked with leeks, cream and stem ginger. Medallions of fillet steak with a red wine, onion and pickled walnut sauce. Rack of lamb with an Arran mustard and whisky sauce. Hot spiced Lanark pears in a rich butterscotch sauce.

STB Commended 1 Crown
Credit cards: 1, 2, 3, 5

Corriegour Lodge Hotel
Loch Lochy, by Spean Bridge
Inverness-shire PH34 4EB
Tel: 01397 712685
Fax: 01397 712696

Follow A82, 17 miles north of Fort William; 47 miles south of Inverness - between Spean Bridge and Invergarry.

A charming former hunting lodge set in breathtaking scenery.

- A small, personally owned and managed country house hotel.
- Excellent modern Scottish cuisine.
- "The charm of yesteryear with the comforts of today."

Corriegour was built in the late 19th century, now extensively and tastefully refurbished in an antique style, the hotel commands outstanding views over Loch Lochy. Its six acres of mature woodland and garden include a small lochside beach with jetty and waterfall. Corriegour Lodge's resident proprietors, Rod and Lorna Bunney, place their emphasis on guests' relaxation and comfort. Set with crisp white linen cloths and napkins, their Loch View Conservatory restaurant with its panoramic views, offers a range of high quality cuisine, all home-made, using the very best of Scottish produce. The hotel's wine list is extensive and reasonably priced. Corriegour prides itself on its ethos, its position, its cooking and the friendliness of its staff.

Open all Mar to Nov
Rooms: 8 with private facilities
Bed & Breakfast £30 - £40
Dinner B & B £49 - £59
Special Rates for 2/3 nights + weekly stays
Dinner 7 - 8.30 pm - reservations strongly recommended (c)
Note: Dinner can be served earlier by prior arrangement
Vegetarians welcome
No smoking in restaurant
No dogs

Home-made soup and pâté. Smoked haddock roulade with scallops. Rack of Highland hill lamb with rosemary and honey. Fillet of Aberdeen Angus beef en croûte.

STB Highly Commended 3 Crowns
Credit cards: 1, 2, 3
Proprietors: Rod & Lorna Bunney

Old Pines Restaurant With Rooms

Inverness-shire PH34 4EG
Tel: 01397 712324
Fax: 01397 712433

From Spean Bridge take A82 to Inverness. One mile north take B8004 next to Commando Memorial 300 yards on right.

A family home with a restaurant and guest rooms; winner of the 'Best Small Hotel in Britain 1994' Judith Chalmers Holiday Care Award and 'The Taste of Scotland Scotch Lamb Challenge 1995'.

- Scandinavian-style log and stone chalet overlooking Glen Spean and the Nevis Range.
- Modern Scottish cooking.
- "The set, five course menu is well balanced, imaginative and full of character."

Old Pines is a little jewel set amongst mature pine trees in the Great Glen - an ideal base from which to explore Aanock Mor and the countryside around Ben Nevis. It is the family home of Bill and Sukie Barber - a charming clutter of books, flowers and family mementos, with pine furniture and open fires throughout. Its owners describe it as a 'restaurant with rooms', and dinner by crystal and candlelight in the conservatory will certainly be the highlight of your stay. Member of the Scotch Beef Club.

Open all year except 2 wks Nov
Rooms: 8 with private facilities
Bed & Breakfast £25 - £35
Dinner B & B £45 - £55
Special Rates for 3+/7+ nights
Food available 8 am - 9.30 pm except Sun (a-b)
Dining Room/Restaurant Lunch 12 - 2.30 pm except Sun (c-d) - reservations essential
Supper 7 - 8pm Sun - residents only (c)
Dinner at 8 pm except Sun (d)
5 course menu - reservations essential for non-residents. Unlicensed
- guests welcome to take own wine
Vegetarians welcome - prior notice appreciated
Facilities for disabled visitors
No smoking throughout
No dogs indoors

Home-smoked fish, shellfish and cheese. Broccoli soufflé with a lemon and chive sauce. Haunch of venison with pineapple juice, thyme and juniper berries. Caramelised rhubarb flan with lemon yoghurt ice cream and ginger sabayon. Home-made pasta, ice cream, breads, scones, cakes and preserves.

STB Highly Commended 3 Crowns
Credit cards: 1, 3
Proprietor: Sukie Barber

Chapeltoun House Hotel

nr Stewarton
Ayrshire KA3 3ED
Tel: 01560 482696
Fax: 01560 485100

From Fenwick exit on A77 (Glasgow to Ayr road), take B778 to Stewarton then join B769 to Irvine. Chapeltoun is 2 miles along on right hand side.

A country house hotel in Ayrshire.

- Country house hotel and restaurant.
- Country house cooking.
- "Interesting menus, very reasonably priced."

This attractive house was built in 1900 by a Glasgow shipping merchant when he married a young English girl. It has all the elegant and refined details of its period - rich oak panelling, grand fireplaces and ornate plasterwork (including a splendid rose and thistle freize, celebrating the family alliance). The house stands in 20 acres of gardens. The bedrooms are very comfortable and individually furnished, often with period furniture, as are the public rooms. The dining room is especially fine, with rich colours and tapestry-covered chairs. The table d'hôte menu is extensive (12 main courses) and changes every six weeks. There is also a 'Chef's dish of the day'. Dishes are cooked to order. The cooking draws upon Eastern, French and Italian traditions; creamy sauces are popular, and a lot of care is taken over presentation.

Open all year except 1st wk Jan
Rooms: 8 with private facilities
Bed & Breakfast £49.50 - £85
Bar Lunch 12 - 2 pm (a)
Dining Room/Restaurant Lunch 12.30 - 2 pm (c)
Dinner 7 - 9.15 pm (d)
No smoking in restaurant

Pan-fried noisettes of lamb with baby vegetables and wild mushrooms in a herb tartlet set on a green peppercorn and redcurrant sauce. Ragoût of monkfish tails in a tomato and basil sauce served with a timbale of caraway braised rice. Tournedos of beef fillet with a pâté and mushroom duxelle wrapped in puff pastry and set on a rich Madeira essence.

STB Highly Commended 4 Crowns
Credit cards: 1, 2, 3 + SWITCH, DELTA
Proprietors: Colin & Graeme McKenzie

The Topps Farm

Fintry Road, Denny
Stirlingshire FK6 5JF
Tel: 01324 822471

On B818 Denny-Fintry road, off M80. 4 miles from Denny.

A family run farm guest house in Stirlingshire.

- A farmhouse on a working sheep and cashmere goat farm.
- Excellent home cooking.
- "Who could resist the promise of the 'Farmer's Breakfast' cooked by the farmer himself?"

This is a most informal farm guest house where you cannot help but share in the day to day activities of the country - our inspector found herself present during lambing. The house itself is a modern bungalow with splendid views over the Fintry and Ochil Hills, pleasantly furnished with plenty of family bric-a-brac. The atmosphere is cosy and familiar. A popular restaurant complements the guest house facilities. It has a small bar and a comfortable dining room. Scottish owners Jennifer and Alistair Steel both cook. The menus are straightforward, usually offering a choice of four main courses and as much produce as possible comes from the farm itself.

Open all year
Rooms: 8 with private facilities
Bed & Breakfast £18 - £32
Dinner B & B £30 - £44
Special Rates available
Dining Room/Restaurant Lunch 12.30-2.30 pm Sun only (a) - reservation essential
Dinner 6.30-9.30 pm (b)
Vegetarians welcome - prior notice required
No smoking throughout

Breakfast - trout, oak-smoked haddock, local haggis etc. Spring lamb steaks sprinkled with wild garlic and served with minted pears. Honey poached salmon. Pheasant breast 'recipe no 7' (roasted and served with garlic and cream sauce). Glenmorangie gâteau - feather-light chocolate sponge with a hint of the 'water of life'. Grilled spiced peaches.

Credit cards: 1, 3
Proprietors: Jennifer & Alistair Steel

Stonehaven

Tolbooth Restaurant
Old Pier, Stonehaven Harbour
Stonehaven
Tel: 01569 762287

Off A90, onto A957 to Stonehaven, 16 miles
south of Aberdeen.

Stylish seafood restaurant in a charming fishing
port.

- Informal restaurant in old toll-house.
- Modern Scottish cooking with strong French
  influence.
- "The restaurant exudes a welcoming and
  relaxing atmosphere in which to enjoy
  delicious food."

Situated in the oldest building in Stonehaven - a
16th century tollbooth - the restaurant is on the
harbourside with picturesque views out to sea.
Almost everything on the menu is fresh fish and
seafood, not surprising given the strength of
Grampian's fishing industry. Interesting vegetarian
and meat options are available too. An attractive
decor is given added interest by a continually
changing exhibition of contemporary Scottish
artists. The menu prepared by Dutch chef Jean-
Francois Meder is à la carte to which a number of
special dishes are added daily, depending on the
morning's catch.

Open all year except Christmas
+ Boxing Days, 1 + 2 Jan
Dining Room/Restaurant
Lunch 12 - 2 pm Sun only (b)
Dinner 6.30 - 9 pm except Mon (c)
Closed Mon
Vegetarians welcome

Cockles and mussels steamed with root vegetables
in Orkney beer. Sashimi of fresh tunafish. Fillets of
John Dory with a tomato beurre blanc. Char-grilled
collops of monkfish served with caramelised
shallots in a red wine sauce.

Credit cards: 1, 3
Proprietors: Moya Bothwell, Jean-Francois Meder
& Christopher McCarrey

Stranraer

North West Castle Hotel
Portrodie, Stranraer
DG9 8EH
Tel: 01776 704413
Fax: 01776 702646

Seafront - opposite harbour.

A family-run hotel opposite the harbour at
Stranraer with modern leisure facilities.

- Large Victorian seafront townhouse converted
  into a distinguished resort hotel.
- Good hotel cooking.
- "Roast loin of venison was delicious."

This castellated townhouse was built by Sir John
Ross, the Arctic explorer, in 1820. It has been owned
and run as a hotel by the McMillan family for
many years and has been well-maintained with
comfortable accommodation and function rooms.
It has the distinction of being the first hotel in the
world with its own indoor curling rink and also has
bowling, swimming pool (with spa bath), sauna,
sunbeds and multi-gym. The games room offers
snooker, pool and table tennis. Overlooking Loch
Ryan the large 'Regency' dining room has a grand
hotel atmosphere with pianist playing each evening
and both the à la carte and table d'hôte menus
offer traditional Scottish dishes, treated in a creative
way. The kitchen goes to great lengths to find fresh
local produce.

Open all year
Rooms: 71 with private facilities
Bed & Breakfast £35 - £64
Dinner B & B £42 - £69 (min 2 nights stay)
Special Rates available
Bar Lunch 12 - 2 pm (a)
Dining Room/Restaurant Lunch 12 - 2 pm (d)
Dinner 7 - 9 pm (d)
Vegetarians welcome

Pan-fried scallops seasoned with lemon and thyme
with a potato nest and wild mushrooms. Oven-
baked loin of Scotch lamb served with baby
vegetables and a port and redcurrant sauce. Pan-
fried breast of Gressingham duck on a potato
pancake topped with gingered leeks served with a
Grand Marnier sauce.

STB Highly Commended 5 Crowns
Credit cards: 1, 3 + SWITCH, DELTA
Proprietor: H C McMillan

Strathlachlan

Inver Cottage Restaurant
Strathlachlan, by Cairndow
Argyll PA27 8BU
Tel: 0136 986 396/275

B8000, 7 miles south of Strachur - signposted.

A friendly country restaurant overlooking Castle
Lachlan.

- Small rural restaurant.
- Traditional Scottish cooking.
- "Family service with a smile. The potatoes
  reminded me of childhood, when potatoes really
  had flavour!"

Inver Cottage has a grand view across a small bay
to Castle Lachlan, ancient seat of the MacLachlans
of MacLachlan (who still live in the 'new' 18th
century house nearby). With an open fire and low
ceilings, polished wood everywhere, candles, both
the restaurant and the adjacent lounge bar have a
cosy welcoming atmosphere. Owners Tony and
Gina Wignell and their team provide informal but
efficient service. The cooking is unfussy and fresh;
well contrived sauces accompanying excellent local
meat, seafood and vegetables. The whole place has
a great atmosphere.

Open Mar to 31 Oct (7 days)
Note: during Nov + Dec open Fri Sat Sun only
Bar Lunch 12 - 2.15 pm Mon to Sat: 12.30 -
2.15 pm Sun (a)
Dining Room/Restaurant Lunch
12 - 2.15 pm Mon to Sat: 12.30 - 2.15 pm
Sun (b)
Bar Supper 6 - 9.15 pm Mon to Sat: 6.30 -
9.15 pm Sun (a)
Dinner 6 - 9.15 pm Mon to Sat: 6.30 - 9.15 pm
Sun (c)

Home-made soups. Avocado with prawns. Feuilleté
of mushrooms. Suprême of salmon with saffron
sauce. Char-grilled fillet steak with peppercorn
sauce. Steak and stout pie. Substantial sandwiches
with home-made bread (lunchtime). Sticky toffee
pudding.

Credit cards: 1, 3
Proprietors: Tony & Gina Wignell

Strathyre

Creagan House
Restaurant with Accommodation
Strathyre
Perthshire FK18 8ND
Tel: 01877 384638
Fax: 01877 384319

On A84, ¼ mile north of Strathyre.

Family-run restaurant with accommodation.

- 17th century farmhouse.
- Innovative Scottish cooking.
- "Lovely balance and expert handling of the cooking."

Creagan House dates from the 17th century, and has been sympathetically restored to provide a 'baronial' dining room and five letting bedrooms. The house is eclectically furnished with all sorts of interesting pieces, and one of the bedrooms has a unique four poster bed. Gordon and Cherry Gunn have been awarded an AA Rosette for their cooking. Guests choose from the 'menu of the day' or the 'chef's favourites menu'. The emphasis of the cooking is to allow the fresh local ingredients to emerge. The care and attention to detail in preparation, cooking and presentation is obvious and the overall effect is excellent. Children's tea is at 6 pm.

Open 1 Jan to 27 Jan + 2 Mar to 31 Dec
Rooms: 5 with private facilities
Bed & Breakfast £32.50 - £42.50
Dinner B & B £49 - £63.50
Special Rates for 3+ nights
Dining Room/Restaurant Lunch at 1 pm Sun only (b)
Lunch parties on other days by arrangement
Dinner 7.30 - 8.30 pm (c-d)
Booking essential for all meals
Vegetarians welcome
No smoking in dining hall + bedrooms

Local smoked lamb with warm salad of goats cheese and avocado. Turbot with braised fennel. Scallops and limed garlic beurre blanc. Local game in season. Garden-grown vegetables and fruits. Variations of traditional puddings.

STB Highly Commended 3 Crowns
Credit cards: 1, 2, 3
Proprietors: Gordon & Cherry Gunn

Strontian

Kilcamb Lodge Hotel
Strontian
North Argyll PH36 4HY
Tel: 01967 402257
Fax: 01967 402041

On A861, 13 miles from Corran Ferry (A82, 15 miles south of Fort William).

An attractive house on the shore of Loch Sunart.

- Small country house hotel.
- Traditional cooking.
- "Warm, friendly and relaxing atmosphere, and a lovely position."

'Lodge' is rather too grand to describe the charms of Kilcamb: it is more a substantial West Highland farmhouse, with extensions at each end. Its situation is superb - standing in 28 acres of lawns and woodland, with half a mile of shoreline along Loch Sunart. The hotel is family-owned and run by Gordon and Ann Blakeway, and their son Peter, who is taking over the running of the hotel in 1996. The Blakeways won an AA 'Care and Courtesy' award in 1993 - one of only two in Scotland. The excellence of the food has been recognised by the award of 2 AA Rosettes, and Kilcamb Lodge was a finalist in the 1993 Scottish Restaurant of the Year competition. Peter Blakeway cooks, presenting a short and highly professional table d'hôte menu which changes daily and uses the best of the produce available that day.

Open 29 Mar to 4 Nov
Rooms: 10 with private facilities
Bed & Breakfast £44.50 - £54.50
Dinner B & B £69 - £79.59
Room Rate from £34
Special Rates for 3-5 nights
Light Lunch 12 - 1 pm (a)
Dinner at 7.30 pm (e) 4 course menu
Vegetarians welcome
No smoking in dining room

Open ravioli of wild mushrooms. Confit of Barbary duck. Celery, almond and walnut soup. Roast saddle of venison with port and juniper sauce. Baked monkfish tails with tomato and mushroom sauce. Caramelised bread and butter pudding. Home-made profiteroles with strawberries.

STB Highly Commended 3 Crowns
Credit cards: 1, 3 + SWITCH
Proprietors: Gordon, Ann & Peter Blakeway

Swinton

The Wheatsheaf Hotel & Restaurant
Main Street, Swinton
Berwickshire TD11 3NB
Tel: 01890 860 257
Fax: 01890 860 257

On B6461 Kelso-Berwick-upon-Tweed, 12 miles west of Berwick or a few miles east of A697.

Quaint attractive hotel in small Border village.

- A small country inn on the village green.
- Modern Scottish cooking.
- "Alan Reid's cooking is remarkably good, both in ideas and execution."

That a great deal of care has been taken to preserve the character of a genuine country inn is evident. The result is a welcoming, comfortable and intimate atmosphere, the sort that takes years to acquire. Bedrooms are prettily furnished, light and airy with en suite bathrooms and there is a secluded, private residents' lounge upstairs. The menu is surprisingly extensive, very reasonably priced and changes quarterly with the seasons. Excellent local produce is given added flavour by the chef's individuality and flair.

Open all year except last 2 wks Feb + last wk Oct
Rooms: 4, 3 with private facilities
Bed & Breakfast £22.50 - £32
Special Rates for 3+ nights
Bar Lunch 12 - 2 pm except Mon (b)
Dining Room Lunch/Restaurant Lunch 12 - 2 pm except Mon (b)
Bar Supper 6 - 9.30 pm Tue to Sat: 6.30 - 9 pm Sun (b)
Dinner 6 - 9.30 pm Tue to Sat: 6.30 - 9 pm Sun (c)
Closed Mon
Vegetarians welcome
Facilities for disabled visitors
No smoking area in restaurant

Toasted brioche filled with prawns in a cream sauce with crispy bacon, glazed with cheese. Duet of Tweed salmon and monkfish with a basil herb crust on a red pepper coulis. Suprême of Guinea fowl filled with apricots and sage and served with fettuccine on a light Dubonnet sauce.

STB Commended 3 Crowns
Credit cards: 1, 3
Proprietors: Alan & Julie Reid

Tain

Morangie House Hotel
Morangie Road, Tain
Ross-shire IV19 1PY
Tel: 01862 892281
Fax: 01862 892872

Just off A9 Inverness-Wick, on the outskirts of Tain.

An award-winning town hotel by the shores of the Dornoch Firth.

- Splendid Victorian mansion of character which has been sympathetically and tastefully modernised.
- Traditional cooking with great emphasis on beautifully cooked and presented fish and seafood.
- "A very popular family-owned and run hotel with first class food and accommodation which succeeds in making guests feel welcome and cared for."

Morangie House Hotel is now a beacon of hospitality in the Northeast. Winner of the 1994 Ross-shire Restaurant of the Year award, host John Wynne is justifiably proud of his standard of food and drink. The dining room offers an extensive à la carte menu where local fish and seafood feature magnificently. There is also a reasonably priced four course table d'hôte dinner menu. Quality in the dining room is matched by the comfort of the bedrooms which are all well equipped and well decorated. The new Garden Restaurant is designed to cater for more casual dining.

Open all year
Rooms: 26 with private facilities
Bed & Breakfast £45 - £50
Dinner B & B £50 - £65
Special Rates available
Bar Lunch 12 - 2.30 pm (a)
Dining Room/Restaurant Lunch 12.30 - 2.30 pm (a)
Bar Supper 5 - 9.45 pm (a)
Dinner 7 - 9.45 pm (c)
Vegetarians welcome
Dogs by arrangement

Mussel and onion stew. Salmon steak poached in white wine served with a lobster and prawn sauce. Slices of prime Scottish fillet steak cooked in a port wine sauce. Local seafood and steaks.

STB Commended 4 Crowns
Credit cards: 1, 2, 3, 5, 6 + SWITCH
Proprietor: John Wynne

Tarbert

The Columba Hotel
East Pier Road, Tarbert
Argyll PA29 6UF
Tel: 01880 820808
Fax: 01880 820808

On East Pier Road, ½ mile to the left around the harbour. Hotel on roadside.

A well-appointed family-run hotel on the harbour at Tarbert.

- A Victorian waterfront hotel refurbished by the present owners as a comfortable and pleasant establishment.
- Scottish modern cooking.
- "Good Scottish produce imaginatively prepared, deservedly popular with locals, yachtsmen and other visitors to Tarbert."

This small hotel overlooks Loch Fyne at the entrance to Tarbert Harbour. It has been a labour of love to Gina and Bob Chicken, who have worked hard at sympathetically refurbishing this Victorian hotel and continue to do so. The decor is in keeping with the building; there is a cosy bar with an open fire, which is popular for its wholesomely different bar food (and its 30 malt whiskies). The restaurant has been elegantly restored; it offers a relaxed atmosphere and a menu which makes imaginative use of the excellent local produce - fish and shellfish from the harbour; game from Inveraray Castle.

Open all year except Christmas Night
Rooms: 10 with private facilities
Bed & Breakfast £29.95 - £35.95
Dinner B & B £36.95 - £47.95
Special Winter Rates available
Bar Lunch 12 - 2 pm (a)
Dining Room/Restaurant Lunch 12.30 - 2 pm Sun only (a)
Bar Supper 6 - 9 pm (b)
Dinner 7 - 9 pm (c)
Vegetarians welcome
No smoking in restaurant

Argyllshire venison pâté. Poached Loch Fyne salmon with cucumber and lemon sauce. Seared Loch Tarbert scallops with a mild mustard sauce and a timbale of saffron rice. Scottish cheeses with oatcakes.

STB Commended 3 Crowns
Credit cards: 1, 3
Proprietors: Gina & Bob Chicken

Tayinloan

The Tayinloan Inn
by Tarbert
Argyll PA29 6XG
Tel: 01583 441233

A83, 19 miles north of Campbeltown.

A traditional West Highland pub in an old coaching inn.

- Family-run village inn.
- Home cooking.
- "Unpretentious, friendly place, popular with family parties."

Formerly a 17th century coaching inn, Tayinloan is on the main (A83) Campbeltown-Tarbet road, close to the Gigha ferry point, and retains many olde worlde features. You can eat either in the cosy bar or the adjacent sun-lounge, and there is a separate dining room available for larger parties. The food is wholesome, straightforward and extremely good value. You choose from a well-balanced menu, supplemented by blackboard specials. Fish from Tarbet features largely; there is always a vegetarian dish available, and a children's menu. Everything is cooked to order. A sound, friendly local inn.

Open all year
Note: Closed Mon Oct to Mar incl
Rooms: 3
Bed & Breakfast £19 - £25
Dinner B & B from £30
Bar Lunch 12 - 2 pm (a)
Bar Supper 5.30 - 8 pm (a)
Dinner 7 - 9 pm (b)
Vegetarians welcome
Dogs by arrangement

Loch Fyne herring pan-fried in oatmeal with Drambuie butter. Sound of Gigha scallops cooked lightly in butter and wine. Kintyre salmon served with a fresh herb sauce. Shank of lamb slow baked with fresh rosemary and mint in a tomato sauce. Liver and bacon served with a port and rosemary gravy. Cara Bheag: ice cream with a honey and whisky sauce topped with fresh cream, shortbread and nuts.

Credit cards: 1, 3
Proprietors: Gerard & Mya Holloran

201	202	203

Tayvallich

Tayvallich Inn
Tayvallich
Argyll PA31 8PR
Tel: 01546 870282

On B8025 (via B841 [Crinan] off B816 at Cairnbaan).

> An informal bistro-style restaurant with an enviable reputation.

- Both a popular local hostelry and a destination for the discerning.
- Outstanding farmhouse/home cooking.
- "A place to return to again and again."

John and Pat Grafton's inn deserves its popularity. Beautifully situated with a spectacular outlook onto Tayvallich Bay, its many regular customers are drawn to its friendly atmosphere and excellent cooking. The reasonably-priced menus concentrate on the abundance of local seafood - scallops, prawns, mussels, crab and oysters - but does equally well for carnivores and vegetarians. The cooking is simple, straightforward and unpretentious. Service is cheerful and relaxed.

Open all year except Christmas Day + New Year's Day
Note: closed Mon Nov to Mar
Bar Lunch 12 - 2 pm (a)
Bar Supper 6 - 8.30 pm (a)
Dinner 7 - 9 pm (d)
Vegetarians welcome
No smoking area in bar

Pan-fried Sound of Jura scallops. Baked goats cheese and roasted peppers. Loch Sween mussels marinière.

Credit cards: 1, 3 + SWITCH
Proprietors: John & Pat Grafton

Thornhill Dumfries

Trigony House Hotel
Thornhill, Dumfries
DG3 5EZ
Tel: 01848 331211

Situated off A76, 13 miles north of Dumfries. 1 mile south of Thornhill on the Dumfries-Ayr trunk road.

> An Edwardian country house standing in its own gardens.

- An attractive converted shooting lodge
- Country house cooking.
- "Charming, friendly proprietors."

Trigony is a small country house hotel built of pink sandstone, standing amidst its own four acres of mature trees and lawns. It was once the home of the oldest woman in Scotland, Miss Frances Shakerley, who lived to be 107, and became an hotel 16 years ago. Its owners, Robin and Thelma Pollock take justifiable pride in their hotel and provide homely comfort and good food made from local produce. Public and private rooms are bright and airy, prettily decorated and with charming views over the surrounding country.

Open all year except Christmas Day
Rooms : 9 with private facilities
Bed & Breakfast £31 - £40
Dinner B & B £47.50 - £61
Bar Lunch 12.30 - 2 pm (b)
Bar Supper 6.30 - 9 pm (b)
Dinner 7 - 9 pm (c-d)
Vegetarians welcome
Children over eight years welcome
No smoking in dining room
No dogs

Escalopes of local venison with a prune and cinnamon sauce. Fillet of beef and pears with a garlic and wholegrain mustard sauce. Salmon fillet poached in white wine herbs with a lime and ginger dressing.

STB Highly Commended 3 Crowns
Credit cards: 1, 3
Proprietors: Robin & Thelma Pollock

Thornhill by Stirling

Lion & Unicorn
Main Street, Thornhill
by Stirling FK8 3PJ
Tel: 01786 850204
Fax: 01786 850306

On A873, 9 miles west of Stirling, between Blair Drummond Safari Park and Aberfoyle.

> A popular old coaching inn.

- Informal restaurant and bar.
- Traditional Scottish cooking.
- "An old inn with great charm and character and unusually good pub food."

The Lion and Unicorn was built in 1635 as a coaching inn - with low ceilings, stone walls and open log fires. It is family-run and friendly: a popular local pub. A good range of reasonably priced dishes featuring fresh produce is offered on a blackboard. Vegetarian and children's options are also available. The lay out of the pub allows for there to be both smoking and non-smoking areas in the restaurant. Chef/owner Walter MacAulay is experienced and forthright, and his wife Ariane is Dutch and also speaks German. Walter speaks reasonable French.

Open all year
Rooms: 4
Bed & Breakfast £18.70 - £25
Bar Meals 12 - 10 pm (b)
Dining Room/Restaurant Meals 12 - 10 pm (c)
Vegetarians welcome
No smoking in restaurant

Lentil and applemint soup. Sautéed breast of wood pigeon with claret sauce. Langoustine with green peppercorn sauce. Perthshire venison in claret and cranberry sauce. Poached halibut with rhubarb and rum sauce. Apple and toffee crumble. White peach cheesecake. Selection of cheeses.

Credit cards: 1, 2, 3, 5, 6
Proprietor: Walter & Ariane MacAulay

Tillicoultry

Harviestoun Country Inn
Dollar Road, Tillicoultry
Clackmannanshire FK13 6PQ
Tel: 01259 752522
Fax: 01259 752523

Just off A91 on eastern edge of Tillicoultry.

A cheerful hotel with bistro and restaurant and a small number of comfortable rooms

---

- A Listed farmhouse which has been tastefully converted.
- Menus which cater for all tastes.
- "Modestly priced menus offering a surprising range of dishes, from dim sum to mixed grills, imaginatively presented."

Transformations and restorations do not always succeed but this one comes off well. The original farm buildings form three sides of a courtyard, and additions have been fronted with similar sandstone. Behind the inviting frontage lies a pleasant inn offering an excellent standard of en suite accommodation and a choice of dining styles. On the ground floor is the recently refurbished bar-brasserie which has a lively and informal atmosphere, and for formal dining there is an elegant à la carte restaurant. The food is sound and well-presented, with an unusually varied menu.

Open all year except Christmas Day + 1, 2 Jan
Rooms 10 with private facilities
Room Rate £34.95 - £59.95
Bar Lunch 12 - 2.30 pm (b)
Brasserie Lunch 12 - 2.30 pm except Sun (c)
Brasserie Supper 6 - 9.30 pm except Sun (b)
Dinner 7 - 9.30 pm except Sun (d)
Vegetarians welcome
Facilities for disabled visitors
No smoking area in restaurant

West coast mussel and prawn croustade. Roast rack of lamb served with two contrasting sauces. Fillet of turbot on a bed of crisp shredded potato with course grain mustard. Glazed seasonal fruits served with a refreshing sorbet. Cloutie dumpling.

STB Approved 3 Crowns
Credit cards: 1, 2, 3
Proprietor: David Lapsley

Tongue

The Ben Loyal Hotel
Main Street, Tongue
Sutherland IV27 4XE
Tel: 01847 611216
Fax: 01847 611212

At junction of A838 and A836, midway between John o' Groats and Cape Wrath.

Comfortable Highland hotel.

- Well-appointed with panoramic views.
- Modern Scottish cooking.
- "Extremely friendly and welcoming place."

Standing in a splendid location overlooking the Kyle of Tongue, the peaks of 'The Queen of Scottish Mountains' and ruined Varrich Castle, this hotel seems to have been designed with the sole intention of enabling guests to enjoy these quite stunning panoramas from the comfortably furnished lounge to the beautifully appointed bedrooms, nine of which are en suite, with their pine furniture, pretty fabrics and four poster bed. But perhaps the best views of all can be had from the dining room. However you will find your loyalties torn between relishing the view and savouring the food. Only fresh local produce - much of it home-grown - is used in the preparation of traditional dishes presented in a modern way.

Open 24 Feb to 31 Dec except Christmas + Boxing Days
Rooms: 12, 9 with private facilities
Bed & Breakfast £25 - £38
Dinner B & B £42 - £55
Special Rates for 3+/7+ nights
Bar Lunch 12 - 2 pm Mon to Sat: 12.30 - 2 pm Sun (a)
Dining Room/Restaurant Lunch - by prior arrangement only (b)
Bar Supper 6 - 8.30 pm (8 pm winter) Mon to Sat : 6.30 - 8.30 pm Sun (8 pm winter) (a)
Dinner 7 - 8 pm (c)
Facilities for disabled visitors

Warm salad of wood pigeon with a cranberry vinaigrette. Poached suprême of Eriboll salmon on an avocado sauce. Breast of honey roasted duck with an orange and port wine gravy. Courgette and sweet potato bake.

STB Highly Commended 3 Crowns
Credit cards: 1, 3, 6
Proprietors: Mel & Pauline Cook

Torridon

Loch Torridon Hotel
Torridon, by Achnasheen
Ross-shire IV22 2EY
Tel: 01445 791242
Fax: 01445 791296

The only hotel on the A896 (do not turn off to Torridon village).

A Victorian country house set on the shores of Loch Torridon; AA 'Best New Hotel in Scotland 1993'. Good Hotel César Award 'Best Newcomer 1995'.

- A 19th century hunting lodge, converted into an opulent hotel.
- Creative country house cooking.
- "The food is excellent; the menus well-planned".

This sizeable baronial shooting lodge was built by the first Earl of Lovelace in 1887 and is set in lovely parkland which stretches down to the shores of the loch. The Victorian character and many original features of the hotel have been restored or kept intact, with ornate ceilings and panelled rooms, many of which enjoy stupendous views of classic Highland scenery. The food has earned the hotel two AA Rosettes and it is typical of the first rank of Scottish country house hotels in using fresh fish, meats and game from the surrounding area. The short menus offer a well-balanced selection; the cooking is classic; the service is professional.

Open all year but restricted service 3 Jan to 28 Feb
Rooms: 20 with private facilities
Bed & Breakfast £40 - £110
Dinner B & B £70 - £150
Special Rates for 3+ nights
Bar Lunch 12 - 2 pm (b)
Note: Bar Meals served in Ben Damph Lodge, 100 yards from main hotel
Dinner 7.15 - 8.30 pm (f)
Facilities for disabled visitors
No smoking in restaurant

Gressingham duck confit glazed with a chicken sabayon. Grilled local lemon sole and salmon lattice on a warm balsamic vinegar dressing. Warm banana and dried fruit bread with Amaretto ice ream.

STB Highly Commended 4 Crowns
Credit cards: 1, 2, 3 + SWITCH, DELTA
Proprietors: David & Geraldine Gregory

Troon

Highgrove House
Old Loans Road
Troon KA10 7HL
Tel: 01292 312511
Fax: 01292 318228

Off A759 near Loans.

High on a hill, with splendid views and good cooking.

■ Country house hotel.
■ Classic cooking.
■ "There are three key words in Bill Costley's vocabulary: quality, freshness and value for money."

The name of this hotel well describes its situation, on the top of a hill outside Troon and commanding panoramic views across the Ayrshire countryside and over the Firth of Clyde to Arran and the Mull of Kintyre. The view of the sunset from the dining room can be spectacular. Bill Costley and his award-winning brigade present well-priced and balanced menus in both the restaurant and the bar. The food is very fresh, and the cooking is 'haute cuisine'. It is no wonder that Highgrove has such a strong local reputation.

Open all year
Rooms: 9 with private facilities
Bed & Breakfast £45 - £65
Dinner B & B £55 - £80
Bar Lunch 12 - 2 pm (b)
Dining Room/Restaurant Lunch 12 - 2 pm (b)
Bar Supper 6.30 - 9 pm (b)
Dinner 7 - 9 pm (d)
Vegetarians welcome

Warm salad of langoustines and red snapper with dill butter dressing. Steamed turbot with fresh asparagus, crab and orange mousseline.

Credit cards: 1, 2, 3 + SWITCH
Proprietors: William & Catherine Costley

Lochgreen House
Monktonhill Road, Southwood
Troon KA10 7EN
Tel: 01292 313343
Fax: 01292 318661

A79 from Ayr, or A77 from Glasgow to roundabout near Prestwick Airport, take road for Troon (B749). Lochgreen is ½ mile on left.

An Edwardian country house close to Troon with a first rate restaurant.

■ Country house hotel.
■ Modern Scottish cooking.
■ "The meal was light, interesting and exciting: great combinations of flavours imaginatively brought together."

The house was built by a Glasgow lawyer in 1905 as a country retreat and has many of its original Edwardian features and a charming, relaxed atmosphere. It stands in 16 acres of gardens (with a private tennis court); all bedrooms are individually furnished and decorated; the public rooms are sumptuous, and there are four dining rooms (conservatory, library, loggia and main dining rooms - the latter is formal and very elegant). Lochgreen is owned by one of Scotland's leading chefs, Bill Costley, and his wife Catherine. His cooking is professional and accomplished. The lengthy table d'hôte and à la carte menus (and a separate vegetarian menu) are ingenious and wide-ranging. A gastronomic treat.

Open all year
Rooms: 7 with private facilities
Bed & Breakfast £55 - £95
Dinner B & B £70 - £120
Special Rates available
Bar Lunch 12 - 2 pm (b)
Dining Room/Restaurant Lunch 12 - 2 pm (c)
Dinner 7 - 9 pm (e) 5 course menu
Vegetarians welcome
Facilities for disabled visitors
No smoking in restaurant
No dogs

Warm quail and wild mushroom salad with toasted pine kernels and served with a crispy bacon and garlic dressing. Marinated rack of lamb with a tomato, spinach and Mozzarella tart with a roasted garlic and rosemary sauce. Salmon and sole soufflé with fresh langoustine and crayfish and brandy sauce.

STB Deluxe 5 Crowns
Credit cards: 1, 2, 3 + SWITCH
Proprietors: William & Catherine Costley

Marine Highland Hotel
Troon, Ayrshire KA10 6HE
Tel: 01292 314444
Fax: 01292 316922

South end of Troon overlooking golf course and sea.

Highly commended hotel overlooking Royal Troon golf course.

■ 4 Star resort hotel.
■ Traditional Scottish cooking.
■ "A classic resort hotel in a splendid location with first class standards of food and accommodation."

The Marine Highland overlooks the 18th fairway of the Royal Troon Golf Course with beautiful views over the Firth of Clyde towards the Isle of Arran. With 20 courses situated nearby, golf is the major attraction of the area but there is plenty for non-golfers to do and you don't even have to leave the hotel to enjoy the superb leisure facilities of the Marine Leisure and Sports Club. The hotel is luxurious and public rooms are tasteful and relaxing. The food is highly commended with a good choice of interesting and imaginative dishes available in the main restaurant, The Fairways. There is also a brasserie/bar, Crosbies, which is open all day.

Open all year
Rooms: 72 with private facilities
Bed & Breakfast £76 - £96
Dinner B & B £55 - £69 (min 2 nights stay)
Special Rates & Breaks available throughout year
Crosbies Brasserie open all day for meals and snacks
Bar Lunch 12 - 2.30 pm Mon to Sat:
12 - 5.30 pm Sun (a)
Dining Room/Restaurant Lunch 12.30 - 2 pm (c)
Afternoon Tea (Arran Lounge) 3 - 5 pm
Bar Supper 5.30 - 10 pm (b)
Dinner 7 - 10 pm (d) 4 course menu
Vegetarians welcome

Fairways: crayfish soup laced with cream and brandy. Pan-fried scallops on a bed of shredded snow peas and smoked bacon. Roasted loin of marinaded lamb with a port wine and redcurrant essence. Escalope of Highland venison in a juniper berry sauce. Crosbies Brasserie: grilled delice of Scotch salmon. Fresh mussels marinière.

STB Highly Commended 5 Crowns
Credit cards: 1, 2, 3, 5 + SWITCH

Turnberry

Piersland House Hotel

Craigend Road, Troon
Ayrshire KA10 6HD
Tel: 01292 314747
Fax: 01292 315613

South corner of Troon.

A fine country house hotel in the town of Troon.

- A beautifully restored Tudor-style mansion in the heart of Ayrshire golfing country.
- International cuisine.
- "A haven from the pressures of modern life."

Piersland was built for Sir Alexander Walker, grandson of the Johnnie Walker who founded the whisky firm of the same name. Tudor outside, inside the house has some fine Jacobean-style features. It stands in four acres of immaculate grounds that include a Japanese water garden. With ten championship courses within a 30 minute drive, this is a golfers' paradise. In the dining room, both table d'hôte and à la carte dishes justify the hotel's reputation for fine and varied cuisine. The Garden Room caters for private functions.

Open all year
Rooms: 23 with private facilities
Bed & Breakfast £48.75 - £59.50
Dinner B & B £66.25 - £77
Room Rate £59.50 - £120
Special Rates for 2+ nights Oct to Apr
Bar Lunch 12 - 2.30 pm (a)
Dining Room/Restaurant Lunch 12 - 2.30 pm (b)
Bar Supper 6 - 10 pm (a)
Dinner 7 - 9.30 pm (c)
Vegetarians welcome

Beef and venison terrine with a redcurrant preserve. Sirloin steak topped with duxelle and asparagus on a Drambuie sauce. Poached fillet of salmon in a lemon and herb cream sauce. Roast saddle of lamb on a garlic croûton set on a sherry and pimento sauce.

STB Highly Commended 4 Crowns
Credit cards: 1, 2, 3, 5, 6 + SWITCH, DELTA
Proprietor: J A Brown

Malin Court Hotel

Turnberry
Ayrshire KA26 9PB
Tel: 01655 331457
Fax: 01655 331072

On A719 Ayr-Girvan, south of Maidens.

A country hotel with spectacular views.

- Popular, purpose-built country hotel.
- Modern Scottish cooking.
- "Malin Court provides a relaxing atmosphere enhanced by the opportunity to enjoy the best of modern Scottish food."

Overlooking the famous Turnberry Open Championship Golf Course and close to Culzean Castle, Malin Court enjoys an attractive situation on the Ayrshire coast with a marvellous outlook over to the Isle of Arran. Accommodation is comfortable and well-furnished with every facility you could wish for. The Carrick Restaurant serves good quality food, carefully prepared and well-presented. Menus are imaginative and complemented by a short, well-priced wine list. The pleasure of dining is enhanced by spectacular sunset views of Arran.

Open all year
Rooms: 17 with private facilities
Bed & Breakfast £71 - £101
Dinner B & B £83 - £126
Special Rates for 7 nights
Dining Room/Restaurant Lunch 12.30 - 2 pm (b)
Supper/High Tea 5.30 - 6.45 pm (a)
Dinner 7.30 - 9 pm (c)
Vegetarians welcome.

Roulade of pork and venison wrapped in bacon, served on a tarragon and apple jus. Lamb cutlets coated in an Arran mustard and garlic crust on a pool of tomato coulis. Baked salmon fillets with a bed of cockles and samphire grass tossed in fresh chillies.

STB Highly Commended 4 Crowns
Credit cards: 1, 2, 3, 5 + SWITCH

Turnberry Hotel, Golf Courses & Spa

Turnberry
Ayrshire KA26 9LT
Tel: 01655 331000
Fax: 01655 331706

A77 - 17 miles south of Ayr.

One of Scotland's most exclusive hotels.

- Resort hotel of international standing.
- Grand hotel cooking; also spa and grill-room styles.
- "An outstanding hotel, beautifully run, friendly, superbly appointed and with magnificent facilities."

Turnberry was purpose-built as a golfing resort hotel at the turn of the century, and retains many opulent Edwardian features. It enjoys an elevated situation overlooking the championship golf courses, with gorgeous views across the Firth of Clyde to Ailsa Craig and Arran. Service is gracious and supremely professional, yet friendly. The hotel's main restaurant offers the best classical cooking - Chef Stewart Cameron is a member of the Academie Culinaire de France - and uses fresh, local ingredients. During the week, lunch is served in the Bay at Turnberry Restaurant, where a blissful menu for the health-conscious is presented. The Turnberry Clubhouse serves roasts, grills, fries and sandwiches. Accolades include RAC 5 Star Hotel of the Year 1990, Caterer & Hotelkeeper's Hotel of the Year 1993, RAC Five Star Blue Ribbon Hotel 1994 and Five AA Red Stars. Member of the Scotch Beef Club.

Open all year
Rooms: 132 with private facilities
Bed & Breakfast £90 - £130
Dinner B & B £129.50 - £171.50
Special Rates available
Bar Meals (Clubhouse Restaurant) 11 am -7 pm
Lunch (Bay at Turnberry Restaurant) 12 - 2.30 pm
Lunch (Hotel Restaurant) 1 - 2.30 pm Sun only
Dinner (Hotel Restaurant) 7 - 10 pm
Vegetarians welcome

Grilled Atlantic sea bass served on a leek fondue with a saffron essence. Suprême of turbot poached in champagne, served in a sauce of crayfish, mussels and colloped mushrooms. Fillet of Ayrshire lamb oven-roasted with potatoes, onions and served with a rosemary sauce.

STB Deluxe 5 Crowns
Credit cards: 1, 2, 3, 5, 6 + SWITCH

209

Turriff

210

Tyndrum

211

Ullapool

The Towie Tavern
Auchterless, nr Turriff
Aberdeenshire
AB53 8EP
Tel: 01999 511201

On main A947, 4 miles from Fyvie Castle, 4
miles from Turriff.

An old coaching inn with restaurants.

■ Village inn.
■ Traditional country-style cooking.
■ "Good use of fresh raw ingredients producing
above average meals."

The Towie Tavern is a charming old coaching inn,
built about 1800, standing close to the beautifully
restored early 16th century Towie Barclay Castle. It
has two restaurants - the Barclay (for dinners) and
the Castle (for suppers). Lunches are served in both;
there is a smaller chamber - the Post Room - off the
Barclay for private parties, family gatherings, etc,
and there is also a diner's bar and a lounge bar. The
cooking makes use of the best of Grampian
produce; à la carte menus are offered, and there are
daily 'Towie Treats' of both supper and dinner
dishes.

Open all year except Boxing Day + 1, 2 Jan
Bar Lunch 12 - 2 pm (a)
Dining Room/Restaurant Lunch 12 - 2 pm (b)
Bar Supper 5 - 8.30 pm Mon to Sat:
6 - 9 pm Sun (b)
Dinner 6 - 9 pm Sun to Thu:
6 - 9.30 pm Fri Sat (c)
Vegetarians welcome
Facilities for disabled visitors

Daily selection of fresh and smoked marinated fish
and seafood served with dill mustard sauce. Fillet
steak with pan-fried sauce of onion, bacon, tomato,
red wine and cream.

Credit cards: 1, 3
Proprietors: Douglas & Eileen Pearson

The Clifton Coffee House & Craft Centre
Tyndrum
Perthshire FK20 8RY
Tel: 01838 400271
Fax: 01838 400330

On A85 just east of junction with A82.

Popular self-service restaurant.

■ Craft and souvenir shopping eaterie.
■ Home cooking.
■ "A simple restaurant, and a welcome refuge."

What began as a simple self-service restaurant has
become a tourist attraction in its own right. The
shopping complex which has grown up around it
sells books, crafts, woollens, gifts and food, but the
restaurant is still the focal point. Friendly and
reliable, offering good home baking and cooking
and a wide variety of traditional Scottish meals and
snacks. Very popular with visitors to Glencoe.

Open 4 Mar to 8 Jan except Christmas Day +
Boxing Day, New Year's Day
Hot Meals + Snacks available from 11.30 am -
5 pm (a)
Vegetarians welcome
No smoking area in restaurant
No dogs except guide dogs

Fresh produce used to advantage, to produce a
range of good food at affordable prices.

Credit cards: 1, 2, 3, 5, 6 + SWITCH, DELTA
Proprietors: L P Gosden, D D, L V & I L Wilkie

Morefield Motel & Mariners Restaurant
North Road, Ullapool
Ross-shire IV26 2TR
Tel: 01854 612161
Fax: 01854 612870

After c. 1 mile leaving village on North Road
(A835), turn left immediately over the river
bridge. Look for sign.

An unpretentious, award-winning establishment
on the outskirts of Ullapool.

■ An inexpensive motel and well-regarded pub
and restaurant.
■ Specialists in seafood, but offer a variety of
cooking.
■ "Ullapool's 'original' seafood restaurant serving
food with flair and imagination."

The Morefield, which has been established for
nearly 15 years, is nonetheless an excellent base
from which to enjoy this beautiful part of Scotland.
The Mariners Restaurant deserves its popularity.
Owners David Smyrl and David Marsh serve the best
of freshly-caught seafood, cooked with flair, and
outstanding Scottish meat. The Lounge Bar and
Beer Garden offer pub grub that proves just how
good this kind of cooking can be.

Open all year except 1wk over Christmas
Note: accommodation closed Nov to Mar
Rooms: 11 with private facilities
Bed & Breakfast £20 - £25
Room Rate £40 - £45
Special Rates for early/late season
Bar Lunch 12 - 2 pm (a)
Dining Room/Restaurant Lunch 12 - 2 pm
except Sat
Bar Supper 5.30 - 9.30 pm Mon to Fri:
6 - 9.30 pm Sun
Dinner (Mariners) 6 - 9.30 pm except Sat -
booking advisable
Vegetarians welcome
Facilities for disabled visitors

Local mussels cooked with a garlic and wine cream
sauce. Halibut cooked with a fish stock and finished
with a citrus sauce. Salmon topped with prawns in
a seafood sauce. Scallops cooked with leeks and
shallots in a Pernod flavoured sauce. Lochinver sole
brushed with herb butter and grilled. Sirloin steak
topped with scallops and prawns in a garlic butter
sauce.

STB Commended 3 Crowns
Credit cards: 1, 2, 3, 6 + SWITCH
Proprietors: David Smyrl & David Marsh

Uphall

Houstoun House Hotel & Restaurant
Uphall
West Lothian EH52 6JS
Tel: 01506 853831
Fax: 01506 854220

Just off A89 Edinburgh-Bathgate at Uphall.

> A 17th century tower house, with additions, in
> an ancient garden.

- ■ Country house hotel.
- ■ Modern Scottish, with continental influences.
- ■ "A powerfully atmospheric place with a superb menu."

The core of the house is a substantial, early 16th century tower, built for Sir John Shairp, advocate to Mary Queen of Scots, and lived in by his descendants for 350 years. Its gardens were laid out in the 18th century, and include a 20 foot high yew hedge planted in 1722 and a cedar tree which is even older. Extensions and additions to the house - including the Houstoun Suite for banqueting and conferences, opened 1995 - have been done sympathetically. The restaurant is situated in the former drawing room, library and great hall on the first floor - each of them delightful rooms, with 17th and 18th century panelling and plasterwork, beautifully furnished with antiques and pictures. Vegetables and herbs for the kitchen are grown in the garden, and Houstoun House's talented young chef, Gavin Young, presents a sophisticated and well balanced table d'hôte menu at lunch and dinner. His cooking is first class, and this is complemented by an award-winning wine list.

Open all year
Rooms: 42 with private facilities
Bed & Breakfast £40 - £102
Dinner B & B £55 - £130
Special Weekend Rates available
Bar Lunch 12 - 2.30 pm except Sun (b)
Dining Room/Restaurant Lunch 12.30 - 2 pm except Sat (c)
Dinner 7 - 9.30 pm (e) 4 course menu
Vegetarians welcome
No smoking dining room available

Rabbit and duck terrine garnished with lambs lettuce and soaked in a port wine sauce. Fine slices of plum duck breast coated with a sweet orange glaze. Lemon and lime parfait with home-made shortbread and fudge sauce.

STB Highly Commended 5 Crowns
Credit cards: 1, 2, 3, 5, 6 + SWITCH

Walkerburn

Tweed Valley Hotel & Restaurant
Walkerburn nr Peebles EH43 6AA
Tel: 01896 870636
Fax: 01896 870639

A72 at Walkerburn - 8 miles east of Peebles and 10 miles west of Galashiels. 32 miles south of Edinburgh.

> Hotel set halfway up the valley overlooking the
> River Tweed.

- ■ An Edwardian country house hotel.
- ■ Scottish country Grill.
- ■ "Just what a small country hotel should be: friendly and comfortable, with an excellent dining room."

This pretty villa stands in its own grounds and has glorious views up the Tweed Valley. It was originally built in 1906 by the Borders wool mill owner Henry Ballantyne as a wedding present for his son, and retains its original panelling and ornate ceilings, although there are now significant modern additions such as a solarium, sauna and mini-gym. The hotel has a walled kitchen garden which provides vegetables, fruit and all the fresh herbs for the kitchen, and its owners, Charles and Keith Miller, also smoke their own fish and meat (these are available for sale). A la carte and table d'hôte menus are presented, and an extensive bar menu. Grills and traditional Scottish dishes abound.

Open all year except Christmas + Boxing Days
Rooms: 15 with private facilities
Bed & Breakfast £25 - £47
Dinner B & B £37 - £66
Snacks + Light Meals available all day
Bar Lunch 12 - 2 pm (a)
Dining Room/Restaurant Lunch 12 - 2 pm (a)
Bar Supper 6.30 - 9.30 pm (a)
Dinner 7 - 9.30 pm (c)
Vegetarians welcome
No smoking in restaurant

Home-made soups. Haggis with whisky sauce. Fillet steaks. Pan-fried loin of pork with stuffed apple and sage gravy. Collops of venison with a rich red wine sauce. Scottish cheeses.

STB Commended 4 Crowns
Credit cards: 1, 2, 3 + SWITCH
Proprietors: Charles & Keith Miller

Whitebridge

Knockie Lodge
Whitebridge
Inverness-shire IV1 2UP
Tel: 01456 486276
Fax: 01456 486389

On B862, 8 miles north of Fort Augustus. 26 miles south of Inverness.

> A charming country house hotel in the
> Highlands: gracious living and good food.

- ■ An isolated 19th century shooting lodge, sympathetically converted into an exclusive hotel.
- ■ Modern Scottish cooking with a most imaginative use of fresh produce.
- ■ "The best run country house I have ever encountered."

Once a sporting retreat for the Frasers of Lovat, Knockie Lodge is splendidly sited high above Loch Nan Lann, with Loch Ness just over the hill at its back. The surrounding Highland countryside is stunning and traditional rural pursuits like shooting, fly fishing, deer stalking and hill-walking are all available to guests in this very special hotel, along with relaxing pastimes like, photography or painting. The atmosphere is that of a private country house, with game-books and ornaments, watercolours and vases of fresh flowers. Logs and peat burn in open fires. Knockie's owners, Ian and Brenda Milward, take justifiable pride in their home and are attentive and enthusiastic hosts. The composition of the five course set dinner menu is excellent - " a matchless gastronomic experience", in the words of this year's inspector.

Open 1 May to 20 Oct
Rooms: 10 with private facilities
Bed & Breakfast £50 - £75
Special Rates for 7+ nights
Dinner at 8 pm (e) 5 course, set menu
Note: dinner for non-residents by prior arrangement only
Restricted Licence
Vegetarians welcome
No smoking in dining room

Cullen skink. Marinated chicken pieces with avocado and red peppers served with a vermouth sauce. Pan-fried sole fillet with langoustine garnish with a piquante sauce. Raspberry pavlova. Gooseberry ice cream with tuille leaves.

STB Deluxe 3 Crowns
Credit cards: 1, 2, 3, 5
Proprietors: Ian & Brenda Milward

SCOTLAND'S COMMENDED
A selection of distinctive Country & Town House Hotels

Scotland's Commended is an Association of Country and Town Hotels of distinction throughout Scotland, all of which are individually owned and managed. Each must attain high standards of ambience, environment and quality of food and service, set not only by the Association but also by The Scottish Tourist Board's Grading and Classification Scheme. The Hotels listed below have been awarded membership of the Taste of Scotland scheme. For telephone and fax numbers and to find out more about Scotland's Commended Members of the Taste of Scotland scheme refer to the index at rear of guide.

Ardanaiseig Hotel
Kilchrenan by Taynuilt, Argyll PA35 1HE

Ardentinny Hotel
Ardentinny, Loch Long, near Dunoon PA23 8TR

Ardfillayne Hotel
Dunoon PA23 7QJ

Auchen Castle Hotel
Beattock, Moffat DG10 9SH

Auchrannie Country House
Brodick, Isle of Arran KA27 8BZ

Balcary Bay Hotel
Auchencairn, near Castle Douglas DG7 1QZ

Balgonie Country House
Ballater AB35 5RQ

Ben Loyal Hotel
Tongue, by Lairg, Sutherland IV27 4XE

Burts Hotel, Roxburghshire
Melrose, TD6 9PN

Channings
South Learmonth Gdns, Edinburgh EH4 1EZ

Chapeltoun House Hotel
Stewarton (off Irvine Rd B769), Ayrshire KA3 3ED

Corriegour Lodge Hotel
Loch Lochy, by Spean Bridge PH34 4EB

Corsemalzie House Hotel
Port William, Newton Stewart DG8 9RL

Coul House Hotel
Contin by Strathpeffer IV14 9EY

Craigellachie Hotel
Craigellachie, Speyside AB38 9SR

Crinan Hotel
Crinan by Lochgilphead PA31 8SR

Darroch Learg Hotel
Ballater AB35 5UX

Dornoch Castle Hotel
Dornoch IV25 3SD

Dunain Park Hotel
Inverness IV3 6JN

Dundonnell Hotel
Dundonnel, by Garve IV23 2QR

Enmore Hotel
Dunoon PA23 8HH

Fernhill Hotel
Heugh Road, Portpatrick DG9 8TD

Garth Hotel
Grantown-on-Spey PH26 3HN

Glendruidh House
Inverness, IV1 2AA

The Golf View Hotel
Seabank Road, Nairn IV12 4HD

Johnstounburn House
Humbie, near Edinburgh EH36 5PL

Killiecrankie Hotel
Pass of Killiecrankie, by Pitlochry PH16 5LG

Knockendarroch House
Pitlochry PH16 5HT

The Knockomie Hotel
Forres IV36 OSG

Loch Melfort Hotel
Arduaine, by Oban PA34 4XG

Loch Torridon Hotel
Torridon, Achnasheen, Wester-Ross IV22 2EY

The Lodge on the Loch
Onich, near Fort William PH33 6RY

Minmore House
Glenlivet, Speyside AB37 9DB

Muckrach Lodge Hotel
Dulnain Bridge, Speyside PH26 3LY

Murraypark Hotel
Crieff PH7 3DJ

Nivingston House
Cleish Hills, near Kinross KY13 7LS

The Old Manor Hotel
Lundin Links, near St Andrews KY8 6AJ

Old Mansion House Hotel
Auchterhouse, by Dundee DD3 0QN

Parklands Hotel
Perth PH2 8EB

Philipburn House Hotel
Selkirk TD7 5LS

Raemoir House Hotel
Raemoir, Banchory, Kincardineshire AB31 4ED

Royal Marine Hotel
Golf Road, Brora, Sutherland KW9 6QS

Rufflets Country House
St Andrews KY16 9TX

Shieldhill Country House
Quothquan, Biggar ML12 6NA

Taychreggan Hotel
Kilchrenan, by Taynuilt, Argyll PA35 1HQ

Tweed Valley Hotel
Walkerburn EH43 6AA

Western Isles Hotel
Tobermory, Isle of Mull, PA75 6PR

RECIPE SECTION

Roast Canon of New Season's Scotch Lamb "En Crepinette"

Topped with a Basil Mousse Set on a Galette Potato and Garnished with a Ragout of
Wild Mushrooms and Baby Vegetables

1995 Taste of Scotland Scotch Lamb Challenge

Gourmet Section: First Runner-Up

Ian Bennett, Head Chef, The Kirroughtree Hotel,

Newton Stewart

Ingredients

2 racks of Scotch lamb
(approx. 4-5 lb) (approx. 2KG)

Basil Mousse

8 oz (225g) chicken breast

1 oz (25g) fresh basil

2 oz (50g) fresh spinach

½ pint (250ml) double cream

1 egg white

crepinette (pig's caul) *(to wrap prepared lamb)*

Pommes Galette

6 oz (175g) potatoes

1 fl oz (25ml) olive oil

1 oz (25g) butter

Baby Vegetables

2 bunches baby turnips

2 bunches baby carrots

1 bunch baby leeks

Wild Mushroom Ragout

4 oz (100g) mixed wild mushrooms

Sauce

¼ pint (150ml) red wine

¼ pint (150ml) white wine

1 medium carrot

1 medium onion

1 stick celery

4 cloves garlic

bouquet garni (thyme, bay-leaf, parsley)

2 oz (50g) plum tomatoes

2 pints (1.2L) lamb stock

1 pint (600ml) fond blanc (vegetable/chicken based clear stock)

2 oz (50g) butter

(serves 4)

Method

1   Bone out the Scotch lamb until left with the fillet, trim out all fat and sinew.

2   Blanche spinach, refresh and squeeze out all water.

3   In a blender, mince the chicken breast, basil and spinach until smooth. Add egg white and mix for 1 minute. Add double cream slowly, take care not to overmix. Season to taste.

4   Season lamb fillet, spread generously with basil mousse and wrap in crepinette. Rest in refrigerator for 30 minutes.

5   Meanwhile, grate the potato, season and make four small galette potatoes.

6   Blanche all baby vegetables and refresh.

7   Clean and saute wild mushrooms and season.

Sauce

8   Chop up lamb bones and roast them. Sweat off mirepoix until soft. Add lamb bones, deglace with red and white wine. Add bouquet garni, stock and plum tomatoes, reduce by half and pass through a fine chinois and skim.

9   Cook in a moderate oven for 10-12 minutes at GM5\190ºC\375ºF.

Leave to rest for 5 minutes.

Oak Smoked Loin of Scotch Lamb

With Charred Vegetables, Heather Honey and
Arran Mustard Jus

1995 Taste of Scotland Scotch Lamb Challenge

Gourmet Section: Second Runner-Up

Rachel MacTavish, Sous Chef,

Glasgow Hilton International, Glasgow

Ingredients

2 best end of Scotch Lamb
(approx. 7 lb) (3½ KG)
uuntrimmed (approx). 7 oz
(200g) trimmed loin per serving

4 oz (100g) oak shavings.

¼ pint (150ml) olive oil

2 medium yellow peppers

2 medium red peppers

2 small courgettes

1 bunch spring onions

1 small aubergine

35 fl oz (1L) lamb jus

2 teaspoons Arran mustard

1 teaspoon heather honey

2 oz (50g) unsalted butter

small bunch of basil

small bunch of flat hat parsley

small bunch of marjoram

salt and pepper

(Serves 4)

Method

1   Trim all the bones, fat and sinew from best end of lamb leaving
     four clean loins. Coat loins in seasoned oil and then seal in hot
     pan. Remove and set aside.

2   Heat oak shavings over low heat until they start to smoke.
     DO NOT SET ON FIRE. Place cooling rack over the shavings and
     place lamb on top. Put in cold oven for 10 minutes.

3   Prepare vegetables, roast, skin and de-seed peppers. Cut into
     quarters. Top and tail courgettes, slice thin lengthways. Cut
     aubergines into rounds, 1 cm thick.

4   Peel asparagus, cut into 4 cm pieces. Trim all roots and most of
     the green leaves from the spring onions. Heat char-grill and roast
     vegetables until soft and charred. Set aside.

5   Place lamb on oiled dish then roast in a hot oven for 10-15 minutes
     at GM3\170ºC\325ºF. Place charred vegetables in lightly oiled dish
     and heat for 5 minutes alongside lamb. Remove from oven. Leave
     lamb to rest for 5 minutes. Meanwhile heat lamb jus in a small
     saucepan. Add the mustard and honey. When sauce is about to
     simmer, whisk in cold butter.

To Serve

6   Arrange vegetables in centre of plate, slice lamb and place around
     vegetables. Pour sauce round edge of lamb. Garnish with sprigs
     of fresh herbs.

Medallions of Scotch Lamb

with Pesto, Garlic Champ, Speck and Puy Lentil Jus

1995 Taste of Scotland Scotch Lamb Challenge

Gourmet Section: Third Runner-Up

John Rutter, Sous Chef, Atrium,

Edinburgh

Ingredients

2 boned racks of Scotch lamb cut
into 12 medallions
 (2-3 oz each 60-70g)

12 oz (350g) fresh spinach

2 oz (50g) packet basil

2 oz (50g) pine nuts

2 oz (50g) reggiano parmesan

2 cloves garlic

¼ pint (150ml) olive oil

3 baking potatoes

2 oz (50g) butter

2 fl oz (50ml) milk

1 fl oz (25ml) garlic olive oil

½ bunch spring onions

1 oz (25g) parsley

4 thin slices of speck (cured pork
leg, then smoked)

2 shallots

2 carrots

2 celery sticks

¼ bottle red wine

1 pint (600ml) stock

pinch of dry mushrooms

dash of balsamic vinegar

salt and pepper

12 oz (350g) lentil du puy

(Serves 4)

Method

1   Bone racks. Cut into 12 medallions. Marinade for 5 days in oil.

2   Trim meat off bones for sauce, reserve bone for stock. Blend
finely all pesto ingredients to a thick pesto.
(Basil, pine nuts, parmesan, garlic and olive oil).

3   Cook lentils until al dente.

4   For sauce, sweat carrots, celery, shallots and meat trimmings until
brown. Deglace with red wine, reduce and add stock. Reduce
gently for 30 minutes and add dry mushrooms.

5   Pass through fine chinois, add balsamic vinegar and salt and
pepper.

6   Cut spring onion into fine slices. Cut potatoes into chunks and
boil until soft. Drain potatoes, blend with butter, milk and add
salt and pepper. Blend to a good puree.

7   Trim speck. Pan fry medallions and rest for a few minutes.

8   For service, add spring onion and garlic for mash potato, cook for
a few minutes, place in centre of plate. Add lentils to jus, heat and
add three large clumps around champ. Quenelle pesto onto lamb
grill, place on lentil. Put speck over champ to finish.

Oven Baked Best End of Prime Scotch Lamb

Encrusted with Scottish Whisky Mustard, Fresh Garden Herbs and Walnuts,
Served with a Timbale of Ratatouille and a Rich Madeira and Rosemary Jus

1995 Taste of Scotland Scotch Lamb Challenge

Classic Section: First Runner-Up

Bruce McLean, Head Chef, North West Castle Hotel,

Stranraer

Ingredients

3½ lb (1KG 575g) best end of Scotch lamb

4-6 tablespoons Scottish whisky mustard

1 oz (25g) selection of fresh garden herbs (mint, rosemary, thyme, parsley)

(225g) 8oz walnuts

2 oz (50g) dried breadcrumbs

3/4 pint (450ml) olive oil

Sauce (jus)

lamb stock (made from trimmings)

2 oz (50g) unsalted butter

1 onion

2 oz (50g) caster sugar

1 tablespoon balsamic vinegar

1 carrot

¼ celeriac

fresh thyme and rosemary

1 clove garlic

½ pint (300ml) Madeira

Ratatouille

2 courgettes

1 large onion

1 aubergine

1 red pepper

1 green pepper

1 clove garlic

2 tablespoons tomato puree

¼ pint (150ml) tomato juice

Garnish

2 bunches baby carrots (16)

16 button mushrooms

(Serves 4)

Method

1   Bone best end of lamb *(leave rib bones attached to meat)*. Trim and scrape meat in between bones. Remove all the fat and sinew from back of meat. Season meat and leave out at room temperature for 30 minutes.

Crust

2   Sieve dried breadcrumbs. Blend fresh herbs *(mint, rosemary, thyme and parsley)*. Toast walnuts and blend. Add herbs and walnuts to breadcrumbs. Season and add a little olive oil.

Sauce *(jus)*

3   Dice onion, carrot, celeriac and garlic. Sweat in butter. Add finely chopped thyme and rosemary. Add caster sugar and balsamic vinegar. Add lamb stock and reduce by half. Finish by adding Madeira and seasoning.

Ratatouille

4   Finely dice courgettes, onion, aubergine and pepper. Crush garlic. Sweat all off in olive oil. Add tomato puree then tomato juice. Season.

Garnish

5   Peel and trim baby carrots and peel button onions. Blanche in seasoned water. Refresh and serve

Roast Loin of Scotch Lamb

with a Confit of Barley, Centred by a Filo Carrot and Coriander Parcel, crowned with Mint Scented Beetroot Ravioli on a Light Beaujolais Essence

1995 Taste of Scotland Scotch Lamb Challenge

Classic Section: Second Runner-Up

David Craig, Head Chef, Chatters,

Dunoon

Ingredients

4½ lb (2KG 25g) loin of Scotch lamb

6 oz (175g) barley

6 oz (175g) beetroot

4 shallots

4 oz chicken fillet

2 eggs

1 teaspoon ground coriander

4 oz (100g) carrots

2 sheets filo pastry

8 oz (225g) pasta dough

2 large carrots

2 courgettes

1 swede turnip

½ teaspoon arrowroot

½ pint (300ml) red wine *(Beaujolais)*

½ pint (300ml) stock

8 oz (225g) mirepoix vegetables *(carrot, celery, onion)*

2 fl oz (50ml) double cream

seasoning and herb sprigs *(rosemary, thyme and ginger mint)*

(Serves 4)

Method

1   Bone out the loin of lamb *(or ask your butcher to do so)*, removing all sinew and skin. Place to one side.

2   Place pre-soaked barley in a thick bottomed pan, cover with chicken stock, bring to the boil and simmer until all liquid is absorbed. Add chopped shallots and top up with stock again. Repeat process until barley is soft.

3   Cut and shape 4 pieces of beetroot ½ inch thick, and about the size of a 50p coin. Poach gently in a pan of slightly salted water till tender. Drain, pat dry and set aside.

4   Blend chicken flesh with egg white in processor. Place grated carrot into a bowl, season with ground coriander, add chicken meat and fold together with a little cream and season.

5   Line four lightly oiled ramekins with filo pastry and spoon in the mixture. Fold over the pastry edges. Half bake them in a moderate oven for 5 minutes at GM5\190ºC\375ºF. Turn onto a tray to finish off and brown pastry.

6   Roll out the pasta very thin, to make two 4 inch squares. Place one piece of beetroot in each quadrant of 1 square, egg wash all round, lay the other square on top and seal all round the beetroot. Cut in 4, blanche in boiling salted water for about 15-20 seconds, refresh in cold water, drain, place on a tray and brush with oil.

Method (continued)

7   Seal lamb in hot oil and cook for 8 minutes at GM8/225°C/440°F.

8   Turn carrots, courgettes and turnip into barrel shapes and cook until tender.

9   Take lamb out of the oven and deglace pan with lamb stock, mirepoix vegetables and herbs. Reduce to half, then add red wine and reduce further to desired consistency. Pass through fine sieve, thicken with a little arrowroot.

10   Reheat ravioli by placing back into boiling water for a few minutes.

Serving

11   On 4 hot plates, spoon barley mixture to one side in a crescent shape and lay slices of Scotch lamb on top in an over-lapping fashion. Place filo parcel in centre of plate, crown with ravioli, pouring the sauce around this. Garnish with turned vegetables and a herb sprig.

Pasta Dough

Ingredients

10 oz (275g) strong white flour or plain flour
2 eggs (1 separated)
1 tablespoon olive oil
1 tablespoon dried mint
2 tablespoons finely chopped fresh mint
pinch of salt

Method

Place sifted flour and salt into blender, switch on and pour in olive oil. Stop machine, add chopped mint and start it again. Add 1 egg and 1 egg yolk. Stop machine and test for consistency. It should be crumbs; take out a teaspoon of the mix, roll it into a ball and press it between thumb and forefinger. If it is too dry, it will crack at the edge. If this is so, start machine again and add the remaining egg white. Tip out, knead into a ball and refrigerate for 20 minutes.

Black Isle Scotch Lamb

Loin of Scotch Lamb Encased in Wild Rice and Woodland Mushroom Farce Nesting on a Sweetcorn Pancake and Served with a Light Garlic and Rosemary Sauce

1995 Taste of Scotland Scotch Lamb Challenge

Classic Section: Third Runner-Up

Walter Walker, Head Chef, Bunchrew House Hotel,

Inverness

Ingredients

2 racks of Scotch lamb (2-2½lb each) (900g-1KG 125g each)

4 oz (100g) shiitake mushrooms

4 oz (100g) chanterelle mushrooms

4 oz (100g) oyster mushrooms

3 oz (75g) lambs liver

4 oz (100g) approx. lamb trimmings (meat only)

4 onions

8 oz (225g) spinach (approx.)

caul fat - weight not relevant

salt and pepper

4 oz (100g) wild rice

½ pint (300ml) chicken stock

Pancake

1 oz (25g) flour

1 oz (25g) butter

½ pint (300ml) milk

1 tin sweetcorn

2 egg yolks

2 egg whites (ribbon stage)

salt and pepper

Sauce

6 cloves garlic

1 oz (25g) tomato puree

2 sprigs rosemary

½ bottle white wine

1 pint (600ml) lamb stock

2 oz (50g) unsalted butter

salt and pepper

(serves 4)

Method

1   Trim and bone out lamb. Seal off and cook for 3 minutes in oven GM9\250°C\500°F.

2   Cook off rice in chicken stock and dry out.

3   Chop mushrooms finely. Process liver and trimmings. Chop and sweat off onions, mushrooms, salt and pepper. Let cook for 3 minutes. Blend into liver mix with wild rice. Blanche spinach and dry off.

4   Open out caul fat, cover in spinach, then cover in wild rice farce. Place lamb in centre, wrap up completely and cook in hot oven until ready - approximately 10 minutes at GM9\250°C\500°F.

Pancakes

5   Make roux with flour and butter, add milk and stir briskly. Cook for 1 minute, take off heat and add egg yolks. Fold in whisked egg whites and sweetcorn, salt and pepper. *(Makes pancakes for 4).*

Sauce

6   Place all ingredients in saucepan, except butter. Simmer gently until reduced to the correct consistency, then gently swirl in butter until dissolved in pan.

Assemble

7   Place pancake in middle of plate. Slice lamb into 4. Place two slices on pancake, then mask in sauce.

Celtic Salmon

Wendy Barrie, Food Consultant

Front Cover Illustration

Ingredients

4 x 4 oz (100g) Scottish salmon escalopes

1 tablespoon sunflower oil

4 oz (100g) each of courgettes, celery, baby carrots *(all cut into julienne strips)* and asparagus

small bunch of dill

4 oz (100g) butter

freshly ground salt and mixed peppercorns

4 medium sized potatoes *(prepared into noisette balls with a scoop)*

2 oz (50g) pinhead oatmeal

4 wedges of lemon

(Serves 4)

Method

1 Boil the potatoes in lightly salted water for the required time - according to their size.

2 Cook the vegetables lightly in the minimum amount of water *(approx. 4 tablespoons)*. Use a pan with a well-fitting lid to ensure the fine strips cook evenly in the steam and do not dry out. This takes 2-3 minutes.

3 Meanwhile, heat the oil in a frying pan and sear the Scottish salmon for an equally short length of time.

4 Using a slotted spoon, remove the vegetables from the cooking liquor and keep warm.

5 Whisk the butter into the simmering "stock", swirl in chopped dill and season.

6 Meanwhile, drain the potatoes and return to pan with a knob of butter and the oatmeal. Stir gently to coat.

7 To serve, stack the vegetables onto heated plates and lay escalope on top. Drizzle over dill butter sauce and lastly the oatmeal noisettes.

Cullen Skink

Gillian Dick, Head Chef

Fins Restaurant,

Fairlie

Ingredients

1 oz (25g) unsalted butter

2 medium onions, finely chopped

2 lbs (900g) Fencebay *(undyed)* smoked cod fillet

1 lb (450g) mashed potatoes

1½ pints (900ml) milk

½ pint (300ml) double cream

freshly milled black pepper

chopped fresh parsley

(Serves 8)

Method

1   Sweat the finely chopped onions in the butter over a low heat for 10 minutes, taking care not to brown or this will colour your soup.

2   Skin the fillets then add them whole to the onions *(no need to chop first)*. Continue to sweat over a low heat stirring occasionally. The fillets will break up as you stir and the fish cooks. Allow to continue cooking in own juices on a slow simmer for 15 minutes.

3   In a separate container add the milk to the mashed potatoes and blend with a hand whisk *(or place in a liquidizer)* until smooth.

4   Add this to the cooked fish and continue to cook for a further 5 minutes.

5   Finally stir in the double cream, season with pepper and allow to cool.

6   This can then be re-heated when required served in warm bowls topped with a swirl of cream and sprinkled with chopped parsley.

7   If time allows, chill and leave in the refrigerator for up to 24 hours - the flavours develop thus improving resulting soup.

Lamb Boudin with Pea Sauce

Jens & Anita Steffen

Cuilmore Cottage,

Kinloch Rannoch

Ingredients

1 lb (450g) chicken meat

2 egg whites

8 oz (225g) lamb trimmings, cubed

1 tablespoon chopped mint

1 teaspoon rosemary

1 clove garlic

1 teaspoon pepper

1 tablespoon concentrated lamb stock (in paste form)

8 oz frozen peas

1 onion

1 clove garlic

1 tablespoon lamb stock *(as above)*

8 oz cream

salt and pepper

(Serves 8)

Method

1 Process chicken meat with egg whites and garlic.

2 Add rest of ingredients and process on "pulse" until lamb is incorporated.

3 Scrape into piping bag without nozzle and squeeze into "sausages" onto cling film.

4 Wrap individually and twist ends of film. *(Freeze at this stage if necessary)*.

5 Put into pan of boiling water and simmer for 15 minutes.

6 Meanwhile make sauce by frying onion and garlic. Add peas. Cover with cream and simmer until done. Liquidise with mint and stock. Add more seasoning if required and keep warm.

7 Slice boudin and fan out. Edge with pea sauce and sprinkle plate with chopped mint.

Roasted Scottish Goat's Cheese in a Herb and Sesame Seed Crust

Kevin MacGillivray, Head Chef

Ballathie House Hotel,

Kinclaven, Perthshire

Ingredients

4 X 3 oz (75g) Isle of Gigha goats cheese

4 oz (100g) fresh breadcrumbs and 2 oz (50g) mixed herbs, thyme, rosemary, flat parsley and lemon balm *(mixed together)*

1 oz (25g) sesame seeds

2 eggs and ½ pint (300ml) milk (mixed together)

2 oz (50g) plain flour

(Serves 4)

Method

1   Coat the goats cheese with the flour and egg, then the herb mix with the sesame seeds.

2   Brush with melted butter and place on a tray in a hot oven for 5 minutes until cheese softens.

3   Serve with mixed salad leaves and homemade herb jelly.

Fillet of Cod with Spring Greens and Smoked Fish

David Wilson, Proprietor

The Peat Inn, Nr Cupar

Ingredients

1 lb (450g) cod fillet *(skin on)*

4 oz (100g) smoked fish

8 oz (200g) spring cabbage

salt and pepper

olive oil

coriander

vinaigrette dressing

(Serves 4)

Method

1 Remove the leaves from the cabbage, cut out the central rib, blanche in boiling salted water.

2 Dice the smoked fish in pieces about (24mm) thick.

3 Cut the unskinned cod fillets into 4 by 4oz pieces. Check to ensure no small pin bones have been left, if so remove with tweezers.

4 Put olive oil in pan, when beginning to smoke sprinkle sea salt on skin of cod then place cod fillets skin side down in pan.

5 Cook for 5 minutes depending on thickness of cod *(skin should be crisp and golden brown)* then turn over and cook for just 1 minute on the other side.

6 Cut cabbage into strips and put in pan with a little olive oil, then add diced smoked fish and heat through. Season then add at last minute the coriander leaves.

7 Arrange cabbage and smoked fish in a soup bowl or deep plate. Place cod fillet on top and spoon a little vinaigrette around edge.

Perthshire Wood Pigeon with Foie Gras and Roquet Salad

Jean-Michel Gauffre, Executive Chef

Sheraton Grand Hotel

Edinburgh

Ingredients

4 X ½ lb (250g) wood pigeon breasts

2 oz (50g) fresh foie gras or chicken or duck liver

2 oz (50g) roquet leaves

½ teaspoon truffle oil

½ teaspoon balsamic vinegar

salt and pepper

(Serves 4)

Method

1   Remove the breasts from the carcass of the birds *(keep the bones for future use)*.

2   Wash and dry the roquet leaves.

3   Slice 4 slices of fresh foie gras, chicken or duck liver.

4   In a saute pan, pour the truffle oil and bring to a high heat taking care not to burn it.

5   Very quickly cook the foie gras, chicken or duck liver slices for a few seconds only.

6   Reserve on a hot plate.

7   In the same pan, cook the pigeon breasts, keeping them pink, then remove from pan.

8   Deglaze with the vinegar.

9   To serve, place the roquet leaves on the centre of the plate and arrange the sliced pigeon breast and foie gras, chicken or duck liver.

10   Add the juices from the pan and serve.

Peppered Venison Liver with Scotch Whisky and Cream

Rita Brown, Proprietor

The Hazelton Guest House,

Crail

Ingredients

2 lb (900g) venison liver

3 teaspoons mixed dried
peppercorns roughly crushed
(black, white, green & pink)

3 tablespoons Scotch whisky

4 fl oz (100ml) stock

5 fl oz (150ml) single cream

butter for frying

salt

chopped parsley

(Serves 4)

Method

1   Dry liver on kitchen paper, then trim and cut into even sized
    pieces or strips.

2   Sprinkle evenly with the crushed peppercorns.

3   Heat butter in large frying pan and fry liver on a medium heat for
    2-3 minutes until just brown but still very rare. Time depends on
    the size of the pieces.

4   Turn up heat, pour in whisky and set alight. Stir gently until
    flames die down. Remove liver which should now be pink and
    keep warm.

5   Add stock to pan and boil rapidly until slightly reduced. Turn the
    heat down and pour in the cream and heat through. Taste and add
    salt if needed. It will depend on the saltiness of the stock.

6   Pour sauce over liver, sprinkle with chopped parsley and serve
    with for example ribbons of blanched leeks with fresh thyme and
    boiled new potatoes.

Pasta Salmon

John Mackay, Chef/Owner
Rock Cafe Restaurant
18 Howe Street,
Edinburgh

Ingredients

1 lb 4 oz (550g) fresh Scottish salmon
bones from 1 salmon
1lb 4 oz (550g) fresh egg tagliatelli or
 12 oz (350g) dried pasta
olive oil
2 oz (50g) butter
4 garlic cloves crushed
1 packet fresh dill
½ teaspoon mixed dried herbs (optional)
1½ glasses dry white wine
½ pint double cream
½ teaspoon paprika
4 pints (1L 200ml) water
12 whole black peppercorns
1 bay leaf
½ small finely chopped onion
salt and pepper

(Serves 4)

Method

Stock

1   Place 4 pints (1L 200ml) water in pan and add salmon bones (broken into 3 inch pieces and any other scrap salmon given by fishmonger. Do not use skin, head or tail-fin as these can make the stock bitter.

2   Add half a small onion finely chopped, 12 whole black peppercorns, 2 thin slices of lemon, half a glass of dry white wine, 2 large sprigs of dill, 1 bay leaf, pinch of salt and a little ground black pepper. Bring to the boil and allow to boil actively for approximately 1 minute. Reduce heat and skim. Simmer gently for approximately one hour occasionally working contents with a wooden spoon. The stock is ideal when the various juices and oils float on top of the stock in a mixture of salmon colours. Pass through sieve with wooden spoon.

Dried Pasta

3   If fresh pasta not available boil several pints of water with a tablespoon of olive oil, pinch of salt and pepper. Add half a teaspoon of mixed dried herbs. Add dried pasta to boiling water and allow to gently boil for 1 minute.

4   Strain al dente and use immediately, if not wash pasta in pot with running cold water to take heat from it. Strain, then mix with approximately 1 tablespoon olive oil. The pasta can be stored like this for several days air-tight. The al dente quality will be lost over time.

Method (Continued)

Sauce

5 Melt 2 oz butter gently and add 1 glass of dry white wine, salmon stock, crush garlic, remainder of lemon squeezed and a pinch of salt and ground black pepper.

6 Reduce approximately by half or until the stock thickens. Add double cream and flaked dill *(from 4 large sprigs - not stem)*. Stir in pasta or cooked off dried pasta.

7 Once pasta in heated add finely cut salmon pieces and cook for approximately 30 seconds until salmon changes colour suggesting it is cooked. *(do not overcook salmon)*.

Presentation

8 Serve in bowls or plates with a sprig of dill on top and a pinch of paprika for colour.

Parfait of Cinnamon and Sultanas, Served with Warm Raspberries in Mulled Wine

Jeff Bland, Executive Chef

Cameron House Hotel & Country Estate,

Loch Lomond

Ingredients

Cinnamon and Sultana Parfait

3 eggs

3 oz (75g) caster sugar

1/8 Pint (55ml) water

½ pint (300ml) double cream *(whipped)*

2 oz (50g) soaked sultanas *(soak for one hour in warm water, wine or cognac)*

pinch of cinnamon

Warm Raspberries in Mulled Wine

8oz (225g) raspberries *(fresh or frozen)*

½ lemon *(juice and grated zest)*

1 orange

¼ cinnamon stick

1 clove

1 dessertspoon blackcurrant juice *(optional)*

1 glass red wine

(Serves 6)

Method

1 Whisk yolks, sugar and water in a bowl over a pan of hot water until stiff.

2 Remove from heat and whisk until cold.

3 Add cinnamon and sultanas to egg mixture and fold through.

4 Fold in cream.

5 Place mixture into a mould or freezer-proof glass dish and freeze for 6-8 hours.

6 Warm wine, orange and lemon juice and zest together with cinnamon and clove.

7 Add honey and blackcurrant juice.

8 Infuse for 10 minutes.

9 Sieve into a bowl and add raspberries. If using frozen raspberries, a little extra honey may be requried.

10 Turn out parfait onto plate or dish and spoon raspberries and mulled wine around. Serve.

Balkissock Brose

Janet Beale, Proprietor

Balkissock Lodge,

Ballantrae

Ingredients

½ pint (275ml) double cream

½ pint (275ml) fromage frais

1-2 tablespoons local runny honey

3-4 tablespoons whisky

4 oz (100g) meusli

2 oz (50g) mixed chopped nuts

9 oz (250g) fresh raspberries or
other fruit

(Serves 6)

Method

1   Whip the cream until it forms peaks.

2   Fold in the fromage frais, honey and whisky.

3   At this stage the mixture can be held in the refrigerator until it is
required.

4   Just before serving fold in the meusli, nuts and most of the
raspberries.

5   Pile into glasses and serve decorated with the remaining
raspberries, mint leaves and a finger of homemade shortbread.

Fouters Bread and Butter Pudding

Robert Brown, Chef

Fouters Bistro Restaurant,

Ayr

Ingredients

8-10 slices of buttered brown or white bread *(spread with a fruit jam or jelly)*

6 oz sultanas covered with a mixture of sherry and brandy

1 pint (600ml) double cream

3 large eggs

3 oz caster sugar

splash of vanilla essence

(Serves 6-8)

Method

1 Layer trimmed bread with sultanas in a buttered bowl.

2 Mix cream, sugar, eggs and vanilla together.

3 Pour over bread and allow to soak in *(2-3 minutes)*.

4 Place in microwave and cook on full power for 2 minutes. Allow to stand without opening door for 2 minutes.

5 Cook until custard is just set.

6 Sprinkle top with flaked almonds and brown carefully under grill.

7 Serve hot with speciality ice cream and whipped cream or good custard.

Using a microwave gives a light pudding. This could also be baked for approximately 40 minutes in a medium oven GM5\190°C\375°F (until custard sets). This should be in a bain marie (roasting tray with water).

Fouters Bread and Butter Pudding can be kept for 2-3 days refrigerated. Portions can be reheated by microwaving for approximately 1 minute or until well heated through but without allowing custard to split.

Rhubarb Crumble Ice Cream

Mark & Elizabeth Grieve, Proprietors

The Granary,

Comrie

Ingredients

1 lb (450g) Rhubarb *(prepared)*

5 oz (150g) sugar

3 oz (75g) powdered glucose
(Do not buy variety with vitamin supplements)

¾ pint (450ml) whipping cream

1 tablespoon lemon juice

Crumble

3 oz (75g) plain flour

2 oz (50g) butter *(softened)*

2 oz (50g) light brown sugar

½ teaspoon ground ginger

(Serves 6)

Method

1   Preheat oven to GM5\190°C\375°F.

2   Put all ingredients for crumble into bowl.

3   Rub butter into flour so that mixture comes together to form small pieces of crumble.

4   Sprinkle on baking tray and bake in oven for 15 minutes. Leave to cool.

5   Cook rhubarb until tender and add sugar, glucose and lemon juice.

6   Puree rhubarb mixture and allow to cool. Cover and put in refrigerator.

7   Combine rhubarb puree and cream together.

8   Pour into ice cream maker and churn for about 20 minutes.

9   If no ice cream maker is available pour into shallow container and freeze for 1½ hours then beat mixture for a few seconds with a sturdy hand electric beater.
Repeat this process at least twice at intervals of 1-1½ hours.

10   Finally add crumble mixture to ice cream.

11   Cover with waxed paper.

12   Label and freeze.

For a great

TASTE OF SCOTLAND HOLIDAY...

Taste of Scotland car touring holidays: Telephone 0141 762 0838

Why not combine the Isles of Skye and Lewis for your Hebridean Adventure this year, or Mull & Iona with the tranquillity of Ardnamurchan, Britain's most westerly mainland point?

"Once again you have come up trumps. Everything worked so smoothly; all we had to do was enjoy ourselves!"

Friendly and knowledgeable experts arrange your travel and accommodation, leaving you peace of mind to look forward to and enjoy your 'Taste of Scotland' holiday.

Take this opportunity to experience the delights of Scotland's Islands and send for your Scottish holiday brochure.

"The details given to assist us were most appreciated. Many thanks for your prompt help."

SCOTSELL,
SUITE 2D CHURCHILL WAY
BISHOPBRIGGS, GLASGOW G64 2RH
TEL: (0141) 762 0838 FAX: (0141) 762 0297

Scotland's northern Viking Isles of Orkney and Shetland can be linked together with 3 days (or more) in each island group. Travel by air or by sea and sample the delights of northern hospitality.

A choice of mainland holidays throughout Scotland are a perfect complement to your island explorations!

- - ✂ - - - - - - - - - - -

For your Scottish Holiday brochures, post to:

SCOTSELL,
SUITE 2D CHURCHILL WAY
BISHOPBRIGGS, GLASGOW G64 2RH
TEL: (0141) 762 0838 FAX: (0141) 762 0297

Name ....

Address ....

....

....

Post Code ....

Ref: TOFS96

The 1997 Taste of Scotland Guide

is scheduled to be published in November 1996

To reserve a copy at a special post inclusive price, just complete the coupon below indicating your method of payment and send it to:

Taste of Scotland (Guide Sales)
33 Melville Street
Edinburgh EH3 7JF

You will be placed on the priority list to receive the Guide as soon as it is published. For your convenience, we accept ACCESS and VISA

- ✂

To: Taste of Scotland (Guide Sales), 33 Melville Street, Edinburgh EH3 7JF

Please send _____ copy/copies of the Taste of Scotland 1997 Guide and debit

my ACCESS/MASTERCARD/VISA (please delete as appropriate)

Card No. [ ][ ][ ][ ][ ][ ][ ][ ][ ][ ][ ][ ][ ][ ][ ][ ][ ][ ][ ]

Expiry Date: Month _____ Year _____

Account Name: _____

Signature _____

Please ✓ appropriate amount:

To addresses		
in UK	£5.75	
in Europe	£7.25	
in North America (Airmail)	£8.25	

Note: cheques in £ sterling also accepted

Name: _____

Address: _____

_____

_____

Post Code: _____ Country: _____

Block Capitals, Please.

Post inclusive prices to other countries available on request

TASTE OF SCOTLAND GUIDE

Taste of Scotland welcomes your recommendations on restaurants and hotels you have visited which you feel merit inclusion but are as yet not listed in the Taste of Scotland Guide.

The Macallan Taste of Scotland Awards 1996

Send to: Taste of Scotland, 33 Melville Street, Edinburgh EH3 7JF

The Macallan Taste of Scotland Awards 1996

I nominate _____ (Establishment)

for a Macallan Taste of Scotland Award for the following category:
(Please tick one category only)

☐ Hotel of the Year ☐ Country House Hotel of the Year ☐ Restaurant of the Year

☐ Special Merit for _____ ☐ Personality of the Year _____

Name _____

Address _____

_____

Date of visit _____

Meal (if appropriate) _____

Closing date for entries: 31 August 1996

✂ -

The Macallan Taste of Scotland Awards 1996

Send to: Taste of Scotland, 33 Melville Street, Edinburgh EH3 7JF

The Macallan Taste of Scotland Awards 1996

I nominate _____ (Establishment)

for a Macallan Taste of Scotland Award for the following category:
(Please tick one category only)

☐ Hotel of the Year ☐ Country House Hotel of the Year ☐ Restaurant of the Year

☐ Special Merit for _____ ☐ Personality of the Year _____

Name _____

Address _____

_____

Date of visit _____

Meal (if appropriate) _____

Closing date for entries: 31 August 1996

The Taste of Scotland

Comments on meals in places listed in The Taste of Scotland Guide are welcomed

Send to Taste of Scotland, 33 Melville Street, Edinburgh EH3 7JF

Establishment visited

Date of visit

Meal(s) taken

Comments

Did the Taste of Scotland Guide meet your expectations?

Are there improvements you would suggest?

Name

Address

✂ —

The Taste of Scotland

Comments on meals in places listed in The Taste of Scotland Guide are welcomed

Send to Taste of Scotland, 33 Melville Street, Edinburgh EH3 7JF

Establishment visited

Date of visit

Meal(s) taken

Comments

Did the Taste of Scotland Guide meet your expectations?

Are there improvements you would suggest?

Name

Address

The Macallan Taste of Scotland Awards 1996

Send to: Taste of Scotland, 33 Melville Street, Edinburgh EH3 7JF

The Macallan Taste of Scotland Awards 1996

I nominate _____ (Establishment)

for a Macallan Taste of Scotland Award for the following category:
(Please tick one category only)

☐ Hotel of the Year   ☐ Country House Hotel of the Year   ☐ Restaurant of the Year

☐ Special Merit for _____ ☐ Personality of the Year _____

Name _____

Address _____

_____

Date of visit _____

Meal (if appropriate) _____

Closing date for entries: 31 August 1996

- ✂

The Macallan Taste of Scotland Awards 1996

Send to: Taste of Scotland, 33 Melville Street, Edinburgh EH3 7JF

The Macallan Taste of Scotland Awards 1996

I nominate _____ (Establishment)

for a Macallan Taste of Scotland Award for the following category:
(Please tick one category only)

☐ Hotel of the Year   ☐ Country House Hotel of the Year   ☐ Restaurant of the Year

☐ Special Merit for _____ ☐ Personality of the Year _____

Name _____

Address _____

_____

Date of visit _____

Meal (if appropriate) _____

Closing date for entries: 31 August 1996

The Taste of Scotland

Comments on meals in places listed in The Taste of Scotland Guide are welcomed

Send to Taste of Scotland, 33 Melville Street, Edinburgh EH3 7JF

Establishment visited

Date of visit

Meal(s) taken

Comments

Did the Taste of Scotland Guide meet your expectations?

Are there improvements you would suggest?

Name

Address

✂ -

The Taste of Scotland

Comments on meals in places listed in The Taste of Scotland Guide are welcomed

Send to Taste of Scotland, 33 Melville Street, Edinburgh EH3 7JF

Establishment visited

Date of visit

Meal(s) taken

Comments

Did the Taste of Scotland Guide meet your expectations?

Are there improvements you would suggest?

Name

Address

Taste of Scotland Alphabetical Index - 1996 Guide

** New Member

E

F

G

H

I

J

K

The Taste of Scotland Guide 1996

EDITORIAL
AMANDA CLARK, ANGELA NEALON, TRACEY WATERSTON

PUBLISHED BY
TASTE OF SCOTLAND SCHEME LTD,
A NON-PROFIT MAKING COMPANY LIMITED BY GUARANTEE TRADING AS TASTE OF SCOTLAND

DESIGN, ILLUSTRATION & TYPESETTING
RUSSELL DESIGN, GLASGOW

PRINTED BY
MACDONALD LINDSAY PINDAR PLC, LOANHEAD

WITH PARTICULAR THANKS FOR EDITORIAL ASSISTANCE
CHARLES MACLEAN, MACLEAN DUBOIS (WRITERS AND AGENTS) EDINBURGH

FRONT COVER & BACK COVER
LANDSCAPE PHOTOGRAPHY BY MICHAEL KUZMACK
FOOD PHOTO BY MORTEN ROSVIK
FOOD STYLING, WENDY BARRIE

COLOUR PHOTOGRAPHY COURTESY OF
FORT WILLIAM & LOCHABER TOURISM (ALEX GILLESPIE)
AYRSHIRE TOURIST BOARD, BUTE & COWAL TOURIST BOARD, EDINBURGH TOURIST BOARD
FORTH VALLEY TOURIST BOARD, INVERNESS LOCH NESS AND NAIRN TOURIST BOARD LTD, MORTEN ROSVIK
MORAY TOURIST BOARD, SHETLAND ISLANDS TOURISM, BOBBY TULLOCH
ST ANDREWS AND N.E. FIFE TOURIST BOARD

PHOTOGRAPHS
PAGE 2 - SANNA BAY, ARDNAMURCHAN. **PAGE 5** - URQUHART CASTLE, LOCH NESS.
PAGES 8 & 9 - THE MACALLAN DISTILLERY, EASTER ELCHIES HOUSE.
PAGES 10, 23 & 28 - PHOTOGRAPHY BY MORTEN ROSVIK. **PAGE 12** - SCALLOWAY FISH MARKET.
PAGE 13 - BURNS TOWER, MAUCHLINE. **PAGE 17** - VICTORIA STREET, OLD TOWN, EDINBURGH AND, POLNISH CHURCH
AND WILD FLOWERS, LOCH AILORT. **PAGE 24** - LOCH ECK. **PAGE 30** - CRAIL HARBOUR.
PAGE 48, LISTINGS TITLE PAGE - VIEW WITH SEA PINKS, THE SHETLAND ISLANDS.

TASTE OF SCOTLAND SCHEME LTD
33 MELVILLE STREET, EDINBURGH EH3 7JF
TEL: 0131 220 1900 FAX: 0131 220 6102

ISBN 1 871445 06 8